The DROWNING of the MOON

A Novel of the 18th Century Silver Nobility in Colonial New Spain

Copyright © 2017 Diana Serra Cary
All rights reserved.
ISBN:1539199630
ISBN-13:9781539199632

The DROWNING of the MOON

A Novel of the 18th Century Silver Nobility in Colonial New Spain

൰ ൱

DIANA SERRA CARY

Cover Illustration by John Ferrara
Interior illustrations by Robert E. Cary

Published on CreateSpace
By Andi Hicks / Word-Werx.com

By the same author:

WHATEVER HAPPENED TO BABY PEGGY?
JACKIE COOGAN, The World's Boy King
THE HOLLYWOOD POSSE
HOLLYWOOD CHILDREN

LITERARY BACKGROUND

Dear Readers,

Over the past few years I have written four books dealing with little known groups or neglected persons who were influential in Hollywood's social history.

My first book, *The Hollywood Posse*, features the historical group of authentic open range cowboys, all expert horsemen, who worked for nearly forty years dong stunts and doubles for popular Western Stars who were themselves not allowed to perform such crippling risks in the course of their dangerous careers.

My second book in the series, *Hollywood's Children*, is a detailed history of performing children, the first inclusive record to be collecting in a single volume, the history and careers of an overlooked group of talented youngsters who worked as long and hard as the adult actors of the nineteenth and twentieth Century American Theater and Studios Hollywood.

Jackie Coogan, The World's Boy King, The only known biography of the first major child star in 20th Century America.

What Ever Happened to Baby Peggy? My autobiography.

I have also written a still unpublished historical novel based on the true family stories of Charles and William Bent who built the historic landmark, Bent's Fort, which has since been restored and become an American National Park near La Junta, Colorado. William was an explorer and successful Indian trader in Nineteenth Century Colorado Territory. During the Mexican War of 1846, Charles Bent was named the first American Governor of New Mexico. A few days later he was brutally murdered by Pueblo Indians in his Taos home as part of a local massacre of several new government officials. His death was witnessed by his wife and children, during what later became the more widely known wartime Pueblo Uprising in the pioneer capital of Taos.

I hope you will enjoy and benefit from *The Drowning of the Moon*, which follows. As the interested author, I would love to see historically accurate motion pictures of both these highly dramatic and 'adaptable for the screen' sweeping epics.

Diana Serra Cary -- Gustine California, 2017

(All of the above books are being republished in paperback and The Hollywood Posse, Hollywood's Children and Whatever happened to Baby Peggy are available on Kindle

ACKNOWLEDGEMENTS

I owe the story itself to Señor Manual Leal of Guanajuato, who in 1957 first related to me the tragic tale of the 1810 rape of Guanajuato during which members of his own noble family suffered greatly. Knowing I was a professional writer he begged me to promise I would write its tragic history for English readers who, except for certain Mexican and American history scholars, most English readers might never have occasion to learnof this little known period of Spanish-American history. I also know that most American readers have never even heard of the Manila Galleon's three centuries of record breaking voyages.

My thanks to Richard Bueller, for his unshakable faith in this story and for performing the painstaking task of transferring the original manuscript from the WordPerfect Program in which it was written, to Microsoft Word after WordPerfect was declared officially obsolete by its owners.

Many thanks to Sue Slutsky for her enthusiasm for this story and to Richard Bueller for helping to design an appropriate cover for its first edition.

I also wish to thank Andi Hicks for having such boundless faith in this book and for taking an active interest in salvaging the completed volume when I believed its computerized version was irretrievably lost and so, was seriously contemplating abandoning this decades-long project.

Most importantly, I wish to recognize the extraordinary love and support given to me by my by now-deceased husband, Bob and our extraordinarily caring and generous son, Mark who has dedicated these last few year to being my in-home caretaker and without whose help this book would not be published.

DEDICATION

*For the silver lords and ladies
of a forgotten Guanajuato,
who cried out to me
from that city's very stones, --
Demanding that their story be told.*

Diana Serra Cary

CONTENTS

DEDICATION i
    The Viceroyalty of New Spain 1819 ii
HISTORICAL BACKGROUND iii
    Intendencies of New Spain from 1786 - 1821 vi
AUTHOR'S OVERVIEW vii
    New Spain's Silver Frontier x
HISTORICAL x
AUTHENTICITY x
HISTORICAL PERSONAGES xi
APPEARING IN THESE PAGES xi
LA FRONTERA xiii
PART ONE -- SILVER DUST AND SPANISH WINE xxvii
PART TWO -- THE MINES OF GLORY 55
    An example of a Reredos Altar Screen. 94
PART THREE -- AWAKENINGS 117
    Baron Alexander Von Humboldt 141
PART FOUR -- MEXICO 163
    The Route of the Manila Galleon 182
PART FIVE -- THE LADIES' SEA 183
PART SIX -- SILVER ROSES 235
    Towns affected by the Hidalgo Revolution 286
PART SEVEN -- THE BLACK FLAME 287
    The Campaign Route of Hidalgo and Allende (1810 – 1811) 300
PART EIGHT -- REAPING HAVOC 353
    The Battle of the Bridge of Calderón 381
LA FRONTERA 429
BIBLIOGRAPHY 437
GLOSSARY 438
ABOUT THE AUTHOR 450

The Viceroyalty of New Spain 1819

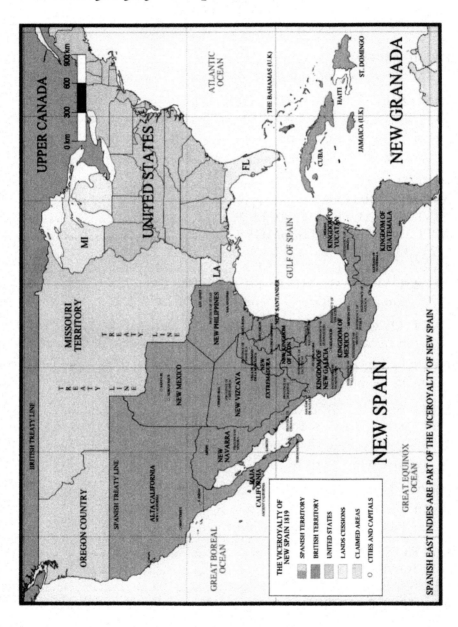

HISTORICAL BACKGROUND

As foretold,
The Gods of Gold departed,
when their Sun dried up at noon.
But the Gods of Silver – Never!
They vowed to stay forever,
'til the Drowning of the Moon.

The "Gods of Gold" deserted Mexico in 1521 when a small band of Spaniards under Hernán Cortés joined forces with 30,000 secretly rebellious Tlaxcalan Indians. Becoming allies of the Spaniards, the Tlaxcalans helped to conquer the tyrannical Aztec Indians whose cruelty had for years oppressed them and all other tribes in the region. After the hated Aztec Empire was ultimately destroyed by the Spanish-Telaxcalan alliance, the fallen Aztecs were quickly replaced by "The Kingdom of New Spain," a colony of the European monarchy. During this same transitional period the name "Mexico" was applied solely to New Spain's Capital City. The Colony itself was ruled directly by a Viceroy, appointed by the distant But her "Gods of Silver" stayed on in what became the Kingdom of New Spain. For nearly three hundred years they lavished unprecedented fortunes upon those charmed few European and American-born miners who comprised the colony's hard-working but aristocratic silver elite. In 1546 the first silver mines were discovered in New Spain's far northern mountains of Zacatecas. A mere two years later, in 1548, there followed a second and much larger rush to the mines of Guanajuato, which proved to be even richer.

By the middle of the 18th Century, Guanajuato was the most important silver center in New Spain. Other smaller mining centers arose to the south of Zacatecas, but by mid-Century Guanajuato alone was producing one sixth of all the silver in the known world.

This thriving, impregnable location, hidden in a central mountain range was, as much as possible, kept a geographic secret from envious European nations, especially the English and Dutch. During the warring Reformation these two nations became predominantly Protestant, which made them view Catholic Spain as their theological and political enemy, and vice versa.

New Spain's seemingly inexhaustible mines were the envy of all Europe, but being located far inland, were impregnable to attack. Their largesse had to be pirated on the high seas or when a silver convoy, awaiting a ship, fell into the hands of buccaneers sacking some port city or defenseless coastal town. Dutch, French and English Corsairs all coveted the Spanish sea-lanes' richest prize -- the annual galleon outward bound from Acapulco for Manila, both cargo and ballast pieces-of-eight and solid silver bars. But, the risk was worth it. The silver lords exploited the curious and financially positive aspect of the Manila Galleon's Oriental trade. By purchasing costly Chinese and other Oriental merchandise for re-sale later at enormous profits in Mexico City's elite shops, silver lords could provide critically needed business loans that were otherwise unobtainable in the colony's severely restricted economy. It was an extremely risky voyage, but even female members of religious orders made the tremendous effort as well, took the bodily risks repeatedly and still miraculously survived.

In Viceregal New Spain, as in British India, the color line was tightly drawn. A white ruling class of less than one million souls presided over the destinies of five million illiterate Indians and other inhabitants of mixed blood. Two distinct factions contended for power within this white society -- ambitious immigrant Spaniards from the mother country and equally well-educated colonists born in New Spain, the latter descended from generations of Spanish, Irish, and French; all of which becoming known as criollos: Many of this latter group, were silver lords of distinguished heritage.

The smoldering tensions between these two factions reached flashpoint in 1808, when the French Emperor, Napoleon Bonaparte, invaded Spain and installed his brother Joseph on the Bourbon throne of Madrid. This distant, but severely disruptive event, rocked Spanish America to its foundations and encouraged a random spirit of rebellion among a small number of discontented colonials seeking independence.

The story that follows begins in Guanajuato, the beautiful "silver city of palaces," in the year 1786, with the dazzling ceremonial christening of Sirena, the First Condesa of Graciana, heiress of the Irish-born First Conde, Don Patrick O'Malley, that city's most successful silver lord. Sirena's birth comes at a time when the nobility is at their peak of opulence and grace, in what has for decades been one of New Spain's most peaceful and prosperous provinces. In this same period, the nobility is becoming unwittingly imperiled by a brewing, catastrophic disaster, stirred up in an unsuspected priest's secret plot to set up his own utopian society. Some of the most forceful characters in Sirena's story are gathered for the important family events of her recent birth and ceremonial baptism in Guanajuato on the Eve of the Stone Mason's Feast Day, the third of May, in the year 1786.

Intendencies of New Spain from 1786 - 1821

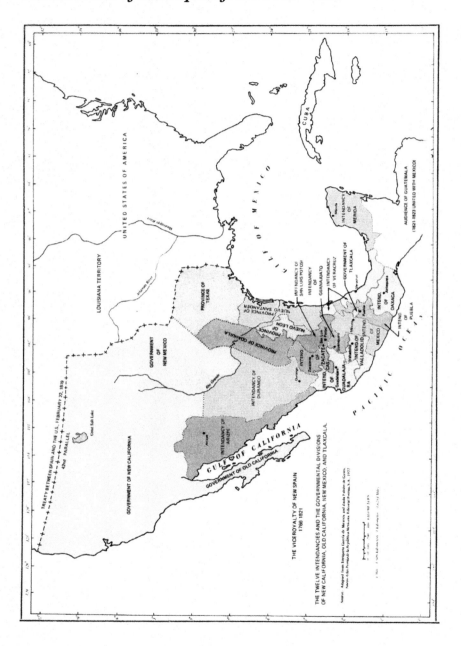

AUTHOR'S OVERVIEW

The Drowning Of The Moon is a vast panoramic novel whose major characters are drawn from the aristocracy of 18th Century Mexico, an upper class made up almost exclusively of immigrant Spaniards and native-born criollo, the latter direct descendants of the first conquistadores, who legitimately lay claim to pure European blood.

While the novel is a work of fiction and all the characters, (excepting historical personages) are entirely fictional as well, it should be understood, at the outset, that everything is solidly grounded in fact. All historical personages and events are treated with scrupulous regard to accuracy: physical appearance, temperament, political stance and chronology. No one is found where he or she could not have been at that time. As for the differing viewpoints of events, they are based on a sympathetic study of letters, diaries and histories of all the nations involved -- The United States, Mexico, Spain, Great Britain and France.

Those already familiar with the histories of 18th Century United States and New Spain will recognize several figures, who play important roles. Among them are Father Miguel Hidalgo, the visionary priest whose daring changed the course of his country's history and Baron Von Humboldt, explorer extraordinaire, who toured the great silver mines of Guanajuato in the autumn of 1804. Antonio de Riaño, Spanish-born Intendent of Guanajuato, who fought on the side of Yankee rebels against the British in Louisiana in 1777 and later took as his wife the renowned New Orleans' beauty and aristocrat, Victoria St. Maxent. And, General James Wilkinson, First Commander in Chief of the American Army, who appears as the hidden hand behind much early American diplomacy.

The story of the main protagonist is set against colonial Mexico's little-known, but incomparably rich silver-mining industry, and the lavish life-style of its "silver lords." A family saga, The Drowning of the Moon is written to be equally fascinating to readers already familiar with Mexico's Spanish past and those coming upon it for the first time. Their drama sweeps from Guanajuato's inexhaustible mines to Mexico City and Upper California, from Acapulco and Manila to Santa Fe and south to an immense plantation above New Orleans. It traces the rise of this titled silver nobility to the brutal destruction of its gracious society -- a Gone with the Wind of Mexico.

True historical figures mingle with fictional characters as both are involved in the daily tasks of such diverse professions as silver mining, silk raising, Church and convent, the Bourbon Army, Viceregal politics, the arts and the now almost unknown, but incredibly lucrative China trade. Annually millions in Oriental luxuries and silver coin were carried from Manila to Acapulco and back, aboard the largest armed galleons afloat. By investing in the China trade many mine owners financed the high cost of sinking their deepest shafts.

But endangering this prospering and peaceful realm hang the dark threats of Napoleonic deceit, a land-greedy, expansionist government in Washington, and the venal prime minister of a cuckold Spanish king. The Drowning of the Moon re-creates Mexico's dazzling silver elite, giving readers a wealth of romance and dramatic conflict that grows directly out of the period in which its story is set to present a true and even-handed view of their vanished world.

Then, between the years 1786 and 1822, Sirena's filigreed world, built on chivalric traditions and sustained by seemingly inexhaustible resources of silver, is torn asunder. She finds herself, her family, the man she loves and the future of the House of Graciana swept up in the maelstrom of insurrection, civil war and personal treachery, as New Spain begins her long, heroic struggle to become Mexico.

Distinctive and forceful characters people Sirena's dazzling world:

DON PATRICK, Sirena's father, the free-spirited Irish-Spanish First Conde of the House of Graciana, whose inherited traditions of frontier hospitality and Christian charity she strives to perpetuate.

DOÑA ISABEL, her pietistic, sensual mother, obsessed by an ungovernable passion for her husband's best friend for whom she recklessly risks honor and her immortal soul.

TRISTÀN DE LUNA, the chivalrous, frontier soldier who adores Sirena, but whose exalted sense of honor traps him in a loveless marriage.

MADRE PILAR, the redoubtable Mother Superior of Mexico City's famed asylum for mentally ill women, hiding a truth that nearly ruins the woman she means to save.

EMILIO SANTA CRUZ, the wild mulatto muleteer who, out of loyalty to Don Patrick and ambitions for his own fair-skinned son, abandons 'the trail', only to return to it with a vengeance.

LORENZO SANTA CRUZ, Emilio's gifted artist son, whose lifelong love for Sirena is poisoned by his envy of her European blood and an implacable hatred for her privileged class.

DON DIEGO LEGÀZPI, the liberal, crusading Spanish-born Bishop of Michoacán, fighting heroically for social justice, political integrity and economic reforms in a colony teetering on the brink of anarchy.

FATHER MIGUEL HIDALGO, the visionary country priest, whose wildly impractical dreams of a Mexican Utopia drive him to destroy the very society in which he longed to rise.

☙ ❧

This novel, has two central, interwoven themes:
(1) The bitter test of change. How strong and weak characters and governments survive or collapse in the face of unprecedented revolutionary change.
(2) The unfolding irony of two great American entities -- Mexico and the United States -- growing from colony to nation side by side, inescapably bound to each others' past and future, their very borders touching, and yet through it all, remaining cultural, philosophical and political strangers.

☙ ❧

The book's commanding characters, combined with a wealth of dramatic incident, bring to life a rich, colorful world, virtually unknown and passed over by other novelists. Just as Gone With The Wind and The Jewel In The Crown dramatize the end of the ante bellum South and the last days of British rule in India, The Drowning of The Moon personifies the fall of white Spanish colonial society in New Spain and the rise of a new order in Mexico. How this occurred will help explain this nearest neighbor, so much in the news but a land about which most Americans know very little.

New Spain's Silver Frontier

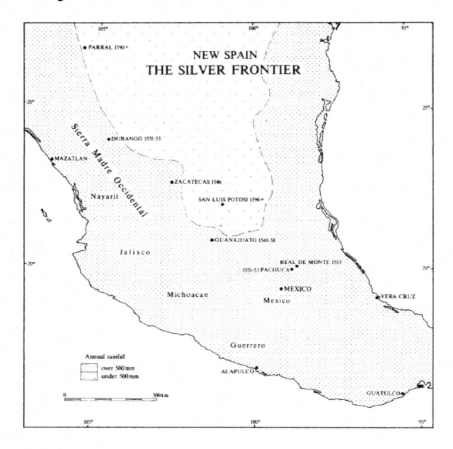

HISTORICAL AUTHENTICITY

I lived in Guanajuato for three months in the autumn of 1957, followed by a ten year residency in Mexico, primarily in Cuernavaca and Mexico City. I also spent the next 20 years continuously studying new and old scholarly works about the 18th century period and personally visiting the most important Mexican cities and sites featured in this story as well as those in Southwestern Texas, Louisiana, New Mexico, and California.

Diana Serra Cary

HISTORICAL PERSONAGES APPEARING IN THESE PAGES
(with key to pronunciation of Spanish terms)

LUCAS ALAMÁN, noted Mexican political leader and distinguished historian.

JUAN AND IGNACIA ALAMÁN, socially prominent parents of Lucas Alamán

IGNACIO ALLENDE, (Ig-nah-cee-o Ay-yen-day) Royalist officer of San Miguel el Grande

FÉLIX MARIA CALLEJA, (Fey-lix Mah-ri-a Cay-yeh-ha)General of New Spain's Tenth Brigade

FRANCISCO CALLEJA, Criolla wife of General Calleja

MARIANA ST. MAXENT DE FLON, New Orleans-born wife of General Flon, sister of Doña Victoria Riaño

MIGUEL HILDALGO, (Mee-gel Ee-dahl-go) Criolla priest, Diocese of Michoacán is considered a national hero of Mexico. A former student of Hidalgo showed himself to be a talented strategist and let the revolutionaly army to victories until a series of defeats in 1815. He was tried and executed by firing squad in December 22,1815.

AGUSTÍN ITURBIDE, (Ah-gus-teen Ee-tour-bee-day) Royalist officer of Valladolid Regiment. Iturbide was named as the presiding officer of a five man political junta in 1821, bestowing upon himself the title of Emperor. His diplomatic priorities -- the ten million dollar loan from the United States and the equitable settlement of the boundary between New Spain and the United States continued to languish.

Iturbide's reign lasted ten months only. In 1809, the Empire had minted twenty-six million pesos. In 1823, it minted a paltry six million, having lost the mines to the Insurrection. Also in 1823, Iturbide abdicated his throne and began a generous European exile. In 1824 he broke the rule of his abdication and illegally returned to Mexico where he was promptly executed by a firing squad.

JOAQUIN ITURBIDE, Spanish-born father of Agustín Iturbide

JOSÉ MARIA MORELOS, (Ho-sey Mah-ree-ah More-rey-los) Mulatto priest, Diocese of Michoacán.

JUAN ANTONIO RIAÑO, (Whan An-ton-io Ree-ahn-yo) Intendent (Governor) of Guanajuato

DOÑA VICTORIA ST. MAXENT RIAÑO Antonio Riaño's wife, sister of Mariana St. Maxent Flon

GILBERTO RIAÑO, son of Don Antonio and Victoria Riaño

BARON ALEXANDER VON HUMBOLDT, renowned German scientist and world traveler, visited Mexico in 1802-3, Humboldt was impressed with Mexico City and pointed to the Royal College of Mines, The Royal Botanical Garden and the Royal Academy of San Carlos as exemplars of a metropolitan capital in touch with the latest developments in Europe. He spent time at the Valenciana silver mine in Guanajuato, at the time the most important in the Spanish empire. He was the first person to describe the phenomenon and cause of human-induced climate change, in 1800 and again in 1831, based on observations generated during his travels. During his lifetime Humboldt became one of the most famous men in Europe

GENERAL JAMES WILKINSON, Roguish and controversial First Commander in Chief of the U.S. Army, mentor of Philip Nolan, associate of Aaron Burr

LA FRONTERA

November 1822

Sitting sidesaddle on her restless grey roan, where the sage-blue plain crested to form a sandy ridge, Sirena gazed anxiously toward the Santa Rosa range. Every morning for the past ten days she had ridden out to this vantage point to scan the distant pass through which Tristán and his father would be riding home.

No reason to panic, she told herself. They were no more than ten days overdue. Considering the great distance they were traveling that was hardly cause for alarm. Still she could not forget the rumor that a passing mestizo trader had brought to her several days ago. She had quickly dismissed it as typical frontier gossip, the sort that always followed the movements of prominent men up here in the North. She was quite certain that if Tristán had not won such renown as Field Marshal of the Royalist Army during the recent wars, and his father were not Commandant General of the Northern Frontier, that trader would not have given a fig if both were six months late returning from this Comanche Council on the Rio San Sabá.

But as the days passed, her concern had deepened and now as her fretful horse tongued the clittering cricket in his bit, the trader's chilling words came back to her.

"I got it from a Comanche headman, dead set against the Alliance," he stated in his spare frontier Spanish. "he said he planned to ambush the two white 'peace talkers' at their first night's waterhole." Taking a last pull on his crudely-made cigarro, he turned a bootheel slowly into the discarded butt, studying the ground to avoid her searching gaze.

"Condesa, I don't like bein' the bearer of bad news any better'n the next man," he confessed drily, climbing back into his high-cantled saddle. "But one thing's sure -- the Indians all know there's not the shadow of an army left to defend these borderlands. Even your so-called 'Comanche allies' savvy there's no 'His Majesty' around anymore to hand out gifts or hold them to their word." He cast a dark look toward the lonely Santa Rosa Pass. "That's why you can count it a miracle if your two men get back alive."

Out here alone on the high plains, where half the world was sky and the wind never ceased its mourning, Sirena felt a tremor run through her. Suddenly her whole being ached for Tristán's protective presence and embrace.

Beyond her own fierce longing for him, she had wanted his even-handed judgment in making the difficult decision to foreclose on the neighboring Àvila estate. But, the time for that had already run out. Before noon today she must confront the notary without Tristán, and somehow make the man accede to the unheard of concessions she was demanding as major creditor of the bankrupt Àvila estate.

She dreaded the encounter, for she had been told the notary was a newly arrived peasant from Spain, a peevish rustic who openly despised New World born nobles like herself. Having survived a decade of insurrection and civil war, Sirena found she had little tolerance left for conflict of any kind, even to crossing swords verbally with a petty bureaucrat, but there was simply no avoiding it.

The scent of rain-wet sage came to her on a rising wind, the familiar breath of a cold norther brewing somewhere beyond the hills. Strong gusts tugged at the wide brim of her sun-bleached straw jipijapa and lifted the fringe of the red wool jorongo which enveloped her from its black velvet collar to the hem of her silk, Roman-striped riding skirt. Wary of the impending storm, her horse kept veering away from the wind's knife-edge, his sharp ears pointed in the direction of La Frontera's snug horse barn.

"You're right amigo mio," she said, stroking the roan's arched neck affectionately, "It's time we started home. We make a perfect lightning rod out here on this high empty plain."

With a last anxious glance at the cloud-covered Santa Rosa range, she gave up her vigil and at the touch of her small spur the spirited animal broke into an eager lope. The exhilarating pace relieved Sirena's tensions and she felt a healing sense of optimism and hope. Then topping a rise softened by scrub mesquite and low huizache trees, the walls of La Frontera rose into view. Reining in her horse firmly, she forced him to approach his home hacienda at the same slow rocking-horse gait by which she kept all Frontera's mounts from spoiling for the barn.

While a far cry from the luxurious palace in which she had been born, this lonely outpost was her last link to that lovely vanished world, her sole warranty against an increasingly uncertain future. Although miles from any city worthy of the name, La Frontera was renowned as a bastion of culture and civility on this perilous Apache frontier. Honor, hospitality and Christian charity -- graces which so many families had discarded since the war, but which her Irish-Spanish father had taught her, were the true hallmarks of nobility -- all received more than mere lip service beneath her roof.

Built in the late 16th Century, fortress-style, La Frontera was enclosed by a stone wall with a lookout above the gate and round crenellated turrets at either side. It served as administrative headquarters for Sirena's six other large haciendas. Its barns, horse corrals, shearing sheds, branding chutes, workshops, wine-press, tannery, flour mill, granary and warehouses made it a hive of productive activity all year 'round, almost a self-contained village in itself.

Within its walls were dozens of adobe houses where Sirena's hundred or more resident workers and their families lived. Many of them claimed ancestral roots at La Frontera, reaching back as many centuries, as her own. In the compound's center stood the imposing two-story casco Sirena now called home. Between this main residence and its surrounding walls rose the slim sculptured bell tower of the family chapel, adding a touch of lyrical beauty to La Frontera's otherwise forbidding aspect.

Half a league distant she could see the looming ramparts of La Soledad, the Àvila family's administrative hacienda, towering above its screen of fresno trees. Here the three Àvila children had grown up together with her own two brothers and herself, more as a tight-knit family than neighbors. Suddenly, she felt a sharp stab of regret: within the hour she would possess La Soledad and everything else this venerable conquistadorial clan had ever called their own.

The heavy wooden gate in La Frontera's outer wall groaned as a young porter swung it wide at Sirena's approach. Dismounting in the stone-paved family patio, she handed the reins to her majordomo, Ricardo, a white-thatched Tarascan Indian who had served as foreman of her father's southern silver mines before she was born.

"Has the notary arrived yet?" she asked anxiously.

"No, Condesa," Ricardo replied, "but Don Gabriel saw him coming from the lookout. He'll be here soon."

Gathering her colorful riding skirt in brown-gloved hands, she hastened toward the stone stairway that spiraled upward to the encircling second floor.

"Oh, Condesa, I almost forgot!" Ricardo called, holding out a small packet in his hand as he limped after her. She smiled to herself. He still proudly refused to use a cane to brace his bad leg, smashed in that mining accident so many years before. "This was just delivered by a special courier riding up from the South."

Mounting the stairs, she withdrew an envelope from the protective oilskin pouch. Her interest immediately aroused because the letter came from Guanajuato, the beloved city of her birth. But, instinctively following her lifelong spiritual discipline of delaying immediate gratification in just such small everyday acts as this, she put off opening it. "Curiosity denied, curbs one's pride," Bishop Legázpi used to say, and she heeded his words now. Over the years she had learned how sage his advice had always been.

When she reached her upstairs office, she tossed the sealed envelope onto the desk and hurried on to her bedroom to bathe and change. When she returned, wearing a formal morning gown, proper to the gravity of the business ahead, she went at once to her desk to glance through the Àvila papers one last time. There the unopened letter caught her eye. Something about the florid handwriting struck her as being eerily familiar and yet the writer's identity eluded her. Curiosity finally getting the better of self-denial, she picked up the envelope and started to break the seal.

"Right this way, Señor Rendón," her Uncle Gabriel was saying, and looking up she saw him coming through the open double doors with the notary in tow. Reluctantly she set the intriguing letter aside, turning her full attention to the folio of Àvila foreclosure documents, for it was imperative she be conversant with every item they contained.

To Manuel Rendón, the province's new notary who had just ridden out from the nearby town of Monclova and now stood warming himself before the corner fireplace in La Frontera's spacious upstairs office, awaiting her pleasure, the Condesa seemed both secretive and proud.

After all, he thought irritably, once the five Àvila haciendas are annexed to the six she already owns, her latifundio will constitute a veritable family empire. She will command farm and grazing lands almost beyond calculating in Spanish leagues. Her cattle, mules, horses and sheep will number in the hundreds of thousands. Moreover, she will be gaining easy access to the three felicitous rivers whose water made this high desert bloom. All in all, it was the largest transfer of land in the long history of the province and the most impressive he had ever been asked to notarize. It nettled him she had declined to surround such a celebrated foreclosure with the public attention it deserved.

Although Rendón had heard many stories about this redoubtable noblewoman since his recent arrival in the province, no occasion to meet her had arisen until today. Now, while her white-haired uncle, Don Gabriel, engaged him in idle conversation, Rendón took the opportunity to observe his hostess from across the richly furnished, high-ceilinged room.

The First Condesa of the noble House of Graciana was seated in a carved 16th Century friar's chair, sheaving through a stack of yellowing parchments heavy with generations of notarial stamps and seals. She was perfectly framed between two matching, five-branched, silver candelabras whose flaming tapers cast her in a pale golden light. Elegant in a long-sleeved, high-waisted gown of burgundy colored silk, a white linen ruff at the throat, her elbows rested on a Persian carpet draped over the Spanish trestle table that served as her desk. A large sapphire ring, set in a baroque swirl of gold, graced the forefinger of her right hand. Ramón knew without asking that the gem was incised with the family crest.

The local magistrate, who had known the Condesa since she was a child, had told the notary she was thirty-six years old. But seeing her for himself, Rendón found that age unacceptable to reason. This willowy young woman with her proud carriage and slim waist, glowed with youthful vitality. Her large black-lashed amber eyes were those of a much younger, woman, and her luxuriant black hair, swept back from a clear broad brow, was still without a trace of grey. Her porcelain-white complexion was as flawless as it must have been the day she turned fifteen and made her quince año debut before the cream of New Spain's silver aristocracy.

Oh, yes, the magistrate had filled him in on all the details of that gala event, unmatched before or since for opulence and splendor. And yet here she was, almost a generation later, still in the full blaze of her beauty!

"Don't be surprised by her shrewdness and business acumen," the magistrate had warned him. "Her father and uncle taught her well how to administer the Graciana haciendas and mines. Don Gabriel collects books in every tongue, so she's widely read, and he took her on the Grand Tour of Europe when she was only twelve. She's been privately tutored in everything from philosophy and music to English and French."

Too much learning for any female, however entitled, Rendón fumed. The degree to which this noblewoman outclassed him only served as a sour reminder of his own failed expectations in this 'Promised Land' of New Spain. While he did not regret having traded his impoverished village in Old Spain for a go at getting rich over here, nothing had so far gone his way. Once landed in New Spain he discovered that Indians and mestizos outnumbered Europeans a hundred to one. Criollo was what they called persons of European blood, who had been born over here, and then there were the castas, a bizarre racial stew of European, Indian, Negro, Filipino and Chinese. Sprung from poor peasant stock, Rendón had counted on being received as a gentleman overnight, simply by virtue of the fact that he was white. That vain conceit had been quickly dashed.

To his dismay he learned pure European blood was a rare privilege which aristocratic families like the Gracianas were born with, and one which their forebears had carefully husbanded for three centuries, keeping their criollo bloodline pristine by means of judicious marriages with their peers. His study of the Graciana documents had revealed a family tree laden with illustrious conquistadorial names -- Cortés, Moctezuma, Mendoza, Oñate, Verdugo. Through her half-Irish father, the legendary Don Patrick O'Malley, the Condesa claimed descent from a first adelantado giving her and her heirs the coveted right to call themselves 'Americans.'

Rendón's initial envy of these lordly fronteristas was fast hardening into an envious resentment, and this haughty First Condesa epitomized the whole feudal lot. Take this morning! When she had need of his services, did she ride into town where this historic public signing would have made him the center of a welcome stir? Not on your life! Instead, she had dispatched a retinue of fiercely loyal Graciana lancers to escort him out to this remote stronghold, imperious as some medieval warrior queen!

СЗ ВО

As Sirena took up a freshly sharpened goose quill she secretly sized up the notary who stood chatting with her father's twin brother. She was struck by the contrast between them: Rendón, short and rotund, in plain black frock coat and knee breeches, white cotton hose wrinkling on his fleshless shanks: Don Gabriel, towering over him as he did most other men. Formally attired for the occasion, as was his custom, in a splendid green velvet suit and gold-embroidered waistcoat, Gabriel stood ramrod straight for all his eighty years. Sirena gazed at him fondly. It might have been 1782 instead of 1822, for his sole concession to the 19th Century was the absence of a dress wig. No matter. His own wavy hair was now whiter than any wig had ever been.

"Sorry to keep you waiting, gentlemen" she said, "but I had to make sure the papers were in order. Shall we begin?" "Well, Condesa," Rendón crowed jubilantly, rubbing his pudgy hands together with relish, "how does it feel, to be picking up a rich plum like the Àvila estate after waiting two hundred years for it to fall your way?"

"It's not our custom to celebrate a neighbor's misfortune," Don Gabriel said reprovingly.

"No offense intended," Rendón replied blandly as they moved toward Sirena's desk. "The way I see it, a winning hand's a winning hand, no matter what the game!"

Pretending he had not heard, Don Gabriel placed two straight chairs at the trestle table, seating himself beside the notary, both men facing Sirena.

"First of all," Sirena announced quietly, handing Rendón a sheet of white foolscap, "I've listed here my own terms, as they affect the future of the Fourth Marqués de Àvila. I insist these conditions be notarized first.

Ceremoniously Rendón perched a pair of square gold spectacles on his nearly bridgeless nose and perused the paper, his puzzlement deepening as he read.

"Am I to understand, Condesa," he blustered, barely able to contain his indignation, "that you are giving the bankrupt Marqués lifetime title to the Àvila family palace in the city of Mexico? Surely you know that property's worth a fortune?"

Sirena lifted her chin imperceptibly. "I do."

"But the other Àvila creditors are not going to go along with seeing an improvident old noble living well, enjoying all the comforts of – of." Lowering his gaze, he read aloud, "'his servants, horses, carriage and an annual annuity to cover all other expenses proper to his title and station.'" Rendón's tone dripped sarcasm and open contempt for all nobility.

"I have satisfied his other creditors," Sirena informed him firmly. "'Bought them out' I believe is the more vulgar term. So I'm quite free to assign any rents and revenues from the Àvila estate that will enable its former owner to maintain a life style proper to the last surviving son of an old and noble house."

Sirena could see Rendón was furious, for it was obvious to her he had come prepared to take immense satisfaction in presiding over the divestment of a criollo aristocrat whose class and wealth he envied. To thwart his intent she had spent every waking hour this past month at La Soledad, poring over ancient deeds, each time-darkened parchment presenting its own special challenge of faded ink, spidery script and antique Spanish terms. Now she was sure she held firm legal claim to every land and water right dating as far back as 1598, when the First Marqués de Àvila had received his title and a generous land grant directly from the Crown.

"Well, it's a very high-handed way of conducting a foreclosure!" Rendón protested. "I find it particularly arbitrary since your long-standing unpaid loan to the Fourth Marqués of thirty-thousand pesos makes you his largest creditor. You alone could reduce the wastrel to beggary!"

"Yes," she replied icily, making her opponent's trump card her own, "fortunately for him it was I who held that note."

Handing him a second quill she asked with a smile. "Now shall we sign?" It was not so much a question as a command.

With poor grace Rendón signed, impressed the document with his notarial seal and pushed it back.

Sirena signed her full Christian name, Mariá Amantina O'Malley de Mendoza, and under it her unique, intricately drawn rúbrica, without which her signature was not legally binding. Dropping hot wax on the document, she sealed it with her sapphire crest. Don Gabriel signed as witness.

Now," Sirena declared expansively, "we can proceed with the routine part of the foreclosure."

"That, my dear, was a gesture worthy of your father," Don Gabriel commented later, sinking into a tapestried bergere to the left of the fireplace. "You knew you would be judged a faithless friend and a heartless neighbor, but you foreclosed anyway."

Sirena stood gazing soberly into the hearth where a green cottonwood log, pouring sap, alternately hissed and blazed.

"God knows I tried to find a less costly way to save him," she admitted, "but his other creditors were determined to throw him to the wolves." A brief smile played across her lips. "Even the notary felt so cheated out of his prey he refused to stay for dinner."

"It's the spirit of spitefulness and envy sown abroad by the Insurrection," Don Gabriel observed sagely. "But at least now, when the Marqués sets out for Mexico, he knows he has a home waiting for him. Your timing was providential for him."

"I hope it's providential for us, as well."

"Suggesting what, my dear?"

"Well, considering the bottom dropped out of both the sheep and wool markets with the Insurrection, and neither of our Guanajuato mines is producing a fraction of its pre-war silver, it's hardly the time for me to layout a king's ransom for five additional haciendas we could live quite well without."

"Now, child, don't go blaming yourself after the fact. You did what you had to do for honor's sake."

"I'm only concerned I may have put our own estate at risk. I've increased our herds, but doubled the borders our lancers must patrol." She was reminded of the grim figures she had entered in La Frontera's Master Ledger today:

LOST TO APACHE RAIDS SINCE JANUARY, 1822
100 horses stolen.
40 mules slaughtered for meat.
200 sheep run off.
One sheep camp burned.
Four shepherds killed.
Three women and two children carried into captivity.
(Requiem aeternum dona eis, Domine!)

"On the brighter side, the wheat market's never been stronger," Don Gabriel was saying, "and today good carriage mules are fetching the highest price in years. Since Ávila wheat ranks among the kingdom's finest, and their mules are as good as ours, I think you weighed your options very well."

"I certainly tried," she said, flashing him a grateful smile. "You and Papá didn't train me to invest in salted mines! Once I saw Soledad's

Master Ledger I knew production could be brought back to where dear Adrian had it before the wars. But it's going to take a lot of work."

Leaning against the mantle, she cupped her chin in her right hand and gazed out the window facing south. It commanded her favorite view, a magnificent vista of cloud-shadowed Graciana pastures, vineyards and orchards ringed by violet-hued hills, the entire panorama sweeping away endlessly toward the far horizon. There, hundreds of leagues to the south lay New Spain's fertile heartland, the Bajío, and the incomparably beautiful city of Guanajuato. Memories of her enchanted childhood there filled her with a sudden longing for that well-ordered time and place.

"I guess it's all the other problems, combined with the Àvila purchase that worry me," she admitted. "And I'm so anxious for Tristán to come home."

Don Gabriel, relaxed in his chair, drew out a fragrant Havana from a dragon-covered Chinese humidor, pared off the end and lit it slowly.

"Well, I'm sure he and Don Octavio have persuaded the Comanche headmen to renew the Spanish Alliance," he said confidently, releasing a great plume of blue smoke and settling back in his chair. "After all, Ecueracapa's people have held the peace for thirty years. No earthly reason they should break it now. Those charged with arranging the formal details know that Tristán was the legal representative for the Viceroy. Everything was ready for their arrival upon his return with the tribal leaders. A new series of commemorative coins had been made by the same mint in Mexico that made the originals, presented at the signing of the first Comanche peace treaty. The medals represent peace to the Indians, who believe that as long as the coins last, so does the peace."

Sirena's housekeeper entered through the open doors, bearing a silver tray with a bottle of Hennessey brandy and two glasses, for a quiet celebration of the Àvila annexation.

Alberta radiated pride as the trusted "mistress of the keys" in a noble house. She wore her customary beige cotton bodice and peplum with an ankle-length skirt of blue Querétaro cloth and silver-buckled leather shoes. Two long, graying braids framed her broad bronze face.

Attached to the leather belt girdling her waist she wore her badge of office -- a large metal ring bristling with keys, one for every door, drawer, chest and cupboard in the casco. But beneath this veneer of

Spanish protocol, Alberta was still pure Tarascan, rooted in pre-conquest Michoacán, solid as a cedar and constant as its shade.

"So has the dear old Fourth Marqués de Àvila shaken off his heartless creditors for good?" Alberta asked anxiously.

"Yes, Alberta and he'll be staying with us a few days before he leaves for Mexico. Please make the guest suite ready with an extra quilt and a scented brazier."

After Alberta left the room, Don Gabriel poured two glasses of brandy. Handing Sirena her drink he asked, "Was there pressing news in that letter that came by courier today?" He sighed. "You don't see many express riders like him up here any more, willing to deliver urgent mail."

"Oh, I set that letter aside when the notary came," Sirena said, going to her desk to retrieve the envelope. "It's from someone in Guanajuato."

"I wonder who is still there that we know."

"It's probably one more British investor trying to lease or buy our mines."

"They are a persistent lot!" he observed tartly. "Just because we've been crippled by the war, they seem to think their sterling pound can buy anything they fancy, short of their soul's salvation."

Returning to the sofa, Sirena opened the letter, curiosity prompting her to glance at the signature first. The elaborately drawn, "Lorenzo Santa Cruz," fairly leapt from the page. The shock of seeing that name after all these years drove every other thought from her mind.

Although they had been children together, she could never forget the harrowing eighteen months she had spent at this man's side. Why was he writing her now? She had been certain that up here she would be safely beyond his reach. Like many others she had known back in the halcyon days before the Insurrection, she had been glad to lose him in its chaotic aftermath. Still her father had always counseled charity. It was possible Lorenzo had changed, perhaps even managed to build a new life on the ruin he had made of the old. The very least she could do was read what he had to say.

> *Most Esteemed and Gracious Condesa:*
>
> *I write you as a Lieutenant Colonel in the proud Army of the Three Guarantees. Since our Emperor has appointed me his Imperial Tax*

Collector, it is my task to raise urgently needed funds to help establish a stable and solvent government after years of civil strife.

I trust the rumor is true you'll be taking over the bankrupt Àvila estate, for it would make you the largest landholder in the North, if not the entire Empire. As I am expected to raise 600,000 pesos in the next thirty days, I assured my Emperor that, thanks to your great wealth and our longstanding friendship, the First Condesa of the House of Graciana can be easily persuaded to donate the entire sum.

Sirena's forced goodwill curdled. How dare this muleteer's son presume on their acquaintance to press such a ruinous loan from her! And to enrich that vainglorious pop-in-jay, Iturbide, who had just overthrown the legitimate viceroyalty and crowned himself Emperor! Damn Lorenzo! If he didn't have an army of 60,000 well-armed men behind him she would rollout Frontera's cannon and greet him with a hail of grapeshot!

But in the event you do not feel disposed to volunteer such a loan, I'm ready to make public that matter which has remained private between us for so many years. When you reflect upon this secret's nature and the devastating effect its disclosure would have on your own happiness and that of those you hold dear -- I'm quite sure you'll agree that your father's renowned prodigality is a virtue well worth emulating.

Sirena was thunderstruck. The deadliness of his intent, the undeniable truth underlying his threat and the awful consequences of her own possible exposure left her reeling. Only her uncle's questioning gaze kept her from giving way to panic.

"My dear, you're white as a sheet. Is it bad news?"

"Oh, no," she lied hastily. "It's what I thought it was. Another Englishman making the usual outrageous demands."

"Well remember, time is on our side. As long as our Zacatecas mines are still in full production up here in the North, we can afford to let those in Guanajuato lie idle a while longer." He studied her pensively. "Besides, I know you don't want to see foreigners working your father's tunnels and galleries any more than I do."

He finished his drink and rose from the chair. "Well, it's time I washed up for dinner," he said, and then turning in the doorway added, "Remember, things always right themselves in the end."

If only they would, she thought desperately. Alone, in her office, she began pacing as she read the rest of Lorenzo's letter.

☙ ❧

I expect be at La Frontera within the week to pick up your libranza, and as always, I look forward to seeing you.
Ah, yes, my dear Condesa, how roles and fortunes change when kingdom's fall!
Respectfully, Your Friend,
  Lt. Colonel, Lorenzo Santa Cruz

So, after all these years, Lorenzo's lust for power had finally culminated in the ultimate treachery -- blackmail!

Move with extreme caution now, she told herself fearfully, one step at a time, as though descending one of those perpendicular 'chicken ladders' in the mines. Lorenzo has no real evidence to prove his claim. It's your word against his. Only Madre Pilar and Bishop Legázpi knew the whole truth and not even a second Diocletian could have wrung it from either of them.

Suddenly exhausted, she sank down in the friar's chair that had belonged to Doña Graciana, the family's foundress. Out of long habit her fingers closed around the familiar carving on the arms, its dark walnut stroked to a lustrous black by generations of caring hands. Merely touching the satiny wood renewed her spirit and resolve. Somehow she would find a way to keep Lorenzo from destroying that which, over the years, he had come to envy and despise - the House of Graciana.

She glanced up at life-size portraits of her parents, facing each other from opposite sides of the bookcase behind her desk. The artist had captured both in their prime - Doña Isabel at twenty-three, Don Patrick, -- forty-two -- in that spring of 1786, the year of her own birth. The likenesses were so lifelike they seemed about to speak.

Her father, with his marvelously expressive smile and deep blue eyes brimming with merriment -- how would he confront such black ingratitude, after all the money and education he had lavished on Lorenzo?

"Appeal to his honor," she could almost hear him say. "No matter how low a man may fall, honor burns on in his soul, a deathless ember of the Divine!"

And the lovely titian-haired Doña Isabel? "Admit to nothing!" would have been her mother's intuitive advice. How often had she heard her say, "A lie that saves family honor, even God accepts as truth!"

She walked over to examine more closely the seed pearls sewn into the lace of her mother's gown. How exquisitely they had been rendered by the maestro's young apprentice! Who would believe an eight-year-old child capable of such mastery? And who would have guessed that boy would grow up to become the traitorous Lorenzo Santa Cruz?

Moving away, she recalled the haunting words of her mother, now a noble inmate of Madre Pilar's Asylum for Demented Women in Mexico City. As regal in dress as she was unsettled in mind, she paced the cloisters daily, delivering the same solemn speech to any who would listen.

"Our world was a fragile peristyle of silver filigree, easily toppled by a storm," she would intone. "But the hail that fell on the Second Day of May in '86 was no ordinary storm. It was beyond the strength of mortal man to bear! Only the first in the long train of calamities that continue to afflict us! Alas, from that day forward, nothing in my world was ever the same again!"

Sirena shuddered. Could that poor mad sibyl have been right? Was it conceivable that the values Don Patrick had given her, values she had risked her life to preserve, and which she was determined to pass on to her posterity, were no longer valid? Could the end of such things as honor, nobility and even the Spanish Empire itself have been foreshadowed by a portent so commonplace as hail?

But it was undeniable, she recalled, gazing out the narrow fortress-like window, so many significant events had occurred in the wake of that storm. The following day witnessed Don Patrick's incredible bonanza, her own lavish christening, the fateful entry of Bishop Legázpi into their lives! On that day too, Lorenzo's brilliant future was mapped out for him by his father and her own, while the two men stood on the broad atrium of the Graciana chapel. And at their feet lay that which had made everything possible -- the rich and noble city of Guanajuato, with its torrent of silver.

PART ONE

SILVER DUST AND SPANISH WINE

1786

*The Conde's family chapel
was dearly built and fine,
For its mortar was not mixed
with ordinary lime.
He used instead a priceless blend
of silver dust
and Spanish wine.*

18th Century Guanajuato Legend

1

In the Graciana palace, high on a stony *bufa* overlooking the canyon-cradled city of Guanajuato, the pampered young wife of Don Patrick O'Malley, First Conde of Graciana, the richest silver lord in Spanish America, awoke with a start.

For a moment Doña Isabel lay still, listening to the beguiling patter of desperately needed rain. Sitting bolt upright in bed she glanced eagerly at her shuttered bedroom window. An errant shaft of sunlight, brazen as the serpent in Eden, stole across the flowered Aubusson carpet. With a sinking heart she realized what she mistook for rain was the usual bickering of iron-shod hooves on cobblestones, as the first mule train of the day toiled along the *Veta Madre's* ore-rich spine, bearing mercury, machinery and tools to the upper mines of La Graciana, La Sirena and El Rey.

It was already the second of May, eve of the Feast of the Holy Cross, and still no break in the longest drought in living memory. Even as she steeled herself for one more day as tinder-dry as all the rest in this long and anxious spring, she was painfully aware that continuance of the drought was not the worst that lay ahead for her.

Today, as on every other since her marriage to the Conde nine months ago, she must expect Don Francisco Durán, her husband's business advisor and dearest friend to call. Once again she must treat him as the casual acquaintance her husband thought him to be, when in fact he was the only man Isabel had ever loved. Each time they met in Don Patrick's presence she yearned to throw herself into Francisco's arms. The strength of will it took to keep from doing so had kept her in a perpetual state of emotional exhaustion.

Sinking back onto the pillows, she indulged the long-forsaken luxury of lying abed without the bulk and burden of an unborn child. Submissive to God's Will in most other matters, Isabel had never resigned herself to the many indignities of pregnancy. Bearing this fourth child at twenty-three had been far worse than bearing her first at sixteen. In spite of that, she silently offered up her morning thanksgiving prayers to Saint Anthony and Saint Anne.

Not that it was a delivery any sane woman would give thanks for, she thought grimly. Her labor had lasted two days and nights, with agony enough to earn a martyr's palm. Crowning it all, a reverse presentation proved so excruciating she had begged to die. Although she knew she owed her life to her Parisian-trained surgeon, Juan Pinal, Isabel was scrupulous. She always took care to give her saints their due.

When Doctor Juan told her the fruit of all this pain was *not* the son she'd been storming heaven for, she had burst into tears. God -- for some inscrutable reason of His own -- chose to waste the priceless Graciana title on a girl!

"Come now, your baby's sound as silver," Doctor Juan had said consolingly. "There's no question that she'll live."

Although he had misread the reason for her grief, Isabel was deeply touched. For the space of a heartbeat she had been tempted to open up her soul to this kindly man who was also one of her husband's oldest friends, but the words refused to come. She was not really surprised. Being honest, even in the confessional, was not in her nature. Confidences that could be used as weapons against her, were luxuries she could not afford, desperate though she was to share her guilt. No, a Condesa counted enough potential enemies among the envious poor, so why arm one's peers with indiscreet disclosures of family scandal and sin?

But one momentous decision did emerge from all her suffering. Isabel vowed this fourth child would be her last. Don Patrick had his heir, even if it was only a girl. So, from now on, if God were good and she herself -- resourceful as many virtuous wives knew how to be -- she would never endure such agony again for any man.

She found herself glancing guiltily at her husband's side of the carved and canopied *matrimonial* although she was well aware he always rose an hour before dawn. Having shaved and dressed in his own chamber, he would now be in the hushed house chapel at the head of the stairs. There, before its triple-tiered reredos, where a dozen wood-carved saints reigned in gold-leafed glory, he devoted the first half hour of this and every day, to a prayerful recitation of matins and lauds.

That done, he then strolled along the upstairs corridor to the formal dining room, his roguish blue eyes downcast, his soul recollected as a Camaldolese. Observing him was a long gallery of magisterial forbears -- portraits of first conquistadores in plumed helmets, their lordly sons, grandsons and great-grandsons equally imposing in velvet, lace, and the long grey wigs of later centuries -- mentors all, whose judgments Patrick heeded as if everyone were still alive. There too, hung a few prized *retablos*, each painting capturing for posterity the deliverance of some distinguished ancestor from entrapment and death in cave-in, flood or fire in mine gallery or shaft. Above each graphically illustrated miraculous event, floated the painted image of whichever Lord, Virgin or Saint it was to whom the rescued miner and his heirs owed eternal thanks.

Breakfasting alone, Patrick would sip his morning chocolate the way he liked it best, scalding hot and whipped to a froth by Alberta's expertly spun *molinillo*, while he read the latest issue of the *Gacéta de Mexico*. This daily newspaper, linking him to New Spain's economic hub, came by courier from the distant City of Mexico each Tuesday and Friday morning without fail, at a cost that Isabel, who had been raised in impoverished circumstances, regarded as appallingly extravagant.

With her eyes closed Isabel could see Patrick cutting a gallant figure in his frock-coat, waistcoat, knee breeches and fine Cordovan boots, tripping lightly down the stone staircase to the family patio. There, welcomed by a corps of worshipful servants, his day, and Isabel's as well, began the instant Indian maids lifted silken covers from a dozen cages made of silver filigree. Scores of canaries, mockingbirds and silver-tongued clarines flooded the *palacio* with birdsong and of course, there was no sleeping after that.

Isabel knew exactly when the groom led out a hot-blooded Spanish Barb and Don Patrick swung into the saddle. The repeated ring of well-shod hooves on stone told her he was caracoling his mount out through the huge brass-studded gates before setting off at a fast trot up the mountain road.

Halfway between his own Graciana and La Sirena mines he would draw rein before the family chapel, a triumph of the roccoco style in sculptured pink stone. Now, as the triple chimes of the Angelus came drifting down to her, Isabel pictured him doffing his tricorn and pausing long enough to recite a proper *Ave* before spurring on up the mountain to his favorite -- but still barren -- La Sirena mine.

Patrick was a good man, Isabel admitted to herself as she slid out of bed and slipped into a silken robe. But that fact did nothing to sweeten the bitterness of life with him. Kneeling at her *prie-dieu* before a small image of the Virgin of Montserrat her father had brought with him years before from Spain, Isabel composed herself for prayer. But the moment she closed her eyes the image of Francisco's face swam before her. The more she struggled to put him from her, the more hauntingly real he became.

Oh God, how she loved him! How she had always loved him! Her whole being thrilled again at the memory of their one night spent together during the final year of her miserable first marriage to old Don Jeronimo. Neither remorse nor confession after her husband's death had been enough to draw out the thorn of this illicit passion, so deeply embedded in her soul. The braid in which her red-gold hair was strictly confined slowly came undone. With a soft despairing cry, she lay her head on her arms and wept.

"*Cuidado!*" a woman's strident voice rang out from below, a voice that was somehow scolding, cajoling and comforting all in one. "Gaspar, *do* be careful with those trunks! You know I'm godmother to the infant First Condesa tomorrow and all my gifts are packed in them!"

Mother of God, Isabel thought frantically, dashing the tears from her eyes, Aunt Amantina's here already! She rushed to the window to let in the light, re-plaiting her hair as she went. With the velvet drapes drawn and the shutters open, the splendidly furnished room came alive. Wide white window reveals reflected the bright morning sun, coaxing fire from the prisms of a crystal chandelier, from a dozen silver candelabras and every piece of ornately carved and gilded French furniture in the room.

With cold water poured from a gaily decorated Majolica pitcher into its matching wash basin she splashed her face, then scrutinized her reflection in the glass, seeking any trace of tears, for if anyone could flush out deception it was her father's widowed sister, Amantina.

Pleased with what she saw Isabel was grateful that years of rigid self-control had given her features their hard, cutting edge. Hooded grey eyes, straight nose and pronounced widow's peak combined to cast an aura of austerity about her. Only her mouth betrayed her true vulnerability, even now when trying hard to look severe. She humbly thanked the Virgin and saints that she'd been born beautiful and sin didn't show.

Stepping out onto the corridor Isabel looked down into the flower-filled family patio as Aunt Amantina emerged from the second, or 'servant's patio' beyond. There carriages entered and Patrick's prized

Arabian's were stabled. Her aunt's arrival had brought the entire palace staff on the run and the energetic dowager was trailed by a cortege of servants, her own and Isabel's. Each was lugging some piece of the mountain of baggage she always brought when she came over from Linda Vista, her hacienda near the village of Dolores, a short ride of only four leagues from Guanajuato.

"Don't risk the stairs on my account," Amantina called to Isabel. "They don't bother me. Why, I climb more stairs than a sacristan with four bell towers does in all of Holy Week!"

Watching the spare old lady lift her trailing brown velvet riding skirt at the head of her procession of carriers, Isabel noticed how much more vivacious her aunt was at fifty-five than when she first knew her as a widow of thirty-three. Her chestnut hair was gun metal grey now and drawn back severely in a knot, her narrow face weathered by sun and wind, but her blue-grey eyes shone with a fierce self-esteem she had not possessed when her husband was alive.

"I'm sorry I wasn't here for your labor," she apologized, embracing Isabel at the top of the stairs, "but the drought has worked havoc with my trees. And at the worst time, too, when the cocoons were in their third molt! I've spent the last weeks running between my mulberry groves and my silk houses, making sure the trees have water and the delicate young worms enough tender new leaves."

Turning to the retinue of servants who had come to a halt on the steps behind her, Amantina issued a flurry of fresh orders. "Everything goes into my suite at the end of the corridor," she exclaimed emphatically, the out-of-date triple-tiered white-linen cuffs of her brown bolero making her gestures more emphatic still. "No, not you, Gaspar! Those two trunks go with me into Doña Isabel's bedchamber." With a firm step she led the way.

The olive-eyed Indians nodded mutely, having learned from experience that Doña Amantina's bountiful gratuities, dispensed at the end of each visit, repaid their patience.

"Of course, I knew you were safe in the care of Doctor Juan," Amantina rattled on. "Thank Heaven Don Patrick was his childhood friend up North and persuaded him to practice here instead of Mexico City! What would any of us in this province have done these past ten years without him?"

Embracing her niece a second time, Amantina held her at arm's length, scrutinizing her more closely. "My dear, you're much too pale! Isn't anyone taking care of you?"

5

"Of course they are," Isabel laughed. "Alberta plies me with teas all day long, and Don Patrick caters to my every whim."

"Well, that's nothing new for the Conde," Amantina mused, hovering over Gaspar until he put down the two trunks and left the room. "Don Patrick's a perfect saint, but I do believe he pampers you to the point of folly."

Although her tone was scolding, Amantina made no secret of the fact she adored the Conde and regarded Isabel's marriage to him an unqualified blessing. Isabel could not help wondering what the proper old lady would think if she were to tell her how shameless he was in bed? While her first husband, old Don Jeronimo, had scarcely touched her body in five years of marriage, siring two sons and a daughter in stygian darkness without so much as lifting her gown, Patrick was a man of strong sexuality and passion.

On their wedding night he had astounded Isabel by coming to their matrimonial as natural as Adam and persuading her to cast aside all modesty as well, while candlelight played on their nakedness. Even now the memory caused her to burn with shame. And as if that were not bad enough, he had stunned her by confessing that she was the one true love of his life. Convinced he had married her merely to perpetuate his title, Isabel had eased her own guilt by assuming their union was safely loveless on both sides. His declaration had placed one more straw of remorse on her overburdened conscience.

"Well, if you think the Conde spoils *me*," Isabel said aloud, casting a glance of mock despair heavenward, "you should see him with the little First Condesa!"

"Fathers *ought* to spoil their daughters," Amantina declared authoritatively, settling into a green damask chair. "Believe it or not, my own father spoiled me. But he also expected something back. *That's the trick.*"

Isabel perched nervously on the foot of her chaise longue, trying unsuccessfully to imagine Amantina as a little girl.

"Because Papá taught me to reason and cipher as well as any man," Amantina continued, "I was able to take over running Linda Vista after my husband drowned. No fortune-hunting immigrant from Spain got his peasant hands on the pittance I was left. I invested it in my groves and silk houses and in growing wheat for Guanajuato's bakers of fine white bread. A woman never knows what she can do until she must."

While Isabel admired Amantina's keen business sense, she openly disapproved of women mixing in the affairs of men. It justified her ignorance and guaranteed no man would ever bother to solicit her advice. So far the ploy had served her well.

"Well, if Don Patrick spoils the baby," Isabel said, bringing the subject back to herself, "maybe it means he's not too disappointed with me for giving him a girl."

"Whatever makes you think he's displeased?"

"Because *I* am!" she shot back resentfully. "Felipe's my eldest son, and by rights *he* should have the title. Instead he'll spend his life being lorded over by a titled baby sister. It seems so unfair that all his own father left him claim to was a mountain of debts."

"Don Jeronimo was never cut out to be a financier!" Amantina parried. "I warned your mother before she signed the marriage contract that the old man had ventured everything but his immortal soul on helping out-of-pocket miners sink new shafts and deepen barren ones." Armantina sighed and then added quickly. "Just compare Don Jeronimo's poor performance to that of the Conde's own advisor, Don Francisco Durán. Now *there's* a born *aviador*, a real wizard at making money grow!"

At mention of Francisco's name Isabel felt herself grow faint. "Yes, I suppose he is," she murmured trying to sound disinterested. "All I ask is that he looks after our affairs well enough so the Conde won't need to be asking *my* advice."

"Ah, but there *are* times when a wife's counsel is sounder than any outsider," Armantina cautioned. "Not even Don Francisco has been able to keep the Conde from sinking all his ready cash into La Sirena, trying to turn that salted mine into another Graciana. Don Patrick should know bonanzas as big as that simply don't strike twice in one lifetime!"

"But Auntie, I never discuss the mines with him.

"Simply explain to him his soundest course lies in declaring the Graciana estate, a *mayorazgos*, including both mines here, those up North, this palace and the one in Mexico City, all the haciendas administered by La Frontera, and yes, even the family portraits, silver and jewels."

Isabel was lost in talk of money at any time, but Armantina's mention of Francisco had unnerved her completely. "I've got no head for such things" she hedged.

"Child, it's the only way to keep a great estate intact when a founder dies. Otherwise lawyers will grow fat on the suits your children file against each other. The King will take his fifth, a canon will offer up a thousand Masses for the repose of your soul and the whole grand scheme that took generations to build will go a-glimmering!" Amantina sighed as though she had personally undergone the whole exhausting process. "That's where your own father failed you," she added sharply. "I don't care if he was my brother -- he failed to protect his legacy."

"But Tia, poor Papá died before he could even draw up a will!" Isabel protested.

"All the more reason to make sure it gets done this time. Tomorrow's the First Condesa's christening, so you should see to it she isn't pauperized by some unforseen family tragedy the way you and your mother were."

"That's another reason I wish the baby were a boy," Isabel said, circling back to her first premise. "Sons know how to get things done. Girls are so helpless in everything!"

Isabel rose to her feet. "You know yourself they're always the first to catch those deadly fevers that come up from Mexico with the promptness of the mail. I lost my three dearest cousins to that one unpronounceable Aztec plague. Only Inéz survived, and she was the plainest of them all."

Isabel had been hotly jealous of Inéz ever since the childless Amantina adopted her husband's niece after the girls' parents died in the same epidemic. Until then Amantina had been like a second mother to Isabel and she resented being made to share her aunt's affections with Inéz.

"Now, now," Amantina chided her, "no need to be uncharitable. After all, I survived and so did you, delicate though you've always been. My concern for a titled heiress like yours is not her health, but arranging a proper marriage."

"I know, I know," Isabel nodded absently, seating herself again. "It's not an empty saying, 'A son whenever you wish, a daughter when you can.'"

"May God spare you from a willful girl bent on marrying below her station or -- God forbid! -- taking the *paso atras*!"

Isabel stared at her aunt in disbelief. It had never even crossed her mind that any daughter of hers might risk that gravest of all perils to befall a woman of the silver elite, taking the "backward step" by marrying a mestizo, an Indian -- or worse, a casta! In her circle the color taboo was so much a part of life no one need put it in words.

"But such a thing would be unthinkable to her!"

"A mother can only pray," Amantina said tartly, her eyes deep wells of wisdom. "The *dueña* hasn't been born who can't be gulled by a lovesick girl." As she spoke she got to her feet purposefully and opened one of the trunks Gaspar had deposited in the room. "But first things first!"

Amidst the whisper of crumpled China paper, she lifted out a cloud of sheer white crepe de chine and Chantilly lace.

"The infant Condesa's christening dress!"

"Oh, Auntie, it's heavenly!" Isabel exclaimed.

"Only the overture to the *zarzuela*," Amantina remarked, opening the second trunk and unfolding a pale grey taffeta gown whose lace trim was sewn with scores of seed pearls.

"For the most beautiful woman in the province," she announced, "the loveliest dress in the kingdom! My Estella, made it from a French pattern not yet a year old, that was sent to me by a friend who lives at Versailles."

"Why, it's even more beautiful than my wedding gown!"

Amantina smiled and then fixed Isabel with a questioning glance. "Speaking of your wedding gown, Estelle had it all sewn and waiting three whole months before you finally set the date. May I ask *why* it took you so long to say 'yes' to the richest and best looking silver lord in the kingdom?"

Isabel flushed nervously, afraid to risk the necessary lie. "Oh, I just thought I'd make him wait and wonder. He's always had everything his own way."

Amantina paused to close the trunk lid before pursuing the subject. "I think what surprised me most was that Francisco Durán didn't come forward and ask for your hand again this time, as he did before your first marriage."

Isabel blanched. "Francisco?" she stammered. "But why?"

"Oh, I don't know. I argued against him with your mother at the time, but I did *like* him even then and I felt sorry he had lost his father the same tragic way you lost yours."

Amantina closed the lids of both trunks softly. "Of course he *was* poor as Job's turkey back then and your mother was in such dire need of money." She looked directly at her niece and Isabel dropped her own gaze defensively. "But in those days how could any of us have dreamed a penniless clerk would become almost a millionaire overnight?"

Isabel would never forget that mysterious stroke of fortune that had taken Francisco from her. After his father died tragically and left him an orphan he had been forced to work as a clerk for Don Jeronimo. Once Isabel was married to Francisco's employer the two childhood sweethearts were thrown together constantly and soon found themselves hopelessly in love. The night she spent in Francisco's bed he had vowed on his honor he would marry her if ever she were widowed. Given Don Jeronimo's age that was not unlikely.

"It surprised me when he suddenly left town to sail for Manila and go into the China trade," Amantina was saying.

"Yes, I remember," Isabel murmured, vividly recalling the day, barely a month after Francisco left, when Don Jeronimo toppled over in San Roqué Plaza, dead of a massive stroke. Later, when the will was read she-learned she had been left almost destitute. Still she was sure Francisco would return, and when he did would marry her.

Knowing the galleon's annual round trip took at least twelve months, Isabel was secretly glad that her enforced year of mourning made it easy to put off all other suitors. Whether Francisco came back rich or poor, she was counting the days.

"It still seems incredible to me that he came home inside a year with enough money and merchandise to buy and stock his own Chinese import shop." Amantina marveled." As I said, he's a wizard at making himself and others rich."

Isabel reflected bitterly upon those weeks of waiting for Francisco to pay his respects after his triumphant return from Manila. By then she was being courted by the two wealthiest silver lords in town and he couldn't help but know it. At last Don Patrick gave her an ultimatum. Being in desperate financial need, with three small children to care for, she could wait no longer. With a broken heart she accepted the Conde's proposal, and then was deeply shocked when Francisco appeared as a well-wisher at the wedding.

Why had he abandoned her? Now that he was her husband's partner and a daily visitor in her home, she realized it was not because he no longer loved her. One day recently he had dared to stop her on the stair. "My dearest," he whispered, "please forgive me. It was not possible to keep my word!"

"Oh well," Amantina was saying, "I suppose it all worked out for the best, because your cousin Inéz tells me she's determined to charm him into marrying her."

"*Francisco marry Inéz?*" Isabel cried filled with such a bitter sense of loss and-betrayal she had to bite her lip to keep from breaking into tears.

"I know! I've warned her she may be in for a longer wait than she expects," Amantina observed. "At twenty-eight she's over ripe for marriage, while at the same age Durán still thinks himself too young. You know how Guanajuato's merchants and miners are -- they almost never marry 'til they're well up in their forties."

Isabel stood up suddenly, cradling the grey silk dress in her arms. She could feel Amantina's eyes upon her, but she was too stricken to speak.

"You look exhausted, child," Armantina noted solicitously. "I forget how weak you still must be."

"Yes, I think I ought to lie down," Isabel lied.

"I'm tired too," Amantina, said, "I was up at two this morning so I could drive my mule train over the hills from Linda Vista in the cool of night. I didn't want the midday sun pressing wrinkles in those two gowns -- not after poor Estella went to so much work." Her face softened. "She's such a treasure. It's almost as though God made up to her for being born a *mulatta*, by making her so gifted with a needle."

"Be sure and tell her how pleased I am with the gowns!"

"You can tell her yourself tomorrow. She's riding over from Linda Vista for the christening. She wouldn't miss it for the world. She's never seen a real live bishop before, let alone one who is a cousin of her mistress and comes directly from the court in Madrid."

Isabel's eyes widened. "Oh, the Bishop! Dear Lord, I'd forgotten all about him! I haven't heard a word since he wrote me from Mexico a month ago, accepting my invitation to baptize the baby when it was born. Have *you* had any news?"

"Yes," Amantina said, pausing in the doorway. "Father Hidalgo was the visiting preacher at Dolores this past Sunday. He told me he was meeting the Bishop's coach at Querétaro and would be acting as his guide. According to him they should be arriving sometime late this afternoon or evening."

ॐ 2 ॐ

When Amantina left her room, Isabel stepped out onto the balcony, drawing in great drafts of clean mountain air in an effort to choke back another flood of tears.

Almost without seeing it, she took in the usual morning concourse of mule trains, muleteers and vendors hawking everything from a load of charcoal to baskets of giant red strawberries fresh from the Bajío. A few bold-eyed servant girls sauntered past the men, holding tall black clay jars on their shoulders, their upper arms provocatively bare as they fetched household water from the public fountain. For some reason the brazen girls reminded her of Inéz and she was inflamed with jealousy at the realization that her cousin was utterly free to seduce Francisco, while she herself had to cruelly repress her own carnal cravings for him.

Turning angrily to go inside, she caught a quick, disquieting image of a young boy riding pell-mell astride a flaxen-maned chestnut stallion. Singly, horse and rider were well known to her, but together they were cause for alarm. The artist's apprentice riding Francisco's horse? Something must have happened at the mines! Her hands flew to her mouth to stifle a frightened cry.

"Lorenzo Santa Cruz! What in God's name are you doing on *El Cid*?" The words welled up from the depths of Isabel's own concern, but they were spoken by Alberta as she came rushing into the street from the second patio door directly below Isabel. "Has there been an accident at La Sirena mine?"

"No, nothing's wrong, Alberta," Lorenzo replied airily, bringing the beautiful animal to a fast, showy stop before a crowd of curious Indian and mestizo boys who had suddenly materialized from nowhere.

"Don Francisco would never give you his permission to ride that horse except in an emergency."

Concealed behind the shutter, Isabel watched the cocksure boy draw himself up proudly in the saddle, his shoulder-length mahogany hair and immense brown eyes making his chalk-white complexion seem whiter still.

"He told me I could ride him," Lorenzo said stubbornly, dismounting with ease, and taking hold of the headstall to pull the animal's noble head closer to his own. "He says, 'I'm more to be trusted with a valuable horse than some grown-ups he knows.'"

"Then what news was so urgent you had to race here on the fastest horse in town to deliver it?"

"Uncle Matiás sent me on ahead to set up his easel and paints, and remind Doña Isabel her sitting is at ten o'clock this morning." Then, with an air of self-importance intended to impress his youthful audience he boasted, "I'll be rendering the lady's lace and jewels -- the hardest part!"

Isabel could not help but smile as the audacious boy passed from her sight, leading the stallion as he followed Alberta into the patio below. "You just wait and see," he told Alberta, "one day I'll be a gentleman like Don Francisco with a prize Arabian stallion of my own."

"Hah!" Alberta chided him, "I'll be married to the Viceroy before any muleteer's son is accepted as a gentleman by this town's silver elite!"

Stepping inside, Isabel held the open-robed taffeta gown against her. Studying her reflection in a pier glass she was pleased to see the grey silk matched her eyes exactly, while the *fichu's* bows and rosettes were the same red-gold as her hair. Striking various poses she felt her spirits rise.

Yes, she did have her figure back, the slimmest waist in town. And the new wet nurse was working out so well her own breasts had dried up completely. Then from somewhere deep inside, a girlish voice told her to look as bewitching as possible at tomorrow's christening ceremonies. Make Francisco suffer the same agonies of lust and longing as you!

Her cheeks turned crimson as a sudden hot rush of desire and guilt swept through her at the thought. Such a deliberate flaunting of her beauty would be wicked and cruel, and yet -- why not? Was she supposed to hand him over on a silver platter to her spinster cousin Inéz?

"*Mi alma*, may I come in?"

At the sound of her husband's voice Isabel gasped. Good God, he wasn't half a league away at the bottom of that worthless mine! He was at her very door! For one wild, unreasoning moment she believed she had been surprised in her lover's arms and instinctively cast about for some place to hide him. Then, recovering from her mindless panic, she found her voice. "Of course, Patricio, *pasa*!" she called, holding the gown against her like protective armor.

The double doors flew open and Don Patrick burst into the room. At sight of his disheveled appearance Isabel started. "Patricio! Whatever has happened to you?"

His wavy black hair was limned with a fine white dust, his usually immaculate white lawn shirt and embroidered silk waistcoat both streaked with grime. Even his Cordovan boots that reached to mid-thigh on his lean muscular legs were caked with half-dried mud.

In three long strides he was beside her, his blue eyes dancing with restrained excitement, the dimples at each corner of his square generous mouth deepening as his smile spread. That was the trouble with Patrick, Isabel thought irritably. No matter how serious something was, he always turned it into a celebration.

"Oh, I'm all in one piece," he assured her gaily, "but there was some -- well, unexpected excitement at La Sirena, and I had to go down into the shaft."

"I'll bring fresh clothes so you can change."

"No, mi alma, I've the rest of my life for that!" he shouted almost angrily. "I've come to give you the most princely gift any mother of a First Condesa could wish for!"

Holding his right hand behind his back teasingly and being mindful not to brush her with his muddied shirt, he covered her parted lips with his own.

"Everything they say is true. I'm the luckiest man alive to have such an angelic wife. And now that you've," he groped for a properly discreet term, " -- recovered. . ." After a second kiss he whispered, "Surely you must know our wedding night was only a taste of what we can now enjoy *every* night?"

Isabel paled, lowered her gaze and then painstakingly laid the gown over the back of a chair. Damn! I *am* well enough, she told herself in sudden terror. What new excuse *could* she invent, now her precarious pregnancy was ended?

"Well, I must say your appearance frightened me half to death," she replied deviously, as though she had not heard a word he said. "You know how I worry about all the terrible things that can happen in the mines."

Looking up at him, she tilted her head to one side like an impatient little girl and asked. "Well, where's my surprise? What is it you're hiding behind your back?"

Beaming, he stretched his closed hand toward her and opened his upturned palm that held a folded white linen handkerchief. This he opened carefully with his left hand to reveal the priceless gift within.

There was a long moment of total silence between them and then Isabel asked tonelessly, "What is it?"

"Behold!" he announced dramatically, "Pure rosicler!"

Isabel was pierced by a keen sense of disappointment as she stared at the lump of blackish-grey ore, faintly streaked with pink, which he now placed ceremoniously in her own hand.

"What you see before you, *mi consentida*, is a perfect specimen of almost pure argentite or silver glance. It's so rich and sectile it cuts like butter with a table knife!"

Isabel studied his sun-bronzed face. The deep lines had been burned away by a dazzling inner radiance. The forty-two year old man before her seemed more like twenty-five. Fearful of shattering his exuberance, she tried to think of the few mining terms she recalled, whose technical meanings had always escaped her.

"It must be a high grade of rock -- I mean, ore?" she stammered, trying to sound both interested and knowledgeable, neither of which she was.

"My dear," he said hoarsely, "you're looking at the richest, rarest silver ore in the world. And can you guess where this flawless specimen was found?"

"No."

"In the deepest Santa Cruz shaft!"

"Oh?" Her mind made no real connection.

"*La Sirena mine!*" he repeated, a trumpet call that resonated through the room. Then, as though transported into another world, one utterly alien to Isabel, he strode about gesturing grandly, trying to convey in mere words the immensity of his good fortune, while Isabel stood motionless, staring mutely at the ugly lump of grey clay in her hand.

"Four brutal years of blasting, digging and spending!" he crowed triumphantly. "Four years in a shaft that fought us every step of the way. But, as God's in His Heaven, it's happened at last! Oh, Isabel, don't you understand? *I've brought in my second bonanza!*"

Stunned, Isabel set the ore down on a tabletop as Patrick swung around to face her, his countenance aglow. "And you should have seen

Francisco's face when I told him he was now a full partner in the richest silver mine in the world! He had to admit I'd been right all along and I fully deserved to win our wager."

"You bet him half of La Sirena?" she asked numbly. It was bad enough now, but as co-owner of a bonanza mine he'll be here at the palacio all the time! She could barely manage to get through his occasional visits now. How could she endure being near him almost all of every day?

"Let me explain. A year ago when he advanced me the capital to deepen that shaft, I made him promise that if we struck a really rich vein I could build the miners' hospital before I repaid him the full balance of what I owe. So now I can begin the hospital at once, and with his half interest in La Sirena, Francisco will earn his money back right away."

The way miners did business was as bewildering a maze to Isabel as their tunnels and shafts. "You're going to build a hospital!" she cried. "But what on earth for? The Jeronymite Fathers have run a good hospital in this town for more than two hundred years."

Patiently the Conde explained it was his plan to provide a charity hospital exclusively for sick and injured mine workers. "They get bad lungs and fevers working underground, and those who bring up the ore that enriches you and me are injured on the job every day. Doctor Juan and I have shared this dream for years. No mine owner's ever done this for our men, and before God, we think it's time someone did!"

"But -- the expense!" Isabel stammered, and then recalling Aunt Amantina's advice about entailing the estate, she ventured blindly, "Maybe Don Francisco is right, advising you to be cautious about money." Patrick looked at her curiously as she blundered on. "Well, there's the little First Condesa to inherit everything now. Perhaps you should put the entire Graciana estate into a -- a mayorazgo -- for her."

Don Patrick placed a hand playfully under her chin. "And why are you talking about mayorazgos at a time like this when we're sitting on a mountain of pure silver! Come with me right now to La Sirena! You've simply got to see that outcropping of rosicler with your own eyes!"

"But I couldn't possibly do that!" she cut him off sharply. "Women don't belong in the mines!" Suddenly troubled by the wounded expression in his eyes, she hurried on. "You know miners consider it bad luck for a woman to visit underground."

"Not in the North, we don't," he retorted. "That's a superstition only popular in the South."

"Well," Isabel continued in a more conciliatory tone, "true or not, I've never set foot in a mine in my life. I'm terrified of being trapped in some awful cave in!"

"Forgive me," Patrick said thoughtfully. "I keep forgetting you weren't raised a fronterista like me." His voice was tender but she saw the merriment had gone from his eyes.

"I've told you, Patricio, that world is frightening to me. I realize that women raised on your Godforsaken Apache frontier -- even when they're aristocrats -- are expected to haul water, mine silver, load muskets and fight off savages as well as any man. Well, I'm not your heroic ancestor, Doña Graciana! These are some things I don't intend to learn!"

"But my dear, you're perfect as you are!"

Isabel paused and her mood softened. "Patrick, what really worries me is that the workers will take advantage of your generosity," she said quietly, tenderly wiping the grime from his face with a cloth. "Everyone says you spoil them. A mine owner can be too generous, especially with the lower class of *vagos*. You already allow your men to take home a good piece of ore every Friday night, in addition to paying the highest weekly wage in town. Such things encourage them to step out of their place and could lead them to stage the same sort of violent riots and strikes this city saw in my father's time."

Don Patrick's eyes widened in surprise. "*Mi preciosa!* I've never heard you hold forth on social conditions in the province before. That speech was worthy of being delivered before the Council of the Indies back in Spain!"

She shook her head impatiently and went to the cedar-lined armoire, returning with a fresh linen shirt.

"There's an old proverb in the Northern mines," he told her as he pulled on the shirt. "'A wise owner makes his workers his friends: a miser makes them thieves.' Francisco and I intend to make our crew our friends."

Isabel nodded silently and then, eager to change the subject, she announced. "By the way, Amantina tells me Bishop Legázpi should be arriving later on today. Father Miguel Hidalgo is serving as his guide through the Bajío."

"Ah, good old Father Miguel!" he exclaimed, "I haven't seen 'the Fox' around much since he became rector of San Nicolas College over in Valladolid."

Isabel's dark brows gathered in a frown. "I can't say why, but I've always disliked that man."

"Well, he's never really been anywhere, not even made the Grand Tour, so he can be a bit of a bore. But then, that's true of most of the lower clergy. Still, he's a good philosopher and I enjoy arguing the theological fine points between Thomas Aquinas and Duns Scotus. Theology's one game he never seems to tire of."

"It's not Hidalgo's rustic ways that bother me. It's because he's so obsequious, always fawning on those above his station, implying they regard him as their peer."

"Well, he comes from the poor country creole class. It may be his way of getting a leg up on the social ladder."

"Every instinct tells me to distrust him."

Don Patrick brushed the dried mud off his boots. "Women are entitled to their intuitions. It's what makes you such fascinating creatures. But it's not Hidalgo who interests me so much. It's the new Bishop himself that I'm most eager to know."

"What makes him so interesting?" Isabel asked. She had never thought her husband all *that* religious.

"It's not everyday one gets to meet a prelate who's lived six years at the Bourbon court in Madrid. It will be a rare treat indeed to discuss politics and the Enlightenment with someone as liberal as Diego Legázpi."

"Liberal?" she asked, surprised again.

"Oh, yes, *very* liberal," Don Patrick said, glancing in the mirror as he combed his hair. "I hear he promises to be a champion of the poor in the heroic mold of our great bishops Zummáraga and Tata Vasco. He's also known as a very holy confessor. New Spain can certainly use a churchman who combines genuine social reform with apostolic zeal."

Until this instant Isabel had known no more about the Bishop than that he was the son of Amantina's older brother who remained in Spain years ago, when she and a younger brother, later to be Isabel's father, sailed to New Spain. Legázpi had been little more than a sprig of ecclesiastical parsley decorating tomorrow's christening. But once her husband left the room she began weaving pious fantasies as she dressed for her sitting. Star-crossed in love, was she destined to become a penitent saint? Other great sinners had been led to sanctity by holy spiritual directors -- Rose of Vitterbo, Margaret of Cortona, Magdalene! As in many mundane events, Isabel saw God's moving hand in this holy confessor's entry into her life, and her mystic vision soared.

3

Inside his episcopal coach, lined with crimson velvet and drawn by ten matched black carriage mules, His Excellency, Don Diego Legázpi Salinas, newly-appointed Bishop of the Province of Michoacán was engrossed in reading the breviary that lay open in his hands. Conversing with each other on the seat facing his were Father Miguel Hidalgo, a middle-aged priest of Legázpi's diocese, and Don Cosmé Medina, a twenty-six year old Spanish mining engineer. The youthful Medina had sailed from Cadiz on the same ship with His Excellency and now, having placed his bride with friends in Mexico, was bound for the city of Guanajuato on a mission of his own.

Although the prelate appeared to be reading his Office, he had discharged that priestly duty hours earlier. However, after three months of incessant travel he had learned this innocent deceit accorded him a much-needed respite from conversing with fellow travelers. It also permitted him to practice, undetected, two functions indispensable to a prelate -- introspection and observation. At the moment, observation had priority, for it was imperative he assess, as speedily as possible, the curiously contradictory character of Father Hidalgo. His own future bishopric could hang on this country priest's insights and advice.

Hidalgo had worked for Legázpi's deceased predecessor as seminarian, professor of theology and college rector. He was familiar with diocesan administration, whereas Legázpi knew next to nothing about the diocese and people he had come to serve. Although grateful to Hidalgo for offering to be his guide on his first journey into the interior provinces, Legázpi was hard-pressed to keep up a relentlessly cheerful façade before a fellow religious whose superior he was as well. To make matters worse, for the first time in his priestly life Legázpi found himself beset by the twin demons of homesickness and spiritual aridity.

Cheerfully and with his blessing, he had consigned hundreds of other religious to lifelong exile in this same kingdom of New Spain. Why then, he wondered, was it proving so painful to go himself? He needed to hear -- and above all *believe!* -- one of those rousing *ferverinos* he had routinely preached to bands of quaking young missionary friars on the eve of their embarkation. "Divine consolation is the crown of apostolic zeal," he had blithely told them. But exhorting was a far cry from doing, for now he found himself a missionary shorn of consolation, an apostle without a pinch of zeal.

From his days as a young *ordinandus* Legázpi had cultivated the mien of a cleric mature enough to attract a rich bishopric. He was grateful that, at thirty-five, he was already portly and his hair turning prematurely grey. While his face was disappointingly youthful, he was hopeful his keen hazel eyes, prominent Roman nose and straight mouth lent the necessary sternness to a countenance otherwise too genial for a prince of the Church. He had been reassured on that point before leaving Spain when he overheard his friend, the respected Count of Floridablanca, remark to his Majesty, "If young Legázpi had not taken Holy Orders he could have shone as a marshal on any battlefield."

Born into a noble but wretchedly poor Vizcayan farm family, Legázpi had found little meat on honor's bones. After ordination, his eloquent preaching attracted the attention of King Charles III and a post at court that had proved a sinecure. But after six years as Royal Confessor to a doltish Crown prince, he became infinitely bored and leapt at his monarch's offer of a suddenly vacant see in America. No comparable plum was likely to fall his way in Europe for decades to come, and the annual stipend of 130,000 pesos was a windfall to one who had grown up poorer than the proverbial friars' servant. Best of all, it offered him the opportunity to put his avant garde theories of social reform to use in a kingdom which he understood had a crying need for them.

But tempting as this far-off bishopric was, the natural man within him quailed before the heroic renunciation of home, family and friends that it demanded. In the end, it was His Majesty who tipped the scales.

"New Spain is the Crown's most peaceful and prosperous colony in America," Charles had informed him brightly over a stirrup cup. "It's also the most like Spain. Once settled there my viceroys tell me they feel as if they've never left home."

The king was right. The Viceregal Court in the city of Mexico, where Legázpi and the newly-wed Medinas spent two months recuperating from their voyage, proved nearly as splendid and sophisticated as its Spanish model. But once outside the capital all similarity vanished. Now, in the bounteous Bajío, a week later and eighty leagues northeast of that 'City of Palaces', he found it alien as the steppes of Tartary. He missed the intellectual brilliance of the Francophile Spanish court. The bittersweet memory of a morning spent in the company of the Count of Floridablanca -- while the artist, Francisco Goya, worked on that grandee's portrait, and the wit and wisdom flowed -- brought Legázpi to the brink of despair.

"You should at least be prepared for the mine owners' resistance," Father Miguel was advising young Cosmé Medina. "Guanajuato is the crown jewel of American mining cities. She produces *one-sixth* of all the known silver in the world and believe me, her silver lords know it."

"I've served as inspector of mines in Saxony, Germany, Scandinavia and Wales," the blonde, brown-eyed Medina replied with self-assured modesty. "I've learned that all miners resist innovation."

While he had just met Hidalgo, Legázpi already knew Don Cosmé well. He had been present the day His Majesty named this gifted young engineer to head the King's Royal Scientific Mission to New Spain. Medina's prickly task was to introduce new mining techniques of the European Enlightenment into that kingdom. Charles felt such methods would double its already prodigious output of ore. That in turn would raise 'the king's fifth', that time-honored crown tax that had been levied on every bar of gold and silver mined in Spanish America since the Conquest.

"The first silver strike in Guanajuato was made back in 1548," Hidalgo continued, "and they've been doing things their own way there ever since. No matter how scientifically sound your innovations may be, if they run counter to local custom and pride you'll be opposed."

As the two men conversed, the Bishop quietly observed Father Hidalgo. What at first he had thought to be his very fair complexion, he now noticed, was overlaid with a pale brown tinge, belying his claim that both parents were pure criollo. Well, in a kingdom where color defined class that was a forgivable vanity.

Until today he had judged Hidalgo to be a reclusive man. He carried his head, with its high-domed brow and bald pate fringed with grey, habitually thrust forward, which gave him the 'scholar's stoop' of a true contemplative. But once engaged in debate he became passionately involved, his temper short and hot. One moment his green eyes were beclouded as if pondering some abstract concept, the next they were ablaze, his full lips parted and nostrils flared, avid as a general in the heat of battle. Yes, he sensed two natures at odds within this complex man -- the visionary and the warrior. So far, neither one seemed to have the upper hand.

At Medina's remarks, Hidalgo turned thoughtful, brows drawn together above his long, angular nose, hands grasping the time-worn lapels of his black frock coat, "I think your first move should be to win over the two most influential men in Guanajuato," Hidalgo advised Medina. "Don Patrick O'Malley, the First Count of Graciana, and his financial advisor, Don Francisco Durán."

At mention of Don Patrick, Legázpi looked up from his Breviary. The Gracianas were one of his few touchstones with colonial society. Since he had traded the enlightened Bourbon court for these benighted provinces, he was grateful to at least be kin to one of the colony's first families.

"That reminds me, Father," Legázpi said, closing his Breviary with a flourish. "I've been meaning to ask you about the Gracianas. Have you known the family long?"

"Don Patrick and I met ten years ago when he first came to Guanajuato from the North. I didn't meet your cousin, Doña Isabel, until last summer when I served as deacon at their nuptial Mass."

"I've been told the wedding was a dazzling affair," Legázpi observed.

Hidalgo nodded. "Oh, yes, the costliest the city has ever seen. But given Don Patrick's lavish hand, you can expect tomorrow's christening to be even more munificent."

"What a pity his firstborn is a girl," Don Cosmé Medina said, with the undisguised prejudice of a bridegroom hoping he has sired a son. "Surely he must have wanted a male heir?"

"Most nobles do," Hidalgo conceded, "but don't expect Don Patrick to fit the classic mold."

"Is it true he's Irish?" Legázpi asked.

"Yes, pure Irish on his father's side. His Gaelic forbears found life under the yoke of Protestant England intolerable so, like other 'wild geese' they fled the Emerald Isle and settled in Catholic Spain. There the O'Malley's prospered for generations, but Don Patrick's father was born a 'second son'. Unable to inherit, he came to New Spain to seek his fortune in the mines of Zacatecas. He met and married that city's leading silver heiress, who became Don Patrick's mother. On the maternal side the Conde claims direct lineage to a First Conquistador."

"Is the name Don Telmo de la Huerta familiar to you?" Legázpi inquired. "The Viceroy says he is Guanajuato's most important silver lord."

Hidalgo laughed aloud. "He *was* before Don Patrick arrived. Surely the Viceroy knows about their feud?"

"He made no mention of a feud to me."

"It all started when Don Patrick first came to town looking for mines to buy," Hidalgo began with relish. "Don Telmo's 'El Rey' was then the city's richest mine, but he also owned two others that were barren. He cleverly unloaded both on the newcomer from the North, at a neat profit."

Wasn't Don Patrick outraged when he found he'd been sold two worthless mines?" Medina asked.

"Oh, not at all! You see, less than six months later one of them -- the great Graciana -- brought him a bonanza. It's the most productive silver mine in the kingdom and has made the Conde a millionaire many times over."

"What irony!" Legázpi exclaimed.

"And irony to spare," Hidalgo added, "for last year both men courted the widowed Isabel and the Conde won her hand. For Don Telmo that turned rivalry into open war."

The coach lurched sharply as their driver maneuvered around a train of some two-dozen mules strung along the right side of the broad, stone-paved *camino real*.

"Now that's a first-rate mule train!" Legázpi exclaimed appreciatively, "The finest one I've seen in New Spain."

"I must say, Excelencia, you have the unjaded eye of a newcomer," Hidalgo remarked half in jest, half-patronizing. "Since this kingdom has no navigable rivers, mule trains must transport everything. They're as ubiquitous as fleas on a wild dog. I wager after you've been here a while you won't even bother to tell good from bad."

"Well, I grew up in the mountains of Viscay, so I consider myself something of an authority on pack mules," the Bishop replied with a twinkle. "Every mule in this train has a balanced load and there's not a lame one in the lot!"

"Ah, *now* I understand why this outfit passes your inspection," Hidalgo remarked. "It belongs to Emilio Santa Cruz. He's the giant mulatto you see riding at its head." The priest smiled knowingly. "Emilio's something of a Ulysses among our *arrieros*."

"And the handsome gentleman riding at his side?" Medina put in. "Surely he's no common muleteer?"

"Hardly!" Hidalgo chuckled, "That's the man I was just telling you about, the young financier, Francisco Durán."

☙ ❧

Astride his favorite saddle mule and riding at the head of his train, Emilio Santa Cruz was the finest arriero in the kingdom, and he knew it. He also knew that an entire army of muleteers, plying their trade between Acapulco and the Apache frontier, acknowledged him as their unofficial chief. Emilio's inherent gift for leadership won their fealty and his powerful physique discouraged contenders. Although tomorrow was only his thirtieth birthday, the packs he had lifted, the fights he had won and the legion of virgins he had brought to bed had all passed into legend.

He owed his broad, kite-shaped face, high cheekbones and lynx-like eyes to Pamé Indian ancestors. His giant frame, stamina and passion for freedom were the legacy of a black slave forbear who fled the cane fields of Vera Cruz to become his own master in the Bajío. Emilio's light-blue eyes were the gift of an unknown Spanish progenitor, man or maid he knew not which, who for love alone took the fateful paso atras and 'married down' to color. Restless, unlettered, suspicious of everyone, he was the classic casta male in whose veins Indian, European and African blood quarreled so incessantly he could not confine himself to any one place for long.

His dress was as flamboyant as his spirit: a full-sleeved cotton work shirt, buckskin bolero and the short leather apron that was the hallmark of his trade, to which he added the defiance of six gallant silver buttons where boot-top and knee-breeches met. A bright peacock plume floated from the sweatband of a wide-brimmed, flat-crowned sombrero that he wore at a cocky angle over the flowered kerchief that covered his hair except for the clubbed pigtail in back. A grey wool *serape* fell from his right shoulder to the top of the leather *tapadera* capping his wooden stirrup. Huge, spike-rowel spurs hung at his heels, ringing when he rode, growling when he walked.

In striking contrast, the elegant young man riding at his side was fair-skinned, aristocratic and slender. He wore a plain, but expensive

Dresden brown silk suit with matching cape and tricorn. The fingers of his left hand, holding the ribbon-like reins of his sorrel horse were, like all the rest of him, slight but surprisingly strong. While Emilio was unpredictable as lightning, Francisco Durán's whole being exuded an air of spiritual and intellectual mastery, as if by will alone he could sustain the universe.

"So Don Patrick's brought in his second bonanza!" Emilio marveled, shaking his head in disbelief. "As the old saying goes, 'Money may not be a saint, but it works miracles like one!'"

Don Francisco smiled. "Money's not the only thing that 'makes the dog dance,' my friend. Surely it doesn't tie you to this vagabond existence of yours, when you could earn twice as much by coming back to work for the Conde."

Emilio flashed his friend a smile as wide as the sky, and winked. "Well, as they say, 'a change of pasture fattens the calf.' I find more pretty girls in every *mesón* along the trail than I ever did in Guanajuato." Then his forced smile clouded over and he added soberly, "But Francisco, you ought to know 'A scalded cat runs even from water that's cold.' That town holds too many sad memories for me."

"But Felicia's been dead five years now," Durán reminded him gently. "Lorenzo's already eight. Is it fair to deprive a motherless boy of his father as well?"

"My brother Matías is like a father to him."

"Matías has children of his own and more commissions than he can fill, even with Lorenzo helping him. Why do you waste your life out here when both have such need of you?"

Emilio winced, sensing the real reason his old friend had joined him half a league back. It was not merely to hire him to pick up the usual two-dozen pigskins of pulque from the nearby La Torre mesón and take them up the mountain tonight, so Don Patrick's mining crews would have it fresh for tomorrow's celebration of the feast of the Holy Cross.

"I was born to the trail," Emilio said evasively. "'til I got married and went to work decorating the Conde's family chapel I never knew another life."

"But think of Lorenzo. He has his mother's light complexion and sensitive nature. He's a born artist." Durán glanced at his friend's face, scowling under the black brim.

"Only last week he told me one day he'd be casting bronze!"

"*Verdad?*" A spark of pride flashed in Emilio's dark eyes. "And is it true what Matías says, that his criollo and Spanish patrons all take the boy for white?"

"They do indeed!" Durán said warmly. "And having been criolla herself, think how Felicia would like that! Yes, Emilio, times are changing in New Spain. Lorenzo's not an ordinary craftsman, he's a true artist with a rare talent that will enable him to -- ," Durán searched for the most discreet way to phrase his meaning, " -- rise in colonial society." He reached across and pressed his fingers into Emilio's powerful forearm. "But, to do all that he needs his father near him."

Emilio shook his head, and his blue eyes blazed angrily. "You mean well, Francisco, but sometimes I think you're blind. Take a good look at me. I'm a casta! I'm called Santa Cruz for my Feast Day because I've got *no legal name*! Why? Because I'm the bastard son of a bastard son! So why saddle Lorenzo with all that? He'll rise faster without me."

He rode awhile wrapped in gloomy silence then he looked back and shot Durán a fierce look and added with a sardonic grin, "Better he says his father's dead. Noble, mind you, but dead."

"The years are flying by Emilio," Francisco continued doggedly. "He's your son -- your only son."

Wearied by the unaccustomed effort of trying to express complicated ideas in a small vocabulary, limited mostly to oaths and obscenities, Emilio became as obstinate as one of his mules. An illiterate who resented being drawn beyond his depth, he fell back on the easy eloquence of familiar proverbs that formed the verbal currency of his class. "'Only the one who carries the coffin knows what the body weighs!'" he growled defensively.

Don Francisco lifted a gloved hand to cover the compassionate smile he was unable to suppress.

08 80

Less than a league beyond the point where they had passed Emilio's mule train, Bishop Legázpi felt the steady forward motion of the great coach gradually diminish until it came to a complete halt on the side of the road.

"Why is Manuel stopping here?" Father Hidalgo snapped irritably.

As if in response to his question, there was a rap on the carriage door and Hidalgo opened it to their driver. Manuel had worked most of his life for the Bishop's predecessor and Legázpi liked the man. He was already in his debt, for Manuel had taken it upon himself to skillfully paint the Legázpi Coat of Arms on both coach doors. The stocky, saturnine mestizo in neat gold-trimmed livery appeared now with his red tricorn tucked smartly under one arm.

"Your orders were to go all the way to Silao," Hidalgo addressed him sharply. "Why are you stopping here? Has one of the mules gone lame?"

Legázpi had already observed that Hidalgo had a rather lofty way of executing any order given him, as though he were executing a self-appointed task. But when in a position of authority he demanded the full spirit of obedience that he himself declined to give. Perhaps his superior intellect made him intolerant of less nimble minds, Legázpi reasoned, but in a thirty-six-year-old professed religious it was a warning sign of rebellious pride that warranted watching.

"Nothing's wrong with my mules, Padre," Manuel explained, "but an ugly storm is bearing down upon us from the north. I won't expose Your Mercies to it here in the road, so I propose we. . ."

"I propose we don't waste any more time!" Hidalgo cut him off. "I've arranged for dinner in Silao at a first class inn and it's only half a league away."

"With all due respect," Manuel corrected him, "Silao is two leagues on. La Torre hacienda is only five minutes from here, so I suggest. . ."

"La Torre!" Hidalgo scoffed, his green eyes suddenly hard as glass. "You know La Torre's been turned into a common pulque plantation and mesón! Muleteers and vagos are hardly fit company for His Excellency and Don --"

"With your permission, Padre," Manuel persisted. "God will judge me more harshly for exposing His Bishop to thunderbolts in the open road than for finding him shelter with rough but honest men."

Manuel turned his black eyes expectantly toward the Bishop. It was clear to Legázpi the man had not worked for religious all his life without having learned a thing or two about using pious arguments to get his way.

"I find no objection to the mesón," the Bishop offered affably. Then, quick to redress Hidalgo's wounded pride, he added lightly, "Since muleteers and vagos are all members of my flock, I may as well get to know them now as later."

"Muchas gracias, Excelencia!" Manuel beamed, his white smile an upturned crescent in the dark firmament of his face. Clamping his tricorn firmly on his head he shut the carriage door. A moment later he had his mules moving along at a fast pace that set their harness bells a-jingle.

"You mustn't let Manuel's terror of storms disturb you," Hidalgo said disdainfully, flicking a speck of dust from his dark coat sleeve. "You'll soon learn that humildes like him take fright at everything. Spin the wildest fantasy and they'll take it all as Gospel. I grew up here in the Bajío so I know how these country people think. I also know these first rains of the season seldom do more than lay the dust."

Legázpi began observing the countryside with an increasingly anxious eye. Only moments ago the passing fields of ripening wheat and corn had been glowing gold beneath a brilliant sun. Now, in the time it took to recite a Pater Noster the rising wind had launched an armada of black thunderheads, plunging the golden landscape into an eerie blue-green twilight. Checking his pocket watch he was shocked to see the two hands stood at noon!

Others on the road seemed equally alarmed. He saw farmers leave their plows standing in the fields to goad their wall-eyed oxen homeward. Bronze-skinned peons in white cotton suits, straw hats and homemade sandals trotted along the footpath paralleling the highway, driving bands of bleating sheep and goats to the safety of home corrals. Coachmen urged their teams to an ever faster pace, the animals already dark with sweat and their bit rings trailing wisps of foam.

Be-wigged and booted horsemen in tricorns and silken suits, spurred their nervous mounts to a gallop. Legázpi was edified to note that, even in their haste, they took time to hail each other with "Amar a Diós", that admonition to "Love God" which, until Martín Luther's day, had been the universal salutation of pilgrims and travelers throughout Christendom.

All at once, jagged spears of blue-white lightning were blazing all around them, punctuated by cannonades of thunder so powerful the heavy coach shuddered. It seemed incredible to Legázpi that so many flaming bolts could be streaking down from greenish clouds above, while others flared up like tongues of flames from the surrounding horizon, illuminating the smoked-glass darkness of midday.

When Manuel turned his lead mule sharply to the right and onto an old stone bridge, a searing white light exploded on the very spot where their coach had rolled seconds before. The earth-shaking thunderclap that followed seemed to come from directly beneath their wheels. Legázpi heard the mules scream in fright, and as they bolted he was catapulted forward, all three men grabbing for the passenger straps beside their windows. The coach flew across the bridge and careered along a lane bordered with giant ash trees, their writhing wind-lashed branches testifying to the ferocity of the storm. As the trees began to flash by more slowly the Bishop realized Manuel had regained control of his runaways. All three men breathed more easily, but the air was so charged with electricity Legázpi could actually taste it on his tongue.

"Is that crenellated tower up ahead La Torre mesón?" Don Cosmé asked Hidalgo.

"Yes. Dominican friars built it soon after the Conquest," he replied. Then, calmly ignoring the storm, he continued like a schoolmaster expounding on the lesson for the day. "The old church and monastery has changed hands many times. A poor criollo called 'Old Martín' runs the place now, trying to make ends meet selling pulque and raising blooded horses on the side."

Father Miguel's voice was drowned out by an unholy hammering overhead. Looking out, Legázpi saw hailstones half the size of cannonballs rebounding from the top of the coach and quickly turning everything white. With an encouraging cry of "Aay, mulas!" Manuel drove his frenzied mules through La Torre's open corral gate and under the welcome protection of an immense shed roof.

Instantly the driver was at his Bishop's side, opening the coach door and holding an umbrella above his head as they ran across the open center of the corral to the lighted door of the mesón. A half-ruin the place might be, Legázpi thought, but he noticed that even Father Miguel, who openly despised it, was racing toward the door, eager as himself to escape being savaged by the monstrous hailstones.

Once inside, Legázpi was greeted by their astonished host, Old Martín, himself, who led him and his party to a scarred wooden table with benches as seats for lack of chairs. The courtly old criollo apologized as he genuflected and kissed the Episcopal ring, deploring the fact that he was sadly unable to offer service befitting a prince of the Church.

Seating himself on a bench, Legázpi could see this dining room had once served as the Dominican's refectory. On one wall hung a carved, Gothic-style stone pulpit where the friar-lector formerly read aloud from pious works while his brothers ate in silence.

How that meditative scene had changed! The room was jammed with travelers of every class, color and dress, all driven inside by the hail, but muleteers outnumbered the others ten to one and Legázpi could see they claimed it as their own. It reeked of sweat, wet wool, mule manure and the soapy sour-sweet breath of pulque. Above the crowd hung a blue fog of tallow candle and cigarette smoke. Here and there on the dingy walls, pious travelers had tacked up blessed palm leaves woven into crosses, now brittle with age, and small faded prints of popular madonnas -- Our Lady of San Juan de los Lagos, Zapopán and the Indians' own Dark Virgin of Guadalupe.

Two or more pitchers of fermenting pulque stood on every table, replaced by vigilant Indian barmaids the instant one ran dry. Boisterous muleteers danced with whores or country girls on the little patch of floor, singing lustily to the music of several guitars, guitarrones and homemade wooden harps. The din of human voices, music, banging dishware, rolling thunder and the relentless barrage of hail pounding on the roof was deafening. But despite La Torre's many crudities the Bishop was grateful to be safely inside the walls of such an impregnable fortress.

While the Bishop's party was still being seated, Don Francisco and Emilio appeared and Legázpi invited them to join his table. Old Martín treated them all to a round of imported cognac on the house, a lordly gesture that the Bishop knew his poverty-ridden host could ill afford.

When his glass was placed before him, Emilio's face lit up in a sunrise of pleasure. "This hail may be bad," he announced, lifting his glass in a cheerful toast, "but 'Since the house is on fire let's warm ourselves at the flames'!" He downed his drink in a single greedy gulp, then, grabbing a pitcher from the next table, he poured the same glass brimful of foaming white pulque.

The Bishop leaned close to Don Francisco's ear and shouted amiably above the roar, "I've never seen hail as destructive as this anywhere in Europe!"

"I'm sure, Excelencia," he agreed. "But our first missionaries had their own rationale for these uniquely ferocious storms of ours. Certain the Devil had held the pagan Indians in thrall until the Spaniards came, they concluded these tempests were periodic outbursts of Satanic rage over having had that multitude of condemned souls snatched from his grasp by the Gospel's saving grace."

"A rather quaint argument for grace," Legázpi replied with a doubtful smile. "But in the light of this diabolic tantrum, not entirely without merit!"

His words were barely spoken when there was an earsplitting explosion and the Bishop saw a powerful bolt of lightning strike La Torre, blasting a hole in the tower wall large enough to drive his coach and team through. Rubble, thick as shrapnel on a battlefield, filled the air. Because the breached wall was across the room from their table, his own party was merely pelted with spent debris, but Legázpi saw others who were nearer to it had been badly wounded by falling stone or were half-buried under masonry. Tables were overturned, glasses shattered, smoking candles sent sputtering to the floor. Engulfed in darkness, terrified Indian women screamed and sank to their knees in a panic of prayer. Indian men, even those not seriously injured, were immobilized by shock, unable to make a move to help those who were.

Suddenly the Bishop was aware of Old Martín tugging at his elbow, begging him to give conditional absolution to a luckless muleteer caught outside the walls and struck dead by the same bolt that had just blasted the tower.

When Legázpi returned inside he found Hidalgo directing several rescue crews made up of the same humildes who, minutes earlier, had been paralyzed with fear. With Father Miguel giving the orders they were binding up wounds, digging through the rubble to pull people free, righting upturned tables and re-lighting doused candles. Although Hidalgo had spoken contemptuously of these country people earlier, it was obvious they all saw in him their natural leader. Indeed, he did know how these people thought!

The Bishop's own pride in his judgment of men was humbled by this glimpse into the character of one in whom, until now, he had found precious little to admire. Yes, he admonished himself, let this teach you what a great potential for good lies hidden in those we find the least prepossessing of men!

☙4❧

It was still dark when Legázpi awoke, and for one heart-stopping moment he thought himself back in Spain with good King Charles. His suite was regal and furnished lavishly, his canopied bed almost sinfully wide. The faintest trace of sandlewood hung in the air, emanating from the hammered-brass brazier with which the room had been warmed the night before. Recalling that the charcoal at court was also sprinkled with the same incense, he felt a fresh wave of homesickness wash over him.

Raising himself on one elbow, he lit the small copse of tapers in a silver candelabrum by his bed and settled back on his pillows to reflect on the tumultuous events of yesterday. It had been filled with experiences unlike any other he had ever known, but they had thrust him into the mainstream of colonial life. The men he had met were worlds removed from his European friends, and he reflected now upon their characters, one by one.

Emilio Santa Cruz was a kind of baptized savage, capable of passionate loyalties, but as likely to bite as to lick any master's hand. Old Martín was barely one rung up from the bottom of colonial society, and yet, being a criollo with European blood gave him daily reason to rejoice.

And of course there was Don Francisco Durán, uniquely American in his own way, too. Born of Spanish parents and orphaned in youth, he was the New World model of a self-made man. But, far more than that, never had the Bishop known a layman whose every word and deed breathed such selfless charity. At the same time he sensed a hidden fire burning inside the man, volcanic in its intensity. Recalling the volcano he had passed on the road to Mexico, he equated Durán with Orizaba, only capped with grace instead of snow.

As for the horrific storm itself, it had gone as quickly as it came. By the time Old Martín led the Bishop's party up the winding tower stairs to the roof to view the countryside, clouds were scudding southward and the sun shone even brighter than before. But everywhere they looked, stricken farmers were picking through the wreckage of their fields. The hail had shredded a bumper crop of wheat. Corn, which an hour earlier had stood as high as a plow-ox's back, now lay splintered and strewn upon the ground.

"Such widespread devastation is certain to drive food prices out of sight," the Bishop observed.

"Far worse than that, I'm afraid," Don Francisco replied gravely. "What I see here is -- famine!"

At sundown, changing from coach to saddle horses purchased from Old Martín, and joined now by Don Francisco, the Bishop and his party set out on the last leg of their journey to Guanajuato. Although sobered by the storm's tragic aftermath, the Bishop found the night ride up the mountain pure delight. The pine-sweet air was crisp as white wine, the full moon overhead wondrously bright. Now and then the sylvan hush was broken by a vigilant mockingbird guarding its nest in some towering cedar or pine rising out of deep aromatic canyons that fell away on either side of the trail. Legázpi had never heard a mockingbird in Europe, and he knew its strident song would always remind him of this first magical night in the interior provinces of New Spain.

"This oddity of nature gave the town and province their name," Father Miguel pointed out when they entered a long canyon with a curious toad-shaped rock formation hanging from one wall. "In the language of the Pamé Indians who roamed here before the Spaniards came, 'Guanajuato' means 'The Place of the Giant Mountain Frog.'"

This seemingly trivial bit of information led to the indirect discovery that Father Miguel spoke Pamé, Nahuatl and one or two other native tongues. This greatly increased his value in a diocese, where as Legázpi now learned, there were entire villages of Indians who to this day still neither spoke nor understood a single word of Spanish!

At ten-thirty, the party reached a stone-paved esplanade encompassed by a vast natural amphitheatre of rock escarpments. Here, with the city of Guanajuato lying in a bowl of nearly treeless hills beneath them, they sat their winded horses and drank in the quiet beauty of the place. After their mounts had rested, they started down a steep cobblestone road leading into town. Passing under soaring stone aqueducts and bridges Legázpi judged would make a Roman proud, through city streets so narrow he could touch the walls of houses on either side. Hidalgo said thirty-thousand people resided here but, except for an anxious lamp ambering an occasional watchful window, the sleeping city belied the presence of a living soul.

As they crossed a small moonlit plaza a night watchman emerged from a shadowed lane, himself another shadow in his wide-brimmed *sombrero* and full black cape, staff in one hand and lantern in the other.

"Eleven o'clock on the night of the Second of May, in this Year of Our Lord seventeen-hundred and eighty-six," he chanted, " -- and -- all -- is -- serene!"

The *sereno's* keen falsetto, spiraling upward from the quiet square pierced Legázpi's homesick heart, taking him back once more to the mountain village of his youth. Climbing again, they ascended the heights on the opposite side of town. Before an imposing two-story mansion on a bufa overlooking the sleeping city, Father Miguel drew rein at last and announced they had arrived at the Graciana palace.

In Don Patrick O'Malley, First Conde de Graciana, the Bishop found a host of irresistible courtesy and charm. Although wealthy beyond belief, a veritable crown prince of fortune, he was humble as a friar. His keen wit and intellect matched that of Legázpi's old friend at court, the Count of Floridablanca, without that grandee's acerbity.

The Conde regaled his weary guests with a midnight repast capped with imported brandy. Then, taking the Bishop aside, he explained that Doña Isabel had not regained her strength and retired early, but she had written him a note that the Conde handed him.

Legázpi had accepted it with a warm feeling of kinship, but reading it, he was struck by its pietistic tone. Isabel wrote that she must meet with him privately tomorrow evening after the christening, at six in her husband's library for, "confession and spiritual guidance." There was more than a hint in what followed that her eternal salvation was at stake. While chary of rash judgments, Legázpi had heard enough overly pious women's confessions in his time to recognize a full-blown case of religious scrupulosity when he saw it.

Since Legázpi and the others brought Don Patrick his first news of the devastating hail, attention had quickly focused on the storm and its far-reaching consequences. In fact, the Bishop was astonished at how swiftly the topic moved from impending human tragedy to the shortage of fodder for horses and mules driving water whims and *arrastres* in Guanajuato's mines.

"It takes at least forty thousand *fanegas* of corn a year just to feed our work animals," Don Patrick explained. "The drought has emptied the public granary and now my own private stores are exhausted, too."

"Fourteen thousand mules run the mines," Don Francisco added. "And if they aren't fed the work shuts down. When that happens the city's output of silver drops by millions of pesos."

"As your Excellency can see, it doesn't take the Bourbon Army to keep foreigners from attacking our mines," the Conde said proudly, striding back and forth before a central fountain in the patio. "Dutch and English pirates may seize New Spain's silver cargoes at sea, but the good Lord has hidden away the main source in these rugged hills." He waved his snifter in a sweeping gesture. "Our only enemies here are natural ones -- floods, cave-ins, droughts and a crop failure now and then."

Legázpi found himself distracted by the life-size marble statue of a mermaid dominating the fountain behind his host. Naked, she cradled a guitar in her arms, her long tresses not quite long enough to cover her breasts. He had noticed this same creature on the Graciana Coat of Arms carved in stone above the palace door. Why would such an exemplary Catholic family have so brazen a motif on its crest?

"Your Excellency may be interested to learn," Father Miguel was saying, "that your late predecessor established his own diocesan granary in Valladolid where ample stores of wheat and corn are stored. If it pleased your Excellency, you could easily. . ." Hidalgo left the question hanging and Legázpi snapped it up.

"By all means! I'll order seed corn shipped to the Bajío farmers as soon as I reach my see city. And I'll provide the mines of Guanajuato with emergency rations for your mules."

"Gracias, Excelencia," Don Patrick said. "And of course, you understand, the cost is no object. Please charge the going rate. I'll repay your diocese out of my own pocket."

"No need to trouble yourself," the Bishop reassured him. "I'm sure our bankers can handle such small details later."

Don Francisco and the Conde exchanged surprised glances. After a moment the Conde informed him quietly, "There *are* no banks or bankers here in New Spain, Your Excellency."

"How extraordinary!" Legázpi managed at last.

"You see, over here religious orders and diocesan funds serve as the only banks. They offer mortgages and loans at the usual five per cent interest rate." The Conde grinned. "So you see, this kingdom needs you even more than you may have guessed. If it weren't for the Church, our entire economy would collapse!"

☙ ❧

The Bishop was rudely jolted from his pre-dawn reveries by what sounded, for all the world like a full-scale artillery bombardment. He rushed from his bed to the window to determine what enemy was attacking the city. But when he pulled open the shutters the first thing that caught his eye was the blue-green sky above. It was ablaze with scores of fire-fountains, interspersed with small puffs of pale smoke that looked like hundreds of tiny grey parasols suspended in mid-air.

"*Cohetes!* Of course!" he said aloud, laughing at his own stupidity. The 'enemy cannonade' was nothing more deadly than a pre-dawn spectacle of fireworks!

"Don't let this kingdom's cohetes take you by surprise," the Viceroy had warned him jokingly. "Ever since the first Manila Galleon unloaded its cargo of Chinese fireworks in the port of Acapulco, our people have made a vice of celebrating holy days with more noise than will be heard at Armageddon!"

Recalling that this was May third, Feast of the Holy Cross, he remembered too, it was the patronal feast of stonemasons everywhere. Since they did not work with nails in their trade, they held themselves uniquely innocent of any part in their Lord's Crucifixion. Guanajuato's stonemasons were merely celebrating their day with an appropriately spectacular display. But he was staggered by the cost of *that* many Roman candles going up in smoke. How can a small provincial city spend itself this way, he asked himself? And with drought and famine at the door, how does it dare?

Sleep being out of the question, he began preparing for the eventful day ahead. Last night Don Patrick had urged his guests to avail themselves of the palace barber, but Legázpi now decided to decline. His Carmelite novice master had taught him that no prelate could find salvation without mortification of the flesh and that some magister's *jeremiads* had been branded on his priestly soul.

Hot water was his for the asking, but shaving with cold proved penance enough for a month. In the same salutary spirit he brushed his clerical blacks, polished his own shoes and restrained his ravenous traveler's appetite for an hour to give his daily Office a slow and prayerful reading.

Passing the open door of Father Hidalgo's suite, on his way to breakfast with the Conde, Legázpi noted with secret amusement that the room was abuzz with Indian servants, waiting on the priest hand and foot. Three barbers bent over his shrouded form with flashing razors. One girl was blacking his shoes, another whisking his frockcoat and a third bringing breakfast on a flower-decked silver tray!

Rubbing his tender chin ruefully, the Bishop chuckled to himself. Beware of rash judgment, he thought, and remember, you're Father Miguel's religious superior, *not* his confessor!

CS ∞

Several hours later, as Legázpi and Hidalgo rode up the mountain road to the Graciana family chapel for the christening that was scheduled for noon, the Bishop got his first real view of the famous city by day.

"I would never have believed a mining town could be so elegant and clean!" he exclaimed. Not at all like the grimy centers in Europe filled with slums!"

"Guanajuato is beautiful at any time, but being in fiesta she's at her best."

The Bishop nodded in agreement. Yes, even the weather was in fiesta, he thought, the sky cloudless, the midday sun pleasantly warm on his shoulders. He found the palaces lining the mountain road impressive, each faced with its own distinctive shade of native building stone -- pale green, buff or rose. Wrought-iron window *rejas* and balconies lent a playful hint of black lace to otherwise severely formal neoclassic facades.

Stonemasons continued their steady barrage of rockets from rooftop and bell tower. Every bridge, building and mineshaft under construction, was topped by a large flower-covered wooden cross. Later today priests would bless each site, asking God's protection against accident and injury in the year ahead. Indian women in brightly colored dresses and aprons were already setting up long tables for the outdoor feasts to follow, while nearby whole carcasses of kids and goats slowly turned on spits over open fires. Everywhere Legázpi looked there was movement and color, every breeze laced with the tempting aroma of roast and barbecued meat.

Rounding a bend he caught his first glimpse of the Graciana chapel's tower and was astounded at the density of the crowd. The church looked like a frosted pink wedding cake upon which thousands of ant-like figures were converging.

Handing their horses to a groom, Hidalgo led the way to a secret patio door that opened directly into the sacristy. The Bishop found it a spacious, circular room with several pier glass mirrors reflecting and enhancing the light entering from a dome and lantern above. A wall dividing sacristy from sanctuary was lined with mahogany vestment cabinets, and dominating the center of the room was a large vesting table, its round white marble top supported by four stout, carved legs. On this flawless surface Father Miguel placed a watered-silk cassock of bishop's purple and a white lace surplice.

As Legázpi donned surplice and cassock, Hidalgo swung open the velvet-lined drawer of a fan-shaped chest, lifting out a weighty cloth-of-silver cope. On the back was a circular image of Our Lady of Remedies on a solidly embroidered floral ground.

"What Order of nuns made this vestment?" Legázpi asked. "The needlework on this lunette is the finest I've seen anywhere! It looks exactly like a painting on porcelain."

"Madre Pilar sent it up from her Virgin of Remedies Convent and Asylum in Mexico city, a baptismal gift to the infant Condesa. Her nuns are famous for their embroidery."

Bracing himself to support the heavy cope as Hidalgo eased it onto his shoulders, the Bishop confided on a sudden impulse, "strange to say, Madre Pilar and I grew up together back in Spain. What a hoyden she was, with her Gypsy father's temper and her own iron will! None of us who knew her then dreamed she would ever enter the religious life, let alone choose such a heroic vocation as working with the insane."

Legázpi was tempted to continue, but an inner voice advised him against taking this man into his confidence. "A prelate should avoid giving others easy access to his humanity," his magister once said. "It can undermine his spiritual authority."

"Your miter, Excelencia," Hidalgo prompted. A slight edge of impatience in his tone.

"Of course. I guess I was wool-gathering," the Bishop smiled, setting the stiff cloth-of-silver miter awkwardly on his own head. Hidalgo, a veteran *ceremoniero*, readjusted it, seeing that the two silver lappets in back were neatly spread.

"And now," Hidalgo said in a warmer tone as he led the Bishop through the door into the sacristy, "I'll introduce you to your acolytes."

Two young boys, about seven and eight years of age, rose from their chairs on the Epistle side of the altar where they had been waiting. Both wore white linen surplices with stiff white ruffs at the throat, over dark-red cassocks. With their fair skin, hazel eyes and sandy hair they looked enough alike to be twins. Each carried a lighted processional candle nearly as tall as himself.

"Excelencia, these are Doña Isabel's two sons, Felipe and his younger brother, Ramón."

Both boys genuflected and kissed his ring with almost military smartness. After receiving his blessing they took their places at the head of the small procession, moving slowly up the aisle of the empty chapel to the open front doors where they were to receive the baptismal party. They found only Don Francisco waiting there.

"Excelencia, the coach is on its way from the palacio with Doña Isabel, the godmother and the First Condesa," he explained. "The Conde is waiting for them beside the road and apologizes for the delay."

His words were drowned out by the joyful tintinnabulation of the three bells in the tower pealing as they turned and turned on their yokes. The Bishop caught a glimpse of the approaching open carriage at the same moment the huge crowd lining the road in front of the chapel surged forward sending up a cheer.

"Excuse me, Excelencia, but I must make sure my men have 'laid the bars'," Don Francisco said hurriedly.

"'The bars?'" Legázpi asked.

"Yes. It's the Conde's last-minute surprise for Doña Isabel," he said smiling conspiratorially. "We're paving her path all the way from the road to the chapel with two hundred bars of silver!" With that astounding statement he was gone.

A cadre of the Conde's miners cleared a path through the crowd, giving the Bishop a clear view of the coach as it drew nearer. It was an open Berlin two-seater, drawn by six milk white horses, with high silver plumes nodding above their white bridles. Everything but the tire rims had been silver-leafed. Prominent on the door panel was the painted image of the same guitar-playing mermaid the Bishop had seen the previous night on the Conde's fountain and Coat of Arms.

Unable to contain his curiosity, he turned to the priest at his side. "Father Miguel, is there some redeeming significance to the mermaid on the Conde's crest that I fail to understand?"

Hidalgo's sober expression changed to veiled amusement. "Oh, you're not the first outsider to ask that question!" he murmured. "When the Conde's Irish father first came to this kingdom, he said he was lured North by a silver siren's song. Once there, as he put it poetically, he found himself 'shipwrecked on a sea of silver.' In gratitude he named his first mine in Zacatecas -- *'La Sirena del Norte*. She has graced the family crest ever since."

At that moment Don Patrick, resplendent in white dress wig, silver-trimmed tricorn and French blue velvet suit, blocked Legázpi's view of the siren on the door by stepping forward to hand down his wife and Doña Amantina, who carried the child.

It was the Bishop's first glimpse of Doña Isabel, and even at this distance he saw his cousin's much touted beauty had not been overstated. Her complexion was as pale and finely textured as a pascal candle, her figure almost as slim. She wore a silver lace mantilla over a high tortoise shell comb and a grey taffeta open-robed gown as elegant as any he had ever seen at court. Among the large crowd of relatives and well wishers lining her route the Bishop recognized only his traveling companion, Don Cosmé Medina and Don Francisco. All eyes were on Isabel, as she moved slowly toward the chapel, leaning on her adoring husband's arm and taking her first tentative steps along a path which the Bishop now saw had actually been paved with a king's ransom in solid silver. A lavish hand indeed!

At a word from Doña Amantina, Legázpi saw the Conde momentarily draw his arm away from his wife to take the fretful infant from her godmother. In that same instant Isabel caught the high heel of her slipper in a crack between two silver bars. She lost her balance and would certainly have fallen had not a watchful Don Francisco sprung forward to catch her in his arms. Once again the Bishop was impressed by this young gallant's unfailing chivalry.

03 80

An hour later, to the jubilant pealing of the chapel bells and a fresh barrage of rockets, the baptismal party emerged from the cool church onto the broad, sunny atrium. Having changed from their vestments back into clerical blacks, Legázpi and Father Miguel joined the group, as did Isabel's two sons, now wearing velvet suits as costly as those of their elders.

Don Patrick took the infant Condesa from Doña Amantina and, moving to the edge of the high atrium, showed her to the waiting crowd below. Two Indian boys trailed him, each bearing a large basket brimming with coins. For ten minutes, while the populace roared its approval, he carried out the traditional rite of honoring a new Christian by showering silver down upon the throng of vagos, *beatas*, beggars and thieves who had come from all over the province to join his mine workers in taking part in this massive outpouring of charity and grace. Not even at a royal christening had the Bishop witnessed greater prodigality.

"Don Patrick! Viva los Gracianas!"

The Bishop turned to see Emilio Santa Cruz pushing his way up the crowded atrium stairs to the Conde's side. He watched in fascination as the giant muleteer stretched out his upturned hands in a silent gesture to which the Conde responded by entrusting his tiny daughter to Emilio's huge open palms. As if on a silent signal a hush fell over the crowd.

"I speak for myself and for all of you who are the Conde's men," Emilio declared in a booming voice, visibly weighing the heiress in his two hands before making what Legázpi rightly guessed was a traditional statement of fealty to the Graciana dynasty.

"Small though she is -- weigh what she will -- the new patrona is born!" Almost before Emilio had finished speaking, Doña Isabel stepped forward to take back the child. Smiling broadly, the swarthy arriero handed over the bundle of ribbons and lace with a deep, courtly bow.

Don Patrick caught his friend in a welcoming *abrazo*. "Emilio! I've really missed you, amigo! And so has the central dome of my sacristy. When are you coming back to finish painting it for me?"

Emilio was beaming, unable to conceal his pleasure at being the focus of the Conde's attention and affection. "I've missed you too, Conde," Emilio mumbled, "but I -- well, I've had other -- work."

"Nothing of such lasting importance as painting an Apostle, I'm sure," Don Patrick piqued him. "Why, an artist's work is like a second soul -- it lives on after death, another kind of immortality."

"Oh, Papá, please come back!" Legázpi saw an eight or nine-year old boy with spaniel-like brown eyes push his way across the atrium to Emilio's side and take the giant dark hand in his own small, white one. "Uncle Matías has taught me lots of things, but you know how to carve and lay on gold leaf and use the agate hook."

The Conde smiled down at the boy, touching his cheek affectionately. "Your son is right, Emilio. You *are* a true master at your craft."

"Emilio laid a hand on Lorenzo's shoulder and drew him close. Legázpi noticed the boy's plain grey broadcloth suit and chestnut hair, tied in a simple black ribbon, set him sharply apart from Isabel's two boys and other sons of the silver aristocracy.

"And your Lorenzo's becoming an artist in his own right," the Conde added earnestly. "I'd be proud to have a son with half his talent."

"I do hope to become a great portrait artist someday, Don Patrick," Lorenzo confessed blushingly, then turned worshipful eyes up to his father. "But Papá, I need your help. Please come home!"

"You should do as the boy asks," Don Patrick agreed. "And nothing should stand in the way of his eventually going on to study at the new Royal Academy of San Carlos in the capital."

"Ah, but Don Patrick, I'm not a rich man!" the muleteer protested. "The Academy's for the sons of silver lords like yourself. It would never accept a boy who – "

"I'd *love* to go to San Carlos, Papá!" Lorenzo cut in.

"Lorenzo," Don Patrick said, raising his hand to emphasize the solemnity of his promise. "When that time comes I give you both my word, I'll see to it you're enrolled at San Carlos."

The Conde frowned briefly then brightened." And I assure you there will be no problem about you being admitted. I've contributed a good deal to that institution, so they owe me a student or two."

Emilio betrayed such a rush of emotion that Legázpi thought the gruff arriero might break into tears. Instead he reached out and clasped Don Patrick's hand in a gesture of loyalty and gratitude, transcending the invisible barriers of class and color which colonial society had erected between them.

"Don Patrick," Emilio said huskily, his broad face aglow with pride, "How can I refuse? Lorenzo means too much to me. I'll start work on the sacristy dome tomorrow!"

A large, florid-faced Spaniard, a total stranger dressed entirely in black, suddenly confronted Bishop Legázpi and pressed a full goblet of wine upon him. "Excelencia, please join me! Let's drink to the new First Condesa!" Then as abruptly as he appeared he lost himself in the atrium crowd.

"I can't believe my eyes!" Father Miguel hissed in Legázpi's ear. "That's Don Telmo de la Huerta! He's swallowed his pride enough to attend the christening! He's even toasting his old rival's heir!"

"Long live the First Condesa and the noble House of Graciana!" Don Telmo proclaimed in a loud voice as he handed a full wineglass to the Conde and touched it to his own. Legázpi saw a brief look of astonishment cross Don Patrick's face, then he recovered his usual aplomb and graciously acknowledged the toast.

Legázpi joined his voice to that of all the other guests on the atrium, "Long live the First Condesa!" But even as he did so he asked himself, "Are we drinking to the end of a bitter feud or merely passing it on to a new generation?"

All at once it struck him how intricately involved he had become in the lives of a family and a city of whose existence he had been blissfully unaware of two days ago!

ଓଃ5୫ଠ

"**But why couldn't it have happened** to me?" wailed Inéz. "I'm the one who should have fallen into Don Francisco's arms! Isabel's already had two husbands!"

Isabel, dreamy-eyed and in a mood to be forgiving, overheard her cousin's complaint as she passed the half open door of Aunt Amantina's suite in the upstairs corridor on her way to meet the Bishop in the library at six. Certain that she could not be seen, she slyly observed her least favorite cousin striding angrily about the room.

"Now, Inéz," Amantina cautioned her. "What if Isabel were to hear you saying such things!"

"I don't care!"

"You've been looking forward to this ball for weeks. Why not enjoy yourself? Perhaps young Durán will ask you to dance."

"I don't merely want to *dance* with the man," Inéz snapped irritably, her pink silk skirts hissing as she spun around to face her aunt. "I want to *marry* him!"

Seated at her dressing table, Amantina was pasting an oval black beauty mark to each temple. As Isabel watched, it occurred to her she had never seen her aunt without those two oversized patches that were as essential to her public image as a caste mark to a Brahmin. "Perhaps you shouldn't set your sights so high. There *are* other eligible men in this town."

Inéz turned in mid-stride, blue eyes blazing. "Name one who's as young and virile -- not to mention rich!"

Amantina tucked a white feather into her high white wig. "You'd do well to keep in mind that Francisco has a strong religious streak. He might never marry anyone."

"Oh, I know he belongs to that nocturnal brotherhood and gives Christian burial to drunks and vagos with his own hands in the dead of night. But that's because he's *bored!* If he had a wife and children he wouldn't have time for such silly pietisms."

"Don't be too sure. It wouldn't surprise me if he up and joined some order of strict observance. I've seen that fever carry off more unlikely bachelors than Durán in my time!"

Inéz twisted the long white love-lock of her powdered wig. "He'll do no such thing! " She said with a secret smile. "I'm making a novena to Saint Joseph. Francisco's sure to ask me soon!

Amused, Isabel turned away and continued along the corridor, her whole being still tingling with the thrill of that brief ecstatic moment in Francisco's arms. His hand had grazed her breasts and that touch had set her ablaze, yesterday's vision of herself as a saintly penitent was now cold dead ash. True love was worth any sin! What mattered the risks of discovery, dishonor and even the awful price of them both losing their immortal souls? With her usual penchant for second guessing God's own mind she was filled with the blind optimism of a girl in love. God meant us to be one, she thought rapturously, He's merely leaving it to our own free wills to find the way!

CS ED

When Bishop Legázpi entered the great *sala* shortly before six, he saw that Isabel had not yet arrived, and his eye was drawn to the library beckoning from the far end of that eminently civilized salon. Drifting through the open door he entered a well-lit, narrow room with beamed ceiling, paneled walls and parquet floors. A long rosewood trestle table with wrought-iron spreaders stood in the center, with cushioned friars' chairs set about informally. A newly-painted portrait of Isabel stood on a draped easel. The wall to his left was lined with family portraits, the one on the right held a library of at least three hundred books.

Running his fingers appreciatively along the volumes' spines, Legázpi was delighted to find a brave collection of French *philosophes* whose rationalistic ideas were expressly condemned by the Holy Office. What luck! He had not dared bring his own clandestine copies of these works, having been cautioned by the Count of Floridablanca that even a Bishop's baggage must pass inspection by nit-picking customs in New Spain's port of Vera Cruz.

Yes, he mused, books mirror the man, and today he had seen how easily Don Patrick moved from his underworld of mines, to hobnobbing with the kingdom's highest-ranking nobles. He's as much at home discussing Rousseau with his peers as he is eating barbecued goat and downing *pulque* with the lowliest pick and blast men. Discovering that the Conde was a liberal, meant that life here would not be the intellectual Sahara he had dreaded.

As a clock chimed the hour, he glanced up to see Isabel sweeping across the sala toward him. For the second time today he was struck by her exceptional beauty, but how the mood had changed! She wore her powdered white wig coifed in the latest *á la Columbo*, French style, but with a large silver replica of the family crest's siren, set with diamonds and pearls, nestled among the curls instead of the usual feathered dove. Her narrow-waisted gown was pale blue silk splashed with bright Chinese peonies, its wide panniers edged with black velvet rosettes. It also had an extremely revealing *décolletage*. Could this radiant, daringly dressed fashion plate be the same beata who wrote last night's note?

"My dearest Isabel," he exclaimed, taking her two hands in his. "How fresh you look, and after such a taxing day!"

"Excelencia. . ." she began, directing him to a seat by the trestle table where a silver tray held a Dresden pot with matching cups and saucers.

Interrupting her as he took the friar's chair next to hers, he said, "Since we're cousins, please call me Diego."

"Of course -- Diego. . ." she replied brightly. Then, handing him his steaming drink she asked rhetorically, "I suppose you've noticed we Americanos are as addicted to our chocolate as the British are to tea?"

Legázpi smiled. "Yes, missionaries back in Spain have told me ladies over here have it served to them even during Mass -- which they say works havoc with a sermon."

Isabel blushed becomingly, but fearful his humor might have piqued her, he remarked quickly, "By the way, I've been admiring your new portrait." And then, because his friend Goya had passed on a few insights about art, he made bold to add, "Excellent brushwork for a colonial artist."

"That's not at all unusual," she said with a hint of pride, "New Spain's been blessed with great artists from the outset, and of course the Conde's people always could afford the best." She inclined her head toward an antique portrait on the wall. "For example, that study of Doña Graciana, his family's foundress, was painted as long ago as 1560 by the renowned Juan Gerson."

Cup in hand, Legázpi rose to view it more closely. The face above a stiff 16th Century ruff was regal, the magnificent black eyes still blazed at him across the centuries. "A noble countenance," he observed, "but the smoked ivory color of her complexion I suppose is due to the pigments' darkening with time?"

"Most people make that mistake," Isabel replied affably. "But Doña Graciana was the child of a union between Cortes and a daughter of Moctezuma. No other generation, except that born of a first conquistador and a lady of the old Aztec nobility, ever had that singular coloring again."

Returning to his chair he noticed a full-length painting of a Spanish gentleman and asked, "Your father, of course?"

Isabel nodded.

"No mistaking that he and my father were brothers!"

"He posed for that just before his tragic death." Isabel's grey eyes suddenly grew dark, and the Bishop sat down beside her. "Amantina wrote that he died of fever in Vera Cruz," he said softly. "Was there more she didn't say?"

"Yes, much more!" Isabel cried, rising from her chair in obvious distress. "He was as good as murdered by the King's own hand!" She took a few steps then turned, bringing herself up sharply before him. "He condemned Papá for leading a rebellion against the Expulsion of the Jesuits!"

"No one dares question the Crown's decisions," he said cautiously. "But we *do* live in an age when monarchs -- Bourbons in particular -- believe firmly in absolute rule."

"But the Jesuits educated the sons of our aristocracy!"

"Ironically, that was a major reason for their deportation. Charles was sure they were teaching dangerous ideas to their students, ideas that questioned Bourbon absolutism."

"The Jesuits were treated like criminals, forbidden to take more than their breviaries and the cassocks on their backs! Four hundred of them were criollos *born over here*!" She sat down stiffly, hands clasped tightly in her lap. "When Papá opposed the soldiers, he and many other gentlemen were arrested. Some were publicly whipped in the main plaza. Imagine! People of our station! A hundred more were hanged." She paused for breath, her eyes glistening with unshed tears. "One man who King Charles sent to the gallows was -- the *father of Don Francisco Durán!*"

Legàzpi was stunned. "And *your* father?" he asked gently.

"He was exiled to Cuba for life, and taken in chains to Vera Cruz where he died of fever before his ship arrived."

Isabel's story gave him an unexpected clue to another puzzling facet in Father Miguel's character. Once, when he mentioned, in passing, the expulsion of the Jesuits, Hidalgo became quite emotional, explaining they had been his beloved teachers when he was a boy. He was devastated by their loss. Then he had added hotly, "The Jesuits and other Religious Orders helped keep New Spain at peace. His Majesty's Bourbon Army polices us now."

Isabel covered her face with her hand. "The disgrace of it broke my mother's heart and, being a woman, she let Papá's money slip away. She had no sons, so our survival hinged on me. At fourteen she married me to a sixty-year old *gachupín*."

"Gachupín?" Legázpi asked in bewilderment. I've never heard the word before. Is it the name of some sort of tradesman?"

"No, it's a very old Aztec word that means, 'the heel that stings,' referring to the Conquistadores' boot heel and spurs. But in our time it's applied contemptuously to any Spaniard who enriches himself over here."

"Quite a sweeping condemnation I would say."

"Well, its only lower-class criollos and unlettered Indians who use the term. They're convinced all Spaniards are avaricious, and 'spur' themselves and others on out of sheer greed, especially those who hold high positions in colonial government or in the church, positions which they covet."

"They could well regard *me* as a gachupín, then?" he asked thoughtfully.

"Oh, some would say so, but then look at me! I'm the daughter of one gachupín, widow of a second and will no doubt one day become mother-in-law to a third! Most criollas are raised to honor the old proverb, 'Fine linen and good husbands come only from Spain.'"

She was quiet for a moment and then she said, "Diego, there's something I want to show you before the guests arrive."

Legázpi followed silently as she led him to the far end of the library and through a door that opened into an immense ballroom. The four great chandeliers were not yet lit, but wall sconces cast sufficient light. Red velvet taborets were ranged along three walls, a relic of the eight centuries that Spain was ruled by Moslem Caliphs. A small, canopied dais dominated the fourth. On this platform stood a gilded chair, imposing as a throne. Hanging on the wall above it was an ornately framed portrait of Spain's reigning monarch.

"In palaces throughout New Spain, thrones just like this one await His Majesty's visit. You can see, in spite of everything, I'm loyal and long to welcome him. Papá himself taught me to *revere* the king." Her eyes brimmed with tears.

Legázpi was at a loss for words before this poignant display of colonial innocence and fealty.

Finding his voice at last, he took her hand in his. "Doña Isabel, trust me. I'll personally see to it His Majesty hears of this."

As if emboldened by the semi-darkness, Isabel's eyes searched his imploringly. "Oh, Diego, I have so many problems facing me! I thought that I might confess -- but I find it impossible. . ." She began to weep openly. "I dare not open up my soul to anyone -- not even you!"

The sound of convivial male voices and laughter came to them through the open library door, and the Bishop was amazed at the sudden dramatic change in Isabel.

"Ah, the gentlemen are back at last!" she exclaimed, addressing him as if he were a stranger. Then, lifting her chin imperiously above her open black lace fan, she blinked her tears away and murmured, "Shall we join them?"

Entering the library, they found Don Patrick at the trestle table pouring drinks for a roomful of male guests. Catching sight of the Bishop and Isabel he came forward to greet them.

"Did you think I was never coming back?" he joked, bowing slightly to the Bishop and kissing Isabel lightly on the cheek. "My pick and blast men were prepared to toast their 'new *patrona*' until daybreak!"

"A genuine compliment to her father," the Bishop said, and cast a nervous glance at Isabel. Seconds earlier she had been on the brink of hysteria. Now she appeared as self-possessed as an abbess at her own re-election.

The three of them moved on into the library and Don Patrick said, "Excelencia, I believe you know everyone here." His white lace cuff stirred as his hand traced a wide arc in the air that included Miguel Hidalgo, Francisco Durán, Cosmé Medina, his twin brother, Gabriel, and the handsome dark-haired surgeon, Doctor Juan Pinal, both of whom Legázpi had met earlier today at the chapel. "But three new arrivals have just ridden in from the Apache frontier."

Legázpi beheld a distinctive trio, the oldest of whom was a grizzled frontier trooper of perhaps sixty-five, with iron-grey hair and beard. The second, a man about forty, bore a marked resemblance to the Conde. The third was a slender blond youth whose dark blue eyes, striking good looks and proud carriage gave him a lordly bearing far beyond his twelve or thirteen years.

Despite their disparate ages, Legázpi saw they shared one characteristic setting them apart from the rest -- their rugged frontier dress. Over full-sleeved cotton shirts and black stocks, each wore a sleeveless leather jacket and dark blue twill breeches. Their boots reached to mid-thigh, with soft buckskin tops folded back to form a wide cuff. It was apparent the two older men knew no other dress, for they wore these campaign uniforms as naturally as a horse wears its hide.

"Permit me to introduce Colonel José María Cota," the Commandant General of the Northern Frontier Provinces," Don Patrick said, "and my cousin, Captain Octavio de Luna, and. . ." Turning to the young man he added proudly, "This is Octavio's son, my nephew, Don Tristán de Luna Mendoza."

Mucho gusto, Señor Obispo!" The old commandant was The first to greet him. Even this polite salutation revealed the gruff sharpness of a field command. His younger companions made full genuflections to kiss the Episcopal ring, but he managed only the shadow of a bow. "I'm afraid that's the best I can do for you, Bishop," he stated bluntly. "I took a Comanche arrow in that knee up in the Pimeria Alta back before you were born. But considering how long it's been since I've met a churchman above the rank of friar, I'm surprised I can even remember how the old curtsy goes!"

Legázpi had never met anyone remotely resembling Colonel José María Cota, but his forthright manner and artless speech immediately won his heart.

"So, Pat, congratulations on the First Condesa!" Don José cried, throwing an arm about the Conde's shoulder and hugging the younger man to him. "I guess you know what old custom would prevail if she were a white baby just born and baptized at some frontier outpost like Tucson or Santa Fe?"

"Yes, I do indeed," the Conde replied merrily, handing him a drink. "A criollo or Spanish leatherjacket soldier would ride up and tell me he'd be back in fifteen years to marry her!"

"And a damned good custom it is, too! Kept frontier families free of savage blood all these centuries!"

Don Patrick's brows arched. "Come to think of it, didn't you ride into the Presidio of Tubac the night your Amalia was born to its Spanish Captain?"

"I did that! And I rode back often, so she would grow up knowing me." Turning to Legázpi, he confided in a softer tone, "Ours was a marriage made in Heaven, Bishop. I loved her from that night 'til the Angel of Death took her from me after thirty years."

Legázpi caught the expression of enthralled admiration on Tristán's boyish face. Not surprising, he mused. While the custom originated with Christian knights on the old Moorish frontier during Spain's long Reconquista, transplanted here in the wild New World it seemed even more romantic.

As was his practice, Legázpi sought anonymity in the crowd, always more intent on listening to, than dominating the conversation of laymen. Sipping his drink, he was amused and enlightened by the banter between the Conde, his twin brother, Gabriel, and their cousin Don Octavio. It seemed the three men had grown up almost as brothers on the family hacienda of La Frontera in the distant North, and reunions such as this were as precious as they were rare.

"It's just lucky you've got Francisco here to serve as your syndic," Gabriel chided Don Patrick. "Without him to watch over the ledgers you'd have frittered away *both* of your bonanzas!"

"Listen to the man!" Don Patrick exploded in mock indignation, "And you, the spendthrift, who bought out every bookstall in London and then had to write for passage money home because you'd spent every peso on rare editions!"

"He's right, Gabriel," Don Octavio laughed. "I recall your own father saying it cost more to bail you out of a single bookshop in Paris than it did to send Pat on the entire Grand Tour!"

As the family reminisced, the Bishop noticed Francisco Durán had moved away and was approaching Isabel who was seated on a love seat at the other end of the library, her two adoring sons leaning on her lap. Although he could only guess at their conversation, it was apparent there was no love lost between the two, for Isabel received him icily.

The Bishop was intrigued. Perhaps she resented the fact that a man so much younger than the Conde exerted such influence over his financial affairs? Whatever the reason, her black lace fan came up like a shield against an enemy. Isabel was indeed a willful creature of strong dislikes and wildly conflicting moods! Suddenly his attention was drawn back to the family group by shouts of, "*Viva, Don José!*"

"To the Commandant!" the Conde said, "for getting Chief Ecueracapa to sign the Spanish alliance with Spain! This diplomatic miracle means the Comanches, Utes, Navajos and Pueblos are finally all at peace with us *and* each other!"

Although Legázpi didn't know a Ute from an Apache, he toasted the Commandant, and then everyone fell in behind the Conde and Doña Isabel as they led their guests to the ballroom where musicians could be heard tuning their instruments.

There Legázpi was surprised to find Don Cosmé Medina in the center of a group of Guanajuato's silver lords, that zealous young *scientifico* already hard at work trying to convert them to his new European techniques!

"You'll find Baron Von Born's method costs a fraction of what you're spending now on the patio process," he argued earnestly. "What's your reduction time running? Two weeks? Two months? And with a high loss of mercury thrown in! With this system you apply intensive heat in the *first* phase, and the ore is ready in a matter of days, even hours! You'll save on fodder for your mules and suffer almost *no* loss of mercury. Gentlemen, trust me! This new Von Born method will pay for itself in less than a year!"

"But we already smelt our high-grade ores that way," the crusty Fifth Marqués of San Clemente countered drily, taking a pinch of snuff. "It's the lower-grade ores don't justify the costs of the process you describe."

Don Francisco, who admired young Medina, came to his rescue. "Don Cosmé, our main difficulty is that your method requires huge quantities of charcoal or firewood to bring the ore to the necessary heat. As you saw today, our hills sacrificed their trees to that form of refining centuries ago."

A full orchestra of finely dressed, white-wigged musicians struck up a minuet, and a dozen elegant couples moved out onto the gleaming parquet floor. Shedding golden candlelight upon the assemblage of colorful silk, velvet and taffeta suits and gowns, powdered wigs and the brilliance of many costly jewels, were hundreds of tapers in the four crystal chandeliers. The whole splendid pageant lived a second time, reflected in the half-dozen pier glasses set all about the lofty room.

Legázpi remained a while enjoying the music and gallantry of the ball. Then, having paid his respects to his hostess, he walked through the deserted sala toward the corridor. There, out of the tail of his eye, he saw Don Francisco standing alone on a window balcony. He stood gazing down on the city, an untouched brandy in his hand, his jaw set, his expression infinitely sad. If ever he had seen a man suffering deep spiritual anguish, that man was Francisco Durán.

Continuing on to his suite he was struck by a surprising idea. What if Durán had a vocation to the religious life and didn't even know it? That would square nicely with his virtuous character and explain why one so richly blessed in material things was finding it so painful to remain in the world. Of course! That was it! And he would need spiritual guidance when that hour struck. The Bishop would be there to respond when that happy day came.

At the door of the upstairs chapel he stepped inside to offer up a prayer for this intention. On the tide of that first prayer he was moved to ask God's blessing on his poor troubled cousin, Isabel. The wave of compassion rippled outward until it included generous Old Martín and that unfortunate arriero killed by lightning, without time to confess, and lastly, the hard-to-understand priest, Miguel Hidalgo. Suddenly, as though someone had just knelt at his side, he felt the Divine Presence. For the first time since leaving Spain he tasted the incomparable comfort of inner prayer, which had been the very cornerstone of his vocation. Here then, he thought with a grateful sigh, lies my abiding home, here in the heart of God.

PART TWO

THE MINES OF GLORY

1792

Padre, si me days victoria,
del enimigo importuno,
passar sin timor ninguno
a las minas de la gloria
do gane ciento por uno.

English Translation:
          Lord grant that my soul's story,
          Like those who seek silver and gold,
          Be a triumph of grace
          On that perilous trace
          That leads to the mines of glory
          Where the gain is a hundredfold.

                              Fernan Gonzales de Eslava
      Cologuios espirituales y sacramentales y canciones divinas.

                                            Mexico, 1816

6

Nothing in Sirena's six years of life had prepared her for the electrifying sweep and excitement of the high Northern plains. Dressed in a grey-green velvet riding habit, and seated on a spirited sorrel mare, she rode between her father and Don José Cota, the old Commandant General of the Northern Frontier Provinces. At Cota's right rode the illustrious Marqués de Salazár, grandee and brigadier in the Spanish Army. As her father had explained to her at the outset of their journey, the Marqués was an important man, but his greatest importance lay in the fact that he was the Spanish king's personal representative and the first Royal *Visitador* to make an official crown tour, inspecting New Spain's frontier defenses, in more than forty years.

"Never forget, *your life and the lives of your children's children* will be shaped by every decision the Marqués makes on this historic tour."

She would remember it well. She liked the Visitador, who was a kind man, despite a brusque manner and his funny French accent when he spoke Spanish. He was the first gentleman she had ever seen with bright red hair: even his military brush mustache was red! He wore a fancy French blue uniform, a-glitter with brass buttons and gold braid. He showed up like a beacon on the grey-blue prairie, in contrast to such seasoned fronteristas as her father and Don José, who deliberately wore drab colors that were almost imperceptible from a distance. They made sure Sirena's dress camouflaged her equally well.

"I can't seem to get it through the Visitador's head that we're nearing unpacified Apache country," Sirena overheard Don José tell her father. "The man's all dandied up as if he were the French king sashaying around 'The Field of the Cloth of Gold.'"

The Visitador traveled democratically with the rest of the party by day but camped apart at night, surrounded by his personal entourage -- chaplain, surgeon, scribe, chef, valet and barber. In addition, Sirena counted a dozen arrieros who drove his pack mules and a private *remuda* of twenty fine Arab Barbs. These drovers set up his jaunty blue-and-white striped pavilion every afternoon, placing on its peaked top a small blue pennant, emblazoned with the Salazar Coat of Arms, which snapped in the ceaseless prairie wind.

Sirena and her father were invited often to dine with the Marqués in his tent, where their French-born host treated them to everything *a la français* -- cuisine, conversation and even wine, for he served Sirena watered burgundy with her meal. He and his entire retinue addressed her as Condesa, which made her feel very grown up indeed. Best-of all, the Marqués' kind but temperamental chef always made her a gift of a half-dozen mouth-watering comfits to take back to her tent. It required an act of heroic charity for her to share these with her maid, but it never crossed her mind not to.

The immensity of the plains, the infinite sky and the aromatic sage-sweet air called out to a wildness within that made her feel glad to be alive. But the dark rim of barren mountains far ahead set her heart racing, for she knew Apache warriors prowled those deep ravines, bringing fire and blood to remote frontier settlements before disappearing back into those same hills, leaving no more trace than the wind.

On the trail her father once more became the *norteño* of his youth. A wide-brimmed sombrero replaced his customary wig and tricorn, a dark wool serape the frockcoats of velvet and silk. He rode with a guitar slung across his back; when the way was easy he tied his reins to the saddle horn, strumming the instrument as he sang ancient ballads handed down in his family from the great Silver Rush of 1546.

> *Upon a branch the white moon sat,*
> *An owl with hidden claws:*
> *The mountain, stretched out like a cat*
> *Lay dreaming on its paws,*
> *And the siren's song of riches*
> *Came ringing down the draws.*
> *With her singing she bewitched us,*
> *Headier than Spanish wine,*
> *And she lured us to the silver*
> *That stole your heart and mine!*

Another of her father's favorites was, *"The Mines of Glory,"* a bittersweet cautionary tale composed by a sixteenth century Franciscan, reminding the reckless argonauts that Heaven promised more enduring wealth than the richest ore.

> *Lord, grant that my soul's story,*
> *Like those who seek silver and gold,*
> *Be a triumph of grace,*
> *On that perilous trace.*
> *Leading to the Mines of Glory*
> *Where the gain is a hundredfold.*

Sirena soon made all these songs her own but, on this crisp October morning she was not singing. She was listening instead as her male companions discussed the troubled state of politics on the vast unsettled realms beyond.

"Now that the American colonists have thrown off British rule," Don Patrick was saying, "I hear they're wasting little time moving into Indian territory.

"Spain's ambassador in Philadelphia writes me that the new nation has no money to pay its soldiers who fought and won their Revolution. So George Washington decided to pension them off with free lands in the West, abrogating former Indian-British treaties. Now thousands of colonists are pouring over the Appalachians, driving the Indians out and filling up the great Ohio valley with farms."

"That's a mouthful of land to chew on," Don José observed tartly. "Stumping out fields should keep them from nibbling at our borders for the next hundred years."

"Ah, but you forget sir, these Anglo Saxons are a restless, greedy race." The Marqués raised a cautionary finger. "They desire a waterway for their products and a Gulf port of their own. They'll never rest 'til they acquire both."

"But Spain has prior claim to the lower Mississippi and to the port of New Orleans," the Conde countered.

"These people do not hold treaties with any nation in very high regard," the Marqués observed caustically.

"Mark my words, these land-hungry Scotch-Irish-English farmers pose a grave danger to our entire northeastern border."

"If they move against us, the frontier can't hold," Don José stated flatly. "It's already overrun with Apaches."

"What do *you* suggest we do to strengthen that border?"

"Since you've asked my opinion, Excelencia, I'll give it, sans varnish or paint. New Spain spreads open like a lady's fan, Mexico its hinge and its flirting edge the sparsely settled lands ahead. It's a wide arc, spreading six hundred Spanish leagues from Tampico on the Gulf all the way west to California's San Diego Bay."

Sirena had never heard the Commandant speak at such length. His conversation was usually as cut and dried as the *pemmican* he carried in a small buckskin pouch tied to his belt and which he nibbled on as he rode.

"I'm told there are sixteen *presidios* and perhaps eight thousand settlers holding that frontier for Spain. . ." the Marqués said. Sirena watched as he withdrew a small cloisonné snuff box from his waistcoat pocket and touched a pinch of brown powder to each nostril.

"Apaches have left fewer than three thousand of them alive," Don José corrected him. "And more than half our presidio soldiers have no weapons except the lance. The *barbaros* are well-armed with muskets and ammunition supplied them by French and British traders, and now the Yankees have gotten into that dirty business, too."

"What if we decoyed the Apaches down to fight on a field of our own choosing? Met them with a full array of infantry, cavalry, musket, saber and cannon?" The Marqués was warming to his subject. "If we did that we could bring them to their knees in a single battle -- a true American Agincourt!"

"Unfortunately, Excelencia, such 'battlefields of our own choosing' don't exist up here. Indian fights are all strike and run."

Sirena saw Don José's raisin-dark eyes cast a half-pitying look at the Marqués before gazing at the distant sierras. "This is unforgiving country, Excelencia," he said, coughing into his gloved fist, a dry, persistent cough that had been nagging him for the past few days. "I've seen entire villages wiped off the face of the earth overnight, Spanish horses scattered to the four winds to sow more havoc, brave men butchered, women and children carried off into lifetimes of unspeakable slavery."

The Marqués blanched. "If you were in my place, what would *you* say should be done?"

"The Spanish Alliance has put the Apaches in a nutcracker between ourselves and our Comanche allies. We could crush the enemy tomorrow -- *with enough men.*"

"How many?"

"Give me six-thousand leather-jacket soldiers, mounted and decently armed, with six extra relay horses for each man, and I'll give you a pacified frontier!"

Sirena was surprised to see the Marqués recoil as if in horror. "His Majesty would never finance such an outrageously costly campaign!"

Don José shrugged. "Then His Majesty can kiss the North goodbye."

While the Visitador mulled over this sobering truth, Don Patrick reined his horse close to Sirena's sorrel. "You're very quiet, *angelita mia*," he said softly, his gloved hand touching her shoulder. "Does this talk of Indians frighten you? Are you homesick your Mamá?"

"Oh, no, Papá!" she exclaimed, "I'm happier than I've ever been, just being here with you!"

It still seemed a miracle that she was here at all. Only a month before Don Gabriel sent word from La Frontera that his wife and infant son had both been killed when their coach overturned. When her father began preparations to ride north to comfort his grieving brother, Sirena asked to go along. He refused, saying it would be a time of too much sadness for such a little girl.

But as he was about to set out without her, Don José had appeared on his way north from Mexico, guiding the Visitador on his two-year inspection of frontier presidios. The Commandant not only invited the Conde to travel with them, he insisted he bring Sirena along.

"It's high time to put inside her head a living map of the land and mines she owns up North," he reasoned, and Don Patrick acted on the older man's advice.

"And who of sound mind will agree to go as her personal maid into that wilderness?" Isabel had asked her husband, certain no one could be found.

"I've engaged Ricardo's sister," he replied. "Teresa's young, single and anxious to visit relatives in the North."

Sirena was not surprised at Isabel trying to keep her at home. Her mother had always been like this, trying to coddle Sirena the way she did Mercedes, her older half-sister who, Sirena believed, was a sickly child because her mother over-protected her. By contrast, Sirena was adventurous and daring, qualities she admired in her father, and he in her.

A few days before they set out for the North, Sirena overheard a conversation between her parents that she felt proved exactly how little her mother understood her.

"But the First Condesa was baptized María Amantina," Isabel complained to the Conde over a rare breakfast together in the family patio. 'Sirena' appears nowhere in the Calendar of Saints, neither Virgin, widow or Martyr!"

"Of course it doesn't, my dear," he replied patiently. "It's simply my own pet name for her."

"It may have begun that way, but now everyone is calling her Sirena!"

"And so, where's the harm?"

"Being named after a siren, and worse still, a mine, is sure to detract from her sense of self and self-esteem. Next thing she'll begin to wonder who she *really* is!"

Well, Sirena thought indignantly, she knew very well who she was! She also knew what was expected of her, because Don Patrick had explained it all so long ago she could not remember being told.

Born an aristocrat and baptized a Catholic, there was no doubt where her duties lay. Social rank and title she took as her due. Conserving the House of Graciana was her destiny. But as Don Patrick told her, in return God expected a Spartan brand of nobility. She must honor the family name, care for kinsmen, servants and neighbors, 'see the face of Christ in every stranger at the door', worship God, revere His saints and show Christian charity toward the poor. Only in this way could she accept the unearned privileges of wealth and class. All this proved a sure hedge against her ever being spoiled.

Sirena's first steps had been taken in the sunny Graciana patio, that dream world of birdsong, flowers and fountain spray. In the evenings she lay on the Chinese carpet in the upstairs sala, listening to her mother play one of Mozart's simpler sonatas on the spinet. Other nights she sat at her father's feet as he read aloud from the *Lives of the Saints*, or retold romantic tales of crusading knights and ladies on the Moorish frontier during Spain's Reconquista. At such times he spoke in his distinct, Gaelic-flavored English which made it easy for English to become her second tongue.

Sometimes he talked about the Great Famine, which had cut like a scythe through the Bajío in the fall of 1786. He described Isabel standing on the atrium of the family chapel under a broiling autumn sun, ladling out water and *pozole* to an endless queue of walking skeletons staggering through Guanajuato's narrow streets crying: "Bread for the love of Christ and His Virgin Mother!" Vultures darkened the skies above as the city's nobles worked tirelessly to save a few of the thousands dying every day on the road. He would end by saying, "Your mother never quite recovered from that ordeal."

Sirena knew he must be right, for she could not recall a time when Isabel had been either strong or well. Chronic migraines kept her from sharing her husband's activities, and he had turned increasingly to his daughter for company. By the time she was five, Sirena was not only the apple of his eye, she had become his constant companion as well.

He even took her with him on business trips, and as they rode along he made a game of asking her to guess how and why he was buying or selling certain properties.

"La Torre is an old, neglected hacienda," he had explained when they rode down into the Bajío earlier this year. "Some say it's nothing but a ruin. Why do you suppose I'm thinking of buying it?"

She thought a moment. "Because it won't cost that much to fix up, and it has a use for you that they don't see?"

"That's partly it," he nodded. "Bishop Legázpi tells me the poor old criollo farmer who owns it is barely hanging on and suggested that perhaps I could help. I plan to buy it and offer Old Martín a good salary to stay on as manager." He glanced at her expectantly. "I plan to raise pack and carriage mules there? Can you guess why?"

"That's easy!" she shot back. "If we raise our own mules we won't have to *buy* them to work the mines, or pay outside arrieros to haul our silver to the mint in Mexico!"

He beamed. "Exactly! So, what crop should we plant" She responded at once. "Corn! That way we can feed our own mules our own corn, and fatten carriage mules for sale!"

In May of this same year, when she turned six, the Conde swore his workmen to secrecy lest Isabel hear of it - and took Sirena on her first tour of La Sirena mine. Seated in a foreman's chair strapped to his own back, she descended the awesome depths of the Santa Cruz shaft. Wide-eyed, she beheld the great Veta Madre, and he pointed out the richest outcroppings of rosicler, teaching her the rudiments of recognizing different ores by texture and shade.

Sirena's second favorite diversion was visiting Emilio and Lorenzo while they worked in the sacristy of the family chapel. It was great fun to watch Lorenzo there, carving and gilding statues of saints on sections of the huge reredos he was making for the chapel of the still unfinished Miner's Hospital.

She also watched Emilio put the final touches on *The Reception of Saint James into Glory,* that he was painting inside the large dome of the sacristy.

Although Lorenzo was only fourteen he seemed able to do everything a grown-up maestro could do. She admired his patience in laying little squares of gold leaf on large sections of wood, but sometimes, to tease him, she used her fan deliberately to send the tiny squares fluttering over the red tile floor like golden butterflies.

"How much did it cost to build this chapel?" she asked one day, as she sat on the vesting table hugging her knees, her long riding skirt spread about her.

"Oh, I don't know exactly," Lorenzo replied, balancing on his lap a stone plaque with raised, gold-leafed letters he was burnishing with an agate hook. "But a very great deal I'm sure."

"As much as -- ten thousand pesos?" she persisted, reaching for the highest sum she could count. Lorenzo gazed across at her, his dark eyes holding far more affection than either of her half-brothers, Felipe or Ramón, ever showed.

"Three-hundred-thousand is nearer the truth," Emilio put in from his perch above the marble vesting table. "But it has given work to hundreds of men over the years." He smiled down at her. "Look at your father's motto that Lorenzo's about to put up outside, above the chapel door. Make it your own."

Jumping down from the vesting table she ran over to look at the plaque, reading slowly as Lorenzo held it up for her.

"God Gave To Graciana: Graciana Gives To God."

Riding beside her father on the high plateau north of Zacatecas, she was only now beginning to grasp the true meaning of those words, for here she was seeing the immensity of the far-flung Graciana family empire. Now she understood why as long as two centuries ago the big ranchers left the crowded central valleys and moved up here to the high plains where their great herds had limitless grazing lands. As the Bajío was New Spain's breadbasket, the North supplied almost all its mutton, wool, beef, tallow and hides. She saw this with her own eyes when they met up with drovers from La Frontera, driving sizeable herds of sheep and cattle south to markets in Guadalajara, Guanajuato, Valladolid and Mexico. And all the way, they would graze and bed down their herds on family-owned Graciana pasturelands!

Seeing her father's other world was both a heady and a humbling experience. Now Sirena realized that *God gave to Graciana: Graciana gives to God,* was not a prideful boast but an enduring promise, a vow to be kept by each succeeding generation.

"We'll make camp early today," Don José announced loudly, jarring Sirena out of her thoughtful reflections. "This valley's got the last good grass and water we'll find for the next two days, so we'd better make the most of it."

The Marqués and his retinue moved apart to set up his pavilion for the night, while the Conde's groom pitched the small campaign tent Sirena shared with Teresa, and brought in their mattresses and other baggage from their mules. Because it was the first time on the entire journey they had made camp this early, the Conde persuaded Sirena to take a nap. He sat beside her cot, retelling her favorite tales of chivalry until she finally dropped off to sleep.

When the Conde rejoined Don José he found him fighting off another bout of coughing while he checked his cinch, making sure it was sound before having his horse unsaddled. As he did so a camp guard rode up to him.

A solitary horseman's approaching from the southeast, sir. Shall I challenge, him?"

Don José drew a field glass from its saddle scabbard and focused on the approaching rider. "Give him welcome," he ordered, and slapped his horse's rump, signaling the groom to lead him away. Turning to the Conde he said, "Our visitor is Octavio's son, young Tristán de Luna."

"Tristán!" the Conde exclaimed, "Why, I haven't laid eyes on the boy since the First Condesa's christening."

The old man's brows lifted quizzically. "You mean he hasn't kept coming 'round to visit her like I did my Amalia?"

"No," Don Patrick said slowly. "But then you forget, Tristán and Sirena are too close of kin."

"Ah, that is so! What a pity!" He took off his black sombrero and slapped it against his iron-muscled thigh, loosing a cloud of trail dust. "I saw him last only a few weeks ago at Tumacacori, when his father agreed to carry a letter of mine to the Viceroy in Mexico. By Santiago, I hope Don Octavio brings me the answer I've been praying for!"

"A promotion?" Don Patrick ventured.

"Well, a change *is* due, and so I requested my next appointment be in some settled town or city, away from the Apache frontier." He seated himself heavily on a large log beside the campfire. "I've got two nieces I've raised as my own since Apaches killed my brother and his wife some years back. The girls deserve to live in a real city where coaches roll in the streets and ladies come to call." He was wracked by a fresh paroxysm of coughing.

"That cough seems to be getting worse, Comandante. Why not have the Marqués' surgeon look at you?"

"Nonsense! A cough's not a sabre wound!"

ఆ ɞ

Sirena awoke refreshed from her nap. Her maid, having given her a camp-style bath, insisted she put on a dainty flowered dress, with hose and slippers, instead of her usual riding habit and boots. While Teresa dallied over her own toilet, Sirena waited restlessly outside the tent. It was a luminous twilight, the sky an intense blue-green, a fragile new moon hanging so low it seemed near enough to touch. She was intrigued by the beauty of their campsite nestled here on the warm south flank of a narrow valley, watered by a small stream. A nearby knoll beckoned with the promise of a wider view. At last, bored with waiting and eager to see more before darkness fell, she decided to go exploring.

Scrambling to the crest of a knoll, she looked down on a wide ribbon of water below, its surface reflecting what appeared to be enormous white flowers blooming in the darkening sky above. She was startled by an eerie birdcall, like the cry of the sand cranes she had been seeing along the trail. Looking in the direction of the sound she made out the figure of a man leaning against a grey, stricken pine on the west side of the slope.

In the pale starlight she could see he was young, with finely cut features, and blond hair. Hatless and wearing the quilted cotton armor and dark wool serape of a fronterista, he was playing a long wooden flute. Fascinated and unafraid, she drew nearer. The flutist was so intent on his instrument, he did not look up until she was directly in front of him. He stopped playing and smiled at her. Sirena found herself looking into the frankest, bluest eyes she had ever seen.

"Ah, you must be the First Condesa!" he said warmly.

"They call me Sirena," she replied, inclining her head politely. "Sir, I've never heard music like yours before. Do you live out here all alone? What's your name?"

"Subaltern Tristán de Luna Mendoza, at your orders, Condesita," he obliged with a deep bow, and kissed her hand as though she were a grown up Condesa. "But, if you'll pardon my saying so, this isn't a safe place for a lady to be strolling around alone, and with night coming on."

"*You're* not afraid," she said candidly.

He laughed. "That's different. I'm a soldier."

"What kind of flute is that? It's made of wood."

"It's an Indian flute. It's never heard in theatres or palaces, because it's made to be played outdoors, where you can hear it echoing against the farthest canyon walls."

"An Indian flute?" she asked, the first flutter of fear in her voice. "Did -- an Apache make it?"

"No, Condesita. It's a Cheyenne flute, but I traded it from a Comanche friend at last year's Pecos River fair."

"Oh, that's good! You see, we have an alliance with the Comanches," she confided earnestly, feeling it was an important fact he should know.

"Yes, I've heard," he grinned, taking off his serape and draping it protectively about her shoulders. "It's getting chilly and your father will be wondering where you are. May I escort you safely back to camp?"

"You may, but -- will you play for me again sometime?"

"I'll do better than that, Condesita. I'll teach you how to play the Indian songs my Comanche friend taught me."

"What do Indians call their songs? Ballads? Concertos? You see, I play the piano and guitar, but only -- well, only *civilized* music."

"These are courtship songs. A warrior comes and plays outside the lodge of the maiden he hopes to marry. If she comes out, it means she agrees to be his bride. That is, if he has the required number of horses her father demands as her price."

While they talked, she and Tristán started back down the slope. Sirena was sorry Teresa had made her change into these thin-soled slippers, which certainly weren't made for walking. Dusk had fallen and she was glad to take his hand as she picked her way through the scrub brush. When they were within sight of the camp she stubbed her toe against a knotty mesquite root and stumbled. To her astonishment the coiled root came alive, rising up from the ground and making a rasping sound like dry seeds being shaken in a gourd.

Then all the breath went out of her as Tristán's left arm encircled her waist and jerked her clear of the ground, at the same time he brought down the leather quirt in his right hand with all his strength. She was horrified to see a huge snake writhing at her feet, although its head had been completely severed from its body by Tristán's blow.

"Condesita mia!" he said in a low steady voice, setting her down gently and running his hands over her exposed ankles. "Are you all right? Are you *sure* that rattler didn't strike your feet or legs?"

"No, Tristán, I'm fine," she replied her voice trembling with fright, although she tried to be as soldierly as he. "If he had, would I have -- turned black and -- *died?*"

He nodded silently, his face ashen in the starlight. "I've seen grown men die of snakebite and it's a horrible death. Promise me you'll never leave camp alone again?"

"I promise, Tristán," she said gravely. "What if you hadn't been here?"

"Precisely!" he said sternly, picking her up in his arms. "I think you need someone to look after you."

As they entered the camp Don Patrick came toward them. Tristán set Sirena down and she was grateful he said not a word about how far from camp he had met her, or her fearful brush with a rattlesnake.

"I see you two met up with each other," the Conde said, as they strolled together to the campfire. "How fast the years go!" he added, placing a hand on Tristán's shoulder. "Why, you must be all of eighteen by now!"

"Nineteen, sir, and just promoted to subaltern."

"Congratulations! And where are you stationed?"

"I was at Tucson, but I'll be serving with my father in Chihuahua, now the Viceroy's made him the new Commandant General succeeding Don José. . . " He broke off, as though he had already divulged too much confidential information. "But he will be along in a week or two with all that news. He sent me on ahead to bring the Visitador an urgent report from the *Arizonac* presidios."

"Tell me, are you still stuffing your saddlebags with those histories of Livy and Polybius? I recall as a boy, you always had your nose in some Roman historian's chronicle, no matter where your father and I made camp."

Tristán blushed, drawing a small well-worn leather volume from his tunic. "It's still Livy," he confessed, pleased to know his uncle had remembered. "I find the old Romans have a lot to teach me about pacifying frontiers, civilizing native peoples and bringing new nations into the Empire."

In the fortnight that followed, Tristán and Sirena became fast friends. They sang as they rode, or he told her true stories drawn from his fund of Roman frontier history, which she found an endless source of pleasure.

At fortnight's end Tristán's father, riding north from Mexico City overtook their party. That night, with dinner over and Sirena safely in bed, the four old friends gathered around the sinking campfire.

"It's not the answer I'd hoped for," Don José confided glumly, the Viceroy's letter to him open in his hand.

"I'm still going to be stuck on the frontier. This time he's named me to the Governorship of *New Mexico*. I'll be headquartered in Santa Fe!"

"I'm sure he meant it as a generous reward for negotiating the Spanish alliance with the Comanche head man, Ecueracapa," Tristán offered.

"At my age Santa Fe's as good as Paris, but my poor nieces will be as isolated there as they are in Tubac!" He fell silent for a long while. "This is the *only* favor I've ever asked the crown in more than forty years of campaigning." The hand that stroked his iron-grey beard trembled. "How could the Viceroy have refused my one request?"

Around midnight, the Conde was shaken awake by Octavio, who was sharing Don José's tent. "The Comandante's cough has gotten steadily worse and he's burning up with fever. I sent Tristán over to bring the Visitador's surgeon at once."

Emerging from the Comandante's tent a short while later, the surgeon told them soberly, "There's nothing I can do. At best he has a few hours. It's bronchial pneumonia."

His words fell like a death knell on the ears of his three companions. Among fronterista's, pneumonia was the dread 'Fourth Horseman'. When that Pale Horse appeared not even the hardiest survived.

Throughout the following day Don José drifted in and out of delirium. During the Conde's watch he even broke down and wept at the Viceroy's refusal to grant his request.

"I'd give anything to relieve his mind on that score," Don Patrick told Tristán. I'm sure he'd die happy if he knew those girls were settled in a decent town."

The midnight watch fell to Tristán. He found the old man weak, but his mind surprisingly clear.

"Don José," Tristán began slowly, "I've been thinking what might be done for your two nieces. . ."

"Yes, I too," he broke in hoarsely.

"What are their names and which one is the eldest?"

"Catarina's sixteen -- a good, strong girl, a true fronterista. Gertrudis, is younger, thirteen, I think."

"The Luna-Mendoza palace in Mexico city belongs to me. It's right downtown, near the Cathedral. My great aunt lives there now with a few servants, but it's very large . . . "

"Ah, yes," the old man smiled faintly, "A house in Mexico city is nearly as good as -- well, you know the old saying, 'Whom God loves, He gives a house in Seville!'"

Tristán took a deep breath and said forthrightly. "Sir, if you don't think it too forward of me -- I would like to ask for Catarina's hand in marriage."

Don José raised himself stiffly on one elbow, his eyes bright with fever and disbelief. "You would -- do this for -- *me*?"

"I do it gladly for you, Sir, and for honor's sake." Then he added. "I'll be away campaigning most of the time, so Catarina should have her younger sister come live with her there."

"But in the Name of God, son," Don Octavio protested later when Tristán asked his father's help in writing up a binding marriage contract. "Do you understand what it is you're doing? Don José is a man deserving of such a noble gesture, I agree. But Catarina! None of us has ever laid eyes on the girl. We don't know who her mother was --"

"What your father says is true, Tristán," the Conde put in cautiously. "You're only nineteen with your whole life before you. This is a rash promise, made under highly emotional circumstances. You might well live to regret it."

"But I'm the only one of us who can grant his dying wish!" Tristán said fervently, staring down into the fire. "That makes me duty bound.

As for marriage. . ." His voice trailed off. "I know the kind of wife I want. A woman of spirit, courage and nobility, a norteña descended from a fine old Conquistadorial clan. . ."

"That's what we both want for you too," Octavio argued.

"The little Condesa is the one I would choose if things were otherwise. I would ride back in nine years and claim her for my bride, just as Don José claimed his Amalia. But, marriage between second cousins is forbidden by the laws of consanguinity, so. . ." He paused. "Well, we all know that, so what difference does it make who I marry? This way at least it lets a man of honor die in peace."

Don Octavio exchanged a deeply troubled glance with his cousin. There was a long silence while he traced an imaginary river with a dry twig in the dust at his feet. "You're man enough to fight Apaches, son," Octavio said at last. "I guess you're man enough to decide who will bear your children. I can't give this union my blessing, but I can't in good conscience withhold my consent."

Signing Tristán's marriage contract was the final act in Don José's long career. Witnessed by the Conde and Don Octavio in the first light of dawn, it stipulated the nuptials must take place no later than one year hence and, until the bride was notified and the banns read, it would remain confidential among the three signatories.

That afternoon, having confessed and received Viaticum from the Royal Visitor's chaplain, Don José Maria Cota gave up his soul to God. Sirena knelt with the others beside his cot, reciting prayers for the dying. Her father had long ago told her that a pious, exemplary death should be the crowning accomplishment of every Christian's life. Having witnessed Don José's peaceful passing she felt sure he was safely bound for the everlasting Mines of Glory.

A week later, a few miles south of the town of Monclova, a sudden thunderstorm boiled up from nowhere, like an angry genie escaping a bottle. The Marqués, eager to reach their first town in weeks where he could bathe and sleep in a real bed, was all for pushing on. But Don Octavio convinced him it was wiser to make camp right where they were, in the lee of a swale sheltered by a small stand of cottonwoods.

"One learns to respect the elements up here on the plains, Excelencia," Don Patrick said persuasively, "Or he doesn't live to tell about it."

The Marqués reluctantly agreed, but his temperamental chef flew into a towering rage because an Indian servant was afraid to go outside and refused to cut fresh wood for his cook fire. The irate chef snatched the hatchet, marched over to the nearest tree and began cutting branches for kindling.

Watching the amusing scene through the open flap of her tent, Sirena was silently applauding her French friend's independent spirit, when a dragon's tongue of flame darted down hungrily, as though it found the uplifted metal blade sweet to its taste. Sirena watched in mute horror as the chef's body stiffened and arched over backwards, the hatchet still clutched in his upraised hand. The surgeon said later he had died of heart failure and it was just as well, for it spared him a long and painful death. Lightning had burned almost his entire body. The French chef's death was a soul-searing lesson in survival that six-year-old Sirena was to remember the rest of her life.

On the last day of their journey, as the high ramparts of La Frontera appeared before them, Tristán drew rein beside Sirena. Catching the cheek strap of her sorrel mare he brought her up sharply. Hatless, Sirena turned her face up to his as the prairie wind rippled through her wavy black shoulder-length hair.

"We'll be saying good-bye to each other soon, but I have something that I made especially for you, a gift to remember me by."

From his saddlebag he drew out a small flute, carved of red cedar heartwood, in the shape of a sand crane's neck and slender head. Taking it she ran her fingers over the smooth tawny wood, the cedar scent headier than any perfume. "Oh Tristán! she exclaimed. "It's exactly like your own flute only smaller!"

"Will you play the Comanche song for me?" he asked.

Lifting the flute to her lips, she picked out the familiar notes. Then, realizing their happy days together on the trail were over, a tear starred her black lashes and slid down her cheek. She was too proud to admit it was there, but Tristán brushed it away with his gloved hand and bending down he planted the tenderest of kisses on her brow. "I'm going to miss you, Condesita mia," he murmured. "Don't forget me."

Sirena nodded but was unable to see or speak for the sudden flood of tears that blinded her.

⊰7⊱

"Rodrigo is very lively, Doña Isabel," the Conde's groom, Mariano, cautioned as he led the majestic rosewood-colored gelding with flaxen mane and tail, into the family patio. "He hasn't been under a saddle for weeks and he might try to run with you."

"I can handle him," Isabel said, stroking the handsome animal's blazed face. "After I stop by the family chapel I'm going on over to Linda Vista for the holiday. That ride should serve to settle him down again."

Dressed in a black velvet riding habit, her burnished red-gold hair caught up in a dark snood beneath a black tricorn with snow-white plume, Isabel was restless. Because she felt better than she had in years, she knew her edginess must spring from the fact that today was the Feast of All Souls, for her the saddest day in the whole Church calendar.

In addition to the always melancholy duty of offering up her Mass and Communion for the repose of the souls of both parents and a host of departed relatives and friends, this particular November Second marked two months since the Conde and Sirena set out for the North. The palacio had been depressingly empty without them, and today it was even more so. Alberta and Ricardo were spending the week in their home village, Felipe and Ramón were with the Bishop at school in Valladolid, Mercedes was visiting Aunt Amantina at Linda Vista and Isabel had given the entire household staff the rest of the week off. Only Mariano remained to guard the palace and care for the Conde's stable of valuable horses.

Now, as he laced the fingers of both hands to form a stirrup, boosting her gently into the sidesaddle, she noticed the groom was scowling at her disapprovingly.

"Is something bothering you, Mariano?"

"*Si*, Doña Isabel," he began gravely, twisting a short lead-rope nervously in his hands. "Everyone in the palacio is pleased at how your health has been restored these past few weeks. Alberta calls it a miracle. A month ago you would have ordered out the carriage for a trip to Linda Vista. Now you're well enough to ride Don Patrick's own Rodrigo. But, well -- the Conde would have my head if I let you ride that dangerous Dolores Road to Linda Vista without an escort!"

"Oh, *that!*" she laughed, "Don't worry, I'll be traveling with friends. But thank you, Mariano, for your concern. And remember, don't expect me back until next week."

Once away from the palace and riding toward the Graciana chapel, Isabel felt greatly cheered. The weather was perfect, the domed sky an unbelievable cobalt blue. The summer rains had ended in late October and the sere topaz hills were cloaked in their usual fleeting mantle of grass, as well as an infinity of small cactus leaves that glittered like oval mirrors of carved jade in the warm November sun.

Yes, she mused, what Mariano said about her health was true, but not thanks to any miracle. She owed this recovery to her own strength of will. When Don Patrick told her he would be away three months visiting his twin brother at La Frontera, she saw that long separation as a God-given opportunity to gain physical and spiritual control of her life.

Without consulting a confessor -- true to her always mistrustful nature -- she undertook a Spartan regimen of the sort practiced only by religious of an Order of Strict Observance, under the guidance of a seasoned spiritual director. She began wearing a hair shirt and taking the discipline every day, penances that would have been unthinkable when her husband was at home.

Above all else she avoided any contact with Francisco, as she could never do when he was constantly visiting the Conde. He, too, was careful to avoid any public or private place where they might accidentally meet. No longer worn out by the relentless struggle against temptation, her appetite returned and the chronic migraines vanished. For the first time in years she enjoyed the domestic and social duties of her state.

Now as Rodrigo tossed his head and tried to take the bit so he could run, she was filled with a rare sense of inner strength and self-worth. Imagine Patricio's surprise when he comes home and finds I'm strong enough to master his fastest Barb? At the thought of his return, she was swept with a rush of joyful anticipation that almost verged on love.

She found the road and the city below deserted, for the Day of the Dead was the one feast day of the year that emptied streets and churches instead of filling them. Bearing candles and flowers, the faithful flocked to cemeteries to visit the graves of relatives and friends. Except for such crises as pulling the proverbial ox from the ditch, every business in town was shut down. But in the reduction patios of the mines a minimal crew of men and mules kept treading ore, while at the collar of every shaft, whim horses were held to their ceaseless task. Holy Day or no, ore had to be processed and water must *never* flood the shafts!

After tethering Rodrigo to a stone post on the terrace in front of the family chapel, she found a barefoot Indian girl about Sirena's age on the atrium, selling the sacred Aztec *cempasuchil* flowers for the dead. Isabel paid ten times her asking price for the entire stock. The wide-eyed child blessed herself with the rare coin and raced for home.

Cradling the giant marigolds in her arms Isabel entered the hushed chapel. The interior was still sweet with incense from the morning Mass, swags of lilac smoke shimmering in the shafts of midday sun streaming down from above. Placing the flowers on her parents' graves in the floor of the sanctuary she silently thanked Don Patrick for having had her father's bones brought from Vera Cruz and re-interred here beside her mother's crypt. What a thoughtful man he was!

As she knelt in prayerful silence, her eye was attracted by an almost imperceptible movement, somewhere inside the sacristy, just beyond the open door. She felt a twinge of fear. There wasn't another soul around. She knew the old sacristan took his siesta at this hour and, being deaf, slept like a stone. Could some passing vago have chosen this perfect time to break into the sacristy and steal the family's gold and silver chalices?

Emboldened by a sense of proprietary concern, she glided soundlessly through the open door, gripping her leather quirt as her only weapon should she catch a thief red-handed at the safe. Reaching the marble vesting table she paused, stood frozen there almost without breathing. Daylight filtering through cream-colored onyx panes in windows above, cast a scrim of light between herself and the far side of the room, but gradually she made out the shadowy figure of a man. His back was to her, as he gazed up at Lorenzo's unfinished reredos for the chapel of the new Miners' Hospital. She waited, one gloved hand starkly black, resting on the chaste marble, the other pressed to her wildly beating heart.

As if sensing a presence behind him, the intruder turned, his dark eyes wide with surprise, his face pale in the gloom. "Condesa!" he exclaimed softly, bowing with icy formality. "I did not expect to find you here!"

The dulcet sound of Francisco's voice, his captivating smile and masterfully controlled self, after all these weeks apart, struck her like a physical blow, like the day she fell from the swing as a child and had all the breath knocked out of her. Here, surmounted by Emilio's painting of Saint James being received into glory in the dome above, Isabel felt caught up in some infinite Beatific Vision. For the first time in years they were alone, no outsider present to be deceived. She reached for all the familiar restraints and one by one felt them all give way.

"Oh, Francisco!" she cried, "None of it was any use! I didn't stop loving you after all!"

"No, Isabel, no!" he protested. "We've both fought well for too long! We dare not throw it away now!"

Helpless to resist the magnetic pull of his body, she moved around the table toward him, but he caught her shoulders, holding her at arm's length. "I can't do this to Patrick, and I won't let you do it either," he ordered with the sternness of a confessor. "It's up to me to see that no one else is hurt."

"I don't care about anyone else!" she stormed, struggling to throw herself into his arms. "I only want to be with you. Oh, please hold me, *please!*"

Grasping her gloved fists, he cupped them in his own strong hands, restraining her as though she were a spoiled child in a tantrum. "Isabel, can't you understand? He's my dearest friend! I'll break off the partnership if I must, and move to Mexico. Maybe once I'm gone you'll be able. . ."

"No! Don't ever leave this town if you love me!" Then, searching his face, she whispered, "You do still care about me. I can see it in your eyes."

"Of course I do," he admitted wearily, "but it's not a case of your love or mine."

"You know I've never wanted anyone but you! I'll come to you anytime, anywhere!"

"Isabel, for the love of God, don't do this to me!" He released her hands abruptly, pushing her from him forcefully. "It's over between us -- *It's over forever!*"

Recoiling from him as though he had struck her across the face, she watched numbly as he turned on his heel and rushed out the side door. Sagging against the table, which alone kept her on her feet, she listened to the sound of his horse's hooves circling slowly while he mounted. Then the stones rang out as he galloped across the side patio and out onto the road.

A surge of white-hot anger replaced her grief, anger at herself for having lost her bitter struggle for freedom, rage at Francisco for his cruel rejection. Furiously, she lashed the marble table with her quirt, that violent gesture of retaliation salvaging something of her pride. Then, picking up her long velvet skirts she ran back through the empty chapel to the terrace.

Mounting Rodrigo, she cut him sharply with quirt and spur. The high-spirited animal reared wildly and set out at a dead run for the palacio. Then, responding to a sudden mindless impulse, she took the bit from him, reined him sharply to the left, sent him lunging straight up a steep embankment flanking the road. When he reached the crest she spurred him on mercilessly, not following any trail but setting off heedlessly across the rough mountain spine.

CB ED

Halfway up the sierra's western slope, overlooking the winding Dolores road and a league beyond Guanajuato, stood a small earth-colored adobe. The one-story dwelling all but disappeared into the surrounding earth and shale. Neither the house, well-house or small, rustic stable could be seen from the road above.

Ever since he built this retreat he called the Hermitage, Francisco had made a practice of spending at least one weekend of every month here. Although its existence was not unknown to intimate friends, to a man they honored his privacy, shunning it as they would an Anchorite's hut. His sole companion was a wild dog he named, *Dulce*, a beautiful golden-haired hunter in these hills. At first she had attacked him, but over time he gentled her with affection, as Saint Francis tamed the ravenous wolf of Gubbio. Now, whenever he visited the Hermitage, Dulce always seemed to know and came scratching at the door.

The Hermitage satisfied its owner's desire for prayer and solitude. The whitewashed walls were adorned with rough shelves that held favorite religious books. On a pine table between two worn bergeres stood a hurricane lamp. Above the stone fireplace hung a painting of saint Francis of Assisi, the work of the Spanish court painter, Francisco Goya, a gift from Bishop Legázpi. On the floor was spread a magnificent buffalo robe, taken in winter when the fur was in its prime. It was given him by Don José Cota, who had received it as a treaty gift from Ecueracapa, when the Comanche chief signed the crucial Spanish Alliance.

It was nearly sundown when, riding like a man possessed, Francisco reached his sanctuary. After unsaddling and stabling his horse, he went inside and sank into a chair, sick with remorse at having hurt Isabel. Why in God's Name had he stopped by the chapel after checking on the crew at La Sirena mine? Why today of all days? Now, thanks to the folly of admitting he still loved her, the fabric of honorable deception he had so carefully woven, was about to come apart.

With bitter regret, his mind went back to the day he left Don Jeronimo's employ lest their clandestine affair ruin Isabel. Penniless, he went to the Conde who, thinking his young friend's only problem was financial, offered to advance him passage on the Galleon so he could enter the China trade, and set up as a merchant with a shop of his own.

Upon his return from Manila his first act had been to call on the Conde and repay part of the loan. But before he could surprise him with news of his successful voyage, his friend had shared some shocking news of his own.

"For the first time in my life, I've fallen in love," he confided. "She's the most beautiful creature I've ever laid eyes on -- pious, virtuous and skilled at running a household, the perfect mother of a future Graciana heir."

"And who is this paragon of virtue who has turned a heart of low-grade ore to silver?" Francisco twitted him.

"The angelic Doña Isabel, widow of Don Jeronimo. He dropped dead shortly after you sailed."

Dumbfounded, Francisco dared not reveal he had vowed to marry Isabel himself. Fearful any other course would betray Isabel and break the Conde's heart, he quietly stepped aside, convinced that it was the Will of God for everyone. But his passion for Isabel refused to die. It bedeviled him, smoldering within his soul like an unquenchable fire in the mines.

Now, as a bright sunset flared, he closed the shutters, changed into a velvet lounge coat and lit the kindling and logs already laid in the hearth. Pouring himself a brandy he heard Dulce's familiar and insistent scratching. Setting down his glass on the mantle, he strode quickly to the door, opening it wide to let the tawny creature in.

The dark figure of a woman stood there instead, silhouetted against a Watteauesque sky of crimson, violet and gold.

"You remembered our signal!" Isabel said, rushing into the room and standing with her back pressed against the closed door. Her grey eyes were enormous with pain, her hair torn from its snood by the wildness of her ride, fell loose about her shoulders. "Once before, when I threw pebbles against another door, you let me stay. Will you let me stay tonight?"

With a cry that was half despair, half jubilation, he caught her in his arms, pressing his lips into her hair. "Isabel! May God forgive me, I cannot let you go!"

Oblivious to everything except her presence, he drew her down beside him onto the deeply furred buffalo robe before the fire, covering her face and hands with kisses.

After years of cruel denial, his every sense was aflame with desire. He was drunk with the scent of her skin, the taste of her lips, the faint but haunting perfume of her hair. Isabel lay without resistance in his arms, utterly content as he stripped away the black velvet jacket and the peplum under it, exposing her alabaster shoulders and breasts to his famished gaze. He did not even know what he had done until the blissful moment when she rose before him, pale as Botticelli's Venus rising from a night-black sea. "Ah, but, only one night together," he groaned in an agony of soul. "After years of longing for you, so little time will be like the torments of the damned!"

"Not one night," she cried ecstatically, her hands stealing away his velvet lounge coat. "I'm not expected home until next week. We have three whole days and nights to be together!"

ଔ ଓ

Over the years in this same room he had alternately begged God and the Devil to give him the bread of this woman's flesh, and both had given him a stone. Now he feasted. Isabel was stunned by her lover's Byzantine sexual repertoire, hallowed though it was by the spiritual purity of his love. What surprised her most was his gift for making their every coupling a drama or a game. Terrified as she was of Indians, she loved being taken captive and ravished by an Apache chief who then 'passed her on the plains' to other warriors, for it was Francisco who *became* them all, each one ecstatic as he mounted her anew. In each other's arms they escaped reality, but it was Isabel who plunged deepest into that rainbow-colored sea of fantasy.

"At one time I did not believe that a corsair could live for nothing more than looting galleons for their silver," he whispered ardently, "but now I have become a pirate with another man's wife as my prize. All I live for is to board and plunder her!"

Isabel thrilled to the brutal language he used to kindle her passions, and a shiver of anticipation ran through her as she wondered what new games her inventive lover had in store.

As they knew it must, their final day and hour came at last. They stood facing each other before the open door, cruelly estranged by mutual shame and remorse. Rodrigo waited outside, saddled and ready to carry Isabel away. Once again the tireless satyr of the Hermitage became the morally circumspect merchant-financier. The nymphomaniacal Isabel, who had not worn a stitch of clothes in three days and nights, was once more the Conde's irreproachable wife.

"I can recommend a gentle confessor at the Church of San Diego," he offered, not wanting her humiliated needlessly by some unfeeling rustic priest.

"No, it's best I confess at Our Lady of Sorrows in Dolores," she said, her voice barely audible. "The old Cura is blind and living out his last days there. With him I can be sure my identity is safe." Then, with a touch of customary hauteur she added. "The least I can do for Patrick is protect his honor and his name." She lifted her brows quizzically. "And you?"

"My confessor is not a heartless man," he said with a wintry smile. "He knows what pity is. But for whatever excesses happened here -- I take all the blame."

She reached up and clasped his head in her two hands, kissing his eyelids, savoring his tears, memorizing every bone and contour of that finely chiseled profile.

"Dearest, will you be safe on the Dolores Road?"

"Of course. I'm a woman, not a child."

She tore herself from his arms and ran headlong out the door. Mounting Rodrigo she reined him firmly onto the tortuous mountain road to Dolores. Francisco watched her ride away, her back straight, the small white plume in her tricorn nodding gallantly. As horse and rider disappeared around the bend, Francisco's buckskin nickered after Rodrigo from his stall.

Inside the Hermitage Francisco realized he was not alone. Inescapable images of Isabel were everywhere. With a sinking heart, he could see the Hermitage was lost to him forever as a retreat. He knew now Isabel was not a cedar but a fragile vine, utterly dependent on him for nearly everything but breath itself. And yet, that helplessness was the core of his helpless obsession for her – it reinforced his own pride of complete self-mastery!

Gazing at the buffalo robe, he thought, "I'm no better than poor Ecuaracapa, who traded his birthright for the white man's gift of horses, glass beads and steel. And as he blames the Spaniards for his own cupidity, I'd like to blame Isabel for my fall from grace." But he knew it was far more than a fall, for he had knowingly betrayed the trust of a friend. Dear God, what havoc they had wrought with grace!

Slowly he took a sheet of paper and a quill from a drawer in the table and lit the hurricane lamp's wick.

Don Cosmé Medina,
Director of the Royal School of Mines,
The City of Mexico,
The Kingdom of New Spain

My Esteemed Friend and Colleague:

It pleases me to write that I have decided to accept your repeated invitation to join the faculty of the new Royal School of Mines that you so ably head.

It will take me a few weeks to appoint a man here to run my shops, and I will terminate my interest in La Sirena mine. I expect the Conde back from La Frontera in the next six weeks, and will make my decision known to him then.

I look forward to the pleasure of working with you in this noble undertaking.

Wishing you health and continued success,
Respectfully,
Francisco

⊰8⊱

Isabel stood before the full-length mirror in her bedroom, brushing her hair and gazing apprehensively at the image reflected there. Although she was almost thirty, she looked nearly as youthful as the day the Conde married her at twenty-two. The only thing that bothered her was the faintest of dark shadows under her eyes. Not even Alberta seemed to notice them, but they troubled Isabel.

Still, she felt confident of her beauty, especially when wearing this favorite negligee of dark blue Chinese silk trimmed with wide flounces of aquamarine crepe de chine. It was a gift from Patricio, but it came from Francisco's New Manila Shop. She suspected he chose it for the Conde so he himself could visualize her in it, perhaps even fantasize he was stripping it from her and exposing her naked body to his exploring lips and hands. Remembering their wanton games in the Hermitage sent desire coursing through her like a searing flame. Oh God, she thought despairingly. I *must* pretend it's him tonight! How else will I endure it?

Patrick and Sirena had returned home late this afternoon, and Isabel knew when he dashed into the patio and swept her into his arms, he was eager as a bridegroom and would take her the first moment they could be alone.

But first there had been Sirena to welcome home with affection and gifts, followed by the mutual exchange of news over dinner, and then listening to Sirena describe all the exciting things she had seen and done in the wonderful North. By the time they finished the family Rosary in the house chapel, Sirena was drowsy, but she refused to go to bed unless her father took her there and told her stories until she fell asleep. Isabel could see the closeness between the two was even stronger than before.

Now, as Isabel waited before the mirror, her long hair shining and loose, she caught her breath at the fateful sound of the bedroom door opening and closing.

"This is how I dreamed of you every night on the trail," Patrick murmured into her ear as he slipped up behind her. He was wearing a white satin banyan and his smiling, sun-bronzed face gazed back at her as his hands stole possessively about her waist. "I even envied this robe that covered you and the very bed that held your weight."

"I've missed you too, mi alma," she whispered, instinctively closing her eyes to shut out her own image as she lied. The hairbrush dropped from her hand and the silken robe accidentally fell open as she leaned back against him.

Breathless from the panic of the moment, she opened her eyes to find him gazing transfixed at her reflection in the glass. Never in seven years of marriage had she failed to wear a modest white gown beneath every robe. He was trembling as he turned her around to face him, his dark hands slowly pulling down the silken robe to bare her ivory-white shoulders and then letting it whisper to the floor. Blushing, she wrapped her arms about his neck, hiding her face in the thick quilting of his banyan.

"I would go away ten times a year for such an ardent welcome home," he said, leading her to the bed and placing her gently on the matrimonial's scarlet cover. "This will be our wedding night all over again," he promised, casting off his banyan and falling on his knees beside the bed, his hands caressing her hungrily while murmuring half-incoherent endearments she was grateful she could not understand.

"Remember," he whispered, "how freely we made love in those first months before Sirena was born? -- before I agreed to withdraw before -- well -- because of your fear of pregnancy?"

"Yes," she admitted, "But it isn't that I don't love you." She kissed him with an unfeigned affection born of guilt and a loyalty she had been incapable of showing. "You're so generous to me, so *kind*. I never meant to hurt you in any way!"

Patrick folded her gently in his arms, as though he were gathering a bouquet of fragile blossoms that would be shattered by a less careful embrace. "Interrupting my pleasure has been a small sacrifice to make for your sake. I always knew any coolness you may have shown was born of modesty and your dread of bearing another child."

"I've tried to be a loving wife despite my fears. . ."

"You've been the very best of wives!" he assured her. "God knows, if I should die tomorrow I'd have had more happiness with you than most men taste in a lifetime."

☙ ❧

Pretending Patrick was Francisco had not worked at all. She had ended up simulating a sexual pleasure she did not feel, and trying not to appear alarmed when he was unable to restrain his ardor for the usual *coitus interruptus*.

"Oh, mi alma, I've never known greater ecstasy," he said as he lay drowsing in her arms. With his eyes closed, he stroked her hips. "You're as smooth as Chinese silk," he whispered, "and I'll take you this way again tomorrow night, and the night after that." He broke off in mid-sentence. "But what if I've gotten you with child?"

Isabel shivered slightly. "Well, at least I'm stronger now," she said hesitantly. "And I guess a wife who can master Rodrigo should be able to -- bear her husband a son."

He glanced down at her with a dreamy smile. "I believe you're turning into a real fronterista after all!"

Moments later he was fast asleep upon her breast. She lay utterly still beneath his weight, wide-awake, infinitely sad but grateful too. Six weeks after their *idillio* in the Hermitage, and with her husband absent *three whole months*, Isabel had known as surely, as she knew there was a Hell, that she was pregnant. With each passing day she had moved inexorably closer to that bottomless pit of scandal and shame she had always thought the exclusive lot of ignorant servant girls and common whores. She had not dared confide in anyone, Francisco least of all, having already weathered a few of his grievous attacks of conscience in the Hermitage, in which he had castigated himself for brazenly betraying his dearest friend, once nearly banishing her from the Hermitage. There was no telling what he would do if he knew he had fathered a child! Much as she dreaded pregnancy, she dreaded her lover's reaction to the truth even more.

Lying here now, flooded with her husband's pent-up seed, her terror began to recede. He had returned just in time to snatch her back from the abyss. And, delicate as she had always been, no one would think it strange if she were to deliver before full term. No one, that is, except dear Doctor Juan Pinal.

Thoughtfully she envisioned that good man's honest brown eyes fixed upon her in the unspeakable query. Well, if it came to that, hadn't she always trusted him more than any confessor? He was too kind and sensitive to hurt another living soul, especially Don Patrick or Francisco. Providentially for her, they were his two closest friends.

The following morning a splendidly attired Don Francisco arrived early at the Graciana palace to welcome Patrick home. In honor of the festivities being celebrated later today he had foregone his usual Third Order Franciscan brown in favor of a pale-green silk suit, elaborately trimmed in gold, with a waistcoat of rich gold brocade, a white dress wig and a tricorn of forest green.

He had completed the preparations for a gala dedication of the Miner's Charity Hospital and the unveiling of Lorenzo's chapel reredos. In a note delivered to Isabel by Lorenzo's hand -- for Francisco did not trust himself to call on her alone -- he had asked her to inform Patrick these events were scheduled for the day after whatever day he got back from the North. She had dutifully done so over dinner and the Conde was looking forward to the ceremonies.

"Ah, Panchito, how good it is to see you again!" Patrick exclaimed, welcoming his friend with an affectionate *abrazo*, and the endearing name he employed only on rare occasions.

"The town was empty without you," Francisco murmured.

"Well, as you can see, Isabel gave me your message last night and I'm dressed and ready for our big fiesta."

Francisco had never seen the Conde look more handsome. He was wearing a rich burgundy velvet suit edged with silver galoons, his dress wig tied with a wide burgundy ribbon. The frilled jabot and cuffs of imported French lace were a dazzling white against his face and hands, deeply tanned after long weeks on the trail.

"So, now then," Don Patrick said, as the two friends seated themselves at the table Alberta had set up in the patio. "Let's eat while we catch each other up on the news!"

With undisguised pleasure Patrick poured hot chocolate while he relished the colors and aroma of Alberta's tempting breakfast delights: large strawberries fresh from the Bajío, drowning in cream, scrambled eggs ranchero-style, with side dishes of red and green chile, steaming white buns swimming in butter and clover honey from Amantina's Linda Vista hives.

A cornucopia of tropical fruits was heaped on a silver tray in the center of the table -- papayas, mangos, mameys, pomegranates, sliced melons, bananas and glossy garnet-colored grapes. The fountain's silvery jet veiled the marble siren in a rainbow-colored mist as it splashed and purled, while a clarine in an ornamental silver cage, filled the patio with the exquisite sweetness of its song.

"Ah, Francisco, it's so good to be home!"

"Well, I see the North has worked its usual magic. You're in positively champagne spirits this morning."

"Indeed I am! You know, dearly as I love La Frontera, I've put down roots here in a way I would never have thought possible when I first came to Guanajuato."

"You've created your own family here," Francisco observed soberly. "That makes any place a home."

Don Patrick smiled as he plucked a grape absently from the tray. "That's true. And you know, it's something you should consider starting soon, as well. Nothing on earth compares to the joy of being welcomed home by such a loving wife as Isabel."

Francisco closed his eyes briefly as he sipped his chocolate, a thousand glowing images of his own private Isabel flooding through his mind. Then, forcing a playful smile he quipped, "I daresay I would not be so fortunate in my choice as you."

"Nonsense! There's Isabel's cousin Inéz. I hear she's only waiting for you to muster up the courage to propose."

Francisco set his cup in its saucer with studied care.

"Patrick, there's something I must tell you." He spoke with an almost alarming seriousness. "While you were gone I took a solemn vow in the presence of my confessor -- a vow of celibacy -- for life."

The Conde was astounded. He had heard of laymen, most often reformed rakehells, who threw themselves into religion out of guilt or scrupulosity. But Francisco wasn't a member of that lunatic fringe. He was a man of exceptional common sense and extraordinary self-control. Patrick, too, prided himself on being a truly rational man. He believed the Virgin and saints worked miracles, that the Lord heard prayers and that Heaven was not unlike a splendid baroque court where Christ the King reigned in glory and received the Blessed.

On the other hand, a man could be a good Catholic without picturing God the Father as some cranky Bourbon deity, enthroned on high instead of in Madrid. The Creator was the very soul of logic, order and reason, the supreme watchmaker who had put this great universe in motion and kept it ticking like the faultless clock most enlightened gentlemen of today knew it to be. The scientific spirit of the age was living proof of such a Creator. Francisco's gesture of heroic sexual renunciation struck him as something from the medieval past.

"I must confess I stand in awe of your moral fortitude," Patrick managed at last.

Francisco shrugged. "You used to visit the *zona* with me, so you know I'm weak-willed where sex is concerned. A vow is all that keeps some men from falling from grace. As the friars say: 'The Rule keeps him who keeps the Rule.'"

The two friends ate in thoughtful silence for a time then Francisco ventured humorously, "So, now that my 'religious solemnities' are out of the way, would you like to hear some really interesting news?"

The gravity dispelled, Patrick grinned. "All right! My first question: did permission come from the director of the Royal Academy of San Carlos?"

"Yes, I have the document here," Francisco beamed, handing him a scroll of parchment tied with a red ribbon. "The director agreed to waive the usual restrictions against Lorenzo's lowly birth and accept him as a first class student. His tuition -- thanks to you -- has been prepaid for the full five years."

"Splendid! I didn't want him getting the shabby treatment of a mere 'quota Indian' or charity case."

"He'll have access to the entire curriculum and attend classes with the sons of aristocrats."

"I think I'll present this to Lorenzo today after the unveiling of his reredos. By the way, you've seen the work. What's your opinion?"

"It puts every altar of Borda's Santa Prisca in Taxco to shame!"

"*Touche!* Now my second question: The China trade? Did the galleon have a safe voyage home from Manila?"

"She had a close brush with English pirates, but the cargo was unharmed. Unfortunately, my agent over there has just died. Replacing him won't be easy. An honest agent in Manila is rarer than a Moor at Mass."

"What would you say to our sending Felipe next year?"

"Doña Isabel's son?"

"Yes, Bishop Legázpi tells me he's anything but a model student at San Nicolás. The boy's been pestering me to buy him a commission in the local militia, but Isabel's against it. Maybe the China trade would bring out a hidden talent?"

"Well, for this year, I've employed the dead man's assistant, a certain Señor Woo. He's a sharp negotiator and being Chinese himself, he's trusted by the mainland merchants who supply us with our finest ceramics and silks."

"You know best. There's more profit in the China trade than in any other investment we can make. And I, too, hesitate to entrust it to anyone as young and green as Felipe."

"Tell me about Gabriel? How is he holding up under his double tragedy?"

"He's devastated. You know how he worshipped Desireé, and they'd only been married a year. He had such grandiose plans for his little son." Patrick shook his head. "He's already left for Vera Cruz to take ship for Europe. He hopes the voyage and change of scene will help him recover from his grief. He'll stay in London a few months, shopping for rare books -- as always! Then he plans to go on to Paris."

Francisco's eyebrows shot up. "Paris? Isn't it pretty dangerous there right now? The Gacéta reports that the rabble is threatening to behead the king!"

"Doctor Juan's son, Daniel, is over there studying medicine at the Academy. Desireé had relatives there, too, whose safety Gabriel hopes to secure. But he says there's no danger for foreigners."

"By the way, you'll be pleased to hear that Cosmé Medina's Royal School of Mines is progressing well." Francisco was determined to steer the conversation to the topic he was so anxious to broach, although he knew his decision to leave Guanajuato would be a difficult one for Patrick to accept.

"I'm happy for Cosmé. What other man would have been big enough to admit that his 'scientific European techniques' simply wouldn't work in New Spain? When the Von Born method proved outrageously expensive here, then failed just as badly in the Zacatecas mines, it took courage to face the truth. But instead of sailing back to Spain in a sulk, Cosmé found a way his great talents could benefit the kingdom."

"Yes. As president of the silver consulado in the Capital, he's shown the patience of a saint. And who else but Cosmé could set up and run an institution as complex and exacting as the Royal School of Mines?"

"I'm delighted he and Sophia have decided to make their home in Mexico."

Francisco saw the ideal opening and seized it. "While on the subject of Cosmé and the School, I've also made a very important decision that we need to. . ."

"Don Francisco! I was hoping you'd be here!" Looking up, they saw Sirena flying down the stairs, dressed in a blue velvet riding habit and shiny black boots. "You'll never guess what Tristán gave me!"

Realizing his own perfect moment was lost, Francisco resigned himself temporarily, turning his attention to the little girl who came bouncing up to his side.

"I swear you've grown an inch since you've been gone!" he exclaimed, kissing her cheek and lifting her to his knee. "So what have we here?"

"It's a Cheyenne flute," she told him, her amber eyes sparkling with pride. "Tristán carved it just for me and taught me to play Indian courtship songs. Listen!"

Slipping off his lap, she seated herself on the edge of the fountain and played the entire piece from memory. When she was done the two men applauded.

"Bravo! You *are* becoming a first rate musician," Francisco complimented her. "First the guitar, then the spinet and now an Indian flute!"

"Well, *mi consentida*," her father announced, rising from the table, "Don Francisco and I have to leave for the mines."

"But you can't go to work today!" she protested. "Today's the dedication of Lorenzo's reredos!"

"Oh, we won't be working, merely riding up to visit the crews before the unveiling. I've been gone a long time."

"Can I come along?"

"Your mother planned for you to go to the chapel with her and Mercedes in the carriage. You can be there just in time for the Solemn High Mass at noon."

"I don't want to ride with them, Papá," Sirena said, looking pained. "Mercedes has a fever. I *know* she'll make us late. And I hate riding in a coach like some dowager who's too old to sit a horse!"

She held out her skirt with both hands and pirouetted gracefully. "Besides, you can see I'm already dressed up in the brand new riding habit that Aunt Amantina's seamstress Estella made for me? Oh, Papá, please!"

Don Patrick fingered a warm, glossy ringlet of her hair and she knew he would relent. "All right, *mi reina*, I'll have Alberta tell your mother that you've come with us."

As they waited for the groom to bring their horses around, Sirena pulled on her riding gloves and set a bright red tricorn on her head.

"This way," she said, casting a knowing glance at Don Francisco, "we don't have to say good-bye. You see, back on the trail we were together all the time, weren't we, Papá?"

"Well, back here at home we won't be able to be together that much. I do have to go to work every day."

"I have it!" Sirena said with sudden inspiration. "Why not let me start working with you at the mines? I can learn the things I need to know, and like Don José said, it's time I did! That way we can be together every day!"

Don Patrick picked her up in his arms and pressed his cheek to hers. "When you're a little older, my queen. One day they're going to be *your* mines and you'll need to know how to run them -- but not just yet."

ॐ ॐ

After visiting the workers at the lower Graciana mine, the three riders headed up the mountain road toward La Sirena. Francisco was riding his fleet buckskin gelding and Sirena, her sorrel mare, while the Conde was mounted on a rare *prieto azabache*, a jet black stallion that Old Martín had bred and raised on what was now Don Patrick's Hacienda La Torre. As they were about to pass the family chapel Sirena noticed her father pull up on his reins.

"Maybe we should stop in here first," he ventured, as though asking Francisco's approval. "It might be better to present Lorenzo with his admission to art school before the dedication."

Sirena watched Francisco appraise her father with a knowing grin. "You Irish are such poor liars! Why not admit you can't resist seeing your reredos before the others do?"

"Maybe!" Don Patrick conceded. "So lets all three of us go in and look. That's the privilege of being donors."

"You and Sirena go on without me," Francisco hedged, an anxious edge in his voice. "I want to get to the upper mine and see Ricardo as soon as possible."

"Something's wrong?" Don Patrick queried sharply. "There's something you're not telling me."

"Well, I didn't want to worry you on your first morning home. But, yes, while you were gone we did have some problems at the lower level of the new shaft."

"What kind of problems?" Don Patrick sensed instinctively that Francisco was -- as always -- trying to put a good face on bad news.

Francisco rested both hands on his saddle horn. "The truth is we've discovered an underground fissure, but it doesn't appear to be due to natural causes. Ricardo and I don't have solid proof, but we suspect Don Telmo de la Huerta of tunneling across from the adjacent shaft of his El Rey mine."

Sirena and her father listened as Francisco explained that on the Day of the Dead he had visited the upper mine to make sure the small holiday crew had things running smoothly. Although neither pick nor blast men were working that day, Francisco swore he heard pick axes at work far below. Ricardo said he also heard blasting on the following two days, which were holidays, as well.

"Of course, Patrick, you know the maze of Guanajuato's underground works has never been properly mapped. It's almost impossible for one mine owner to prove another is poaching."

"Don Telmo *always* knows what he's doing! That's the very spot where three rich veins may converge. I believe we'll find a pocket of very high-grade ore there. Don Telmo must think so too."

"Probably. But at the moment, I'm more worried about the safety factors."

Sirena saw her father's jaw harden as his renowned concern for the welfare of his workmen took possession of him. "If you sense the slightest danger or weakness in the wall of that shaft, order every man pulled up from underground at once," he commanded. "I'd rather lose a month's worth of ore than a single man's life."

"Ricardo and I will check everything."

"And don't do anything foolhardy yourself, my friend," he cautioned, half-jokingly, laying a hand on Francisco's shoulder. "I don't want Don Telmo making any martyrs."

"I'll do everything you would do," Francisco laughed. "My business with Lorenzo won't keep me here long. I'll join you at the collar of the shaft within the hour."

⚜9⚜

"**Praise God and all His saints,**" the deaf sacristan shouted delightedly as he limped down the atrium stairs to welcome Sirena and her father, "They brought you safely home!"

As a young assistant sacristan led their horses away, the white-thatched, arthritic Julio grasped the Conde's hand in both his own. His deeply seamed, earth-brown face reminded Sirena of the rain-scoured arroyos she had ridden through on the far northern plains.

"Thank you, Julio, for taking such good care of the place while I've been gone," the Conde said, pressing a small buckskin pouch of silver coins discreetly into his hand.

"It was nothing, Patron!" Julio squared his narrow shoulders and expanded his bony chest under the thin white cotton *camisa*. "I'm proud of this chapel as if it were mine."

"Well, you stood with me against those who tried to keep us from building it, remember? I've not forgotten that."

"Yes, it *was* a hard fight!" Julio chuckled as the three of them began ascending the stairs. Sirena noticed her father slow his brisk pace to match the old man's painful ascent and she followed his example.

"But Papá, why did you have to fight to build your very own chapel?"

"Oh, there were some who. . ." her father began, but Julio cut in boldly, "It was mostly Don Telmo de la Huerta, child. He envied your father's good fortune, and when we were breaking ground he snatched the shovel from my hands and cried out to the crowd: 'It's a crime to waste a hill of silver on a useless church!'"

Julio's eyes grew black at the memory. "Ah, little Condesa, never before or since have I seen your father raise his voice in anger to anyone, but he did that day, and I was *glad!* He grabbed the shovel back from de la Huerta and ordered him off this property, shouting: *'The silver on this hill is mine, and if it pleases me I'll give it ALL to God!'*"

When they reached the top of the stairs, Julio was called away by a workman and Sirena was surprised to see her father remain standing there, one foot poised on the top step, a hand resting on the stone newel post. It took her a moment to realize he was simply admiring the chapel, as though seeing it for the first time. She in turn could not help admiring him. What an elegant figure he cut in his wine-red suit and black tricorn, framed against the soft pink stone of the ornate facade and tower.

"Always be proud of this church, mi reina," he said with uncharacteristic gravity. "Long after we are dust and ashes, these bells will summon generations yet unborn to worship here. And if this hill holds more silver than all the mines in town, I will have kept my word: *God gave to Graciana: Graciana gives to God*."

"I understand, Papa," Sirena said with an earnestness matching his own. "I know it wasn't *really* built like that silly story says, 'with silver dust and Spanish wine'. It stands for what Our Lord has a right to expect in return for all He's given us."

"You put it well, child," he said. "Every noble worthy of the name is duty bound to be a living channel of Divine Providence. If the flow of Christian charity from rich to poor were ever cut off, our society would collapse and sheer anarchy would prevail. Always remember, without charity there is no honor, without honor one forfeits the Grace of God."

Sirena stood thoughtfully at his side, and for a moment longer the two of them drank in the lyrical beauty of the slender pink spire floating against the gloriously blue sky. Then the familiar spark of humor returned to his eyes as he asked, "Well, Condesa, shall we surprise Lorenzo with his letter of admission to San Carlos now or later?"

"Oh, let's do it now!"

Inside they found Lorenzo's tall, three-tiered reredos, temporarily set up in the sanctuary for the formal unveiling. Several workmen were busy testing the curtains concealing it, curtains made from the violet throwcloths Julio used to cover the saints during Lent. Lorenzo, looking more aristocratic than she had ever seen him, in a suit of black watered silk, was directing the work, shadowed by an anxious Matías and a remarkably well-dressed Emilio.

"Maestro," the Conde said placing an arm about Lorenzo's shoulders, "may I steal a look before the big event?"

"Of course, Conde!" Then, flustered by the Conde's unannounced visit he added nervously, "I hope you'll be pleased." Lorenzo himself slowly pulled the cord revealing the work of four long years.

An example of a Reredos Altar Screen.

At first glance all Sirena could see was the overall dazzle of gold-leaf and the swirl of saints' tunics and robes which, although carved of wood, had been *estofadoed* to simulate the folds and swags of silks, until every figure seemed to spin and soar in space. She recognized six saints identified with the miners' trade, in the peripheral niches, while the center niche held the True Cross, patronal symbol of stonemasons and those miners who worked with stone.

Crowning the reredos was Sirena's favorite, the Holy Child of Atocha, seated on his chair and holding his little basket and water gourd. His story she knew by heart, beginning in 8th Century Spain when Christian captives of the Moors were starving in the dungeons of Atocha. The Christ Child brought them food in a basket never short of bread, and water in a gourd that never ran dry. From then on his aid was invoked by captives, prisoners and persons trapped underground. Spaniards brought the devotion to New Spain and the first silver miners took it north, where He became their most powerful intercessor. Lorenzo had carved Him perfectly in his tunic, cape and wide-brimmed pilgrim's hat. She had already been told that the pure silver sandals on His feet were the handiwork and gift of her father's pick and blast men.

"I'm truly impressed, Lorenzo," Don Patrick said at last. "You've not only carved each figure to perfection, you've organized the entire reredos superbly."

Sirena saw Lorenzo's face glow.

"But that silver frost-like finish, misting over the gold? I've never seen that done anywhere."

"In places I burnished the leaf down to the red bole, glazed it with oil and dusted it with the fine powder called rottenstone. Emilio helped me to create that effect."

The Conde reached inside the breast pocket of his frock coat and drew out the small parchment scroll, while inviting Sirena, Lorenzo, Matías and Emilio into the greater privacy of the sacristy. "Lorenzo, the First Condesa and I wish to present you with something you richly deserve."

Fascinated, Sirena watched Lorenzo take the document, untie the silk ribbon and read the scroll. Although she knew Emilio could neither read nor write, he gazed studiously over his son's shoulder and studied it.

Small beads of perspiration appeared on Lorenzo's brow and upper lip. When he glanced up at the Conde all his hopes and future ambitions were in his eyes. "To be admitted to San Carlos Academy personally," he breathed, "and by the Director himself!" He paused a moment to compose himself and added, "Conde, this means everything to me. How can I repay you?"

"The only favor I ask in return is that you become the best artist you can be," Don Patrick said with a wink. "A second Juan Gerson or Juan Cabrera, nothing less!"

"I can make an artist of myself, but you, Sir -- with this paper you have made me what I could not otherwise have become -- *an hidalgo!*"

Emilio stepped forward silently to engulf his patron in a large abrazo. "You kept your promise, Patron."

"Lorenzo kept his," the Conde parried modestly.

"I thought I heard familiar voices!"

Sirena looked up to see Bishop Legázpi coming through the door from the sanctuary with Doctor Juan Pinal, followed by her half-brothers, Felipe and Ramón.

"I decided to declare a holiday at San Nicola's for this gala event," the Bishop explained jovially. "And I thought Doña Isabel might be pleased to have her sons home for a few days, as well."

"We were all out there on the atrium," Doctor Juan laughed as they all left the sacristy for the chapel, "laying bets that Patrick couldn't resist stealing a private look before the official unveiling."

"Of course!" the Conde agreed, "And I assure you, this reredos will be the envy of silver lords from every mining center in the kingdom." He cast a curious glance at a still unexplained cloth-shrouded figure that stood directly in front of the reredos. "Lorenzo, is this the statue of some saint you couldn't find a decent home for?" he teased.

Lorenzo cast a questioning look at his uncle and Matías shrugged. "The Conde will see it in a few hours anyway," he suggested smilingly.

Lorenzo stepped forward and lifted the cloth, revealing a life-size kneeling figure. It was carved and gilded like the saints, but was apparently the portrait of a modern gentleman in contemporary dress, hands folded before him in prayer.

Sirena stared at it, completely bemused. What made it seem both so strange and so uncannily familiar?

The Conde was equally perplexed. Then all at once Sirena recognized who it was. "Why, it's -- it's a statue of *you* Papá!"

"Don Francisco commissioned it as his personal gift, Conde," Matías explained. "He said it wasn't fitting that the Miners' reredos be installed without an image of the donor kneeling before it."

Sirena could see her father was deeply touched and she moved closer to clasp his hand in hers. "I think it's wonderful, Papá! And it looks exactly like you."

"For the second time today," Don Patrick said, embarrassed by the depth of his emotion, "I'm overwhelmed. . ."

As he reached out to shake Lorenzo's hand, everyone in the chapel was transfixed by the disquieting clamor of a wildly pealing bell, a sound Sirena had never heard before. It came from far away, but rang urgently and clear, as though crying frantically for help. They stood motionless, as frozen as the panoply of estofadoed saints gazing down at them.

"It's La Sirena's disaster bell!" Don Patrick cried, turning on his heel and running toward the open chapel doors.

Instinctively, Sirena blessed herself before hitching up her skirts and racing after him. She reached the sunny atrium just as a workman led her father's jet-black stallion at a fast trot to the foot of the stairs. As he started to mount, they both caught sight of Francisco's buckskin pounding down the road at a dead run. Sirena felt her blood freeze. It wasn't Don Francisco in the saddle, it was Ricardo's youngest son!

Seeing the Conde, the boy pulled back so hard on the bit he set the buckskin down on his tail in a globe of shining dust. "Come quick, patron!" he shouted, his bronze face ashen. "There's been a cave-in! My father's badly hurt at the bottom of the shaft!"

"We'll get him out," Patrick promised, "but you'll be of more use here. Help Doctor Juan set up saw horses and fiesta tables for litters -- in case there are others."

"That's not all, Patron!" the boy explained, choking back tears as he dismounted. "Don Francisco went to help my father and he's trapped down there, too. . ."

Don Patrick did not wait to hear more, and as she watched him vault into the saddle Sirena called out, "Papá! What can I do to help?"

He turned and fixed her with an expression of such anguish it wrung her heart. "Pray with all your soul to the Holy Child of Atocha to save them!"

With that he spurred his fleet *prieto* and streaked up the road in the direction of the bell's incessant tolling, Emilio, on the buckskin, riding hard at his side.

10

For what seemed an eternity Sirena knelt before the unveiled reredos, praying fervently to the *Santo Niño* for a double miracle, never doubting for a moment that He could perform this prodigy. She was only half aware of hushed voices in the sacristy as workmen set up boards and Doctor Pinal cleared the marble vesting table making a place for him to examine the injured.

Then without warning, the quiet chapel was filled with noisy miners all talking at once. Two men bore the unconscious Ricardo on a blanket, shouting orders as they surged past her and through the open sacristy door. Jumping to her feet to follow the crowd and see what was happening, she felt strong hands from behind close around her waist and hold her in their vise.

"No, Condesa!" Lorenzo ordered her. "Stay here with me!"

Emilio's giant frame brushed past her. He was holding one end of a canvas litter on which a second injured miner lay.

"In here, Emilio!" Doctor Juan directed him urgently from inside the sacristy.

As this second litter went by Sirena had a sudden glimpse of burgundy velvet and torn white lace. "Papá!" she screamed, straining with all her strength to break Lorenzo's hold. "Lorenzo! My Papá is hurt! Let me go to him!"

"No, Condesa! You mustn't see these things."

Wild as a treed river panther, she was kicking, screaming and pummeling Lorenzo with her fists, when she heard a man's commanding voice order Lorenzo, *"Let her go!"*

Looking up Sirena was thunderstruck to see Tristán striding toward her.

"And who are you to give me orders?" Lorenzo flashed back, still holding her in an iron grip.

"Let her go," Tristán repeated more softly. "Before I take her from you!"

Slowly Lorenzo released his hold, his dark eyes burning with resentment and rage. "Then *you* be responsible for the consequences," he snapped. "It could mark a child for life!"

"Not *this* child," Tristán told him hotly, kneeling to catch Sirena as she ran into his outstretched arms. "She has more mettle than you know!"

Throwing her arms around his neck, Sirena buried her tear-stained face in his sage-scented quilted-cotton armor, grateful beyond words that he had appeared like an avenging angel from on high. "Tristán, take me to Papá!"

He lifted her in his arms, and as they moved into the crowded sacristy she asked him brokenly, "How did you know I needed you?"

"I didn't, Condesita. I'm on my way to Mexico with a secret dispatch from the Marqués to the Viceroy. I merely thought I'd stop by and surprise your father and you. I never dreamed I'd walk in on anything like this."

Doctor Juan was examining the Conde's motionless body in the bright midday light from the dome.

Tristán found a step stool so she was high enough to see. Taking up his vigil behind her, he braced her body firmly against his own.

"Are you able to go through this?" he asked her gently, scrubbing away her tears with balled fists, she squared her shoulders manfully and took a deep breath. "Yes, Tristán. I can do it."

Solemnly she studied her father. His velvet coat was muddied, but there were no cuts on his face and no visible wounds. She glanced up at Doctor Juan. He appeared puzzled, but not deeply concerned. She let a small sigh of relief escape her lips.

While the doctor worked over her father, there was another small commotion and she saw Don Francisco carried in and laid on a picnic table nearby. Although severely cut about his head and chest, he dragged himself to a place beside the doctor, where he took the Conde's hand in his.

At the sight of Don Francisco, wounded but alive, her spirits lifted. The Holy Child had more than answered her prayers. She had only asked Him to rescue two miners, and He had already safely brought up *three!*

11

Isabel had been wretchedly nauseous all morning, but now, dressed in a new ashes of roses open-robe gown with a floral-panel and half-farthingale, she began to look and feel restored. The rose color and her wine-red mantilla imparted a healthy glow and would complement the Conde's burgundy suit when they danced together at tonight's palacio ball.

A fever kept Mercedes from accompanying her mother, but Isabel was not disappointed. These long Masses were tedious enough without having a sulky child to bother with. Since it was the dry season, she had ordered a closed carriage to shield her from the burning December sun and the all-pervasive rust-colored dust that drifted down from Guanajuato's ore-rich hills on every breeze.

Being enclosed, and busy pretending Francisco was making love to her right here in the perilous semi-privacy of the coach, Isabel was in sight of the chapel before she noticed the unusually large crowd milling about the atrium. At first, she thought they were gathering for the Mass, which was due to begin. It was only when the dread tolling of the sadly familiar alarm bell reached her ears that it sank in on her there had been a disaster at one of the mines.

Lowering a window, she asked a youth running past what had happened. He called out there had been a cave-in at La Sirena and the foreman was hurt. Oh, God, not Ricardo! He was Alberta's husband and Patricio's strong right arm.

"Is he -- alive?" she asked fearfully.

"I don't know. I heard they took him to Doctor Juan in the chapel's sacristy," the boy said briefly, running on.

When her driver stopped Isabel did not wait for him to hand her down. She fairly flew out of the coach, up the atrium stairs and through the chapel.

She found the sacristy, crowded but ominously quiet. Her gaze went at once to the vesting table, awash with noonday light. Emilio's back was toward her and his huge form half-obscured Doctor Juan, who stood facing her. With sleeves rolled up and sweating profusely, he was bent over Ricardo, the lower half of whose body was covered with a swag of violet Lenten cloth. At the surgeon's side stood a stricken Don Francisco. Seeing him, her eyes took in nothing more.

A mere ghost of the man she loved, his face was deathly white and streaked with blood and grime. His head was swathed in a blood-soaked linen that had once been the sleeve of his shirt. The rest of it hung in tatters from his lacerated shoulders and chest. His gentle eyes were two dark wounds, his expression that of Lazarus emerging from the tomb. "Jesucristo!" she gasped, and felt her knees begin to buckle under her. Bishop Legázpi steadied her and led her to a chair beside the celebrant's *prie-dieu*.

"Oh, Diego, thank God you're here! Please, tell me, what happened to poor. . ." Afraid to utter Francisco's name she choked out, "Ricardo?"

"He was in the shaft examining its wall," Legázpi explained in a tense whisper. "An entire section gave way and he was badly injured. Don Francisco bravely rode a whim bucket down and brought him back up in his arms, but just as he was handing Ricardo to safety the whim rope suddenly burned through; hurtling Don Francisco down the shaft.

Isabel groaned aloud, feeling every cut and bruise as if it were her own flesh.

"When Patrick arrived and heard young Durán was trapped below, they say he went berserk. Not even Emilio could hold him. He went down, with nothing more than one whim rope tied around his chest and his feet braced in the loop of another. They got caught in a second rock slide but he managed to get them both out alive."

While Legázpi was speaking, Isabel's gaze was riveted on Francisco. With an eerie sense of *deja vu* she saw herself standing at this same vesting table and, dismal as the distant tolling of the disaster bell, she heard him say again: "I won't do this to Patrick! It's over between us -- It's over!" Shaken with the chill of guilt, she took out her Rosary and began praying fervently that Francisco's wounds would heal soon, and poor Ricardo's life be spared.

Even at this distance she could see Doctor Juan Pinal begin scissoring away the sleeves of Ricardo's shirt. She saw drift unheeded to the tile floor those insignificantly small but tragic reminders of the brief mortality of men who spent their lives in the mines -- pitiful wisps of torn lace from an elegant French jabot, crimsoned remnants of a linen shirt, the muddied sleeve of a wine-red velvet coat.

"Oh, God no!" Isabel cried aloud, sinking to her knees on the nearby prie-dieu as the searing truth burned into her brain. Jesus, Mary and Joseph! It *wasn't* Ricardo who Doctor Juan was working so desperately to save -- *it was Patricio!*

"It can't be true!" she sobbed hysterically, "I can't bear it!" Oblivious to Legázpi's words and Francisco's eyes mutely pleading with her to keep silent, she began reciting a litany of promises, in exchange for her husband's life. "Dear Mother of God, I'll go on my knees to the Santo Niño in Fresnillo and to your shrines at Zapopan and San Juan! I'll give both my sons to the church. Oh, God, please, please, *strike me dead, but let my husband live!"*

Sirena stood stoically at her father's side, only half hearing her mother's loud lamentations as they gradually waned into muffled sobs. She watched the doctor's every move and gave an occasional encouraging smile to Don Francisco who was holding himself upright by will alone.

But as the minutes ticked by she saw Doctor Juan was becoming alarmed at Don Patrick's condition. Having cut away what was left of her father's coat and shirt, his skilled hands began gently probing the injured man's throat, neck and rib cage. Blood began bubbling up from some sinister hidden spring inside, and each time it did Don Francisco wiped it away with the remnants of his own jabot.

"If only it were a surface wound, or a bone I could set," Doctor Juan told Francisico helplessly. "But several of his ribs are broken and I'm certain one of them has pierced a lung."

He stood a moment with eyes closed, both hands spread impotently on the cold marble surface. Then, addressing no one in particular he muttered softly, "God help me! He's drowning in his own blood and there's absolutely *nothing* I can do!"

Sirena saw her father's eyelids flutter and realized he was trying to move, but the effort made him groan aloud with pain. At an urgent signal from the doctor, Legázpi handed him a velvet foot-pillow that was kept in the sacristy for visiting dignitaries. With his head raised, the Conde breathed more easily. Although his blue eyes were clouded with pain, she saw them light up at the sight of Francisco smiling down at him. "Panchito mio! You're alive!"

"Thanks to you, my foolhardy friend," he said accusatively, but with an affectionate grin. "And you told me not to let Don Telmo make any martyrs!"

Except for the blood that kept rising relentlessly, and which Francisco deftly wiped away, Sirena was surprised that her father's face was so clean and unbloodied. He looked as neatly groomed as if he just set out for Mass.

His lips moved, but for a time no more words would come. Then he said quite clearly, with a touch of his customary wit, "Death – surprised me! I always thought I'd have time to get ready, so I'd be sure to – do it all properly."

He reached across to pat Sirena's cheek. "My brave little Condesa! Remember what I told you when Don Jose was dying? Death should be the crowning. . ."

Unable to speak, Sirena nodded. Fearfully, with a deepening sense of doom, she knew her father was aware he was dying. The thought of being separated from him forever was so excruciating she felt she must be dying too, and she began to cry. Then she felt strong hands on her shoulders and Tristán whispered, "He wants to do it well. *Help him!* You've the rest of your life for tears."

"Juan, you did your best," the Conde was saying consolingly to his lifelong friend whose stricken eyes were still hoping for a miracle. Then, seeing that Patrick was trying to convey a confidence, Juan placed an ear to his lips.

"Look after Isabel. I'm afraid last night -- I got her with child. You know how she fears. . ."

The doctor nodded, "I'll take every care."

Turning to Sirena, her father said, "You're head of the House of Graciana now, Condesa. It's my last wish care for your sister and brothers as if they were mine. And -- watch over your mother." He struggled for breath. "She's willful -- but fragile as spun glass."

Turning anxiously to Francisco he murmured. "I left my estate -- too many loose ends. Please set them right?"

"I'd move Heaven and Earth for you!" Francisco replied, tears coursing down his face."

Bishop Legázpi appeared at the doctor's side, anointing Patrick, giving him absolution and softly reciting the slow, stately prayers for the dying.

"Death surprised me," Don Patrick said again, sweeping the faces of everyone around the table with an almost merry glance, "but – it came on a – *very* – good day!"

After that he seemed to take leave of them, his gaze going beyond, to focus on Emilio's painting of the Spanish crusaders' Warrior Saint inside the dome. The martyred saint was being received into glory by the Most Holy Trinity, his crimson cloak, like giant wings, lifting him upward into the blinding light of pure Divinity.

Sirena saw an expression of great dignity and peace infuse her father's face, as though he were entering some opulent baroque court and being received by influential friends. Then simply and slowly he whispered, "Into Thy Hands -- I commend my spirit."

His head turned wearily, coming to rest in Francisco's embrace. Sirena felt as if a sword had cleft her body, the pain unendurable, and yet somehow she must bear it. Tristán took her in his arms and held her close, rocking her gently as she tried to stifle the sound of her sobs in his dark cotton armor.

Francisco gave a single, agonized cry and threw himself across the body of his friend. Hearing it, and aware only that the man she adored was in mortal pain, Isabel rushed blindly from the prie-dieu to comfort him. Reaching the table she was stunned to behold her husband lying dead in her weeping lover's arms. Uttering a long, blood-chilling scream she sank in a dead faint to the floor.

12

"**If I weren't carrying this urgent dispatch** to the Viceroy," Tristán said, kneeling beside Sirena in the Graciana patio and hugging her to him, "you know I wouldn't leave your side today."

"I understand. You're duty bound." Then, forcing a wan smile, she added on a note of hope, "Maybe, on your way back from Mexico, you could stop by Guanajuato again -- ?" Her chin began to tremble. "By then we should know for sure if Mamá will get well."

Folding her in his arms Tristán held her tightly a moment longer, trying to will his own strength and stamina into her small body. It seemed almost too much to ask of such a little girl: to watch her father die and her stricken mother faint, strike her head on the table where her husband lay, and lapse into a coma. Still, Sirena had carried herself like a queen throughout last night's public wake in the palace ballroom, and at this morning's Solemn High Requiem Mass in the parish church.

But he would never forget the sight of that small, straight figure walking behind the open hearse with its four matched blacks, marching to the beat of muffled drums and wailing fifes, as the long funeral cortege serpentined up the mountain to the Graciana chapel. She was followed by himself and Don Francisco, Isabel's two sons, Amantina, the household staff and the city's entire populace: the silver elite with their families in unrelieved black, and members of the city's religious Orders in less doleful tones of blue, white, red, brown and grey. Behind them surged the mines' muscle and bone, three thousand of the Conde's own ore carriers, processors and pick and blast men, trailed by those from all the other mines, the upper left arm of each man banded in black.

Every church bell tolled, every household mourned -- swags draped great, brass-studded doors, cheap black China-paper flags graced the low lintels of the poor. From all sides beatas praised the

Conde's piety, hopeful beggars hinted, no señor had ever received such an outpouring of grief and gratitude.

The body was interred in the chapel's sanctuary. Francisco had blanketed the casket with scarlet noche buenas, a flower Patrick had loved, and these were massed beneath the marble wall crypt, which on Sirena's order, bore the simple epitaph: Don Patrick O'Malley Oñate, First Conde of Graciana, 1744-1792: *God gave to Graciana – Graciana gave to God.* Only there, Tristán now recalled, kneeling at his side with her hand held tightly in his own, had Sirena broken down at last, weeping inconsolably as the choir sang *The Mines of Glory.*

"Of course I'll stop on my way back up North," Tristán said, fighting back tears. "My solemn promise!" He made the Sign of the Cross over her then, putting her from him, rose to his feet and strode to his waiting dappled grey.

Sirena, in her black watered-silk gown waited numbly. Her gaze fixed on his spurs, each silver rowel bright as a snow-crystal at the heel of each boot. She knew she would never forget their sound, ringing like small chimes against the flagstones. Once in the saddle he paused and looked back, touched his fingers to the wide brim of his norteño's dark sombrero and gave her a soldier's salute.

After watching the road until Tristán was out of sight, she turned and slowly climbed the stairs. In the upper corridor she found Aunt Amantina and Doctor Juan outside her mother's bedroom door. "Is Mamá ill?"

Amantina shook her head and cupped Sirena's face in one hand. "She'll awaken soon child, I'm sure. Can Alberta get you something? A cup of bougainvillea tea?"

Sirena shook her head. "No thank you. I think I'll just walk around for a while."

Seeking the comfort of her father's presence among his books and ledgers she crossed the sala to the library. She was surprised to find Francisco there. His head was wrapped in a clean bandage and a long, stitched cut, running from his left temple to his jawline, stood out angrily against the pallor of his face. He sat slumped in a chair beside the trestle table, staring in morbid silence at a dying fire in the hearth. The utter bleakness of his expression filled her with dread.

Drawing near she asked softly, "Don Francisco?"

He glanced up and then, for the first time since her father died in his arms, his unshakable composure deserted him. Burying his face in his hands, his body was shaken with great tearing sobs as he gave vent to his anguish.

She rushed to his side, drawing his head down gently onto her shoulder, her own river of sorrow seeming a mere trickle compared to this grown man's torrential grief.

"I'm here, Don Francisco," she whispered, wrapping her arms around him. "Please, please don't cry!"

"Oh, Sirena," he sobbed, and the desolation in his tone frightened her. "I can't bear the guilt, the pain! First your father and now your poor Mamá! And all of it my fault! Oh, why didn't God take me instead?"

She had never seen anyone so torn with remorse, so terrifyingly close to losing the saving virtue of Hope. She wished there were some grown-up to care for him, but his parents were dead and he had no wife. I'm only a little girl, she thought helplessly, but who else is there?

"Poor Don Francisco," she murmured as soothingly as she knew how, her own tears raining down unheeded because the one who had been her model of moral strength through all of this was now clinging to her like a drowning man.

"But you don't understand!" he groaned, lifting his head and staring hopelessly into the flames. "Patrick was my friend, he trusted me and I. . ." He covered his face. "Not even God, Himself, can forgive me for what I've done!"

"Our Lord forgives everyone," she cried. "You know that! Remember Saint Peter, the Good Thief! Papá died to save you, but how can that be your fault?"

Francisco drew out a white handkerchief, wiped her own tear-stained cheeks first then pressed it to his own eyes. "I'm sorry, child. You don't need any more grief than you've been through." He paused. "But I loved your father very much and. . ."

"And he loved you," she said almost scoldingly. "So now that the Bishop says he's in Heaven, you know he's forgiven whatever little thing it is that worries you."

Francisco stared at her, as though her own blind faith in him held out a valid reason to go on. "God knows, I'd like to believe that your words are a sign from him, what he might tell me himself, if he were here." He took a deep breath and said obliquely, "I've got to find a way to live with what I've done or go complete mad."

"You could keep Papá's promise to me."

"His promise?"

"Don't you remember? He said he would take me to work with him every day. Couldn't you take me instead?"

He picked her up gently and put her on his knee. "Maybe I could. After all, I don't plan to be in town much longer, and he wouldn't want you dependent on the advice of strangers." After a thoughtful pause he added, "Maybe -- just for your own protection, I could."

A tear slipped down her cheek and she whispered, ". . . and Don Francisco I just know we'd both feel closer to him there than anywhere."

Inside Francisco's troubled soul, Sirena's need to find solace in her father's world, indirectly offered him a chance to repay some part of his crushing moral debt to Patrick. While not enough to expunge such betrayal or gain his own redemption, at the least this opportunity for redress could occupy his mind enough to save his sanity.

"As God is my witness, Sirena, I'll teach you everything about the mines you can grasp at your age. After that, Don Cosmé can take you the rest of the way."

❧ ❦

"I think it was a mercy Doña Isabel did not emerge from her coma until the wake and funeral were over," Sirena overheard Doctor Juan tell Don Francisco a few days after her mother regained consciousness. "But I'll have to break my iron-clad rule against giving opium for anything short of surgery. She cannot sleep or face the pain of each new day without some kind of sedation. Never in all my years of practice have I known a widow so passionately attached to her spouse."

"I'm sure she must have -- worshipped him," Francisco offered weakly, in a voice so low Sirena barely heard him. Moving away from the open door, Sirena was puzzled. When her father was alive, her mother never seemed that devoted to him. How had she kept it so well hidden until now?

For the next two months, Alberta and Aunt Amantina ran the household. Ricardo, despite a badly smashed leg, spent part of each day overseeing the mines. Francisco's body healed far more quickly than his soul. Added to his crucifying burden of guilt, was the task of putting the Conde's estate in some kind of order. He could see it would take months and it meant postponing his move to Mexico. This, in turn, kept him near Isabel, who was now more emotionally volatile than ever.

Working through the pragmatic Amantina, who approved his plan, he obtained Isabel's approval to take Sirena with him to the mines, as long as she gave her tutor the first two hours of each day. He began with simple tasks suited to her age. She memorized a few basic geological terms, types of ore, and some chemical formulas. All the rest she picked up, as he himself had done, by observation. After a few weeks of watching him in the reduction patios, she was bold enough to say when she thought the mix was ready to add more mercury, pyrite or salt. Many times her guess was right. Best of all he found that Patrick did seem closer when they were working together at the mines.

By February Isabel had regained her strength enough to undertake the penance imposed upon her by the blind priest in Dolores. He had been severe, even though her confession was an expurgated version of what had gone on in the Hermitage. He directed her to make the Stations of the Cross, every Friday for a year. With the old fear of death in childbirth hanging over her again, came the terror of losing her immortal soul by failing to carry out her penance. But getting downtown to the only Church where the spiritual efficacy of this devotion could be obtained was a penance in itself.

On Guanajuato's narrow cobbled streets no coach had ever rolled, so ladies were carried in sedan chairs, and this drew undue attention to her visits to church. Unhappily, too, the stations were widely known for being most confessors' first choice when assigning a penance for mortal sins, so Isabel felt all eyes were seeing right through her.

But despite all this, on a Friday afternoon in mid-March Isabel found herself in church again, making the obligatory round. The deep, double-genuflections were becoming more difficult as she grew heavier. Now in the fourth month of her pregnancy she had still not told a living soul. She had not even visited Doctor Juan, but planned to get up enough nerve to do that next week, still terrified he might not swallow her blithe lie of being a scant three months along.

While making her sixteenth genuflection she was stricken with such excruciating pains she had to lean against the wall to stand at all. She glanced about seeking someone to help her, but there was not another person in church. Oh, why hadn't she brought Mercedes along! As the pains grew worse she wrapped the hooded cloak around her and collapsed on the floor.

"Señora, are you ill? May I help you?"

A man was bending over her. Oh, thank God! Someone had seen her fall! Her hands clasping his shoulders eagerly as he helped her to rise, Isabel was shocked to find herself looking directly into the eyes of Francisco Durán.

"Isabel! My God, what's wrong?"

"Oh, Francisco! I'm in terrible pain! Take me across the plaza to Doctor Juan at once!"

Lifting her in his arms, Francisco hurried from the church and across the small plaza to the corner mansion that served as Doctor Juan's office and home. Juan took her from him and into a small infirmary off the sala, leaving Francisco to wait nervously alone. Soon he was joined by Doña Emma, the doctor's plump and chatty wife, who diverted him with light conversation, an art her husband's profession gave her considerable practice in.

"Have you heard from Don Gabriel?" she asked, over a cup of steaming chocolate.

"Not yet. I sent word of the Conde's death by fast packet boat to London. But losing Patrick so soon after the death of his own wife and child is sure to be a terrible surprise and a killing blow."

Francisco glanced anxiously at the infirmary door. Then, returning his attention to Doña Emma, he asked, "And what do you hear from your son, Daniel, in Paris?"

"Juan and I are very proud of him!" Emma swept a strand of blond hair from her brow with delicate fingers. "He's working on the battlefield with France's greatest surgeon. Juan says its the best training a medical student can have."

As they talked, twilight fell and still the infirmary door remained closed. The lamplighter went about the dark square until it was aglow with torches and candlelight.

Finally Emma rose discreetly and left the room just as Juan entered, his sleeves rolled up, his expression grim.

"It was providential you happened upon her when you did," he said seating himself on a settee across from Francisco. "If she had been left unattended any longer – he shook his head gravely."

"Is she . . .?"

"She's very weak. I'll have to keep her here at least overnight."

Francisco nodded and got to his feet. "I'll tell Doña Amantina."

"So much tragedy in one family in so short a time," Juan soliloquized. He sighed heavily and, gazing hard at his long time friend, his dark eyes took on an expression Francisco had never seen there before. Was it curiosity, compassion or a look of well-veiled contempt? Or was it his own distress, making him see what wasn't there?

Juan looked away. "So much that's hard to believe!" Bringing his hands down on the knees of his fawn-colored breeches in a gesture of finality, he got to his feet. "Doña Isabel asked to see you before you go. But please be brief. She needs to rest."

Entering the room, Francisco approached the narrow cot on which Isabel lay with her pale hands folded on her breast, and seated himself stiffly on the chair beside her.

"Doctor Juan says you'll be fine. You just need complete rest." He felt strangely uneasy in her presence.

Slowly she turned her head on the pillow and fixed him with huge grey eyes. "Lucky for me you paid your daily visit to the Blessed Sacrament when you did."

"Remember, now, no more Stations of the Cross! If it's a penance from that priest in Dolores, I'll do it for you."

She nodded gratefully. "I'll do anything to keep from losing this child."

Francisco caught his breath in genuine surprise. "Juan didn't tell me! That's wonderful!" He paused and then continued effusively, "Imagine how happy Patrick would be!"

Isabel's worshipful, unwavering gaze never left his face and he saw her eyes fill with tears, overflow and fill again. "Yes, that's exactly what Juan said when I told him." Reaching up she ran her fingers tenderly along the angry scar on his handsome face.

"I'm sure having his child will bring Patrick close to you again," Francisco ventured, trying hard to distance himself emotionally.

Her brows lifted and she smiled as though she saw right through his gallant attempt at deception. "But surely you understand?"

"Understand?

"I was a month pregnant when Patricio came home! It's not his child -- it's yours!"

Francisco looked as though God Almighty and the Devil had both read the Last Judgment over him.

"Oh, Francisco, you know how much I love you!" she cried happily, lifting herself on one elbow. "We can marry now and make a real life together! I'll give you a son! Why else do you think I want this baby so?"

He stared at her, numb with shock. Her devastating honesty -- the sordid truth, completely unmanned him. This was no shattered vow of chastity to be confessed away. A man's seed carried an irrevocable commitment of a sort he had never intended to make. In the light of this single act, all that had gone before was reduced to playing roles in a series of Eastertide Passion Plays -- scarlet sinner one week, celibate saint the next!

"Merciful Christ, Isabel!" He lowered his head until his forehead rested on her pale folded hands. "I'll do everything possible for this child, but – the two of us . . . ?" He raised his eyes and studied her in disbelief. "I can't even bear the guilt I carry now, alone. Together, Pat's accusing eye would be everywhere. Don't you see? We can never marry! It would be a living Hell for both of us!"

Isabel fell back on the pillow. She had gambled and lost, pitted herself against a side of him she could not fathom. Incredibly enough, his passion for purity of soul outweighed even his insatiable carnal passion for her.

But while she had been brutally honest with Francisco, Isabel dared not lie to God or leave the utterly honest Doctor Juan alone to firmly establish Don Patrick's departure date and explain how he also seemed to be inexplicably absent when her pregnancy began. Belatedly, she now told the doctor her own impromptu version about a mysterious Spanish stranger she had surprised inside the family chapel on the Feast Day of All Saints. Entering the sacristy alone, she found the man stealing a costly gold chalice. Armed only with her quirt, she lashed him across the face and he retaliated with a hard blow to the side of her head, knocking her unconscious. When she came to, the stranger had disappeared and she realized she had been raped. She slowly made her way back to where she had left her horse and then she rode Rodrigo back to the Graciana barn and handed him to the groom. She closed her tale to the doctor with the casual remark, "It's just been too embarrassing to mention these humiliating facts even to you!"

Although he distrusted Isabel's typically histrionic delivery, the French-trained Dr. Juan Pinal pretended to swallow what he considered her blasé description of the child's critically important sire. However, by this time in her life the doctor had heard and pretended to believe many still more far-fetched experiences in Isabel's fantastically unreal, make-believe religious life. What made this episode of greater consequence than the others was that it concerned the future of a real unborn child, whose mother knew it was a boy whom she had already named Crispín. The perceptive, French-trained Doctor Juan Pinal, found himself suspecting that "Isabel's sympathetic role of 'little girl lost' may have sexually enslaved their unsophisticated and, perhaps until now, morally irreproachable young friend, Francisco Durán, whom both the doctor and Don Patrick loved and trusted in every business aspect of their lives.

※ ※

Tristán was riding north from Mexico City, bound for the west coast port of San Blas, but he was looking forward to visiting Guanajuato on the way. He was deeply remorseful that nearly eighteen months had passed since the Conde's death, and it had been impossible for him to stop by on his way north as he had so solemnly promised Sirena. But, acting on a whim of the Royal Visitor, the Viceroy had sent Tristán on a wild goose chase to Cuba, recruiting volunteers to soldier on the Apache frontier. When he returned empty-handed from that fruitless quest, the Viceroy ordered him to go by ship instead of overland to rejoin the Royal Visitor's party on the lower Rio Grande.

Now Tristán entered Guanajuato and made the familiar climb up the mountain to the Graciana palace, he began speculating about what he would find. Sirena would have changed, of course, and grown. By now she probably had her own tutor. Bright as she was, it would be a joy to see how her mind had flowered.

When he reached the palacio he found the gate open and the patio eerily quiet. He dismounted and, since no groom appeared, led own his horse as he walked about slowly. The place seemed deserted, and he was amazed to find that even the fountain was dry!

"Alberta! Ricardo!" At first no one answered his call, then a moment later an Indian youth came down the stairway, a broom and a feather duster in his hand.

"Something I can do for you, sir?"

"Can you tell me where I can find the family? Doña Isabel and the First Condesa? I'm a kinsman."

The boy seemed confused. "I'm Ricardo's son. He and Alberta are the caretakers here, but they've gone on a pilgrimage to San Juan de los Lagos." He leaned on the broom.

"But the family? Doña Isabel and the child, Sirena?" Tristán repeated. "What has happened to them?"

"Oh, the First Condesa moved North months ago, to live with her Uncle Gabriel," he volunteered. "That happened not too long after her mother remarried."

Tristán stood rooted to the flagstones still holding on to his horse's reins. "Doña Isabel?" he mouthed incredulously, far more prepared to hear she had died in a coma than that she had married again. "And — whom did she marry?"

"Don Telmo de la Huerta," the boy told him. When Tristán could not help staring at him in shocked disbelief, he elaborated. "Don Telmo is an important silver lord. He owns the upper mine, El Rey, and now, thanks to Doña Isabel, he owns the great Graciana mine as well!"

"You must mean he's running it for her," Tristán suggested, but Ricardo's son was adamant.

"No Sir! He owns it, lock stock and barrel!"

Tristán could think of nothing more to say. What questions were there left to ask? Virtually nothing the boy had told him was good news, and what little information he had given only filled Tristán with a terrible sadness. The disappointment of not finding Sirena was almost the same as finding her dead. But why did she go north? Why would her mother let her? And how Doña Isabel bring herself to marry a man as loathsome as Don Telmo?

"Are Emilio and Lorenzo Santa Cruz still around?"

"Oh, no, Señor. Emilio's gone back to his mule train and Lorenzo's at San Carlos Academy in Mexico."

Tristán mounted his horse, but before riding out he turned in the saddle to ask one final question.

"Do you know Don Francisco Durán?"

"Oh, yes. He was the Conde's partner."

Good, Tristán thought, now I'm getting somewhere. Francisco was one man who would be able to explain everything.

"Where can I find him?"

"He left town very suddenly — almost a year ago."

☙ ❧

Tristàn continued on his journey with a leaden heart. At San Blas, he embarked on the small packet boat that carried supplies up the west coast to the Missions which a handful of Franciscan friars were establishing for heathen Indians living along the barren coastal lands of Upper California. His father, Don Octavio, now Commandant General of the Northern Frontier, had assigned him to serve as Captain of the military Presidio of Monterey for the next three years.

Yes, he thought bitterly, as the trim little ship put out to sea, any other man would equate serving time in that pagan wilderness with being consigned to three years in the lowest circle of Dante's Inferno.

But as things stood now, any assignment that kept him in the field and away from his Mendoza palace in Mexico, he counted a blessing. His marriage to Don Jose's niece was a tragic mismatch. Catarina had turned out to be half-Comanche: a wild, illiterate presidio gamin who bragged that their wedding was only the second time in her life she had ever worn shoes! His father and the Conde had been right to warn him against the union. That beau geste was the most disastrous mistake of his life.

Standing at the ship's rail as it fought the steady head winds blowing down from the north, his mind kept returning to Sirena. She must have thought I abandoned her; that I didn't care. She was such a plucky child! Well, at least she didn't have to face being raised by a stepfather like Don Telmo. Gabriel would give her everything, and maybe she would make up to him for the loss of his own infant son. But when, in God's Providence, he asked himself again and again, was he ever to see her again?

PART THREE

AWAKENINGS

1803

Love is like war:
You begin when you please
And leave off when you can.

Spanish Proverb

13

"Oh, Excelencia!" Monsignor Alonso Crespi exclaimed as Bishop Legázpi entered the spacious sala of his handsome neo-classic Episcopal palace in the city of Valladolid. "You just missed the noblewoman who came to call while you were out."

"Did she give her name?" The Bishop inquired absently, seating himself at his large Venetian-style desk.

"María Amantina O'Malley, First Condesa de Graciana. She said she was sorry to miss you, but promised to see you tonight at the Iturbide hacienda."

"Little Sirena! Why I haven't laid eyes on that dear child since her father's funeral!"

"She's quite grown up now," the Monsignor remarked. "She is on her way to Guanajuato to manage her father's mines."

"Really?" He rubbed his chin thoughtfully. "No one seems to know *why* she moved up north with her Uncle Gabriel while still a child. But then, I've had no contact with the family since the posthumous birth of the late Conde's son, easily ten years ago.

Sirena's mother, Doña Isabel, is my own cousin, but once she remarried she locked me out of her confidence and her life -- completely!"

"From what I've heard, nothing about that family has been the same since the good Conde died."

The Bishop gathered several loose papers on his desk and arranged them in two neat stacks. "Perhaps now that Sirena and I will be in Guanajuato at the same time, I'll find out what actually did happen between them."

"That reminds me, Excelencia, your trunks are all packed and ready to load first thing in the morning for your trip to Guanajuato." Crespi advised him crisply. "And Manuel will bring the coach around this afternoon at five to take us to the Iturbide fiesta."

"Thank you, Alonso. Believe me, I'm looking forward to getting away from this paperwork for the next two months!"

"And I don't want you giving a thought to Episcopal matters," Crespi told him smilingly, "I've prepared for every eventuality straight through to Advent!"

Legázpi beamed as he studied the silver-haired Monsignor standing in the center of the room, poised as always to move efficiently in any direction to attend to any task. His black cassock and wide cerise silk cincture accentuated his slender build. His strong, even features reflected the dignity of equal parts Spanish and Tarascan Indian blood, and the contrast between his up-tilted ice-blue eyes and pale bronze skin remained a daily surprise to Legázpi. He was not only a faultless canonical assistant, but had become the Bishop's most trusted friend. What a treasure the man was!

"Alonso, I couldn't have survived these past fifteen years without you!" Legázpi" told him warmly. Then, recognizing a familiar silent signal in the thick dossier of documents cradled in Crespi's left arm, he asked. "Are those last minute papers I need to sign before I leave?"

"Unfortunately, they bear upon a rather -- sordid matter that cannot wait until your return."

The Bishop sighed in practiced resignation. "Well, I've still got half a workday left. What have we?"

"A number of serious accusations against one of our own diocesan priests -- Father Miguel Hidalgo." The Bishop's thick grey brows lifted. "And who is bringing charges against *him*?"

"A potpourri of rather bizarre witnesses, I'm afraid," Crespi replied. A faint glint of humor lighting his otherwise sober gaze. "The first is a Carmelite nun, in the city of Puebla. She states she entered religious life to make amends for what she calls 'the unrestrained existence I lived for many years in this priest's company.'"

Legázpi knew Monsignor Crespi was incapable of bearing personal malice toward anyone. He was scrupulously fair, his life giving the lie to that demeaning gachupín myth that all mestizos were lazy and malicious. If someone else had handed him this lighted grenade he might have doubted its veracity. If a scandal got past Alonso to Legázpi, it *had* to be true.

Crespi turned a page. "A second woman claims she lived with him here in Valladolid while he was still rector of San Nicolás" College and she bore his child." He paused for a short breath. "A third woman, from

Guanajuato, says she was his mistress there for some years – and bore him two sons."

Legázpi left the desk and strode the full length of the sala in silence, his eyes fixed on the deep blue Chinese carpet, his right hand nervously fingering a large pectoral Cross, set with amethysts, that lay on his breast.

"A fourth woman has come forward with the unsolicited declaration that they carried on a long affair, commencing when you made Hidalgo curate of San Felipe. She says her conscience caused her to confess that she and Father Miguel 'had an evil compact, in which she sought out suitable women for him to enjoy, and he found ardent men for her, so she could sin with them.'"

"Dear God!" Legázpi sucked in his breath and demanded angrily. "Who else accuses this Mexican Abelard?"

"Two Mercedarian friars, claim he scandalized them by describing – and approving of – a practice he calls 'the mechanism of human nature'."

"And what, pray tell, is that?"

Crespi coughed discreetly into his fist. "To be candid, he justifies his own lack of chastity by claiming fornication is not a sin, even for a priest, but merely 'the perfectly natural evacuation of every man.'"

The Bishop shook his head in shocked disbelief. His eyes turned momentarily to the Legázpi Coat of Arms, carved in bas relief on the wall behind his desk. It featured a castle tower on a crimson field with eight golden crosses on the border device, each cross signifying a victory won by some intrepid Legázpi over the Moor. While every Bishop displayed his arms, for Legázpi it represented more than family pride. It was a daily reminder that his own crusade was introducing social reforms to vanquish such enemies of the Christian poor as generational poverty and unjust laws.

"Alonso, I wouldn't tell this to any other man," he said emotionally. "But when I first came to New Spain Miguel Hidalgo was my guide and aide. By all rights he should be standing here in your shoes today, for I did *everything in my power* to put him there! I never dreamed he was a womanizer, but his lack of pecuniary responsibility, his gaming, his rebellious streak -- they all defeated me!"

He strode angrily to his desk and struck the gilded top a blow with his open hand. "Right here lies an unfinished letter to the reigning Spanish monarch, whose confessor I was when he was still Crown Prince. It contains suggestions and pleas -- for remedying social wrongs that cry to high Heaven for justice!" He swung around, fire in his eyes. "So why am I wasting precious time on a feckless Sybaritic priest who can't keep his yardarm in his breeches!"

Crespi remained discreetly silent until Legázpi's rage burned itself out and he threw himself into his chair. For the space of an *Ave* he studied the human skull he kept on his desk, a reminder of his own mortality. Then, folding his hands on the desktop he murmured, "I owe you an apology, Alonso. That was an unseemly *and* uncharitable outburst."

"There was due cause, Diego," Crespi said, balm in his tone. "Now, all the rest of these papers cite examples of public scandal – dancing, gaming, staging risqué French plays, hiding the Host at Mass – and a request from the Holy Office for a letter from his Bishop, stating if you wish to prosecute or dismiss the charges against him."

Close personal friend though he was, Crespi observed all the niceties of Church protocol. Inclining his head respectfully, he laid the folio before his religious superior.

"I'm not entirely without fault in all this, you know," Legázpi confided. "I listened to those who praised his work with the Indians and parish poor, but *disbelieved* others who told me he was living loosely and giving scandal."

"Fickleness may be his worst vice," Crespi averred. "He's launched many fine projects to help the *humildes*, but he no more than starts one than he loses interest and drops it for another."

"I'd almost prefer a thoroughgoing renegade I could justifiably defrock." Legázpi pursed his lips and added prophetically, "Unfortunately for us, Miguel Hidalgo is that most dangerously unpredictable of all men -- a self-indulgent visionary astride the runaway horse of pride."

It was twilight when the Episcopal coach made its way through the palace-lined streets of the proud city of Valladolid and out into the spreading valley beyond.

"Well, I finished my letter to His Majesty *and* wrote the Holy Office," Legázpi told his companion cheerfully. "In my opinion they have no solid evidence against Hidalgo on theological grounds, so I asked them to drop the charges."

Crespi nodded his agreement.

"As for the rest?" the Bishop spread his hands helplessly. "What bishop is empowered to absolve a celibate priest of five illegitimate children and only God knows how many less fruitful unions? Sadly, for the women involved, the cries of embittered mistresses and repentant nuns boil down to their word against his. I sent Hidalgo a severe rebuke by special courier. He's to leave San Felipe at once for the village of Dolores, replacing his own brother who died there last month. I'll visit him there while I'm in Guanajuato!"

After a long silence Legázpi spoke reflectively, "You know Alonso, I *am* looking forward to meeting Sirena at the Iturbide ball tonight! I've often wondered how she might turn out without her father to form and guide her. I only hope she doesn't disappoint me. So often the criollo children of industrious silver lords and hacendados grow up ruinously spoiled by their gold-plated, easy- come, easy-go world of privilege and wealth.

⊰14⊱

After passing through a long avenue of fresno trees, the Bishop's coach stopped before an elegant two-story casco. Faced with an ochre-pink native stone, the grilled windows and stone-framed front door were crowned with flamboyant white-stucco baskets and swags. This palatial main house of the Hacienda de las Flores was owned by one of the region's wealthiest and most respected hacendados.

Don Joaquín Iturbide, a Spaniard and long time friend of Bishop Legázpi, had arrived as a penniless immigrant exactly forty years ago to the day. Tonight the unassuming and well-liked Don Joaquín was not only giving a lavish fiesta to mark his fortunate four decades in New Spain, but was proudly announcing the engagement of his twenty-year-old son, Agustín Iturbide, to the daughter of a city *alcalde*.

Legázpi understood better than anyone what a coup it was for this troubled father to marry his heir into the family of a prominent judge. At San Nicolás, Agustín had been a student of idle and vicious habits. Now a peacocky ensign in the town militia, he was said to be an all-around rakehell. To scotch such dark rumors Don Joaquín had engineered this supremely redemptive match. Invited to help him celebrate both signal events was the cream of Valladolid society, with many aristocrats from distant provinces attending as well.

After Don Joaquín greeted the two churchmen and led them to the door of the crowded sala, he was called aside by another new arrival. The Bishop managed to linger a while in the doorway, scanning the finely dressed company in search of Sirena. To his own great surprise he was able to single her out at once, thanks to a striking resemblance to her father.

Surrounded by a pride of young male aristocrats and uniformed regimentals, there was no mistaking her. She wore her thick black hair coifed in a stylish Psyche knot. Her high-waisted Empire gown of opaque white silk clung to her finely proportioned figure, and her fashionably deep décolletage was covered by a costly necklace of sapphires and pearls with matching earrings. She wore white, elbow-length gloves, and a long-fringed paisley shawl graced her right arm. There seemed to be an Attic purity about her quite unlike anything the Bishop had anticipated.

Legázpi recalled the first time he had seen her mother moving toward him as he stood in the doorway of the family chapel. Isabel's blond beauty had seemed like diaphanous silk rippling in the wind. Sirena's beauty was more a bright, steady flame. Her features were patrician and strong, her expression animated, her gestures spirited but composed. She not only bore a strong resemblance to her father, she exuded his same intense passion for life that had made him so charismatic. As he watched her commanding this troop of attentive beaux with her striking topaz eyes, the Bishop suddenly understood how the fathers of beautiful young daughters must feel -- proud, sad and more than a little jealous.

Although uniformly gracious to all her admirers, she remained slightly aloof, her black-lashed eyes intent upon the one addressing her at the moment, but intermittently glancing about the room, as though searching for someone.

With a sudden bright flash of recognition she caught sight of the Bishop. After a quick murmured excuse to those around her she hurried across the room to greet him.

"Excelencia!" she cried, dropping effortlessly to one knee to kiss his ring and as quickly rising again. "How wonderful to see you again!"

"Well, I see my little Sirena is no more!" he said ruefully, taking her gloved hand. "You've grown into a lovely young woman. How proud your father would be!"

She blushed, but smiled appreciatively. "Please come and meet some special friends," she smiled happily, leading him through the crowd to the group she had just left.

She introduced him to a well-dressed, sandy-haired aristocrat whose face was tanned from exposure to the elements and who looked uncommonly accustomed to hard physical labor. "Excelencia, this is my childhood friend and neighbor at La Frontera, Don Adrian, the Fifth Marqués of Ávila."

The young man genuflected expertly, and when he stood up the Bishop noticed the possessive – almost jealous – gaze the young Marqués bent on Sirena.

"And this is Monsieur Noel LeClerque," Sirena enthused. "Noel came from Paris with my Uncle Gabriel after the Terror and has been my poor, long-suffering tutor ever since!"

The slender, blond LeClerque who nodded silently, impressed Legázpi as an extremely shy and insecure young man.

"Noel is also a wonderful composer and musician," Sirena said proudly, "and the orchestra will be playing one of his own sonatas later this evening."

Legázpi found himself admiring the poise with which the young Condesa maneuvered the crowd of young men to whom she introduced him. Obviously they all found her enchanting, but her candor and gracious manner kept them from becoming overbold.

"We're all riding together over to Guanajuato," Sirena was saying. "I will be consulting with Baron Von Humboldt over the next two months while he's there inspecting all the mines in the region."

"I leave for Guanajauto tomorrow, too," he said. "I'll be staying with the governor of the province, Don Antonio Riaño and his lady wife. Surely, since we're both there for such a long stay, we'll have time to visit."

As the orchestra struck up one of the popular new German waltzes, young Agustín Iturbide broke impetuously into the circle. "My pardon for interrupting, Excelencia," he said with a hasty bow, "but if your host doesn't steal this fair Condesa at once, he'll never get another chance!"

❧ ❦

"Condesa, you are beyond all doubt the most beautiful woman here tonight!" Iturbide declared, holding her daringly close. It was clear to Sirena that young Don Agustín was very sure of himself, both as a dancer and a lover. He was taller than she by several inches, imposing in his flashy militia uniform and charming in a supremely self-confident way.

"Where have you been all my life?" he asked, brushing her cheek with his lips.

"On the Apache frontier," she replied, a remote address that usually dampened most Lotharios' ardor. Then parrying politely she ventured, "Is it true you'll be announcing your engagement tonight?"

He never flinched. "Were I married twenty years, you would still tempt me to stray from my vows. And you? I hope you'll stay a while. Tell me you're not promised to anyone?"

"No."

"Good! I was worried the thin young French composer who volunteered to play later on, might be your fiancé. He looks at you as though he owns you -- or might care to."

"Noel?" She laughed. "That's because he's been my tutor for so long. He and my brother are chaperoning me on this trip, so perhaps that's why he's being overly protective.

Suddenly Adrian de Ávila stepped between them. "A proper host always defers to his guest in cases like this," he blithely informed Agustín as he swept Sirena away in his arms. "You didn't save a single waltz for me," he said teasingly. "I've courted you longer than any local regimental!"

"I thought you preferred an old-fashioned *contradanza*," she parried. Having grown up with the three Ávila children, she still thought of Adrian more as a brother than a beau.

"You know only a waltz lets me hold you this way." He tightened his grip on her waist. "*Please* tell me you've changed your mind! You know you'd be happy as mistress of La Soledad, and you could add 'Marquésa' to your title. Everything would be the way it's always been except. . ." He pressed his cheek to hers, " – except you'd be my bride!"

"Dear Adrian! I've been saying 'No' to this same proposal for the last two years! I love both you and David dearly, but I've still got many other things to do before. . ."

At that moment Adrian took a backward step and Sirena turned to find herself in the arms of an officer she knew to be even more brazen and vain than her swashbuckling host.

"Captain Allende!" she exclaimed. "I had no idea you were going to be here this evening!"

Allende gazed down at her almost hungrily. "So you *do* remember me! You were a pretty bit of fluff when I danced with you last, at your *quince anos* in Guanajuato two ago," he said smoothly, "but by God, you've turned into a more dazzling enchantress than Circe! Your father knew what he was about when he named you after a Siren!"

Sirena remembered Allende well. From a good family in the town of San Miguel El Grande, not far from Dolores, his father was a wealthy gachupín merchant. When this dashing officer showed a great interest in Sirena at her debut, several dowagers said he was a catch worth going after. But wise Aunt Amantina told her to avoid him like the plague.

Married, in his mid-thirties and powerfully built, with red-blond curly hair and intense blue eyes, he was Captain of the same San Miguel militia to which her brother, David belonged. Although David idolized him as a model soldier, his renown for drinking and chasing every woman was even greater than that of her over-ardent host, Agustín. A bull in a village *corrida* had given his otherwise chiseled profile a flattened Michelangelesque nose. A second country bull had crippled his left arm. Even if she were desperate for a man, no lady would trust Allende as far as Easter Sunday Mass.

While she was hoping Adrian would cut in again and rescue her, Allende began whirling with dizzying speed. Before she realized it he had deftly waltzed her through a hidden arch and along a shadowy cloister that opened unexpectedly onto a secluded garden.

Dark cypresses framed a row of white Grecian columns along a gravel path edged with flowers. A small artificial stream rippled just beyond several white stone benches set at intervals along the path. The moon was nearly full, the garden awash in its light. With a sense of foreboding she realized the garden was deserted except for the two of them.

"A virginal Grecian maiden in a Grecian garden. . ." he whispered passionately, locking her in a fierce embrace.

"Captain Allende," she whispered softly, "I'm afraid you overstep. . ." His mouth closed over hers, his crippled left arm holding her in a vise-like grip, while his right moved upward expertly to fondle her breast. His lustful kiss filled her with anger and revulsion, but she could not break free.

"My own sweet virgin, don't fight me!" he said hoarsely. "Your chaperon is busy making music. We have time! I know a place nearby where we can lie together. I'll drive you wild with acts of love, the likes of which you've never even dreamed."

Even more outraged by this lewd proposal than by his crude physical assault, Sirena marshaled the same hidden strength with which she mastered a runaway horse. With a rush of fury she broke his grip, pushing him from her, at the same instant delivering a stunning blow to the side of his head. Unbalanced by the unexpected force of her blow, Allende stumbled backwards, fell across a stone bench and ended up sprawled on his back in a bed of begonias, his head and shoulders immersed in the cool waters of the twinkling stream.

Trembling with rage and mortification, Sirena started to go back into the house when, without warning, an officer burst from the darkness of the shadowed arches. To avoid colliding with him she stepped into the concealing shade of a cypress and he strode angrily past her to where Allende lay.

"Captain!" the officer said in a voice taut with suppressed fury, "you've already given General Calleja enough cause to cashier you. I suggest you go inside at once before I report this disgraceful incident to him."

Too embarrassed to reveal her presence, Sirena hastily assessed the stranger standing over Allende. He wore the Turkish blue uniform of a lieutenant colonel, with scarlet cuffs, lapels and piping, and a wide silk sash at his waist. Judging from his silver epaulets he commanded a cavalry unit of lancers in Calleja's renowned Tenth Brigade.

Incandescent with rage, Allende got to his feet, his bull-like chest heaving. Water streamed from his auburn curls and his dress tunic was drenched. For a second it looked as if he would lunge at his superior. Instead he balled his fists at his sides and spat out contemptuously, "Calleja's nothing but a tight-assed gachupín!"

He's your commanding general, who expects his men to comport themselves as Christian gentlemen, whether on – or *off* –the field!"

"I was a fool to think I could serve under any goddamned stinking Spaniard," Allende fumed. "When I get back to San Miguel I'll be my own man again!"

"Until that happy day, Sir, you answer to me! Now, I order you to leave this noble lady in peace."

With what shreds of dignity remained to him, Captain Allende combed his hair with his fingers and moved furiously toward the house, gravel grating loudly under his tread.

"I'll not soon forget you!" he hissed at Sirena as he passed. "*Someday I'll even this score!*"

When certain he was gone she moved forward to make her presence known, extending her gloved hand to the stranger, angry at herself because she was unable to keep from trembling. "Sir, I am the First Condesa de Graciana. And who is the consummate gentleman to whom I owe my gratitude?"

The lieutenant colonel stepped forward, took her hand, and, with a deep bow, raised her fingers to his lips. "Ah, my dear Condesa," he exclaimed reproachfully, "have you so quickly forgotten the frontier subaltern who gave you a Cheyenne flute?"

"Tristán?" she cried, staring incredulously at the blond, trim-bearded stranger smiling down at her. "It really is you!" For a moment she stood frozen in shock and then impulsively, as though she were a little girl again, she threw her arms around him. "Oh, Tristán, I'm so glad to see you! The beard, the uniform -- they fooled me completely!"

Suddenly embarrassed by her own forwardness, she drew away. "So," she continued with a nervous laugh, "what did you do with your dear old quilted cotton armor? It was so nice to lean against – and weep into – when you used to hold and comfort me."

"Oh, I assure you, I put it away safely, in case you ever needed it again."

Resting his hands gently on her shoulders he held her at arms length and studied her. "Ah, Condesita, what an Irish beauty you are! I couldn't believe my eyes when I saw you on the dance floor tonight." With a wicked grin he added, "But who else has those eyes and that determined O'Malley chin?"

As he moved into the light of the brilliant moon, Sirena saw his face clearly at last. He was the same as she remembered him, only a little taller and heavier in the shoulders. The same proud head and deep blue eyes, his mouth still firm but tender, the bold line of his jaw somewhat softened by the short blond beard.

Suddenly she was mortified to realize it was he who had stumbled upon her in a strange man's arms. "Tristán, I know how it must look, but I can explain about Allende . . . "

"Please!" he said, laying a finger on her lips. "I know him all too well. I've served with him. He's a fine soldier, but not a man to be trusted with a lady. When I saw him try his usual 'ballroom escape' with you I knew what was coming, and took it upon myself to – well – to look after you."

"It was very sweet of you, Tristán."

"I must say, you defended yourself quite formidably without me. I'm sure the bold Captain will think twice before he risks rousing another Irish fronterista's wrath!"

They sat down together on a stone bench facing each other. He took her two hands in his and held them. "Sirena, until I saw you tonight, I thought I had lost you for good."

"Oh, Tristán, I was so afraid we'd never meet again! Where have you been all this time?"

"Well, since I saw you last, I've been to Cuba, Texas and Alta California. Then I served quite a while patrolling the northeastern frontier." His eyes were sober. "It was there I began to understand the real dangers New Spain faces from expansionist Yankee filibusters and land-hungry Kentuckians. More important, I met Félix Calleja while he was making a military reconnaissance of that entire border. I became his aide-de-camp and, I'm proud to say, his very close friend."

Sirena found herself hanging on his every word, drinking in the remembered timber of his voice, the warmth and solace of his presence. "And then?" he told her tremulously, "Calleja sent me to study modern European military tactics and field command at the best academy in Spain."

"How long were you there?"

"Nearly five years -- but I also studied armies in Italy, England and France. After seeing Napoleon's veterans in action. . ." he shrugged. "Well, I saw what we needed to do over here to keep this kingdom safe."

He gazed down at her for what seemed an eternity. Sirena felt herself drawn toward him, filled with an overpowering desire to somehow become a part of him. What would he think if he knew her favorite day dream as a child had been of him riding into La Frontera, asking Don Gabriel for her hand and then riding off with her to some wild province like Texas or New Mexico? She was afraid to move for fear she would lose what little self-composure she had left and throw herself headlong into his arms as she had done so easily as a child.

"And my dear, what about you?" he asked, the same disarming sense of genuine concern in his tone. "I've thought of you so often, wondered where and how you were."

"Well, after Mamá married Don Telmo things were very hard for me. He tried to make me give up my title and my inheritance in favor of my baby brother, Crispín."

"But that's absolutely illegal under Spanish law!"

"I was only seven, so he thought if he locked me in my room and fed me dried tortillas and water long enough he'd force me to give in." She looked down. "Well, I didn't."

Tristán covered her hand gently with his. "You always were a courageous child," he said, eyes alight with pride. "But your mother? Why didn't Doña Isabel help you?"

"That's a long story. She re-married to spite Francisco for not staying on to manage Papá's affairs for her. I was a part of her anger and revenge. But when Uncle Gabriel returned from Paris and found how sick and weak I was, he flew into a towering Irish rage. Because he is my godfather he fought for custody over me and won. Then he took me north with him."

"And so you grew up at La Frontera?"

"Yes, and summers in Zacatecas assisting Uncle with the family's northern mines. Then we spent two years on the Grand Tour. Except for that, and having my quince años in Guanajuato, at Mamá's insistence, I've tried to fill the shoes of that cherished little boy Uncle Gabriel lost in infancy."

"Yes, I remember his grandiose plans for his son -- world travel, the best education money could buy, everything!"

Sirena spread her hands. "Well, I got it all!"

"So what are your plans for the future?"

"After I re-open Papá's palacio in Guanajuato I'm going to attend the School of Mines."

"Really!" His voice betrayed his surprise.

"I'm taking over operation of La Sirena, and I need to sink a new shaft soon." She looked at him curiously. "Does that surprise you?"

"No," he said with quiet amusement. "Actually I was referring to your marriage plans. Judging from the regiment of suitors hovering about you in there, you've only to choose which one you want and -- march down the aisle."

"Oh, but I don't want -- I mean there's no one I've even considered except --" She had to bite her tongue to keep from adding 'for you!'

Sensing her embarrassment he changed the subject. "Sinking a new shaft is pretty expensive, isn't it?"

"*Very!* To help finance it I sent my brother, Felipe, to Manila to invest in Chinese trade goods. That was two whole years ago, but Felipe's disappeared without a trace, and every centavo of my investment money vanished with him."

"Not too large a sum, I hope?"

"Large enough, Tristán. A hundred thousand pesos!"

"Good God! Are you sending someone to look for him?"

"Yes," she replied, delighted to be able to confide her own secret thoughts with him, "possibly, Ramón."

"I know that brother well, because he's in Allende's regiment. Do you think he's man enough for such a mission?"

"No," she replied honestly. "I sent him to Mexico on important business recently." She shook her head in dismay. "He got in a duel over an officer's wife! If Don Francisco hadn't hidden him away 'til his wounds healed, the scandal would have cost him his commission. The way he worships Allende, that would have been worse than death for him!"

She smiled and looked into Tristán's eyes trustingly. "I think I'm going to do what I should have done in the first place -- take the galleon to Manila myself."

"The galleon!" he exclaimed angrily, "I absolutely forbid you to do such a hair-brained thing!" He sprang to his feet, walked a few yards down the path and then stopped abruptly, one hand resting against a moon-silvered column. Bewildered, Sirena rose and followed him.

"Please forgive me," he said unhappily. "I had no right to order you about as though you were my. . ." He passed a hand over his eyes. "I don't know what possessed me."

She took a tentative step toward him and touched his sleeve. "I don't mind. I know you're only concerned for my safety. It's nice that someone I care for, also cares what happens to me."

He turned toward her, and there was a sadness in his expression she could not reconcile with her own outrageous happiness at being with him.

"Sirena, this is why I was so afraid of ever finding you again -- much as I wanted to." His meaning was shot through with contradictory undertones she did not understand. "I was afraid all the admiration and affection I felt for you as a little girl might come back again, but in a dangerously different way." He gave her an enigmatic smile. "Well, I was right. It has."

His words sank in on her slowly, but there was no denying their meaning. He was confessing he loved her, no longer as a child, but the way a man loves a woman! Suddenly she felt herself aglow with an indescribable happiness. Oh, thank God, she thought wildly. Dare I confess I love him too?

"But Tristán," she asked, half-fearfully, "Why do you think of it as 'dangerous'?"

Taking her gently in his embrace, his beard brushing her cheek, he spoke deliberately. "For your own second cousin who is also a married man – it's *very* dangerous!"

She felt herself turn to stone in his arms. "I had no idea you were married." Her voice was toneless.

"It was a tragic mistake. She lives in my Mendoza palace in Mexico, and I'm away all the time." He gazed down at Sirena. "God, I was miserable before. But now I understand just how miserable I've been -- and why."

She leaned her head against his breast and he drew her close to him. "I love you, Sirena, but it simply cannot be." He fell silent, as if trying to summon the courage to say what must be said. "But you're very young. Someday you'll fall in love with a worthy man of your station and marry."

"No, Tristàn!" she cried, shutting out the finality of his words. "I'll never marry anyone but you!"

"Well," he said soothingly, "What law says we can't be what we were before -- kinsmen and good friends?"

"Oh, yes," she said, "I need your friendship, your advice, someone to confide in! Please be my 'protector', again, if you will!"

"I'll love being all those things," he said, framing her face in his hands. "God knows, I too, desperately need someone who cares about what happens to me!"

Sirena closed her eyes, feeling utterly safe for the first time since her father's death. "I care what happens, Tristán! You know I care."

"It's risky," he said, his voice husky with emotion. My God, he thought, after tonight, any confessor would tell me that just seeing her constitutes a serious occasion of sin! You know it's impossible even for two saints to remain mere friends, once they're in love! Aloud he said, "I'm afraid watching over you, my dear Condesita, is a risk that -- I'm more than willing to take."

He drew a deep, hesitant breath. "So now," he said, putting her from him, "your *protector* had better get you safely back inside before he loses his head as completely as poor Allende lost his."

Walking toward the casco together, only the rasping of the gravel breaking the silence, he turned and asked with a sheepish grin. "Please promise me one thing?"

"Anything!"

"Promise me you won't make that voyage on the Manila Galleon? Please?"

"I promise!" She took his hand and pressing her lips gently into his palm she murmured, "And I've even sealed it with a kiss!"

15

"Good linen and good husbands come only from Spain'" Doña Isabel admonished Sirena smugly.

"Mercedes has acted wisely in following that rule, and you should, too."

Sirena sat on a heavy 17th Century porter's chair in the suite of her half-sister, Mercedes, on the top floor of the De La Huerta mansion in Guanajuato. Isabel was helping her older daughter prepare for this morning's sitting with the artist, Matías. It was Mercedes' pre-nuptial portrait and she was nervous as a *maturescent* royal, whose image was due to be peddled through the courts of Europe and bid for by the neediest crown prince.

"Actually Mamá, I'm in no hurry to get married," Sirena said, "I explained that to you when you asked me to consider Neto two years ago and I turned him down."

"Your father merely wanted to keep the title in the family," Isabel replied testily. It irritated Sirena that her mother insisted on referring to Don Telmo as 'your father', but let it pass.

"Anyway," Sirena added as a conciliatory gesture, "now I'm glad I refused Neto, since Mercedes is so in love with him."

Sirena had not even considered this forty-year old immigrant fortune hunter. Poor Neto and his brother were the brow-beaten nephews of Don Telmo, who had brought them from Spain to work as his clerks and drove them like galley slaves, paying little more than bed and board. As a result, Neto was literally poorer than the proverbial friar's servant.

But for Mercedes -- vain, self-centered and painfully insecure -- Neto was someone she could lord it over. Having been a sickly child, her plain looks compared unfavorably by others to her beauteous mother and sister, Sirena, was pleased to see that at twenty-one the ugly duckling was finally a swan. She had fine features, spun-gold hair and, in place of her once sallow coloring, a complexion as translucent as mother-of-pearl. Unfortunately, it had become her crowning vanity, causing her brother, Ramón, to hint she carry a hand mirror and save having to pause before every pier glass she passed, to gaze upon her own luminous complexion.

Although the two of them had never been close, Sirena was still trying to bridge the gulf between them. For this same reason, she had accepted Isabel's invitation to stay in the De La Huerta mansion during this visit to Guanajuato, 'under your own roof', as her mother archly put it. Uncomfortable as she was around Don Telmo, Sirena was striving to honor the promise made to her dying father, by forging a bond of trust and affection with her mother and with Isabel's three badly spoiled children.

"I suppose that rough-cut norteño, Adrian de Àvila, is more to your taste," Mercedes observed, "since marrying him would tack a string of haciendas onto those you already own."

"Adrian's merely a childhood friend," Sirena replied.

"We've heard rumors you've even considered marrying your own French tutor!" her mother said reprovingly. "I do hope that's not true!"

"Noel?" Sirena laughed. "Really, Mamá!"

"Well, why else would he be traveling with you all the way to Mexico?" Mercedes put in suspiciously. "Besides, when your own bosom friend, Alicia Àvila, stopped by here on her way to Mexico last year to marry a mariscal, *she* said you were in love with Noel."

"We found it hard to believe you couldn't do better," Isabel said, seconding her surprise, "but then I guess up North what real choice is there?"

More amused than angry, Sirena recalled her inauspicious meeting with Noel when she was seven and he a solemn youth of sixteen. With his proper speech and regal manners she thought him a polished snob, until her uncle explained.

Noel was a distant cousin of Gabriel's dead wife, and he had found Noel hiding in a Paris basement at the height of the Terror. Noel's parents, tutors to a noble family at Versailles, died on the guillotine. Gabriel gave Noel a home at La Frontera, and to save the young orphan's pride and fill an urgent need of his own, engaged the youth as Sirena's tutor. He was well-educated, richly gifted in music, played several instruments, knew Latin and was fluent in Spanish, English and, of course, his native French.

Noel was a strict maestro: Sirena was made to memorize whole passages from Caesar in Latin and read Shakespeare aloud in English. Noel accepted no French less perfect than his own. Thanks to his patient coaching, she could dance every minuet, polonaise, contradanza and waltz as expertly as any lady-in-waiting to his poor martyred Queen. Sometimes the Àvila children took classes with Sirena, and it was the capricious Alicia Àvila who enchanted Noel. Alicia's arranged marriage to a wealthy older man in Mexico had left him desolate. But now Sirena was happy, for he would soon be seeing Alicia again, and under circumstances ideal for Noel.

"The real reason he's going to Mexico," Sirena explained to Mercedes with satisfaction, "is because Mexico's renowned *Teatro Coliseo* has engaged him to be resident composer-conductor for all their future productions."

"I see." Mercedes shrugged, thereby dismissing the topic of Noel. "Well, I'm glad *I'm* marrying well," she said, returning to her favorite subject, herself. "I pity poor cousin Inéz, still not married at forty-five." She pulled the neckline of her violet gown lower, exposing more of her milk white throat and shoulders. "Would you believe she's still mooning over that awful Francisco Durán who treated us so shabbily right after Crispín was born?"

Sirena winced at her sister's barbed reference to her own oldest friend, and noticed that Isabel set her jaw stubbornly at mention of Francisco's name.

Mercedes moved away from her vanity and settled into an armchair by the window to take her pose, "Maybe, since you've no better prospects, you should pursue Baron Von Humboldt. He seems to be the most popular bachelor in the Americas right now."

Sirena laughed. "My sole interest in the man is his knowledge of metallurgy and mining." Then, turning to her mother she asked, "Are you and Don Telmo attending the dinner and ball being given for the Baron tonight?"

"Absolutely not!" her mother retorted heatedly. "Your father and I wouldn't attend even if we *had* been invited! A man of Don Telmo's experience doesn't need some pompous foreigner telling him a better way to mine!"

Sirena was relieved. Don Telmo's presence would have spoiled the entire evening, for she was hoping to see Tristán there. Although she hadn't seen him since that night in the Iturbide garden, she knew he was in Guanajuato with Félix Calleja, serving as his senior officer during the General's continuing military inspection of every town regiment as he journeyed through the Interior Provinces.

Just as Sirena felt herself growing giddy at the prospect of seeing Tristán again, there was a rap on the door and Isabel opened to the maestro, Matías.

He was the same grave maestro she remembered, in his open-necked shirt, rolled up sleeves, and a dark blue shop apron covering his grey waistcoat and knee breeches. He still wore his iron-grey hair long, drawn back the old-fashioned way and tied with a wide black bow.

While he set up his easel and laid out his paints, Isabel was busy making last-minute changes in Mercedes' hair, so Sirena had a few minutes to visit with Matías.

"Tell me about Lorenzo," Sirena asked. "Has he finished his studies at San Carlos?"

"Si, Condesa. He graduated with the highest honors. He's taken over the family atelier in Mexico and is working at the foundry with the great maestro, Manuel Tolsá!"

"So he's realized his childhood dream of learning to cast bronze!" she enthused.

"Not just learning," he said proudly. "He is now First Assistant to Tolsá."

"Then Lorenzo must be helping him with construction of the building for the new School of Mines?"

"Yes, that and a heroic equestrian statue of His Majesty as a Roman Caesar." He paused. "But Condesa, I never forgot, it was your dear, noble father who made all of this possible for our Lorenzo."

"Lorenzo made an artist of himself by working hard, I'm sure," she said and then asked, "And Emilio? Where is he?"

Matías stuck his lower lip out in an indignant scowl. "Emilio went back to -- the trail," he said, as though loath to admit what he regarded as his brother's crime.

When Mercedes was finally ready and Matías began painting Sirena left and went downstairs to her own bedroom to change. In the corridor she almost collided with Don Telmo who came hurrying toward her, arm in arm with Neto.

"Well, if it isn't Sirena!" he said condescendingly. "Finally got your fill of the outer marches and came back to civilization, eh?"

"Not quite," Sirena replied, a matching edge of sarcasm in her voice behind her smile. "I've come to watch Baron Von Humboldt bring civilization to the provinces."

She found she still viewed Don Telmo the way she had as a child, imagining his round head was a bean pot and his large ears the handles on either side. His face was more florid than she remembered it, webbed with purple veins. Obviously time had not mellowed him. Dressed as always in what her father had called 'executioner's black', he was the same cold-hearted Basque peasant she had grown to hate during the weeks he was starving her. She marveled that her mother could share the same bed with such a bestial man.

"I can't for the life of me see why everyone acts as if that German prig's visit were the Second Coming!" he bellowed. "What entitles Von Humboldt to dip his Austrian horn spoon in our affairs and stir?"

"Exactly!" Neto agreed, his Uncle's echo as well as his shadow. While she disliked Neto almost as much as her stepfather, she had once felt a certain pity for him. He led the life of a slave, and had to beg his Uncle's nod to even take a stroll, but cruelly treated as he was, he showed no compassion for others. Crewmen who worked for him at the Graciana mine told her he showed them even less mercy than Don Telmo de la Huerta himself.

"Will you be visiting the offices of La Sirena mine while you're in town?" Neto asked politely.

"Oh, yes," she assured him. "In fact I'm taking the Baron on a tour of its patios and shafts in about an hour."

"I won't have you doing that!" Don Telmo exploded. "You know full well it's bad luck to have a woman underground!"

"Well, I'm afraid you'll have to get used to it, Don Telmo. I'll be running La Sirena mine myself very soon."

"But I've arranged for Crispín to manage that mine when he turns eighteen!"

Sirena's eyes flashed angrily. "It does not belong to you or to Crispín. My father left it to me!"

"But as God's in His Heaven, Sirena," Neto said in a weak attempt at conciliation. "That's impossible. You can't be a miner. *You're not a man!*"

"No, but I am a Condesa! You both may as well know this now," Sirena said, enraged, "when I come back from Mexico I'm going to run my *own* house, my *own* life *and my own mine!*"

Don Telmo stared at her as though she had turned into a serpent before his eyes. "I'm sure you've heard of the Guanajuato mining consulado," he said slowly. "Well, *I'm* its President, and I'll *never* let them admit you to the board. I'll fight you every step of the way. You won't be able to turn a water whim above, or blast a peso's worth of ore below. I think you need to learn just who runs this town!"

"I will indeed, sir! And you can tell the Consulado for me that whenever I'm ready to do so, I'll take my rightful place on that board. I'm my father's daughter and heiress, and I'm going to pay fair wages and fight for the workers' rights the same way he did. I think you forget, it's not being a man that counts. It's having the title!"

"We'll decide all that later," Don Telmo said coldly, resuming his business-as-usual mood. "Come along, Neto, we're due at the Consulado in ten minutes." He drew out a heavy gold watch and chain from his waistcoat. Snapping open the ornate gold case with deliberate ostentation, he made sure Sirena saw the great, gaudy showpiece and its value. Peering at its face through the quizzing glass he carried on a grosgrain ribbon around his neck, he growled. "We'll find out how long our crewmen will watch their families starve before they agree to work for what we are willing to pay."

Rapping Neto sharply on the elbow with the heavy gold head of his cane he shouted crankily at his forty-year old nephew, "Neto! *Don't lag boy, don't lag!*"

                                                     ಶ ಆ

"I've visited mines all over Europe," Alexander, Baron Von Humboldt exclaimed, "but I'm impressed with the sheer beauty of yours."

Sirena stood beside the visiting dignitary in the largest of La Sirena's two processing patios. She had been prepared to meet a much older man. The Baron was only thirty-four and looked ten years younger. His blue eyes were large and candid, his high-bridged nose full at tip and nostril, his sensuous lips red as a child's. His fair, pink-cheeked complexion, shielded by a wide-brimmed felt hat, showed no sign of exposure to the fierce tropical weather of the South American highlands and jungles he had been exploring over the past two years.

With his loose-fitting trousers and open-collared shirt he looked more like a German peasant in haying season than the world's most respected scientist. It was easy to see why the women of three continents had found him irresistible. The mystery was how he remained impervious to their charms. It was rumored he had three pet hates -- concert music, orthodox religion and romantic love. Perhaps that explained it.

Baron Alexander Von Humboldt

"There are twenty-three arrastres in perpetual operation in these two patios," Sirena explained, gesturing to the mule teams, harnessed four abreast, patiently plodding an endless circle inside shallow vats, paved and curbed with stone. The mules turned a heavy, central pole to which were chained four huge blocks of stone. By dragging these through the muck, the great mass of half-pulverized ore was ground to a greater fineness with every turn.

"And this has already been crushed in a stamp mill and strained through copper screens first?" the Baron asked.

Sirena nodded and led him into a second stone-paved patio where some three-dozen piles of ore were spread out in circles about two English feet deep and some thirty feet across. An *azoguero* was busy scooping up samples in a horn spoon and testing the consistency of the mix between thumb and forefinger. At intervals, mule teams were led through the *tortas* to trod in the pyrite, mercury and salt being added occasionally to the mass by the azoguero.

"When I came to visit the patios as a child I used to call these tortas 'mud pies,'" Sirena told him.

"And aren't they?" he asked with a wicked grin.

Sirena found him the most informal man she had ever met, the very antithesis of the cold scientific genius she had expected.

"When the ore is finally processed, it's carted to those huge masonry washing vats you see down there along the river," she continued. "After the water has washed away the base metal, we process the amalgam in these bell-shaped iron ovens, separating the mercury from the precious ore." Pointing to the 'bells' she added, "Of course, I'm sure this whole process seems pretty primitive to you after the scientific works you've headed as Chief Inspector of Mines at Beyrueth."

"Not at all, Condesa. I find La Sirena's galleries outrank the best in Freiburg -- wide and high enough to house five choirs of angels, veritable cathedrals underground. But of course, not entirely without flaws."

He looked at her keenly, as though measuring her tolerance for criticism. "I find it hard to speak harshly to a Condesa. It's difficult to remember I'm talking to a silver lord."

"My dear Alexander," she chided him, "do you think I rode three hundred Spanish leagues to hear compliments? I invited you here to give your honest opinion and advice. Harsh as it may be, I expect to profit by it."

Within the hour she would regret her request that he be candid. The faults he found were legion. Guanajuato's maze of completely unmapped workings underground outraged his exacting German soul. On that they were agreed. The rest were much more bitter pills for her to swallow.

"One costly error is the excessive size of your pits and galleries. They do nothing to renovate the air, which I'm sure was your father's intention."

Happily, he had only high praise for the sixteen small, portable forges in the interior of La Sirena, for most other mines had only three. He admired the ease with which her fifteen hundred underground workmen employed these forges to re-sharpen the stone-dulled tips of their *pointerolles*. "But," he added, "German miners haven't used pointerolles since Emperor Charles the Fifth abdicated his throne – 1556 was the year, as I recall."

Sirena winced at the antiquity of the date.

The Baron said her blast men wasted powder, and advised she use wooden casks to lift water and ore, since leather ones wore out within a week. He was unaware that wood was scarce in Guanajuato, or that cattle roaming the northern plains in the hundreds of thousands made hides both plentiful and cheap. But on this point she kept her own counsel.

Sirena led him to the collar of the great Santa Cruz shaft. Cut octagonally, and lined with dressed stone, it measured ninety feet across. It was her father's proudest engineering achievement. It was also the shaft that had cost him his life.

"Is it true you plan to sink another shaft even deeper than this one?" Von Humboldt inquired.

"Yes, sixteen-hundred English feet. But I estimate my annual profits from it should average a hundred thousand British pounds."

He shook his head disbelievingly. "Despite my carping, Condesa," he murmured apologetically, "I'm awed by the depth and inexhaustible productivity of your great mine."

She grinned back at him. "So, if I change all her engineering vices to virtues, will you admire her thrift as much as her beauty?"

"*Touche!*" he said. "I deserve that!"

Laughing, they walked back through the patios to where their horses were tethered. As they rode together down the mountain, he asked with an intriguing smile, "Will you save me a waltz at tonight's Riaño ball?"

"Of course, Baron Alexander."

He laughed heartily. "I want to be able to tell them back in Beyrueth that I actually danced with an honest-to-God American silver lord!"

16

The heavily laden metal ring at Alberta's belt jangled as she fit a key into its matching lock, opened the door and led Sirena into what had been her parents' bedroom in the Graciana palace. The shutters stood open and the spacious room was flooded with fresh air and light. Red gladioli, spiked with fragrant white nard, graced a Sèvres vase on a center table. The gilded Louis XV French furniture and crystal chandeliers were dustless, the flowered Aubusson carpet and the canopy of the matrimonial clean and bright.

"It's hard to believe the palacio hasn't been lived in all these years," Sirena told Alberta appreciatively, "you and Ricardo have taken such wonderful care of everything."

"Don Gabriel told us you'd be coming home someday."

Sirena moved from one familiar object to another, touching the carved cedar shutters, trailing her fingertips across the creamy surface of a marble-topped table. Plucking a spike of nard, she breathed in its heavy scent as she drifted about the once familiar room.

"Alberta, when I come back from school in Mexico and really settle in, we'll turn back the clock and make this old palacio as lively as it was before my father died."

Sudden tears appeared in Alberta's dark eyes. "Si, mi preciosa! And may the Virgin bring you a husband as noble as your father to share it, and as worthy of your love!"

Sirena looked at the older woman dubiously as she tossed her hat on the bed, stepped out of the riding skirt and pulled off her boots and pants. "I'm afraid not many men are going to be drawn to a female silver lord," she said half-humorously. "Even Baron Von Humboldt had trouble with that."

"Well, you have your father's blessing!" Alberta countered, as she tossed a few fragrant blossoms of nard into a warm bath she had prepared in the square, colorfully tiled tub built into a corner of the bedroom. "As for this German Baron," Alberta continued petulantly, "I don't see why the whole town's turning out for him. You'd think he was the Viceroy himself!"

"The Baron is one of the world's greatest living scientists," Sirena explained, sinking into the welcome bath.

"But the Conde de Rul's housekeeper swears he's not a *true Christian*," Alberta said darkly, laying out the gown Sirena had chosen to wear to the Riaño ball.

"Well, it's true he's not Catholic, but the king himself made this exception, inviting the Baron to make a scientific tour of all Spanish America and report on everything he finds. Whatever facts he learns about Guanajuato, its people and mines, will be written up in an *Essay on New Spain*."

Emerging from her bath, she wrapped herself in a towel and stepped behind a shoulder-high screen to dress. Alberta deftly worked her damp hair into a Psyche knot, then helped her into the Empire-style ball gown of jade-green silk, with short shirred sleeves, a low neck and the graceful train she would carry draped over one arm.

"I don't know," Alberta sniffed suspiciously, as she clasped a necklace of fiery black opals around Sirena's throat. "Who beside the king will ever read what a non-believer thinks about New Spain?"

"Oh, lots of people, Alberta!" Sirena laughed. "Most Europeans would give anything to know what goes on inside our mysterious kingdom, which has been closed to all but a handful of foreigners ever since the Conquest." She drew on long black elbow-length gloves and affixed the opal earrings that matched her necklace. "Englishmen and Yankees especially are *dying* to find out the exact location of our elusive silver mines!"

She gave a last quick glance in the mirror and picked up a small black and gold fan. "Of course I'm sure the Baron won't disclose *that* kind of secret information about us. We'd have the whole English Navy landing at Vera Cruz!"

☙ ❧

At twilight Sirena alighted from a hired sedan chair before the three-story Riaño palace that topped a low rise on the west side of the city. It had a grey stone neo-classic facade, with a large stone statue of the French Crusader King, Saint Louis IX, in a niche above the door. The spirit of those who lived here was inscribed beneath a flaming heart on a wood-carved banner held by two bas relief brass angels: *The door of this house is a heart always open.*

A block away to the south Sirena could see the rising walls of the unfinished *Alhóndiga*, that imposing new municipal granary that the governor was building with surplus revenues from city taxes. Since it was his own most ambitious project it seemed ideal that he could look down every day from his rooftop office above and watch some two-dozen stonemasons at work giving substance to his dream.

A French-speaking criollo servant ushered Sirena across a family patio, announcing her full title, in French, at the door of the inviting sala, which was ablaze with the candlelight from several brilliant chandeliers.

Sirena recognized the blonde, graceful matron with dancing grey-green eyes who came forward with her husband to greet each new arrival. Doña Victoria was a St. Maxent, a New Orleans French family of five sisters, all renowned for their beauty, when she married Don Antonio Riaño. She was still dazzling now, in a gown of yellow silk, accented by topaz jewels that shone as brightly as the candles overhead.

Sirena had met them both years before when, as a child, she and her father attended their inaugural ball in this same palacio. The Conde had been a close friend of Don Antonio, a Spaniard who had risen through the ranks as a career soldier. Now, despite his ample girth and a blaze of white at either temple, Riaño retained his military bearing, together with the intense dark eyes, black hair and fair complexion of his earlier years. His erudition, like his French, was impeccable, and it was easy to see why everyone of culture in the kingdom regarded it an honor to be considered his friend.

After a warm greeting, Doña Victoria led Sirena to a group of chairs, settees and wine tables, all in the new French *directoire* style that was sweeping the Americas as it had already done the Continent. There Sirena was greeted by the Riaño's two house guests, Bishop Legázpi and a tall grey-haired gentleman Doña Victoria introduced as, 'my dear brother-in-law,' the North American Captain James Lowell, who is here on a rare visit from his plantation home in Louisiana."

Sirena had visited Captain Lowell years earlier in New Orleans while making the Grand Tour, because Uncle Gabriel was also related to him by marriage. Lowell had met and married Doña Victoria's younger sister in 1778, while he was a rebel soldier fighting the British during the American Revolution. Doña Victoria then married Riaño, his comrade-in-arms, who was leading the Spanish force that helped

Americans oust the British from Pensacola. On a book-buying trip to New Orleans, Don Gabriel later met and married the third sister, Desireé, and brought her home to La Frontera as his bride.

Sirena greeted other old friends, Doctor Juan Pinal, his wife Emma, and their son Daniel, back from years of study and practice in France, now a surgeon like his father.

"Brigadier General, Don Félix María Calleja!" the servant announced in stentorian tones. Sirena shot an eager glance toward the door to catch her first glimpse of the renowned Spanish General of the Royal Bourbon Army, who had taken such a personal interest in Tristán.

The moment Calleja entered, his dynamic presence dominated the room. Wearing a white dress uniform with high collar, cuffs and lapels faced in red, and gold-fringed epaulets, he seemed a truly formidable personage even when merely standing at ease: *Madre de Diós!* Sirena thought, what must he be like in the midst of battle?

" -- And," the servant announced in almost the same breath, " -- Lieutenant Colonel, Don Tristán de Luna Mendoza!"

Sirena's whole body stiffened and she resolved not to even look at him when he entered, fearful her worshipful gaze would give her away to everyone in the room. But she could not resist. And, the sight of Tristán poised in the doorway at the General's right, clean-shaven and breathtakingly handsome, in a white dress uniform with French blue lapels and silver epaulets, Sirena felt all her resolve melt away. All at once his marriage to someone else was only a dream -- their kinship a cruel fiction. Being in the same room with him sent her into near panic, but when his searching eyes found hers and held, the undisguised affection she saw there ravished her.

Incredibly enough, when he bowed to kiss her hand and introduce his Commander and good friend, she was able to find her voice. "Don Félix," she said as the General bent over her, "We are all very proud of you and your famous Tenth Brigade!"

"I have fine men under me!" he replied, casting a proud glance at Tristán. "That's what makes any army great."

As the two soldiers moved on to greet other guests, Sirena watched Calleja with fascination. He seemed to be that rare anomaly, a gentleman of silken manners welded to a character cast in bronze. His features were bold, as though the Creator meant to make a strong statement with a few broad strokes -- uncommonly large and intense grey eyes under heavy dark brows, ruddy complexion, a prominent arched nose and a wide mouth, generous but strong. With a resourcefulness not entirely devoid of vanity, he had adopted a forward-brushed hair style that concealed his partial baldness with a full hedge of iron-grey hair. For all his fifty years, when he smiled he looked disarmingly boyish. In his more reflective moments, however, Sirena noticed he seemed to be as hot-eyed and restive as a tethered falcon.

When Baron Von Humboldt arrived moments later, all the members of this intimate dinner party were present. But as their hosts rose to lead them into the formal dining room, a belated guest appeared. Sirena did not recognize the graying, slightly built priest in clerical blacks who came rushing across the sala, unannounced and -- she somehow guessed -- uninvited.

"I'm sorry to be late, Doña Victoria," he said with enormous self-possession, "but it was difficult to break away from my new Indian parishioners in Dolores!"

"Father Hidalgo!" Doña Victoria exclaimed graciously, releasing her husband's arm and turning back to introduce the newly appointed Cura of Dolores to those who might not already know him.

"Ah, yes Condesa," he assured Sirena as they met, "your dear father, the Conde and I were the dearest of friends. I'm sure you must have heard him speak of me."

Being herself a frontier hostess, often surprised by brazen guests, Sirena read the silent signal Doña Victoria sent her majordomo. As they all drifted slowly into the *comedor,* Sirena saw the silver plate service and wine goblet materialize instantly out of thin air. Somehow Sirena sensed Father Hidalgo was aware of the magic wrought by his hostess and enjoyed the deference it implied.

The dining room was long and narrow, but with a ceiling high enough to accommodate a small choir-loft, where an excellent string quartet now began playing selections from Mozart, Hayden and Bach.

The table was spread with a rich white cloth, their hosts seated side by side at its head. A magnificent silver pineapple formed the centerpiece, rising out of a low bed of fresh flowers, with a silver obelisk at either end, and some three-dozen lighted white tapers in between.

Sirena sat on Don Antonio's left, directly across from Baron Alexander. She was grateful Doña Victoria seated Tristán farther down on the opposite side next to Calleja and facing Father Hidalgo. She glanced across at Baron Alexander to see if the concert music he claimed to hate was sawing on his nerves, but he gave no hint of it, wearing what seemed to be his customary expression -- one of avid interest in everything and everyone around him.

"Don Antonio, I must say your new Alhóndiga is coming along well since you began work four years ago," Father Hidalgo enthused, as the piping hot French onion soup was being served.

Riaño beamed. "Well, Father, the walls are only halfway up, but then it is an enormous enterprise. My architect tells me it may take five more to complete. However, it will have the capacity to hold four times more corn and wheat than the present granary."

"It's built with an eye for beauty, too, I noticed," the Baron observed. "A spacious inside courtyard with Ionic columns and two fine stone staircases leading up to an encircling second floor."

"Well, I don't lack critics on that score," Riaño said, smiling good-naturedly. "Some of them have accused me of building *a palace for corn!*"

"For one who arrived in this kingdom on the eve of the worst famine in our history," Bishop Legázpi offered, "I can testify to the wisdom of building a granary large enough to meet such crises. The Alhóndiga will be an enduring monument to the generous, humanitarian spirit of its builder."

"Well, well, Excelencia!" Don Antonio said, laughing to cover his embarrassment at this accolade. "Such a speech obligates you to preside at the dedication when it's completed!"

"Doctor Daniel, I've been wanting to congratulate you on taking over your father's practice," Doña Victoria said, turning to Doctor's Juan's handsome son. "We were all delighted to have you home from your studies in France, but taking your father's place is an unexpected development."

"Unexpected for both of us," Daniel replied.

"Is it true you've been serving with the French Army's field surgeons?" Tristán inquired. "What with the wars raging now, that could be an unforgettable experience."

"Definitely an eye-opening one, Sir! In peacetime French medicine had remained almost medieval. The recent wars have had the merit of shaking up the entire French medical profession and forcing it to modernize."

"Medical care on the battlefield is a subject much neglected in the Bourbon Army," General Calleja said earnestly. "Doctor Daniel, I'd like for Tristán and myself to get together with you while we're here and have you help us form a good medical corps in the Tenth Brigade."

"I'd be happy, Sir." Daniel replied. "Without going into detail at such an inappropriate time and place, I can assure you, General, that more than any other thing, prompt amputation on the battlefield has saved thousands of French soldiers who would otherwise have died of gangrene. Young doctors like myself have grown expert in the art of such emergency surgery."

"It will be hard for this city to lose its beloved 'Doctor Juan' after all these years," Don Antonio said, addressing the elder Pinal. "When must you leave for Mexico?"

"New Spain's sudden death of the chief surgeon has left no one in charge of Mexico's Department of Public Health. I'm to leave at once to take over as head of the *protomedicato*."

"Won't next year's small-pox vaccination program present the protomedicato with some formidable problems?"

"Oh, yes indeed!" Doctor Juan replied. "Getting Indian children vaccinated over their superstitious and terrified parents' protests will be a real battle, but somehow it must be done!"

"Ironic isn't it?" Father Miguel put in. "Can you guess how different the course of this kingdom's history would have been if we'd had this vaccine three centuries ago?"

Sirena saw a satisfied smile light up the priest's narrow face, as though the thought had truly given birth to the deed and the past, itself, been re-written.

"The first friars could have vaccinated the Indians after baptizing them, and the epidemics that carried off so many million natives would never have occurred!"

The look Von Humboldt bent on Hidalgo fell little short of pity. "I've just completed a study of the long history of birth and death statistics in Mexico," the Baron said, taking a sip of burgundy, "and I've come across some facts which pose a grave threat to the future of this kingdom."

"That the Indians are being mistreated by Spaniards and are ripe for rebellion?" Father Hidalgo suggested boldly.

"Your Indians have what is known as an 'Asiatic birth rate'," Von Humboldt continued, unperturbed. "If they ever become immune to measles, smallpox and all the other European diseases which wreak such havoc upon them now, births among your country's poorest ranks will skyrocket, at the very same time as their infant mortality rate declines."

Sirena saw both doctors glance at each other and nod knowingly.

"How then," Von Humboldt asked rhetorically, "will New Spain, with so little arable land, be able to feed the children created by such a remorseless birth rate? Can you even guess what your Indian population might be by -- well, let's say, by the year two thousand?"

"Sir, it's my conviction the poor Indians need far more than vaccine," Father Miguel stated hotly. "They need the hated tribute lifted, their own lands given back to them, the large latifundios broken up..."

"There are a multitude of sides to that thorny question," Bishop Legázpi reminded Hidalgo, stepping in firmly to head off an impolite attack on the Spaniards present, one of whom was their host. "We all know reforms are needed, but any form of radical change takes time."

"I think, Father Miguel," Tristán said coolly, "you've only to look around this table to find men noted for their efforts to eliminate social and economic inequities. Your own Bishop Legázpi has introduced the silk industry to the Indians around Valladolid, and planted a grove of *forty thousand mulberry trees* there to help them ply that trade and prosper. Doctor Juan and the late Don Patrick have been tireless in their efforts to improve the health and welfare of all miners here."

"Well said, Don Tristán," Riaño concurred. "Besides, hasty, ill-considered reforms often do more harm than good."

"I couldn't disagree more," Father Miguel persisted angrily, ignoring all the signals cooler heads were sending his way. "I say we need sweeping political change, and *we need it now!*" He waved his arms dramatically. "Only radical land reforms or a genuine Indian *Reconquista* can ever..."

Hidalgo's broad gesture caught the rim of his goblet, tipped it over and shot a great gout of burgundy across the table, staining the front of General Calleja's white tunic with what looked exactly like fresh-spilled blood.

A servant appeared instantly, with a damp sponge and salt to remove the stain from tunic and tablecloth, while Doña Victoria assured the priest no damage had been done. But Sirena was intrigued by the General's reaction. He made light of the spill itself, but his expression was as forbidding as a gathering storm. For a long moment he studied the fiery priest with a fiercely discerning, almost prescient light in his restive falcon's eye.

"General, you just completed a tour of the border lands," Don Antonio ventured, changing the subject tactfully, "can you inform us about conditions on that frontier?"

"Actually the Indians are quieter than they've been in years," Calleja replied. "The big problem is securing our northeastern boundary against invasions from -- ," he glanced at the American Captain Lowell. "My apologies, Captain, -- I should say against *illegal* invasions from the United States."

Calleja put down his knife and fork and looked about him thoughtfully. "I think you should all know that I received an official dispatch today from the Spanish ambassador in Washington. Despite the Spanish-Franco treaty forbidding such forfeiture, Napoleon Bonaparte has just sold Louisiana to President Thomas Jefferson for fifteen million dollars!"

A murmur of shocked dismay went around the table.

"In New Orleans we've been expecting this for months," Captain Lowell volunteered. "As you all know, Don Antonio led the Spanish troops who helped our thirteen colonies throw off British rule. We were brothers then, and we still are. But while I admire my country's love of liberty and the justice of her laws, I don't like what I see in this affair of Louisiana. It shows a flagrant disregard of Spanish rights. And General, I know of secret *government sponsored entradas* into the known territory of New Spain. That kind of disregard for legitimate boundaries dishonors any nation, even when that country is my own."

"Philip Nolan alone made five such entradas in as many years," Tristán said, "all of them under the guise of rounding up wild Spanish mustangs to sell in the United States. We know he acted under the protection of men in very high places -- George Washington among them."

"We also know," interjected Calleja, "that Philip Nolan was raised in the home of General James Wilkinson, Commander in Chief of the United States Army, Washington's friend and favorite. Wilkinson, Nolan and Aaron Burr have been playing a dangerous three-handed game against their own country, against Spain and against each other, for a good many years."

"What appears to be at stake," Tristán added, "is a private empire carved out of their own nation's unsettled West, and as much of New Spain's territory as they can steal."

"Not long ago," Captain Lowell related, "when Philip Nolan promised an especially fine mustang *gratis* to President Jefferson, citizens asked, 'Why such a gift for such a man?'"

"But before that horse could be delivered," Tristán chuckled, "soldiers of General Calleja's Tenth Brigade surprised Nolan in a fortress he had built on Grand Prairie."

"Did Nolan escape?" Sirena asked, guessing Tristán had been one of the frontier soldiers who discovered the fort.

"No, Condesa, unhappily for him he tried to fight his way out and was killed, along with some of his men. Those we captured said they were following Wilkinson's orders to build a chain of forts inside New Spain to assist a future invasion."

"In the past six months New Orleans has been overrun with a horde of wild, backwoods Kentuckians," Captain Lowell revealed. "These brutes grew up killing Indians for sport and survival, and each other out of sheer meanness. In the streets I've heard them say, 'Let's go grab the golden candlesticks and silver plate of Mexico!' If one of their sons does some act of daring they say boastfully, 'Now *that* boy's going to Mexico!' which means, he'll strike it rich."

"But the real irony is this," Tristán said quietly, "that reckless rogue Wilkinson is the man most likely to be appointed American Governor of Louisiana Territory!"

There was a thoughtful silence as dessert was served, then Calleja remarked with a smile, "Oddly enough, Wilkinson and his men all have this wrong-headed notion that New Mexico is the heart and center of our silver mines, when it's actually a desolate, profitless outpost of empire."

"General, how *do* those poor settlers up there manage to survive in such a sterile region?" Doña Victoria asked.

"They survive, Madame, by begging God for what only the Viceroy can give, and begging the Viceroy for miracles which not even the Almighty is able to perform!"

Sirena smiled at the General's better wit as Doña Victoria steered the conversation to a topic closer to home.

"General, will you and Don Tristán be going over to Dolores tomorrow with the rest of us?"

Sirena strained to catch his answer.

"Yes, we'll be inspecting the Regiment there, and the one in San Miguel el Grand, as well."

Sirena noticed the string quartet had suddenly stopped playing, and music was wafting in from the ballroom. The ball, to which a great number of people had been invited, was starting to get underway.

As the Riaños rose to leave the comedor, someone drew back Sirena's chair, and she looked up to find Tristán bending over her.

"Condesa," he asked, offering his arm, "will you do me the honor of dancing the first waltz with me?"

She rose slowly, moving as if in a dream. "Of course," she breathed tremulously, resting her gloved hand lightly on the white sleeve of his tunic. Leading her to the ballroom, he gazed down at her possessively, placing his hand over hers and pressing it firmly.

"As your protector," he told her softly, "I promise not to let you out of my sight – or my arms – for the rest of the evening!"

As he swept her out onto the gleaming parquet floor, she smiled and whispered, "I can think of no other place I'd rather be!"

17

Seated at a small baroque desk in the corner suite that opened off her bedroom, Sirena was engaged in the pleasant task of recounting the joyous events of the past six weeks in a letter to Alicia Ávila in Mexico. As she wrote she glanced up every few minutes to enjoy her surroundings. She had always loved this jewel-box of a room in the Graciana palace, with its *petit* Louis XV furniture, covered in azure blue silk damask. It had five lofty windows, with white stucco shell-arch reveals, which as a child she thought were made of white meringue and, could she reach that high, might be scooped up and licked like frosting from her fingertips.

By day these windows commanded a magnificent view of the green hills and rust-red escarpments encircling the city. Now their panes were luminous with the deep blue-green of a late September twilight, set off by a full golden moon just rising above the darkening sierra.

Dearest Alicia:

How can I begin to describe these past few weeks here in Guanajuato! The Riaños have become like second parents to me. Every other day we've gone on a dia de campo with picnic baskets filled with fruit, fowl and chilled French wines. We usually ride, but yesterday a group of us went by carreta, (its solid wood wheels shrieking with every turn!) It overflowed with dimity and dotted Swiss skirts, while the ribbons of our wide-brimmed leghorn hats floated in the breeze. My own handsome escort assured us we looked prettier than a basket filled with wildflowers!

> *I had forgotten there were so many lovely haciendas with cloistered gardens close by. We've been to Linda Vista twice for Amantina's fiestas, and there's been a banquet or ball in Baron Von Humboldt's honor every other day. You wouldn't believe how the German waltz, (thanks to the Baron's visit!) has taken staid old Guanajuato by storm!*

Sirena brushed the peacock plume of the quill across her cheek, recalling moments too precious to disclose, unforgettable moments spent with Tristán. They had been inseparable since the first Riaño ball, and she had stored up a dozen precious cameos of him that she loved sorting through. The day they toured the Alhóndiga was branded on her mind, for no more reason than she had looked across that patio -- shimmering with stone dust from the masons cutting stone -- and seen him framed against a sun-splashed column, regarding her with that secret smile she now knew was meant for her eyes alone.

Riding through the sun-dappled aisles of Linda Vista's mulberry groves, Tristán at her side, she had memorized every plane of his finely formed profile, half-shaded by a French blue military tricorn. Merely observing his graceful hands fingering the reins or at rest on his saddlehorn, stirred outrageous desires which had never crossed her mind when riding with any other man. She longed to have those strong, sun-bronzed hands moving like cloud-shadows over the unexplored wilderness of her naked body. When he placed his hand over hers on the swell of her saddle and asked what she was thinking, she had crimsoned, lowered her eyes and replied, "I was wishing you were my -- *adelantado!*" His adoring gaze held a promise, as though he had seen what was in her mind and agreed.

That same day they spent several golden hours in the old adobe silk house down by the river, a place Amantina abandoned long ago when the location proved too damp for her temperamental cocoons. Later Sirena had made it into her playhouse on visits to Linda Vista, in the lonely months between her father's death and moving north to La Frontera.

"I pretended it was my Spanish castle on the Moorish frontier," she admitted shyly, "and from this window I'd wait and watch for my lord knight to return from his crusades."

"But why are you blushing?" he asked, his hand beneath her chin, and reluctantly she confessed she had named her make-believe knight 'Tristán'.

Lingering over a picnic lunch that same day, while their servants fished along the river's bank, he opened his heart to her, revealing things about himself he had never told another soul. Because his mother died when he was ten and Don Octavio never remarried, he became an apprentice soldier to his father when he was only twelve, growing up inured to a life of hardship and solitude. In the bitter years since his loveless marriage he had lived the equally Spartan and solitary existence of a frontier trooper.

"Until we met that magic night in Valladolid, I never realized how alone I've always felt," he confessed. "Being with you these past few weeks is the nearest thing to Heaven I have ever known."

At La Frontera, Sirena had grown up in a not too different environment, an only child, living mostly with adults and accustomed to the constant threat of Apache raids, making the two of them more alike in character than she had dreamed. They both bore the hallmarks of those early frontier years -- self-reliance, a passionate love for their native land and a deathless sense of honor.

She found herself chuckling again at the memory of the fiesta where Aunt Amantina insisted the two of them perform a Spanish *jota*. Both in *tipica* Aragonese peasant dress. With her full flounced skirts flirtatiously a-whirl, Sirena's eyes flashed fiery promises and furious denials, while Tristán arched over and pursued her, his imperative castanets demanding the favor of a long-forbidden kiss. At the spirited finale they fell into each others' arms, faces flushed and hearts pounding. And on the ride home they laughed 'til they wept at their hilarious private joke: dancing the jota had saved them from having to attend a corrida where the ever-dauntless Captain Allende was defying yet *another* village bull!

Although at parties, Tristán was careful not to appear too attentive, it was understood Sirena saved each waltz for him, and no matter who served as chaperon, he helped escort her home. One day as a lark, Matías had dashed off a watercolor miniature of each of them: Sirena had the one of herself framed inside a silver locket and gave it to Tristán. Although she did not commit the fact to paper, Tristán had escorted her on every dia de campo, and she would never again see a carreta or a picnic basket without thinking of him. From dawn 'til dark her days were filled with the lilting chime of his spurs as he strode across a patio or bounded up the palace stairs, a sound that set her heart racing and the blood coursing faster through her veins.

She closed her letter, thanking Alicia in advance for staffing the Graciana palace in Mexico with servants, in advance of her arrival. She expected to arrive in mid-October, traveling with Baron Von Humboldt, Noel, Ramón and their servants. Best of all, Tristán and the General were coming as well, to report in person to the Viceroy on their inspection tour of all the town regiments in the Interior Provinces.

As Sirena sealed the letter, she wondered if she had ever felt more pampered than she did in this peignoir, which Amantina's Estella had sewn for her. With its snowy cotton lace overlaying white taffeta, it dripped lace at the cuffs and rustled when she moved. And when, since turning fifteen, she asked herself lazily, had she ever written letters in such elegant *dishabille*, with her hair down as well?

A cool wind sprang up and while she was closing the shutters for the night Alberta appeared, festive in a new silk rebozo Sirena had given her to wear to tonight's fiesta of the Archangel Michael.

"Mi reina, Ricardo and I are going to watch the fireworks in the plaza. Are you sure you won't come with us?"

"No Alberta, I've been out dancing nearly every night this week. I'm going to read a while and retire early." When Alberta was gone, Sirena snuffed out all the candles except those in a wrought-iron floor candelabrum behind the settee, and took down a copy of Thomas Paine's *Common Sense* from the bookcase. Captain Lowell had suggested she read this particular book to gain valuable insights into the sometimes, startling political views of the *norteamericanos*.

❧ ☙

Tristán nearly collided with Alberta and Ricardo as they came hurrying out the palace gate when he was about to enter from the road. "Alberta, is the Condesa at home?"

"She's not 'at home' to company, Don Tristán," Alberta replied, "but you know she's always 'in' to family. You'll find her in the corner suite upstairs."

As Tristán walked across the patio, the only sounds the fountain's spray and a caged mocking bird pouring forth a floodtide of song, the quiet splendor of the palace struck him anew. What a pity the Conde was not here to enjoy it in his golden years! And how tragic he had not lived to see his promising little First Condesa grow into the gracious woman Sirena had become.

Then, as happened all too often these days, he began speculating on Sirena's future. He liked to imagine her spending the rest of her life right here, whether married or single. Of the two, he hardly knew which prospect disturbed him most. The thought of her becoming a spinster and 'staying home to dress the saints,' depressed him. On the other hand, when he imagined her married to *any* man, however noble -- Adrian, the handsome Fifth Marqués of Ávila, always came to mind -- Tristán was beset by envy, jealousy and a helpless rage at not being able to marry her himself.

As he climbed the stairs he glanced down at the yellow flowered Saint Michael's cross in his hand, hoping this simple gift would make it easier for her to accept what he knew she was going to find dismaying news. Even though he was without his spurs she must have recognized his step, for he found she was already framed in the doorway of the suite and waiting for him by the time he reached the loggia.

His heart was wounded at the sight of her. In a long gown of white lace and with her hair down, she was as lovely as Aphrodite rising from the ocean's foam. The impact of such purity, intelligence and beauty unnerved him. All her other gowns and coiffures had made her appear worldly and mature but, Dear God, he thought, she really is only seventeen!

I'm afraid I'm not dressed to be receiving company," she apologized nervously. "My hair isn't up or anything!"

"Come now, condesita, *I'm* not company."

"Of course you're not! But you *are* a very pleasant surprise!" She drew him after her into the suite and then began busying herself lighting more candles.

"No need to bother with more light," he floundered, feeling utterly miserable at being the bearer of such news. "I really can't stay but a few minutes."

She looked at him quizzically, waved him to a chair and seated herself of the edge of the settee. "Is something wrong Tristán?"

His resolution faltered. "Well – first I brought you this, to help *San Miguel* watch over you." He handed her the cross, slightly larger than his palm, made of four clusters of bright yellow pericon blossoms tied in the center with a thread. Each year on Saint Michael's Feast, such crosses were placed above the door of every house, with a prayer asking the Archangel to protect those within from lightning and all other evils.

"How dear of you, Tristán! I'll tack it up right here, above the door into my suite!"

After an awkward pause he began, "I'm afraid I'm the bearer of bad news for both of us. The General and I won't be going to see the Viceroy as we planned." He studied the carpet's floor pattern. "Our report is to be sent on by special courier instead."

"Oh," she said softly.

"This sudden change was brought about by the Louisiana affair. We've learned that President Jefferson is mounting three ambitious exploratory expeditions into that new territory. We expect there will be deep probes into Texas, New Mexico and perhaps as far West as the Pacific."

"I see."

He took a deep breath. "Much of that country lies inside Spanish territory and we think they intend to trespass and map these regions wherever possible. A force from the Tenth Brigade has been ordered to patrol and defend those far northern frontier provinces. Because I know that country well, I've been put in command."

He could see she was fighting hard to appear composed. "So, when do you have to leave?"

He clasped and unclasped his hands, buying time and the moral strength to tell her what he must. "Far sooner than I expected," he said quickly. "At sunup – *tomorrow*."

Sirena's false courage failed her. She turned ashen and buried her face in her hands. "Oh no, Tristán! You can't leave me now? *I can't bear to lose you again!*"

Cut to the heart by her anguish, he sprang to her side. "Oh, my dearest one you know wild horses couldn't drag me away from you if there were any way possible for me to stay!"

"Then, take me with you!" she pleaded, throwing herself in his arms. "Oh, Tristán, I'll simply die without you!"

His own forbidden desires, fanned by weeks of propinquity, suddenly became as unquenchable as a prairie fire driven by the wind, sweeping all sense of duty and honor before it. Cupping her face in his hands, he covered her cheeks and eyelids with wildly passionate kisses and then his lips found hers in a long-denied first kiss that was as fierce as he meant it to be tender. Sirena responded with a sexual hunger that only inflamed his own passion more. He pressed her to him, kissing her repeatedly, while his hands instinctively sought out the tempting curves and hollows of her body, which for weeks he had been burning to expose and explore.

"Oh my beloved Tristán, be my conquistador!" she cried softly, "Let me be your wilderness – let your hands and lips be like cloud-shadows passing over me!"

How did she know he had dreamed of claiming the virgin wilderness of her body, which no other man had gazed upon before? Drunk with the promise of all that lay waiting for him beneath the enticing latticework of white lace and whispering silk, he lost all sense of time and place.

"I never meant to let my passion carry me this far," he whispered brokenly, "but three magical weeks together – confiding in you, riding with you by my side, hold you dangerously close in the German waltz – every day I've been falling deeper in love, even knowing it's impossible for me to ever have a place in your life. I tried to kill what I feel, but I can't."

"But tomorrow you'll be gone! What if we never find each other again?"

"When I was nineteen I thought there was no such thing as a day of reckoning. Don Patrick himself warned me I would live to regret my folly and many times over I have. Now, at whatever cost to me, I must spare you that kind of lifelong regret."

"I would never regret giving myself to you!"

During the years he was training in Spain he had enjoyed affairs with accommodating women. But now a moral tocsin deep inside his soul warned him that family honor ordained he must protect her innocence. He lifted to his lips the silver locket she had given him with her image inside and kissed it reverently.

"Condesita mia, you are with me always, now and forever," he promised. "But as God is my witness, I cannot let my love destroy you!"

"My dearest Tristán! I'll be there protecting you, wherever you may go." After an agonizing last embrace and the kiss they feared might have to last them both a lifetime, he stepped out onto the narrow balcony, slipped over the low wrought-iron rail and dropped soundlessly to the deserted road below. He walked briskly toward the neighboring palace where he and the General were houseguests and where he had left his own horse stabled. There, as he saddled his horse and regained command of himself, he decided to ride down to the palace where Bishop Legázpi was staying. They had once sailed together on what was His Excellency's final visit to Spain and he had come to know and respect him as a man and a confessor. He had never needed grace and the Bishop's wise counsel more desperately than now. Riding slowly toward the city under a moonless, rocket-spangled sky, Tristán beheld in the steady rain of ashes the fearful omen of his own mortality. But would that be so bad, he mused? A life without Sirena at his side promised to be only a longer, slower death of its own

PART FOUR

MEXICO

1803

The city itself was the grandee of all colonial cities and knew itself to be. It was granted, by royal command the right to be called "imperial, significant, loyal and most noble city," and bore in addition the official titles of "capital, court and head" of New Spain.

The Fall of the Royal Government in Mexico City by
By Timothy E. Anna

There are about forty houses in Mexico City that can be considered noble residences of monumental character. One feels that the term. . ."The city of Palaces" (attributed to Baron Von Humboldt) was justified.

Colonial Art in Mexico
by Manuel Toussaint

෪18෫

All twenty-four bells in both towers of Mexico's imposing Metropolitan Cathedral exploded in a storm of jubilant sound. Scores of startled white pigeons, soaring upward from towers, cupola and domes, formed a living re-splendor of wings above the magisterial greystone façade.

Seated in the second tier of a canopied, brightly festooned viewing stand in Mexico's great central plaza, Sirena was one of a gathering of government and Church dignitaries and select members of titled families invited to attend the unveiling of Maestro Tolsá's equestrian statue of the reigning Bourbon king. She was seated between Baron Von Humboldt and Doña María Ignacia Rodríguez, the doyenne of Mexico City society. Beautiful, rich, divorced and scandalous, the flippant name by which Doña María was known to everyone in Mexico was, La Güera -- The Blonde.

Sirena caught her breath as a pompous, Spaniard in gala dress uniform took the supreme place of honor, directly in front of her own chair. It was the Viceroy himself!

A shiver went through her as she recalled her conversation with Bishop Legázpi the day Tristán departed for the North. In the confessional he had given her gentle, but firm reproval backed by sound, common sense spiritual advice. But in their long visit afterward he made an effort to shock her out of her severe emotional depression by making her aware of what was taking place in the larger world around her.

"There are serious problems confronting New Spain, concerns which have occupied Tristán, Don Antonio Riaño, General Calleja, Captain Lowell and myself in our every private meeting these past weeks," he told her. "These are vital matters which, as a Condesa with mines and vast landholdings, you must come to terms with *now*. Tristán

-- being a man deeply in love -- never discussed them with you because he wanted to shield you from any painful realities.

"However, our world is not the pretty, halcyon place you knew as a child. Our kingdom faces an imminent threat of encroachment from the North Americans -- a danger Tristán will soon confront. But sad to say, our gravest threat *comes from the Spanish Crown itself!*"

He described the Spanish Bourbon court as venal and corrupt. The reigning monarch was vain and spineless, a willing tool of his manipulative prime minister, the young and energetic Manuel Godoy. The queen and Godoy were lovers who openly flaunted their affair, making Spain and her cuckold king the laughing stock of all the courts of Europe. It was Godoy and the queen who, for private ends of her own, persuaded the king to retrocede Louisiana to France. For Napoleon to receive his fifteen million dollars from Thomas Jefferson, that French tyrant had only to reward this faithless queen with a small duchy's throne on which to seat a favorite grandson!

When Sirena asked how deeply this scandal would affect New Spain, Legázpi assured her it was already doing great damage, for the present viceroy was Godoy's personal appointee and his political creature in everything.

"Why do you think New Spain's present viceroy keeps imposing new 'Crown taxes' and forced loans upon merchants, miners, hacendados and the Church?" The Bishop asked, then answered his question, "This viceroy is merely doing his master's bidding, knowing he will soon retire to Madrid and a life of ease, taking with him his promised five percent of all these forced levies!"

Now, as the bells fell silent, Prime Minister Godoy's puppet rose and gave a self-adulatory address in which he boasted how he, as viceroy, had toiled twelve long years to erect this monument to his monarch. It was, he said, his own "personal tribute to His Majesty, King Charles the Fourth, and to his Prime Minister, the illustrious Manuel Godoy!"

In the center of the stone-paved plaza, mounted on an oblong pedestal, stood an immense shrouded figure. When the Viceroy finished speaking, four Indian boys tugged on hidden wires instantly unveiling a horse and rider of heroic size. There was a breathless silence, followed by loud expressions of admiration, swelling to sustained applause and cheers as the aristocratic guests gave a standing ovation to its sculptor, the renowned Don Manuel Tolsá.

Sirena had to admit the monumental equestrian bronze of the reigning monarch as a Roman Caesar, was a masterpiece of dynamic movement and strength. The massive stallion with its stylized Florentine mane and tail, seemed about to stride off its pedestal. The imperial rider's flowing toga, laurel wreath and straight right arm extending a baton, was a triumph of Roman force welded to Christian virtue. Instead of portraying his royal model as he truly was -- vacuous, middle-aged, and ponderously overweight -- Tolsá had created a lithe and virile Spanish Constantine.

The gallant, forty-year-old Tolsá took his place at the pedestal's base, bowing grandly. Sirena looked about to see if the maestro had deigned to share a little glory with his first assistant, but poor Lorenzo was nowhere to be seen.

"Superb, Maestro! Superb!" the Baron called out enthusiastically, when all the others had stopped cheering. Then, in the brief hush that followed, La Güera leaned across Sirena and boldly informed Baron Von Humboldt in clear ringing tones that filled the plaza, "Tolsá may have made a conquering hero of our cuckold King, *but he certainly doesn't know the male parts of a stallion!*"

Shocked at La Güera's brazenness, Sirena wished the stones of the plaza would open up and swallow them all. But Baron Alexander, richly amused, laughed -- a loud, lusty, contagious laugh -- that convulsed La Güera and reduced the two of them to helpless tears!

☙ ❧

Heartsick and lonely as Sirena was, having been stripped of the physical and emotional balm of what had been Tristán's abiding presence, she found that not even the heaviest heart could remain so in a city as proud and stimulating as Mexico. There was no denying the august presence of what the Bishop referred to as "New Spain's Imperial Trinity – *Christianity, Civilization and Monarchy!*"

On the long ride south from Guanajuato, Baron Alexander had bombarded Sirena with facts about the metropolis, from facts at his fingertips that he had gathered for his political essay on New Spain. She discovered he chattered on about science and statistics the way ordinary mortals gossiped.

"Did you know Mexico is the Queen City of the Americas?" he asked, then promptly explained, "with a population of one hundred-and-twenty thousand souls, she is twice as big as New York and *three times* the size of Philadelphia!" He said croillos, like herself, comprised nearly half of this population, while immigrant Spaniards numbered a paltry twenty-five hundred, a low figure that surprised Sirena. Having imparted that bit of wisdom, the Baron winked and added drily, "Not exactly what our anti-Spanish firebrand, Captain Allende, of San Miguel el Grande's Regiment calls the *"overwhelming presence of oppressive gachupínes!"* However, most of these Spaniards *do* hold high posts in Church and government, so the Captain may have a point."

There was no question Mexico was the crown jewel of Spanish America. Encircled by a ring of diamond-bright lakes and pearly volcanic peaks, her colorfully-tiled palaces, church towers, chapels and domes sparkled in the crystal clear air of the Vale of Anahuac. Her broad, tree-lined streets and avenues were wide enough for three large coaches to drive abreast, and the Baron had meticulously counted more than a thousand such coaches in Mexico!

The single thing about this capital the Baron deplored was its infamous *léperos*, as the homeless were called. By his estimate there were seventy thousand such scabrous vagos infesting the streets. Driven from village and farm by flood, failed crops, famine or merely man's eternal itch for change, this human flotsam and jetsam had been borne in on the inexorable tides of hope and despair for a good three hundred years -- long enough to be accepted as a time-honored institution and an ineradicable evil.

They slept in doorways, church atriums or under the huge open sheds which the larger pulque parlors were required by law to provide their besotted regulars, constituting a self-perpetuating population of eminently cunning beggars and thieves, which the upper ranks of society understandably feared. But when Sirena asked the liberal Baron to suggest some "enlightened European" cure for Mexico's age-old plague of léperos, he was unable to come up with even one.

Sirena's days were crammed with activities, which helped to numb the relentless pain of not only her separation from Tristán, but -- as the Bishop sharply admonished them both in their respective confessions to him -- a firm mutual renunciation of what his marriage and their close kinship decreed an 'illicit love' for each other. His parting exhortation still rang in her ears, "The pain of denying a great love is the anvil on which the souls of saints are forged!" I don't want to be a saint, she told herself over and over again. But that was not the point: Her cross had been laid upon her, and somehow she must learn to bear it.

Resolutely she took the Baron on tours of San Carlos Academy of Art, the Mint, Xochimilco's colorful Floating Gardens. They visited the great San Francisco Monastery, hub of the Franciscan Order's far flung missionary activities throughout New Spain and the Filipines. There in the sunny patio, they saw aged friars who looked as gnarled and grey as a stand of stricken trees, after serving thirty, forty, even *fifty* years in the Indian Missions of New Mexico, Texas, Arizona and California. It drew her mind back to Tristán, and her heart ached anew, knowing he would be in those remote regions soon.

On the handsome loggia of Tolsá's still unfinished building for the Royal School of Mines, the Baron gave a moving farewell speech and as a final gracious gesture donated to the school his costly collection of scientific instruments which he had brought from Europe and used on his travels. Baron Von Humboldt's final parting with Sirena – whom he still referred to as "my favorite silver lord" – was a mutually tearful one.

From December twelfth, when the city celebrated the Feast of Our Lady of Guadalupe, until January sixth, Feast of the Three Kings, the city's social season was at its height. This year the highlight of the social calendar was Noel LeClerque's debut at the famed Teatro Coliseo, with the opening of an original three-act *zarzuela* composed, staged and directed by himself.

"You were the one who always told me not to be nervous before a recital," Sirena chided her former tutor at the evening soiree Alicia Àvila was giving for him at her palace, following dress rehearsal. "No musician in the kingdom can hold a candle to you, Noel, and the first night audience is sure to give you a standing ovation!

"And if they *don't*," the pretty, green-eyed Alicia cut in saucily, "I'll never invite a single one of them to my *salon* again!"

"Doña Alicia, you always were a hopeless optimist," the self-effacing Noel replied, gazing at her fondly. "Why else would you have invited me here to Mexico?"

Sirena's eyes followed the two as he took Alicia's hand and led her to the floor for a stately polonaise. It did not surprise Sirena that they both danced superbly, for it was Noel -- years before at La Frontera and La Soledad -- who taught Alicia this very polonaise! Sirena was discovering that life had many ironic twists, for it was not Alicia, but her late husband who was responsible for inviting Noel to Mexico and securing for him this high post at the Teatro.

The old Mariscal was a dilettante who wrote reviews of musical performances and drama for the Gacéta de Mexico. He publicly deplored the low level of productions presented at the Teatro Coliseo by visiting European troupes. Then, just at the time Sirena finished her studies and was preparing to leave La Frontera, Alicia's husband wrote Noel inviting him to Mexico where the Mariscal himself would help launch his musical career.

Shortly after writing that letter the aged Mariscal had died, and the Alicia that Sirena now beheld was just emerging from her proscribed year of mourning. She was a beautiful, enormously wealthy widow of twenty-one, with the Mariscal's vast fortune and palace, a flock of young suitors and limitless social clout. She was eminently qualified to enjoy her state, for she loved entertaining, did it well and collected people with a connoisseur's eye. She dressed expensively, and through the help of her socially powerful friend, La Güera, she knew everyone in Mexico worth knowing.

Now as Sirena watched them together she saw they were gazing at each other adoringly. All at once it dawned on her -- Alicia was falling in love before her very eyes! As for Noel, hadn't he been eating his heart out over this coquette for years?

If Alicia's afternoons and evenings were given over to soirees in her salon, her mornings were dedicated to paying calls on noble ladies who had chosen the veil over matrimony. Sirena soon grew accustomed to having Alicia arrive at her door each morning at ten, her auburn hair covered by a rich lace mantilla, a dainty silk parasol held a-tilt against the bright winter sun and her taffy-colored spaniel, Puff, cradled in one arm, all ready to drag her unsophisticated norteña friend off to yet another nunnery.

This was a facet of Mexico which surprised Sirena, for near-atheist though he was, even the Baron admitted no other city in the world excelled it for charity. There were twelve major hospitals, all administered by religious orders. The Royal Indian Hospital was a Crown charity, and like Cortés' own Hospitál de Jesús, dated back almost to the Conquest. Other orders ran three special hospitals for the insane and a dozen free schools and orphanages. Even with bells pealing in her ears all day long, without the Baron's count she would not have believed there were a hundred churches and chapels in this 'American Rome'! She had doubted his claim of twenty-one monasteries for men and twenty-five convents for women, but through

Alicia's tireless efforts Sirena guessed she had seen the interiors of at least twenty convent parlors!

"Today we visit Sister Agatha of the Infante Jesús!" Alicia announced, the morning after Noel's soiree. "You're simply not going to *believe* the nun's parlor at *La Encarnacion*, it's *that* elegant!" Alicia rattled on as they settled into Alicia's sumptuous private coach.

Alicia explained that Sister Agatha had been the Fifth Marquésa of Verdugo before entering the religious life, and Sirena expressed surprise that a woman with a title as old as the Conquest would ever take the veil.

"She wanted no part of the marriage her father arranged. Luckily he's a pious old man whose aunt is a Mother Superior. Sister Agatha's Order wears the *prettiest* burgundy-red habit, and her Papá wept at the clothing ceremony, she looked *that* heavenly!" She sighed, half-enviously. "He promptly gave her three Indian servants to take in with her and a harpsichord to play in her cell. No wonder she adores convent life!"

When they entered the great sala of La Encarnacion, Sirena had to admit it was truly palatial, the walls covered with fine paintings and tapestries, the furnishings regal. The nuns were dressed in trailing wine-red habits and on her breast each wore a painted, gold-framed medallion, large as a dinner plate, bearing the likeness of the spiritual paradigm on whose virtues she modeled her religious life -- Cristo, Virgin or Saint. Each nun presided over her own private brood of visitors as jealously as any Mariscala over her elite *salonistas*.

When the pretty, but vapid Sister Agatha greeted them, Sirena noted her medallion featured a blond Infant Jesús, decked out like a royal *infante* and dangling a golden orb on a chain, as though all Creation were merely His toy!

"Yes, Condesa," she said, in that limpid, bell-like voice Sirena found these titled nuns cultivated, "we've renounced the world of Martha, and like Mary, chosen 'the better part.'"

She rejoiced at being unencumbered by such worldly minutia as pleasing a spouse, giving birth and running a noble house or hacienda. Sipping chile-spiced chocolate made from her own "secret recipe," Sister Agatha trilled, "Here there are no fathers, grandfathers or brothers to dictate our destinies."

Sirena got the distinct impression the nuns at this convent got extra points for drumming up new vocations! Sister Agatha omitted mention of the doting father whose fortune made her own blessings flow, but as Alicia said, rich dowries like hers fueled the engine of the city's charities!

Sirena found she heard more secular than sacred news in these female strongholds. Before Viceroy or Bishop got wind of some new scandal or saint, regulars like Alicia with their 'ever-itching ears', had long since heard it through the convent rumor mill.

"Our secret recipes have been closely guarded and handed down through the centuries," sister Agatha declared, behind a scrim of lowered eyelashes and modest smiles.

As expected, when they left, Alicia's basket was crammed with sweet Rom Popé and other rare liqueurs, each as cloying as their confectioners. For these Alicia left a princely donation, which in turn enabled La Encarnacion to feed a horde of léperos at its own back door! Mexico's byzantine, 'wheels-within-wheels' charities were positively dizzying!

"So, was your marriage to the late Mariscal a happy one?" Sirena asked as Alicia's coach took them toward the Virgin of Remedies' Asylum, where Sirena was paying her first call on Bishop Legázpi's childhood friend, Madre Pilar.

Alicia stroked Puff's silken ears. "Oh, yes. He liked dressing me up and showing me off, and I pleased him by having lots of fun in bed, *without* getting pregnant."

Sirena was bowled over by her candor, but also concerned. "Oh, Alicia, I had no idea you weren't able to have children!"

"Silly! I didn't say I *couldn't!* I meant we agreed not to have them. He wanted me to keep my figure, and so did I!"

Sirena was confused. "But when your mother was teaching us about -- you know, our monthly flux and men and all, she said when a lady marries she *can't help* having children, unless of course, she's barren."

"Sirena my pet, Mamá led a very sheltered life up at La Soledad. Marriage -- the real down-to-earth sexual scrambling isn't at all like her lady-finger version of it."

There was a brief silence, and then Alicia said shrewdly, "Trust me, a smart wife learns early on to put such staples as lime juice and vinegar to good use *outside* her kitchen." She tossed her head. "In fact, I'll give you the magic formula. You never know when it might be useful." She giggled. "Like Sister Agatha's confections, my secret recipe has also been carefully guarded and handed down through the centuries!"

Serious doubts about Alicia's virtue began tumbling through Sirena's mind. The Marquésa de Ávila, God rest her soul, had been a true mother to Sirena all those years at La Frontera. What would she think if she could hear her daughter saying such things?

"Well, now I've told you Noel and I are being married in May," Alicia said with an intriguing sideglance at Sirena. "What about you? You've been silent as a stone on the subject of your own love life and plans for marriage."

Before Sirena could compose an answer Alicia tapped her on the knee with her fan. "But first let me guess! You're here shopping for a titled husband?"

"I *am*?"

"Well, you couldn't have come at a better time. I know two-fourth Condes and one-third Marqués – on Isabel La Catolica street *alone*! – all of them in urgent need of titled wives."

Alicia stopped and looked at her friend reprovingly. "Honestly, Sirena, don't you hear the gossip going on all around you? Don't you know you're the most sought-after 'silver bride' in town?"

Sirena felt as though she were being scolded. "No, I guess not," she admitted weakly.

Alicia smiled. "Well its time you started making the rounds of the more prosperous old houses. You'll find the welcome mat is really out for you!"

Sirena drew her red wool cape around her defensively. "But that wouldn't be – honest of me, Alicia! I'm not the least bit interested in getting married – ever."

Alicia scrutinized her closely. "*So that's it!* You've got a vocation!" Her eyes lit up. "Then, what do you think of La Encarnación? As you can see, it's the only truly *elite* convent in town."

Sirena laughed aloud. "Licia, you of all people should know I wouldn't last a week in there, trading recipes and gossip all day long! I'd go mad!"

"Well, what is it then? You're not in love or I'd have spotted it. I always could read you like a book." Sirena felt unexpectedly pleased with herself. A bucolic milkmaid she might seem, but Alicia, for all her worldly ways had no inkling she was deeply in love, although Sirena felt it must show like a black mourning band on her sleeve.

"Actually, Alicia, I'm here to begin special classes as soon as the holidays are over."

Alicia's green eyes lit up. "Oh? What are you taking up? Dramatic recitations? Violin?"

"No, nothing like that. I'll be studying metallurgy at the Royal School of Mines."

"You're taking up -- *mining*?" Alicia's dancing eyes went blank.

"Yes. You see, I'll be running La Sirena soon."

Alicia looked disappointed. "Then what about Adrian?" she asked pointedly. "I was teasing you about the others, but you know Adrian's been in love with you *forever*." She buried her face in Puff's silky coat. "With Adrian you could marry him and run ten silver mines. God knows, he wouldn't care what you did by day so long as he could screw you every night!"

Sirena turned scarlet, "Really, Alicia!" she admonished her. "I spent a lot of time with Adrian on the road from Guanajuato. I think he finally realizes I don't intend to marry anyone. After all, I'm not the first titled woman in New Spain to settle for running her own business. A condesa can leave other lasting legacies besides children."

"I'm truly sorry. I'd always hoped we'd be sisters as well as friends."

"It's better for Adrian. Perhaps he can meet someone else and marry while he's here in the capital, before he has to go back to help your father with lambing season at La Soledad."

"It's a shame he has to return at all," Alicia said. "He's the one with the title. He deserves to marry well and live comfortably in the Ávila palace, here in Mexico where things are happening. If only David would shoulder his responsibilities as a second son, poor Adrian wouldn't have to live up there in the wilds to help Papá.

"Well, I was at San Miguel el Grande recently and I can tell you, David is obviously under the same spell as my own brother Ramón. Captain Allende is their idol, and his Regiment the only cause they live for! I don't know how Ramón is going to sail to Manila and back on business for me, without Allende always in his sights."

Alicia's always merry face grew sober. "By the way, the other night at dress rehearsal I warned Ramón to keep his hands off that blonde soprano he's been hotly pursuing. I happen to know she's the private stock of a colonel in the City's Royal Battallion. Ramón's begging for a sword through his *cajones* if he tries bedding that old goat's trollop."

After crossing an ancient stone bridge, Alicia's coach drew up before the convent-Asylum of Our Lady of Remedies. "Honestly 'Licia," Sirena said, "David and Ramón are both so feckless and footloose, I hate to think *where* their vainglorious notions about life could someday lead them."

"Now don't forget," Alicia reminded her excitedly as she left the coach. "Tomorrow's opening night! Dinner at my palacio, then we'll all go with Noel to the Coliseo!" She pressed Puff's face against her cheek and holding his tiny paw in her hand, made him wave a playful farewell through the coach window as she drove away.

Alicia was a dear but such a vain and empty-headed doll, Sirena thought, feeling a sudden uneasiness, almost a fearful premonition about Noel's future life with her.

19

Unlike Sirena's convent visits with Alicia, this one to Los Remedios was on business. Bishop Legázpi had advised her to meet Madre Pilar, for he was sure she could prove helpful to her. As it turned out, he was right.

It was a cool November morning and beatas, beggars and vendors crowded the atrium. A lay sister in a black wool habit admitted her into the inner patio and said Madre Pilar would be with her shortly.

Nothing could have been in sharper contrast to La Encarnación than this spare and Spartan convent. Even if she hadn't heard it from the Bishop, she would have known it was an Order of Strict Observance. There were no overstuffed parlors here, and probably, she thought with an ironic smile, no secret recipes either.

There was no mistaking the identity of the lean, handsome woman Sirena saw descending the staircase into the busy patio below. She could only be Madre Pilar. Everyone waiting below, looked up at her approach. Nuns and lay sisters passing her on the stairs paused to ask her advice. Women patients -- Sirena guessed only the less serious cases seemed to be about -- greeted her with transparent trust and affection.

Her eyes were large, very black and heavily lashed, her complexion olive, her face square, her manner brisk but amiable. She wore a wool habit of lively French blue, in honor of the Virgin. The large, framed medallion on her breast bore a painting of Our Lady of Remedies, the same pert and plucky-looking Spanish lady in a fan-shaped cope with scepter and crown, as graced the banners of Cortés when he first met Moctezuma on the causeway not far from here.

"My dear Condesa, forgive me for keeping you," she said, addressing Sirena in French. "I was delayed by that poor Indian family over there." With an almost imperceptible nod she indicated a trio on a bench near the wall. "They're from Cuautla, and faced with tragedy."

Sirena noticed a dark mestizo farmer and his solemn-eyed Indian wife in a grey rebozo. Their adolescent daughter sat sullenly beside them, inanimate as a lump of brown clay.

"When the girl was five a drunken Indian threw a lighted cigarette into the bell tower of a village church where fireworks were stored," she explained, leading Sirena through a door into a second, private patio.

"The explosion deafened her and she soon turned mute. But now she's reached womanhood her parents can't cope with her at home. So we will take her in as a lay sister."

Opening another door she ushered Sirena into a bright but austere office, and once the door closed behind her she quickly changed to speaking Spanish.

"I'm sure the girl will not only *feel* useful here, she will be so, in fact." Madre Pilar seated herself at a plain wooden desk, tall bookshelves stuffed with papers behind her and two comfortable chairs for guests facing her. Sirena selected one of them.

"There's so much to be done for our ladies -- everything from dressing their hair to delivering their babies."

"*Babies?*" Sirena asked. "I had no idea you had patients that young!"

"The tragedy of mental breakdown is no respecter of age," She leaned back in her chair. "Most people see Mexico's old families only from the outside: inside many are iron-clad patriarchies. Fathers and grandfathers may spoil their children, but they can also be repressive." She shot Sirena a confiding glance. "I'm sure by now you have met the famous La Güera Rodriguez?"

Sirena nodded.

"Her first husband beat her unmercifully. I knew it, so did many others. But no magistrate would hear her. So she hired a first-rate lawyer, proved her father married her off against her will, and her husband had stolen her dowry. She won a civil divorce and an annulment from the Church. But until then her only refuge was here at Los Remedios."

"I must say, your Asylum serves many unusual purposes."

"It has to, otherwise noble women would end up in charity asylums, or in those public houses of correction, where unlicensed prostitutes are detained until they are taught to master a more virtuous trade."

Sirena was amazed at Madre Pilar's candor.

"Our most tragic cases are those of sensitive young girls, forbidden to marry the men they truly love."

Sirena felt a deeply sympathetic twinge of pain.

"These caged birds from the best families find their way to me. Some I can mend and return to sanity, but the others -- ," she moved a silver letter opener from left to right of her desk. "The others never leave." She fell silent. "However," she continued on a brighter note, "here at least they receive the respect and care proper to their rank.

"The Bishop speaks so highly of your work, Madre," Sirena said admiringly, "and I can certainly see why."

"Ah, Diego!" Madre Pilar smiled reflectively. "But now I've rambled on enough about my work. Let's get on with the reason you've come." She pulled a folio of papers from one of the shelves behind her. "According to your letter you wish to mortgage an hacienda of yours located in the Bajío."

"Yes, Madre. La Torre has served for many years as a pulque plantation and a ranch for raising mules."

"And you wish to change the nature of that operation?"

Sirena nodded. "As you know, most of the great families here produce pulque on their ranches in the Valley of Mexico, for quick sale in the capital. Being so distant, La Torre can't compete with them in pulque sales."

Sirena leaned forward, elbows on the desk. "I plan to clear the property of magueys and re-plant it with a profitable turnip called *colza*. Most lamps in use throughout the capital burn an oil pressed from its seeds, but its not much grown in this region."

Mother Pilar nodded. "Do you have your own mill for pressing the oil?"

"No, but I have a friend here who has. He also has a contract to supply oil to the municipal lighting concessionaire. Perhaps you know him -- Don Francisco Durán?"

"Oh, Don Francisco!" Her face lit up. "That dear, saintly man! There's not a religious in the city who's not been touched by his goodness." Then, rifling through the papers briefly she said, "Condesa, all your holdings are admirably solvent, unlike most I see, which are mortgaged to the roof-beams from two centuries past."

"I was fortunate to have Don Francisco and my uncle directing my affairs until I came of age. This loan enabling me to plant turnips at La Torre, is less than a third of La Torre's market value. I estimate the annual crop will total a thousand *cargas*, delivered to the mill. The sale of seeds should earn six per cent per carga."

"Like all other religious houses extending mortgages, we charge a five percent annual interest rate. Since your credit is sound, I'll have the lay syndic who keeps my books prepare the papers for your signature right away."

"Thank you, Madre. And I expect to repay this loan in full within a year. I'm investing in the China trade, which earns quick and high profits. My brother sails to Manila next month to purchase my cargo of merchandise for me."

Madre Pilar glanced up quickly. "What an odd coincidence! He and I will be fellow passengers."

Sirena could not conceal her surprise. "You mean you will be sailing on the galleon?"

"Oh, yes," she said off-handedly, stacking the papers neatly, "Our Order maintains a similar house in Manila. One of our sisters there is ill, so I'm taking a nun out to replace her and bringing Sister Rosa home."

Sirena found it incredible. This woman, who must be at least fifty-five, was embarking on what Tristán had said was the most difficult and dangerous voyage in the world, and yet she acted as though it were a boat ride through Xochimilco!

"But Madre Pilar, I've heard it's a killing voyage -- especially for a woman!"

Madre Pilar looked at her serenely. "This will be my first trip, but other women religious make it all the time." Then with an imperturbable smile she added, "And of course, it *only takes a year!*"

❧ ☙

Returning from Los Remedios by cab, Sirena asked to be let out at the Cathedral so she could walk the length of the famed Street of San Francisco and the Silversmiths, back to the Graciana town palace at the end of the block. The architectural details and façades of these noble old palaces were well worth seeing, and she had not had time to enjoy them.

The Cathedral's deep-throated bells began to peal, and Sirena -- like every other man, woman and child on the streets -- stopped in mid-stride and dropped to her knees, reciting the mid-day Angelus. For the space of this short Ave all movement ceased and then quickly started up again. Rising, Sirena found herself in front of an especially magnificent old palace. The walls were faced with the reddish-brown stone the Aztecs called *tezontle*. In pleasing contrast, its doors and windows were trimmed with *chiluca*, a creamy white native stone that lent itself to the carver's art. Wrought-iron grills graced windows and balconies, while three stories above the entrance, on an oval stone medallion, was carved the owner's coat of arms, but far too high up for the legend to be distinguished from this vantage point.

Unlike other residences on this fashionable street, its front door was open to the patio. Catching Sirena's eye was a rough-hewn table where a short, bronze-skinned mestiza in grey rebozo was setting out tin trays of brightly colored cactus candies.

"*Buenos dias marchanta!* Which ones do you wish to buy?"

Sirena was astonished at the woman's brass. Didn't she know vendors were forbidden by law to put up stands on this exclusive street? More brazen still, she had set up her table *inside* the patio!

In spite of this, Sirena found herself drawn against her will by the rare sight of real cactus candy. "Buenos dias," Sirena greeted her, stepping hesitantly over the high threshold into the patio. "It really *is* cactus candy from Sonora!" she exclaimed. "I'm a norteña and I used to love it up north as a child, but I've never seen it here in the capital."

"I make my own, Señorita," the woman replied. "from fresh *tunas* and *pitahayas*, straining the mash for seeds, boiling it in sugar and spices and *ya!* -- *dulces del norte!*"

"I can't resist them," Sirena confessed, glancing guiltily over her shoulder. "I'll buy all you have."

The woman disappeared and while Sirena waited, she cast an admiring glance around the interior soaring up and around the spacious patio. A second mestiza emerged from behind a column, a girl who seemed tongue-tied in front of strangers.

Sirena smiled encouragingly. "I'd love to meet the mistress of this lovely old palace. Is she at home?" The girl nodded, but remained mute, and Sirena tried again. "Please, who is the dueña of this house?"

"The candy-maker," the girl ventured, "she's the *dueña de la casa*."

"No, no," Sirena insisted, "I meant what is the name of the noble lady who owns it?" The girl frowned, and then seemed to remember. "Oh, she's the Señora Luna-Mendoza, wife to the soldier, Don Tristán!"

Sirena went faint with shock and reached out quickly to a nearby column to support herself. At that moment the candy maker returned, her black eyes shining with friendliness. "My sister and I are norteñas, too. We get lonely here." Then, after Sirena paid her for the candy and rushed out into the street, the woman called after her, "Come back often, Señorita. I make cactus candy fresh every day!

In a near panic, Sirena crossed the street, her gaze going swiftly to the stone medallion high above the palace door on the opposite side. Surely there was some mistake, some easily explained mix-up of names. Then her heart sank, for there was no mistaking the distinctive configuration of castles, shells and stars that formed Tristán familiar Luna-Mendoza Coat of Arms.

Mother of God, she thought, walking slowly back to her own palacio, feeling it must be a dreadful dream, could it be that Tristán's half-Comanche wife lived only six doors down from her own palacio here on San Francisco street? Tristán had told her little about his marriage, but Bishop Legázpi had filled in the details. Without question these were Don José nieces, who deserved "to live in a city where coaches roll in the streets and ladies come to call!" What a tragic misjudgment the old Comandante had made! Now, having seen the way Catarina lived in the Luna-Mendoza family palace, Sirena understood the real tragedy of this contract marriage. What a terrible price Tristán had paid for his well-intentioned *beau geste*.

The Route of the Manila Galleon

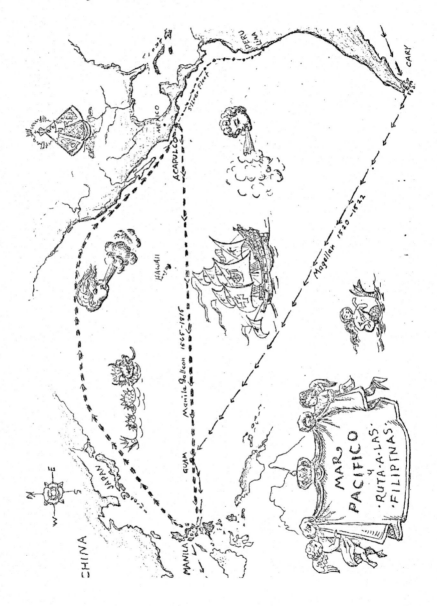

PART FIVE

THE LADIES' SEA

1804 -1805

The first of the galleons crossed the Pacific in 1565. The last one put into port in 1815.

Yearly, for the two and a half centuries that lay between, the galleons made the long and lonely voyage between Manila in the Philippines and Acapulco in Mexico. No other line of ships has ever endured so long.

No other regular navigation has been so trying and dangerous as this, for in its two hundred and fifty year history, the sea claimed dozens of ships and thousands of men and many millions in treasure. As the richest ships in all the oceans, they were the most coveted prize of pirate and privateer.

The Manila Galleon
By William Lytle Schurz

⌘20⌘

"It was gallant of you to accompany me across the sierra from Mexico," Sirena told Don Francisco as they sat together at sundown beneath a stand of fragrant pines, on the last day they would see each other for at least a year.

"My dear, I'd go all the way to Manila with you if I could," he replied. "I couldn't love you more if you were my own daughter, and I know how Patrick would feel about your making this voyage."

On the first leg of what promised to be a journey of high adventure, Sirena felt her heart beating faster as she sat here on a mountainside, gazing down upon the broad Valley of Cuernavaca, the torrid *tierra caliente* glowing like coals in the distance. They had been only two days on the road, their small party comprised of Madre Pilar, a young nun going out to replace the ailing nun in Manila, two lay sisters from Remedios, Sirena, with two Indian maids from her Mexico City palace and three mestizo arrieros serving as packers, drivers and guides.

She had glimpsed this lovely valley earlier from the pine-clad heights of *Trés Marias* -- three lofty peaks now far behind them. But here on the southern slope of the high mountain range dividing the Valley of Mexico from the tropical south, the valley's full splendor lay beneath them. Rippling fields of rice and sugar cane formed a vast inland sea, its chartreuse and amber waves rolling endlessly to a march of far blue hills where lay the silver-rich mining town of Taxco.

To their left Popocatepetl lifted his lordly presence, the western slope of its snowy cone a bright salmon-pink in the sun's last rays. The small, violet-shadowed peaks of a dozen failed volcanoes were strewn across the valley floor, like high-crowned sombreros tossed at random by a playful Creator. Directly beneath where the two friends sat on a knoll, lay the town of Cuernavaca, "place of eternal spring," which Sirena knew to be historic ground. Here, to this delicious clime, Aztec lords brought their favorite wives to be delivered: here too, Cortés -- with Moctezuma's entire realm to choose from -- elected to build his conquistadorial castle in whose shadow Europe's High Renaissance would burn itself out and be laid to rest at last.

An hour earlier the travelers had dismounted before the door of what Don Francisco assured them was the last decent inn they would find on the long China Road leading to the port of Acapulco. While the religious retired to their rooms to read the Little Office of the Virgin before supper, Sirena and Don Francisco remained here to watch the dying embers of this clear December day.

"As you know, this past month has been especially trying for me," Sirena said, reaching over to pat Francisco's hand fondly. "But you've been a real tower of strength and as always, your thoughtfulness has made everything bearable."

"I traveled this same route before you were born, so I know it can be torturous. I also know it wasn't an easy decision for you to make."

"The voyage?" She shrugged philosophically. "That was the simplest part. Ramón made it for me. I warned him twice about that blonde soprano, but he wouldn't believe me until the old colonel caught them backstage in each other's arms."

"Well, as long as they had to have a knife fight over her on opening night, at least the theatre lobby was empty and I got him quickly out of sight."

"And thanks to you, for the second time, the Army didn't get wind of it! But it infuriates me the way Ramón expects you to get him out of one scandalous scrape after another!"

Her anger mounted when she recalled that recently at Linda Vista, Ramón had been openly making free with Estella's pretty young daughter, Analinda. Later, when Sirena quizzed him about the girl, he bragged that Analinda expected him to marry her, then added insolently, "She's become my steady lay, without the vows, but I might just marry her to piqué Mamá!"

He knew Isabel would rather die than see him marry a quadroon, but Sirena was outraged that he would so deliberately debauch and deceive this innocent, trusting girl.

"He was luckier this time than last," Francisco was saying with a wry grin. "Despite his own wounds, the colonel didn't press charges, being even more afraid of scandal than Ramón."

Sirena thought back on her years of trying to salvage Ramón, rescue Felipe, make peace with Mercedes and Isabel, all to fulfill her promise to her father to care for them. It brought to mind the haunting question Bishop Legázpi had put to her before she left Guanajauto. "Has it ever occurred to you that all your caring for them might be your way of denying the sad truth that *not one of them* has ever really cared for or looked after *you*?"

His parting words to her had been equally profound and had troubled her ever since. "You and Tristán are both hostages to honor. You *each made a solemn promise to a dying man, and you've both become the victims of your vows!*"

"So don't give Ramón another thought!" Francisco said, clapping his hands to emphasize his point, bringing Sirena sharply back to the present. "He's safely hidden in my warehouse on the Zocalo 'til he recovers and can report back to Captain Allende's regiment in San Miguel el Grande."

"I suppose I should be glad Ramón wasn't killed," she said irritably, "but he created such a wild last minute scramble for me, getting myself ready and having all the viceregal permits and papers signed in time."

The cool breeze rising from the valley was sweet with the scent of sugar cane, the air softer than Chinese silk against her face. "No matter how it came about this voyage is the necessary business at hand, and going to Manila myself is a choice I'll have to live with. The hardest part of all for me was leaving Guanajuato."

"And parting from Tristán?"

She was taken aback by his insight, but not surprised. He always was able to see into her heart. She nodded, afraid words might bring on tears.

"I felt sure you were both falling in love when I saw you waltzing together at the first Riaño ball."

"Do you think others noticed, too?"

"No . . . I did, only because I happen to be -- well, let's say, more perceptive of such things."

"That's because you're a poet," she chided him.

"On the contrary. Poets and playwrights trivialize what is soul-searing pain by labeling it 'romance.'"

A servant brought a pot of hot chocolate and filled their cups. Francisco sipped his pensively. "Renouncing or losing a great love is the supreme tragedy of life."

It was like Francisco to wax eloquent on the subject of spiritual love, but Sirena noted something very personal in this remark and felt an even deeper empathy for him.

"Bishop Legázpi told me that 'unrequited love is the anvil on which the souls of saints are forged,'" she said, and she thought she saw Francisco flinch at the phrase.

Studying his features now in the twilight, she noted how handsome he still was, looking almost as young as when she first remembered him, his finely-textured skin tautly drawn over the splendid bone-structure of face and head, with only the tiniest lines visible at the corners of his mouth and eyes. But a kind of emotional frost seemed to have settled over him, a certain wounded look in his eyes, reminding her of the mute suffering of animals.

"I agree with the Bishop," he said slowly. "I had a great love once, but to my eternal sorrow I lost her."

This surprised Sirena. She had never heard a hint of any romance in Francisco's life, not even from Aunt Amantina, who knew everything about everyone! Sirena had a vivid image of him as a young man, kneeling at the grave of this sweetheart, carried off by death in the bloom of her youth.

A long, consoling silence followed, reminding Sirena of the wordless companionship that had existed between herself and Tristán, something she missed every bit as much as his physical touch.

"Francisco, I gave Tristán my solemn promise I would never go to Manila," she confessed, "do you think he will forgive me for breaking it?"

"Love forgives everything in the beloved."

Tears sprang to her eyes, and she felt she had to lighten the mood or they would both break down even before it was time to say goodbye. "Speaking of forgiveness," she said brightly, reaching into the pocket of her riding skirt. "I have a letter here from Mamá, and she asked me to read part of it to you."

Unfolding the letter she read aloud: " -- and please tell Don Francisco for me, how much I appreciate all he has done for my darling boy, Crispín, both at the School of Mines and by taking him into his home in Mexico. "

Sirena glanced up to mark his expression of pleasure, but he was staring intently into his cup. "'Please explain to him," she read on, "I'm glad to have him caring for my son, because *I know how happy it must make Crispín's own father!*'"

Sirena looked down at the letter in her lap and observed softly, "It's the first time since Papá died that she's spoken of you both in the same breath!"

Looking up she saw Francisco had turned deathly pale. "Francisco dear, are you feeling ill?"

"No, no," he replied hastily, passing a hand over his eyes, "it's just the dizziness that comes with the sudden change of altitude between Mexico and here. It will pass."

One of Sirena's servants called from the inn to inform them supper was about to be served. Francisco rose from the blanket and helped Sirena to her feet. "I'm starting back to Mexico at sun-up," he said quietly, "and you'll be heading south even earlier, so we'd best say our goodbyes now."

"Thank you again, Francisco for everything!"

"Remember now, you can trust Señor Woo implicitly. He's an honest agent who's worked for me for years. He'll get you the best prices, and he can help you find Felipe." He took her in his arms and hugged her to him. "It's a long hard voyage child, and while I'm sure your own dear father will be watching over you, do stay close to Madre Pilar. She's indestructible."

ॐ ॐ

The tierra caliente was not only an open oven door, it was also a door leading into a vanished, pre-conquest world. The unrelenting heat led to widespread Indian nakedness, with bare-breasted women washing clothes along lush riverbanks while their stark-naked children ran free. Indian men of all ages, bathed in tanks and streams in full view of travelers on the China Road, more free of shame than Adam before The Fall. Never having seen a grown man naked, Sirena was at first deeply shocked, but soon she gave their nudity no more thought than if they were brown trees lining the road.

After they passed Taxco, coconut milk became the official drink of the road. The heat was stifling, even for Sirena in her light dotted Swiss or dimity. For the religious in their heavy wool habits, it was a penance reserved for martyrs and saints. Clouds of ravenous gnats tormented them, and after ten days, mattresses were given up for native woven hammocks that were cooler.

Finally, on an oppressive morning after two weeks of misery, the thorny mesquite forest parted briefly and the exhausted women caught a tantalizing glimpse of the lava-dark cobalt sea. The long-awaited comforts of what their arrieros kept referring to as 'lithe great port of Acapulco' were finally at hand!

Madre Pilar celebrated by blessing herself and uttering an almost silent, "Gracias a Diós!"

From there the trail kept dropping and they found themselves behind another party also bound for the port, the suffocating dust its mules kicked up one last penance to endure. At a bend in the road, Sirena dismounted eagerly before an open-sided jacal with a hand-lettered sign proclaiming: *COLD coconut milk served he*re. The people just ahead had stopped here too, and were already inside ordering their drinks.

Stepping into the thatched jacal, Sirena noticed a gentleman standing at the long counter with his back to her, while an Indian woman filled his glass. In this remote jungle oasis she realized he had to be a total stranger, and yet there was something oddly familiar about him.

"A whole *real* for a glass of coconut milk?" she heard him ask in outrage.

Sirena saw the large Indian woman shrug and remark with a wicked grin, "It's COLD Señor, and you are HOT!" There were entire centuries of hostility in her few tart words.

Sirena smiled to herself. Apparently the poor fellow hadn't yet learned that travelers on the China Road were fair game for innkeepers and vendors all along the way. Last night her Indian host had demanded -- and gotten! -- three whole pesos for merely permitting her to hang her hammock under his scorpion-riddled thatch!

Grumbling, the gentleman at the counter paid the asking price and turned to find a table. When his gaze met hers, Sirena saw his expression turn from marrow-deep weariness to wide-eyed astonishment.

"Condesa?" he asked incredulously, doffing his wide-brimmed Panama as he bowed. "I can't believe it's you -- not here in this godless jungle!"

For a split-second Sirena's memory failed her, then she recognized him - the same chalky-white complexion, the dark hair tied back with a black-ribboned bow. A boy no longer, she guessed he was in his late twenties now, but everything else about him remained unchanged.

"Lorenzo Santa Cruz! What on earth are *you* doing here?"

"I'm on an art and business mission to Manila for the maestro, Don Manuel Tolsá." Sirena saw him flush with pride as the head of every gentleman traveler in the place turned at mention of that famous name. "And you Condesa? Surely *you* can't be sailing on the galleon, too?

Sirena accepted his drink, which he gave her gallantly. Tucking a strand of damp hair back under her Panama, she pressed the cool glass to her temple. "It's a rather long story," she said, basking in even this small relief from the murderous heat, "but, for better or worse, I'm afraid I am."

There was no mistaking his delight at this news. "Well, fortunately the long voyage over will give you time to tell me all the interesting details." He smiled and, touching her elbow, guided her to a rough-hewn plank that passed for a table. He pulled out a bench for her and then seated himself at her side.

"I'm traveling with Madre Pilar of Los Remedios," she explained as the religious entered and seated themselves at a nearby table. Sirena eyed her cold drink greedily.

"Please go ahead," Lorenzo insisted. "I know how thirsty you must be."

She gave him a grateful smile and drank deeply. "I never knew any place this side of Hell, itself, could be this hot. I must have consumed at least fifty liters of this ghastly stuff in the past two weeks."

"So have I," he commiserated.

A serving girl brought a second drink for him and he paid for six more, instructing her to serve the nuns and their servants as well. Madre Pilar smiled and thanked him with her eyes.

Slowly sipping her drink, Sirena felt a profound sense of relief. How nice to have the companionship of someone from home! For the first time since deciding to embark on this odyssey, she admitted to herself how intimidated she had been at the prospect of searching for Felipe and purchasing a cargo of exotic merchandise in a place as foreign to her as Manila. Never had she been without the presence of some protective man at her side, and the more she had thought about dealing with a people as reputedly sly as *Los Indios Filipinos*, not to mention the notoriously crafty Chinese, the more frightened she had become.

"Condesa, I can't tell you how pleased I am that we'll be fellow passengers," he enthused. His genuine, but respectful affection reminded her of the many times as a child she had sat on the marble vesting table in the chapel sacristy, watching him gold-leaf or paint the habit of some carved wooden saint, glancing up from his work occasionally to look at her in this same way.

"And once we reach Manila," he said earnestly," I'll be happy to help you in any way I can. I'm not boasting, but thanks to Tolsá's connections I have access to many influential people, in what, they call the Parián."

"That's kind of you Lorenzo. Don Francisco gave me the name of his agent there, but I might still need your assistance." She laughed and confided self-deprecatingly, "As for my engaging as a merchant in the China trade, I must confess I'm a rank amateur."

"But Condesa," he exclaimed admiringly, in a tone of true brotherly concern, "you are very young and gently reared. I think it's positively -- *heroic* of you to even try!"

Slightly embarrassed by his almost worshipful tone, she busied herself with her drink and drained the glass. Then, anxious to put them both more at ease, she tapped his arm lightly with her closed fan. "Lorenzo, we've been friends since childhood. There's no need for you to use formal address with me. Please feel free to call me Sirena, just as you used to do."

21

Two hours ride from the wayside jacal, the China Road emerged from the jungle and became a dusty trace meandering over a flat, sun-baked plain. On the far horizon the slab of cobalt sea they had seen from afar was now a sheet of silver, mirroring a white-hot sky. Beyond a file of dust-white palms was a savage looking reef of black rocks encircling the shore like a pack of prairie wolves.

A shimmering blanket of dust from dozens of mule trains churning north and south, hung over everything. Its glare was blinding. Shading her eyes, Sirena looked ahead at a scattering of adobe hovels, jacales, and a few wooden shacks made of boards as white as old bones in the sun.

"How much further is the great port city of Acapulco?" she asked one guide impatiently.

"Not much further than I can spit," he replied, "That's Acapulco you see -- dead ahead!"

Sirena was both appalled, and furious at herself. She had been around Mexican Indians all her life and should have known her guides had spun their seductive tales of clean inns and cool baths to make the sufferings of the China Road more bearable. Now their secret was out, all three arrieros let loose a flood of ghastly truths about the real Acapulco.

It was a pest hole. Any criollo or Spaniard lingering longer than the galleon's two-week fair, was 'waltzing Sister Death.' Any white port official who lived long enough to be promoted to a less pestilential post, was held in as much awe by the locals as if he had been assumed bodily into Heaven before their eyes. The dread 'Black Vomit' fever, was its foremost claim to fame. Then, with their horror stories of 'the great port' all told, the arrieros unloaded the women's baggage with indecent haste, received their pay and decamped for Mexico.

Driven by an urgent need to find the galleon's captain and arrange for boarding, Sirena took a quick bath and changed into a fresh dimity. A leghorn hat and a pink parasol were her sole defenses against the remorseless sun. With her two terrified Indian maids in tow, she found a rickety cab for hire, driven by a loquacious Malay, and drawn by a blinkered rail of a horse, so nearly dead even a footsore Apache would have thrown it to the wolves.

"The galleon made port here from Manila six weeks ago," the driver said, "and she'll be outward bound again any day." This information only heightened Sirena's urgency.

They passed a stone church, two well-built convents and a solid-looking hospital, rising from the sand, which the man said, were all run by nuns and friars. Dear God, Sirena thought, their daily miracle must be staying one step ahead of the port's Grim Reaper!

"When the galleon puts in after nine months at sea," the Malay explained, "many passengers are so near dead they're *carried off* the ship! The hospital fills up and stays that way 'til sick folks either go up to Glory or get strength enough to make it back across the hot lands to Mexico."

Well, Sirena told herself fiercely, when we return I'm going to *walk off* the galleon! I'd rise from the dead to get out of here!

"Once the fevers got so bad," the man went on, "one governor had a deep notch cut in the mountain over there to give the 'dead air' a way out." Sirena saw the deep "V" still visible in a hill behind town. "But the air didn't go."

Northeast of town they passed the great octagonal-shaped fortress of San Diego that commanded the entire bay. Its high walls of dressed stone bristled with eighty cannon, manned by black soldiers called, pardos -- the only men alive who seemed to thrive in this lethal climate.

"No pirate ship or British gunboat's ever goin' to take Acapulco!" her driver boasted. Looking back at the squalid port Sirena asked herself, who would even want to *try*?

Then, Sirena caught her breath as the great galleon came into view. She was moored in a little cove, inland from the harbor, tied up to two tall trees. The ship was huge beyond belief, so gargantuan she marveled it could float: her masts reached as high as the bell towers of Mexico's metropolitan cathedral, and dozens of toothpick-thin Malay sailors were flitting fearlessly through a maze of masts and rigging.

Turned now in readiness for departure, her bowsprit was pointed toward the mouth, presenting a clear view of her carved and gilded sterncastle, with its balconies and diamond-bright windows. At this tide the bottom row of gun ports was level with the dock and the ship's cannon drawn back to allow an army of sailors to shove cargo through them into the hold. Across the stern in gold letters, was the ship's name: El Santo Niño de Atocha. What a good omen, Sirena thought, and blessed herself in gratitude.

But the sight of so many cannon reminded her the galleon not only carried passengers and cargo, but was a fully armored fighting ship as well.

"They had to arm her to fight off buccaneers," the garrulous Malay said. "French, Dutch, English or mongrel -- they're all after this richest prize afloat!"

Suddenly Sirena wished the man would desist. Both her Indian maids were getting the glassy-eyed look of terror that always presaged full flight. And she could do without any more grisly news herself. This morning at the jacal when she asked about the risk of pirates, Lorenzo assured her she had nothing to fear. "Why, in two-hundred and forty annual crossings, pirates have taken only *four* galleons."

Then a gentleman at a nearby table had the bad grace to contradict him. "Sir, you forgot to tell the lady that a full *thirty* others were shipwrecked, burned or lost at sea!"

As the cab lurched to a halt in the galleon's shadow, soldiers, sailors and merchants swarmed everywhere, carrying everything from hens in crates to chests of silver coin. Several gentlemen, using special canvas slings, were struggling to hoist four Spanish barbs aboard, the spirited animals kicking wildly and screaming with fright. All at once Sirena became completely rattled. How could she ever find the captain in this melee? She stood up in the carriage, her parasol warding off the sun, searching frantically for the uniform that matched the man.

"Condesa, you look lost!"

Turning her gaze from the ship to the direction of the voice, she saw Lorenzo alight from a carriage and come striding toward her, grave concern for her stamped on his face.

"Oh, Lorenzo, I really am lost!" she said. "Madre Pilar and the nuns are at the inn, prostrate from the heat. And, I'm trying to find whoever's in charge so I can give him our papers. But everything's so confusing -- I can't tell the captain from the cooper!"

"Come, Condesa," he said, offering his arm, "I'll take you directly to the proper authority!"

"It's quite true, the Chinese *are* a crafty race," their Captain, Don Patrick Eagle, was saying as he presided over dinner in the galleon's Great Cabin, the second night at sea. "But be forewarned -- not *all* are equally so."

A stocky, florid-faced Irishman of middle age, Eagle's stance on deck had given Sirena the impression he was as securely affixed to his ship as its own mainmast. With his large, beaked nose, heavily lidded eyes and long-tailed green coat he reminded her of a parrot. But he seemed a born storyteller, who loved to pass his tales on to others over wine.

"In Manila," the Captain continued, "they tell the classic story of a Spaniard whose nose was eaten away by a rare disease. Upon arrival he was told the mainland Chinese were wizards at carving, so he asked one to fashion him a new nose out of wood. The carver made him a perfect nose, and the Spaniard gladly paid a princely sum.

"So that same crafty Chinese carver met the next year's galleon with an entire cart full of wooden noses! Too late he learned there was no demand for this article of trade."

The story made its point, the guests were amused, and Sirena began to feel bolder about dealing with the not-always-crafty Chinese merchants in Manila's Parián.

Sirena and the nuns fell quickly into the routine of shipboard life. The passage was smooth, the Pacific living up to the name the first galleon pilots gave it, *The Ladies' Sea*, because it was far gentler than the boisterous Atlantic. The cabins were small but comfortable, each passenger limited to two servants, two trunks and a chest for personal food. Sirena had no servants. Her two petrified Indian maids had deserted her when they got back to the inn, fleeing to Mexico with the same arrieros who had brought them south. One of Madre Pilar's two lay sisters helped with the few chores Sirena did not do for herself.

Three large bands of religious were on board -- Dominican nuns, Franciscan missionaries and male Hospitaliers of Saint John of God. One of Lorenzo's former teachers at San Carlos was going out to Manila with his wife, to teach in a royal art school there. The highest-ranking government official aboard was the new Captain General of the Islands, sailing with his wife and daughter to take up his post.

As the weeks passed and Sirena got to know Lorenzo, she was surprised to find the mild-mannered apprentice she knew as a boy, had become a moody and rebellious young man, resentful of all authority or restraint.

"It's ridiculous I'm not allowed to smoke on this ship, even in calm weather," he complained to her one day. "Captain Eagle is a second Captain Bligh!"

Sirena knew cigarettes were forbidden, and why, but other smokers seemed able to substitute the permissible pipe or cigar. Why couldn't Lorenzo do the same?

"God knows, a simple game of *mus* is hardly a crime," he exploded one evening, "but Captain Eagle considers gambling for stakes as perilous as blasphemy!"

It was only when she asked how he had enjoyed his years at San Carlos Academy that Lorenzo provided clues to his change of character.

"I didn't enjoy it at all," he replied. "The other students treated me like a pariah from my very first day."

Despite Don Patrick's full payment of his fees, word somehow got around that Lorenzo's father was a casta muleteer. He insisted he was not merely ostracized, but singled out for persecution. The work that won him First Prize and the praise of Tolsá, had been his drawing of a naked Indian, a *cargador*. "That proved which side I was on!" he added bitterly. He claimed the other students worked from plaster casts of Greek and Roman statues, and that only he had "dared to work from life!" This was a false claim, for Sirena knew that all students at San Carlos also worked from nude male models. He claimed the criollo students envied his talent as much as they despised his casta blood, and that his five years there had been 'My Purgatory'.

At other times Lorenzo was the very soul of charm. He did a quick sketch of the Captain General and won a commission to paint three family portraits as soon as they reached Manila. The young mestiza governess to the Captain General's daughter fell completely under his spell, and Sirena was sure she would marry him in a minute if he asked. It was clear he enjoyed being the center of so much attention and respect.

But for all his moodiness, Sirena had not felt uneasy in his company until soon after they stopped at Guam to take on fresh water, vegetables and fruit. She was sitting on deck reading, while Madre Pilar and sister Rita were busy embroidering altar cloths.

When sister Rita left them to pray before the Virgin's statue, enshrined on the quarterdeck, Madre Pilar took the opportunity to address Sirena in confidence. "The Señora Sandoval knows your young friend, Lorenzo Santa Cruz."

"Yes, Lorenzo told me Maestro Sandoval was his favorite teacher at San Carlos." "Please understand, it's none of my affair, but I feel obliged to pass on her remarks -- for your own protection."

"Of course Madre, what is it?"

"According to Señora Sandoval, Lorenzo -- good student though he was -- pursues a private life that is. . ." Madre Pilar's black eyes followed her flashing needle, "I think she used the term 'dissolute'."

Some of the Señora's remarks squared with what Sirena already knew about Lorenzo, but the rest she found shocking and deeply disappointing. In the Capital he consorted with an unsavory class -- gamblers, drinkers, womanizers. He sought out and paid destitute young women to pose for him in the nude, and kept favorite models in his home as concubines. Over drinks with Maestro Sandoval, in port before sailing, Lorenzo said the galleon should revive its former custom of letting each male passenger bring along a female companion for 'carnal solace'. He said he was going to find it 'sheer Hell,' not being able to indulge his 'voracious sexual appetites' daily, as was his custom in Mexico.

"Señora Sandoval passed these facts along to me as a cautionary tale. She knows you're in my care and it's my duty to warn you of danger from whatever quarter."

Sirena felt the careful inner balance she had maintained with Lorenzo beginning to slide, like cargo in the hold that has not been sufficiently well secured.

"Even before the Señora told me this, I observed the way Lorenzo looks at you," Madre Pilar said, stitching steadily. "I've had experience with other men of his class in the city. They resent what most aristocrats are -- industrious, socially secure, with an inborn sense of *noblesse oblige*. They do not wish to emulate such virtues, which in fact they *envy*, but they do ache to possess the aristocrats' wealth and power." She looked steadily at Sirena. "I've seen all these same things in Lorenzo's eyes, whenever he looks at you."

Sirena took Madre Pilar's warning soberly. Yes, where indeed might not the smallest misstep lead? A bungled embrace, an attempted kiss, forcing her to tell him flatly that she did not return his feelings and never could -- all questions of class aside. She would hate for it to come to that, not only because she was fond of him, but because she sensed he had a spiteful side that might even turn vengeful.

The first thing she would do was to stop depending on him for anything. He had been helpful getting them aboard, but she could not risk his becoming overbold. She made up her mind that when they reached Manila she would deal with the Parián merchants *entirely on her own*, not relying on the help of any man, except of course, Francisco's dependable agent, Señor Woo.

22

"Ah, yes!" Sirena exclaimed grandly to her nun companion and any merchants who might overhear. "One can travel the wide world over, but no store can hold a candle to the merchandise one finds here in the shop of Señor Woo!"

Standing in the center of Señor Woo's store in Manila's crowded Parián, she hoped a bold show of knowledge would convince the Chinese agent and his clients that she knew a thing or two about the China trade.

It was early April, but the heat in the shop was tantamount to being inside a glowing brass brazier with its cover on. Although melting, she tried to exude confidence in an Empire gown of ice-blue silk, its deep décolletage screened by a sheer scrim of chiffon drawn close at the throat. Short puffed sleeves left her arms bare and, while she disliked wearing hats, she affected a small bonnet tied with a big taffeta bow, adding a touch of Parisian elán. Behind this cosmopolitan façade she was so intimidated by her exotic surroundings she had to clasp both hands on the handle of her parasol to control their trembling.

The voyage from Acapulco had taken three tedious months. After resting a few days at Madre Pilar's neat-as-a-pin hospital-asylum in Manila, she had set out this morning to meet Señor Woo. She was accompanied by Sister Carolina, a Filipino-Spanish nun who spoke Chinese and Tagalog, as well as fluent Spanish. Except for this concession to Manila's strict social code on chaperones, Sirena was as free to move about as any male merchant. Best of all, with Sister's language skills, and Señor Woo, she would need no help from Lorenzo.

The Parián was an enormous square plaza with a monumental stone cross in its center. Facing the cross from all four sides were scores of shops, all fronted by a common, unbroken arcade, supported by stout wooden posts. Each shop's storerooms and warehouses were located at its rear, all backing against a high wall, which enclosed the entire mercantile compound. The palm-thatched arcade gave non-acclimated merchants, like herself, merciful protection from sun and rain, each of which in its own season, hammered down on the treeless plaza with horrendous force. The Parián offered few amenities, but Sirena knew more money changed hands here in a single day than it did in an entire month anywhere else in the Americas.

Just across a small inlet lay the bustling Spanish port of Manila, with its Baroque and neo-classic stone churches, palaces and shops, all securely locked behind a high city wall. As Madre Pilar had explained to Sirena, in earlier times devastating pirate attacks from without, and bloody uprisings of its Chinese population from within, prompted a wise Captain General to fortify Manila city and harbor. This isolated and contained the volatile Sangleys in their own Parián, safely separate from Manila.

The typical, sly-looking Chinese clerk Sirena expected to find, was not tending the front counter of the shop. Instead a white-haired Chinese, who looked more like a philosopher, regarded her from under snow-white brows. If this man -- her very first Sangley -- was indeed Señor Woo, she meant him to see she had a fat purse and a perceptive eye.

"Señor Woo?" she asked, approaching the counter with sister Carolina at her elbow. The old man inclined his head politely, but did not respond.

"I wish to speak with Señor Woo," she said, re-phrasing her request.

When he still did not reply the nun asked him in Chinese, bringing on a flood of agitated words and gestures. Sister Carolina listened intently, nodded and signaled Sirena silently that they should leave.

Outside under the arcade, jostled by merchants, storekeepers and swarms of beggars, Sirena quizzed the girl impatiently. "Is he Señor Woo? What did be say?"

"It doesn't look good," the nun parried. "It seems agent Woo is a habitual gambler. He's been playing a marathon game of mus at another Sangley's house for the past two days and nights and. . ."

Sirena was baffled. "So?"

"Señor Woo is also a very punctual man, *'muy formal'* as you Spanish say. It's not like him to neglect the shop even for his abiding vice. His counter man thinks some mischief has befallen him."

While Sirena stood helplessly, wondering which way to turn, a Chinese man in dark silk jacket and trousers came rushing toward them, pushing his way through the crowded arcade. Sirena felt relieved. Perhaps this was Señor Woo himself, *formalidad,* having triumphed over his passion for cards. The man raced past them and into the shop, where, in animated and shrill Chinese, he harangued the increasingly distressed counter man. Suddenly the nun, who was taking it all in, grabbed Sirena's arm. "Come!" she ordered her, "there's no use staying now!" In almost desperate haste she pushed her way to the single gate leading in and out of the Parián, dragging Sirena forcibly in her wake.

"But why are we leaving?" Sirena cried, "Perhaps the man has news of. . ."

"He *has*!" Sister Carolina said firmly, forcing their way through the gate. Not until they were well away from the noisy compound and safe inside Manila's walls did sister Carolina deign to impart her news. "All Sangleys are inveterate gamblers," she began, "so indeed Señor Woo is no worse than the rest -- if perhaps more sorely tempted."

"But *where* is he?" Sirena asked, running out of patience. "What's happened to him? Did he win? Did he lose?"

"He lost, *heavily,*" the girl sighed. "And since it's the time-honored custom among Sangleys so disgraced -- ," she blessed herself neatly and added matter-of-factly, "to save the family honor he went home and hanged himself."

"Hanged himself!" Sirena cried, standing stock still in the street. "You mean Señor Woo committed *suicide* over -- over a game of cards?"

"It's common here. The man who came running was his nephew. He had just found the body."

"Merciful God!" Sirena breathed. She had not even laid eyes on Don Franciso's dependable agent and he was already dead by his own hand! She said a silent Ave for his soul, heathen though he may have been. Dear God, what an inauspicious start! Where and how would she ever find another agent she could trust?

"Sister, do you know any agents in the Parián?" she asked, as they made their way along the streets of Manila, "I must find someone to take Señor Woo's place."

"The practice here is to approach a fellow countryman who already has an agent," the nun advised, looking not unlike a Chinese merchant herself, hands tucked into the ample sleeves of her French blue habit. "It's always done 'by reference only' as the Sangley's say."

Sirena was dismayed, but she was not going to admit defeat on her very first day in the trade. Setting her jaw, she opened her reticule and fished out the card Lorenzo had given her with his Manila address. *Just this once*, she told herself fiercely.

☙ ❧

"I hate to trouble you Lorenzo," Sirena began hesitantly, "but I need to find a new agent, and I've really no one else to turn to. . ."

Lorenzo was staying in a palatial downtown mansion with a very wealthy Spaniard, a friend of Maestro Tolsá. He welcomed her with obvious pleasure, and invited her into the cool, high-ceilinged sala, where she sat now sipping a refreshing drink, while he pondered her request with great attention and concern.

"It's already April," she continued, "and I'm told the galleon must sail for Acapulco by the twenty-fourth of June. Time is short and I've no idea where to begin." She paused, wondering if she dared trust him with the even more delicate matter of her search for Felipe. Then, taking a deep breath she plunged into that distressing subject. "Another problem facing me is -- well, my brother Felipe is missing somewhere over here. . ." She was in an agony of embarrassment. She had never meant to tell anyone who knew her family about Felipe's mysterious disappearance.

"Felipe is here in Manila?" Lorenzo asked in disbelief.

"Yes, he came two years ago. He's either dead or being held for ransom by pirates of some sort, but no one has contacted the family to demand the usual ransom."

She told him what little else she knew, and explained that a large amount of her own investment money had vanished with Felipe.

"My dear Sirena," Lorenzo said, "I'll contact Manuel Tolsá's own Sangley in the Parián at once."

"I'm very sorry to bother you with all this," she apologized, fighting down her anger at the luckless Señor Woo for causing her to lean on Lorenzo this way.

"Please don't apologize," Lorenzo said, with an openly admiring glance. "You forget how much I owe the House of Graciana. This gives me a chance to repay that debt in some small fashion."

His remark made her feel vastly relieved. It was true, her father's tactful sponsoring of him had lifted a gifted boy, doomed by lowly birth, into the coveted class of 'criollo gentleman.' No matter that Lorenzo's libertine habits might jeopardize this hard-won status, in class-conscious New Spain, making it possible for a fair-skinned casta to enter white society was no small thing. Yes, the Conde's gesture did counter-balance this modest favor.

When she rose to go he bowed and kissed her hand. "You'll hear from me tomorrow without fail," he murmured, holding her hand in his an uncomfortably long time. She sensed again a virile, leopard-like aura surrounding him, which she first noticed on the voyage. It made him physically attractive to women, but now it filled Sirena with feelings of deep distrust.

However, Lorenzo proved as good as his word. The following afternoon his carriage called at Remedios Asylum to pick up Sirena and Sister Carolina. The coachman drove all the way across town and far out into the countryside, beyond the city walls, drawing up at last before a Chinese-style mansion built of native hardwoods.

Sirena persuaded her nun chaperone to wait in the carriage while she and Lorenzo dealt with a very delicate matter concerning her brother.

As they mounted dark hardwood stairs to the broad veranda surrounding the house, Lorenzo divulged the identity of the Sangley they were about to meet. "Her name is Su Mei. She is a niece of your own agent Woo, but she runs her own independent trading company." Then speaking very softly he added, "She told my Sangley she knows where Felipe is."

When a richly dressed man servant admitted them into the mysterious SU Mei's presence, Sirena was surprised to see a very young Chinese-Spanish mestiza of exceptional beauty. She sat in regal isolation at the far end of a long, highly polished teak table, her pale, tented hands reflected in the glossy wood, a white pavilion mirrored in a dark lake. She asked them to be seated at the opposite end of the table.

"Condesa, I am Su Mei. Welcome to my home." She inclined her head. "Since fate and bad cards have robbed you of the services of my late uncle, family honor obliges me to offer you every assistance."

Her large brown eyes seemed enormous in her small heart-shaped face. Her shining, black hair was wrapped in elaborate coils, and spiked with sticks of jasper and jade. She's not a day older than I, Sirena guessed, but she looks for -- all the world -- like a Ming Empress.

"I'm told you are Don Felipe's sister?"

Sirena nodded, afraid to speak lest some careless word of hers might shatter the fragile hope Su Mei was extending.

"Your brother dwells with me here in this house," Su Mei said quietly, "but do not expect him to return to New Spain with you." She fixed Sirena with an unflinching gaze. "He belongs to others now."

"Who?" Sirena dared to ask in a whisper.

Su Mei rose from the table. "Come with me. You'll see." As she and Lorenzo followed Su Mei down a long corridor, Sirena could not help but admire this delicately formed young woman who carried herself with such queenly grace.

Su Mei led them through a large sala and into a small room opening off of it. On a low table a lamp burned dimly beside a couch draped in paisley silks. There, Sirena beheld an almost unrecognizable Felipe. He was lying propped up against an array of pillows his face sallow and gaunt, black circles beneath his eyes. He was half-drowsing with a long-stemmed pipe in his slack lips.

For Sirena the lamp by the couch cast its light on a totally bizarre world. None of the answers to the multitude of questions bombarding her mind made any sense. This Felipe, who bore no resemblance to the spoiled and carefree youth she remembered, was a disgusting stranger, cloaked in a cloud of sweet smoke, totally beyond the reach of reality.

"He came to me from the galleon," Su Mei was saying in a whisper. "He was suffering from a tropical ague and in unbearable pain. Opium was the only thing that gave him relief." She turned to Sirena with a radiant smile. "Luckily for him, I trade in it."

Su Mei closed the door as though deciding they had seen enough. "Eventually he recovered from the fever," she continued, as they retraced their steps, "but not his need for its cure." Su Mei smiled again, this time a sweet but cynical smile. "I love him and -- in his own way -- he loves me. So I'm willing to share him with what we *Manileños* call 'the flowers in the blood'."

They seated themselves at the table again in the same distant configuration. "I'm a successful merchant, so I had no need of Felipe's investment money. Now that I find it is actually your money anyway, you have a hundred thousand pesos more to spend with me than when you came in."

Very cooly, Su Mei laid out her terms. As Sirena's agent, she would help her select a fine cargo, rare and costly items from mainland China seldom offered ordinary merchants from Spanish America. Their cost would be a fraction of that charged in the Parián. "I do this to redeem my uncle's good name," she said, "and on certain rare articles I can guarantee that your profit, when they are sold in Mexico City, can be as much as a thousand per cent. But," she added with a firmness that belied her lotus-like fragility, *"Felipe stays with me."*

Still stunned by the frightful apparition that had once been her half-brother, and with no alternatives to offer, Sirena agreed to Su Mei's terms.

"You're white as a sheet," Lorenzo said as they walked back to the coach. "Seeing Felipe like that was horrifying!" she said shakily.

Lorenzo placed his arm supportively about her waist. "Try to put him out of your mind, Sirena," he murmured, "there's nothing more you can do for him."

"Oh, Lorenzo, promise me you'll keep this a secret? Please don't tell anyone where he is or what's happened to him? Mamá would die of grief and shame!"

"You have my word as a gentleman," he murmured. Then, looking at her quizzically he asked, "But what *will* you tell Doña Isabel?"

"The same sort of white lie she would tell," Sirena said slowly, speaking as if she were actually thinking aloud. "I'll simply tell her he gambled heavily and lost, and to save the family honor -- as is the custom over here, *he went home and hanged himself!"*

∽23∾

As it turned out Sirena did not give up on Felipe so easily. In the weeks that followed she visited him several times, and once he was even coherent enough to discuss the possibility that he might return with her to New Spain.

"What's back there for me?" he asked, his lips curled in a bitter smile. "You've got the title, Mamá's got Don Telmo, Mercedes has Neto, Ramón's got his fucking Queen's Regiment, and I have -- *what?*"

"You know the Graciana mine will go to you eventually."

"You really *are* a true believer, aren't you?"

Her eyes narrowed. "What do you mean?"

"I mean I saw Don Telmo's will before I left. An old school friend of mine from San Nicolás is the lawyer who drew it up, and as a *very* special favor he showed it to me."

"What has the will got to do with anything?"

"A lot. He doesn't just own title to that mine, handed him on a silver plate by that most astute of businesswomen, Doña Isabel. The son-of-a-bitch is leaving it and everything else that might have come my way-- not to Mamá but to *'my beloved nephew and sole heir, Don Ernesto, who at this writing is affianced to my adopted daughter, Mercedes.'"*

The day before the galleon was due to sail, Sirena and Lorenzo paid a final visit to Su Mei at her home.

"I see you are attracted to the Condesa, "Su Mei told Lorenzo candidly, as soon as Sirena had left the room to bid Felipe goodbye.

"I'm an artist," Lorenzo replied, leaning back lazily in his chair, "I'm naturally attracted to beauty, and she happens to be quite beautiful. However," his dark eyes flickered appreciatively over the ivory skin, delicate features and enticing figure of Su Mei as she sat curled up on a couch facing him, "*you* also hold a very strong sexual attraction for me – from the moment I first laid eyes on you."

Su Mei gazed at him with a frankness matching his own, her eyes eloquently inviting, but when she spoke she surprised him by changing the subject abruptly.

"The return voyage to Acapulco is never so easy as the one coming over. We Manileños have a saying, "On the eastbound galleon Death signs on as Third Pilot.'"

She let a pillow's silken fringe spill through her fingers. "I've never made the voyage myself, but I know that some ladies who survived frightful galleon voyages were driven mad by the terrors they endured. Madre Pilar knows their stories well. I like Sirena, and wouldn't want to see her suffer that fate." She walked to an armoire, took out a small, intricately carved camphor chest and handed it to him.

"This chest contains six vials of liquid sedative," she explained. "In case of storms or God forbid, a shipwreck, make Sirena drink one vial. The sleep it brings will spare her suffering." She stretched out on the couch, observing him with cat-like arrogance. Lorenzo could almost hear her purr.

"It's not opium," she assured him, answering the question in his eyes. "However, since she tells me she'll never marry, and you have her conquest on your mind, you'll be glad to know it is also a strong aphrodisiac. Not for the man," she added quickly, "but the woman. Some gentlemen say it makes prayerful virgins lustier than brothel queens."

"I heard of this potion in Mexico," Lorenzo said, eyes alight, "but its claims were so amazing I dismissed it as some Casanova's fantasy."

"If you care to see how well it works," Su Mei said with quiet urgency, lowering her voice as she heard Sirena's step nearing the door, "come to me tonight." She leaned forward and the low cut gown exposed her full, lotus-like breasts. "I don't let just *any* man give this drink to me," she murmured slowly and ardently, "but I've this sudden passion to have a true sculptor's hands – *all over me!*

Letting his half-closed palm cup and trace the curve of her throat, he whispered, "So have I!"

"Islanders say: 'the man who sets sail with a Manilena's kiss on his lips has all the luck he needs to survive.'"

"I'll be here at nine," he promised, "ready to take all the luck you can give."

On the great dock at the port of Cavite, near Manila, Sirena sat at a small table shaded by sailcloth. All merchants bound for Acapulco sat at such tables, forming two long rows facing each other on either side of the wharf. Between them flowed an endless stream of sailors and cargadores bearing trunks, boxes and bales into the hold.

At Sirena's side stood the General of the Sea, a white-uniformed port official, elected by the merchants to oversee their cargoes. He checked her list of purchases against his own, for no more than any other trader, did Sirena intend to pay a crown duty on goods that were not on board.

Because this galleon was even larger than the Santo Niño, the work of moving such a mountain of merchandise made the loading more chaotic than it had been in Acapulco.

Built here in Cavite and christened *The Santa Barbara*, she was making this maiden voyage under the steady hand of Captain Eagle. The stoutest Manila galleon ever built, her keels, rudders, futtocks and joints were made of hard teak and molave wood. Displacing over two thousand tons, building her had cost the Spanish crown the unprecedented sum of six hundred thousand livres. In addition to her Captain, a piloto-mayor and three minor pilots, she carried a crew of three hundred Lascar and Malay sailors, ninety ship's gunners and soldiers to man the cannon, a notary, a constable and two surgeons. With her record-breaking four hundred, there were close to a thousand persons on board and a cargo valued at three million pesos.

Sirena was not surprised at the cargo's worth for the wholesale cost of her own cargo exceeded two hundred thousand pesos. This galleon's greater capacity tempted passengers to invest in many last-minute purchases. Sirena justified hers, for with the profits she hoped to repay Madre Pilar's loan, and sink the costly new shaft in La Sirena mine.

Sirena had spent eight weeks, eight hours a day, in Su Mei's warehouses. While male merchants typically bought cheap ceramics and loaded up on ginger, painted fans and high tortoise-shell mantilla combs, Sirena had a woman's eye and bought for discriminating women. Thanks to Alicia, she knew the tastes of nuns in Mexico's richer convents, and now picked out many distinctive items with them in mind.

Hand-painted wallpaper depicting Chinese scenes, and oddly 'Orientalized' European landscapes, Chinese carpets and Coromandel screens were in vogue. She also knew Black Tea, so rare in Mexico, was all the rage, especially among snobs.

After centuries of importing ivory from India, the mainland Chinese were the finest ivory carvers in the world. Sirena bought three standing crucifixes, each Cristo carved from a single tusk, the body bent to conform to the tusk's own curve, and the Cristo affixed to a solid ebony cross. However disconcertingly Chinese these Cristos looked, Sirena knew the Abbess of La Encarnación would give half her own dowry to see one of these three rarities gracing her convent altar.

For gifts, she ordered sets of hand-painted porcelain dinnerware with the Ávila, Riaño, Legázpi, Graciana and Luna de Mendoza Coats of Arms, which had yet to be finished and would be shipped to her on next year's galleon.

With Su Mei's help, and her own instinct for what would sell, Sirena selected ivory castanets, embroidered and long-fringed Manila shawls, carved sticks and bibelots of ivory, jasper and jade, finely-crafted portable dressing tables, desks and chests for jewels. Brass novelties such as gongs, lanterns, birds, bells and incense pots were all prized in Mexico. Nor did she despise the commonplace. "Some everyday items *never* go out of style," she laughed, and asked Su Mei to throw in two gross of brass toothpicks.

Just before sailing, Sirena spied a truly magnificent Coromandel screen. Francisco once said he saw one like it when he was in Manila, and had always regretted not buying it. The screen *was* expensive, but what better gift for him!

For unique objects d'art, cloth of gold and silver, and bolts of coveted Chinese white opaque silks, Su Mei instructed their vendors to meet the Santa Barbara at night, while the ship was still creeping through the Filipino archipelago.

"You'll be outside the jurisdiction of customs officials," Su Mei told her. "These Chinese will load your goods directly from their junks to the galleon, duty free."

"Is that – legal?" Sirena asked dubiously.

"It's accepted custom," Su Mei shrugged. "It's the same reason galleon captains can't keep a good pilot more than two years. They turn merchant and retire to Mexico or Madrid!"

As a final gesture, she made Sirena the practical gift of a dozen native-style dresses, made of long-fiber cotton in various solid colors, falling comfortably loose from embroidered yoke to ankles without girdle or sash. As she parted from Su Mei at Cavite, Sirena felt an affection for her she would not have dreamed possible the first day they met.

Having finished checking her own cargo, Sirena looked across at Lorenzo's table and saw he was still wrestling with the problem of how to secure a bronze communion rail, destined for Mexico's Cathedral. Designed by Tolsá and cast in China, it was divided into ten sections which, when assembled, measured all of sixty English feet.

"If even one section broke loose in a storm," the Captain of the Sea was saying, "it could become a battering ram, smashing everything else in the hold."

Deciding to go aboard, Sirena found the decks packed with excess merchandise. The Santo Niño's decks had been clear, but the captain said on the return voyage passengers gladly forfeited comfort and space for profit. Now, to make room, he ordered fifty of the ship's eighty gun ports sealed.

"Well, I finally lashed each section of the rail to a huge spike driven into the bulkhead," Lorenzo told Sirena, joining her at the rail. "They'll hold in a full typhoon!"

"No danger of that," she assured him, "the Captain says we're sailing so early, we're well ahead of any typhoons."

The next day, having followed *Nuestra Señora de los Buenos Aires* in procession from her chapel in Cavite to the quarterdeck of the galleon, Sirena stood next to the bareheaded Captain Eagle, while a priest recited prayers and a pilot placed the revered image in her shipboard shrine.

"Can you believe, Condesa," the crusty Irishman confided to her under his breath, "Protestant officers and men of the English Navy still salute their own quarter decks and don't know why? It's been *that* long since they were Catholic and *their* ships carried an image of Our Lady aboard!"

Hours before they sailed, a fast packet-boat on its semi-annual run from Acapulco, reached Manila. The mail she carried was rushed over to Cavite by courier and distributed among the galleon's grateful passengers.

Sirena immediately retired to her cabin, which was crammed with baggage, two trunks, and a chest of glazed fruit that Madre Pilar's Manila nuns gave her to ward off scurvy.

For lack of space, she had to spread her own six letters on her bunk. Most tempting of all was the one from Tristán. Merely touching the envelope made her want to cry. It had been sent to her palace in Mexico and forwarded, proving he did not know she was here. He need *never* know!

"Curiosity denied, curbs one's pride!" the Bishop had advised as a good way to strengthen her will. Obeying his directives, she opened one letter a day, the Bishop's first and on the second day, a welcome note from Adrian.

He apologized for its briefness. He and everyone else at Soledad and Frontera was working hard building a stone aqueduct from the Monclova River. As she read she could see him framed against the Santa Rosa range. He spoke again of marriage and she almost wished she *were* in love with him. That would make things too easy! Doña Isabel wrote that Mercedes was tiring of the eighteen-month engagement she had wanted, (because so many fetes would be given her) but now she was starry-eyed in love with Neto. Banns would be read in May, the wedding set for June, with Sirena home in time to attend. Isabel asked for news of Felipe, which told Sirena she had not yet received her own letter telling of his 'suicide'. Sirena prayed her mother's shock at this news would have worn off by the time she got home.

Alicia's letter came from Vera Cruz, on the eve of her departure for Europe, where she and Noel would honeymoon. "A year in Spain," she wrote, "then on to Rome and Milan for opera season!" It seemed such a blessing that dear, selfless Noel LeClerque was happily married and financially secure -- happy for the first time since The Terror!

Francisco wrote he was busy with his mill, his shops, and classes at School. He had also volunteered to help the protomedicato in their Herculean task of bringing the new small pox vaccine to the Indians.

> *The Crown sent us its 'Ship-of-Children',' twenty-six small orphans from a foundling home in Spain, bringing the vaccine to the Americas. Before embarking, two were inoculated and on the voyage the vaccine was passed from arm to arm, transporting it the only way possible on so long a voyage, live in their little bodies. Vaccinating began in Vera Cruz, but the local doctors stopped it, claiming the vaccine would kill them!*
>
> *At this point our Viceroy rushed to Vera Cruz, assembling the magistrates for what they thought was a state visit. Instead he brought out his own little son and had him vaccinated before their eyes! The child was brave, his father firm and now all the kingdom is accepting the vaccine!*

Francisco said he could not meet her galleon in Acapulco, but his manager would see her cargo through customs.

At last, on the sixth day, she opened the thick envelope that held her treasured letter from Tristán.

∞24∞

My Esteemed Condesa:

Time has passed slowly for me since we parted. I have been in the saddle continuously, patrolling the Red and Sabine Rivers along the eastern approaches to Santa Fe. Each of Jefferson's expeditions is linked in some way to the infamous General Wilkinson we talked about that night at the Riaños. Each expedition has a misleading 'scientific purpose', but all have a common mission -- to carve land from the living body of New Spain.

Our friend Baron Von Humboldt left Mexico City to visit the United States capital. Learning he had the very maps and facts he needed most, Jefferson lost no time asking to 'borrow them'. Having just sent off his first expedition under Lewis and Clark, he wrote the unsuspecting Baron:

Can you inform me of the actual limits of Louisiana between New Spain and the United States? What population may lie between those two lines, of white, red or black people? And, whether any silver mines lie within them?' (Italics mine.)

Receiving this request from a Republican hero, how could the Republican in Humboldt refuse? He generously loaned everything to the Secretary of State, who had them copied and sent post haste to Wilkinson, who as I foretold, is now Governor of Louisiana Territory -- the wolf watching the sheep!

Thus the Baron gave the filibusters a detailed invasion route into New Spain -- every river, harbor, presidio and fort clearly marked! His documents were returned to him only minutes before he sailed back to Europe, never suspecting the devious purpose they had served!

Disturbing as this news was, Sirena's first thought was not concern that the kingdom was imperiled, but fear for Tristán's physical safety.

> *I think of you often and want to see you, but I wouldn't wish a New Mexican winter on anyone I cared for. Please write, if and when you can.*
>
> *Until then, I remain,*
> *Your humble servant, who kisses your hand,*
>
> *Don Tristán de Luna Mendoza,*
> *this First day of March, in the year of Our Lord, 1804*
> *in the Royal City of Santa Fe,*
> *Province of New Mexico,*
> *Kingdom of New Spain.*

Circumspect and devoid of all emotion though it was, Sirena drank in the consoling presence behind his carefully chosen words. Not until she had re-read the letter half a dozen times did she notice a small object still inside the envelope, wrapped in a note written on a very small slip of paper. It held a gold locket on a chain, with the image of Santiago engraved on its cover, and El Santo Niño etched on the back. Inside was the sharp miniature Matiás had painted of Tristán. Greedily she devoured every word:

> *My dearest Sirena:*
> *Please wear this as a reminder of my undying love for you, so that no matter how far from you I ride, I'll know this shadow of myself lies between your sweet breasts, where my head once rested and my lips once browsed. Brand these burning words upon your heart, and then destroy this note, lest it do us harm. May God and all His saints watch over you, while I'm not able to. I miss you terribly, and feel half my soul has been cut out of me! Pray for me in my loneliness!*

Sirena thought her heart would break with love and pity for this loving, lonely man. She clasped the chain around her neck and felt his treasured image settle between her breasts. For the first time since leaving Mexico, she let herself think about the awesome distance between them, the fearful depth of the ocean and the frailty of this ponderous galleon. Crawling under the covers, she sobbed into her pillow until she finally cried herself to sleep.

"At the outset of each homeward voyage," Captain Eagle announced to his guests at conclusion of the evening meal on their seventh night at sea, "I show my passengers the arc of the long route we'll be taking."

At the Captain's table were Sirena, Madre Pilar and Lorenzo. Looking about Sirena counted far fewer religious and many more merchants than on the outward voyage. Oddly enough, the highest ranking official aboard was another Captain General of the islands. After many years' service to the Spanish crown, the jovial Irish-born Don Kevin Crowley had just handed his baton of office over to his successor, who had come to Manila on the Santo Niño. He was now happily sailing back to Mexico with his pretty wife, Consuelo.

Sirena had met this interesting couple at Don Kevin's farewell ball, and she and Consuelo had become good friends. Despite the disparity in their ages, the older man and his eighteen-year-old bride were touchingly devoted.

The first pilot pinned a large map to the bulkhead and with pointer in hand the captain outlined what lay ahead. "Having left Cavite promptly on Saint John the Baptist's Day we feel we sail under that saint's favor, for water is our prime concern on the long voyage home. Our new water butts hold the purest water in the islands, and the ship's cistern contains the same. The scores of small gourds you see hung throughout the rigging overhead have been placed there to catch what rain might fall."

This preamble ended, he pointed to their present location, halfway through the maze of islands, sailing north by northeast. At this season, he said, monsoons would lie behind them all the way to Japan. In former times the galleons had taken on extra water there, but after 1600, the Tokugawa Shogunate closed her ports to all foreigners. Now the galleon had to bypass Japan and head into open sea.

At thirty-five or forty degrees north-latitude the *Santa Barbara* would pick up what Japanese mariners called the *Kuro Sivo*, or Black River, a benign ocean current that would carry them for about a hundred and twenty days of clear sailing until they sighted the coast of Upper California, near Monterey Bay.

From there, steady winds would drive them south, down the West Coast of New Spain. Putting in at that Coast's port of San Blas, a special courier would be sent ashore. Local couriers would carry his news to every major city, where pealing church bells alerted merchants that the galleon was nearing homeport. From San Blas to Acapulco was only a few more days, but time enough for merchants to meet her there.

The captain's talk over, Sirena retired alone to the taffrail where the wrought-iron ship's lantern shed a cheerful light on the sterncastle beneath her. The myriad empty gourds in the rigging above chunked against each other like muted Chinese wind-bells. Relieved to be alone, she took out Tristán's loving note and forced herself to tear the small slip into tiny bits, consigning them resolutely to the moving black waters of the ship's wake.

"What are you thinking about?"

Sirena started guiltily as Lorenzo materialized soundlessly at her elbow. "Oh, nothing," she replied, her eyes wistfully trying to follow the little flurry of tender words now disappearing from sight. "Thinking of home, mostly."

"Is no one waiting for you?" he asked.

"No, Lorenzo. I was being perfectly honest when I told you I don't intend to marry."

"I still find that hard to believe."

"Many titled women choose to run their own estates and lives. Why wait until I'm widowed, when I can do it now?"

She felt his searching gaze, but it did not disturb her. After his being so helpful in Manila, her trust in him had grown, especially as to the propriety of his conduct toward her. Madre Pilar's warning had lost its initial impact. "So what are *you* thinking?" she asked, feigning a lighthearted tone despite her aching loneliness for Tristán.

"I'm thinking that here aboard the galleon we're beyond the strict social rules prevailing in New Spain."

"Yes, out here we're all equally helpless mortals, at the mercy of wind and sea."

His hand closed over hers. "I'm very glad to hear no Conde or Marqués is waiting for you," he said softly.

She felt a flutter of dismay, not knowing quite how to respond, afraid to retrieve her hand lest she offend him.

"Can you imagine in Mexico, a poor artist like me saying out loud that he admired a *Condesa*?"

"You're hardly a poor artist," she chided him, glad to turn the topic from herself. "You told me you were paid handsomely for your three large portraits of the new captain general and his wife and daughter."

"A mere aperitif for a man like me who's bent on acquiring *real* wealth and position," he replied defensively.

"The China trade's a quick way to acquire wealth. I was surprised you didn't take Su Mei up on her offer to put together a cargo for you. A small investment could have brought you large returns -- more than enough to win the hand of a girl of good family."

"How *could* I invest my commission money?" he asked, "I'd already lost it all at mus!" He winked wickedly. "Those Sangleys have a way of dealing bad cards to strangers."

"Wasn't that a bit -- improvident?"

"Not when I had the chance to triple my money with no effort at all!"

A young grummet came up to ring the ship's bell and chant the hour's prayer. Blessing herself gave Sirena a good reason to draw her hand away.

> *One glass is gone,*
> *And now the second floweth,*
> *More shall run down,*
> *If our God willeth.*
> *To God let us pray*
> *To give us a good voyage,*
> *And through His Blessed Mother,*
> *Our advocate on high,*
> *Protect us from the waterspout*
> *And send no tempest nigh.*

When the grummet moved on Sirena told Lorenzo it was time to retire to her cabin for the night, and he took her arm, guiding her through the maze of bales and boxes cluttering the deck. But when they reached the hatchway, instead of bidding her goodnight, he faced her boldly. "You ought to know I won't settle for just *any* wife," he said quietly but with fervor, "You forget, I'm from Guanajuato, too, where *only an honest-to-God Silver Bride counts for a damn!*" He pulled her close in the darkness. "Don't you understand, Sirena? Ever since we met in that wayside jacal, I've wanted you, wanted to show you my love. What's impossible back home is possible out here!"

"Lorenzo, please!" she said, torn between confusion and compassion, "You're homesick and I understand, but. . ."

He took her in his arms. "You say you're never going to marry," he whispered persuasively, running his hands across the silken back of her gown and down the long taffeta sleeves sheathing her arms, "but that doesn't mean you can never know love! Why not disport yourself with someone who's *already* in love with you? Better a good friend you can trust, than a stranger, no?"

"Ah, Condesa! Is that you there?" Recognizing Don Kevin Crowley's voice, Lorenzo stepped back and dropped his hands to his sides as the dignitary drew near.

"Consuelo wants to show you that book of poems she was discussing earlier. Can you come to our cabin now?"

"Buenas noches, Condesa," Lorenzo said clearly, "we can continue our discussion of quaint social customs in New Spain another time."

ෆ ෮

Five weeks out of Cavite the uneventful voyage was interrupted by an epidemic of fever, vomiting and severe stomach cramps, afflicting both passengers and crew. Sirena was one of those stricken. Before the cause was finally traced to the new water butts, which had been lined with improperly seasoned wood, twelve passengers and twenty sailors were dead, each corpse given a grim and hasty burial at sea. The Captain quickly ordered everyone put on half rations of cistern water for the remainder of the voyage.

For Sirena and Madre Pilar this voyage had already started out badly. The Manila house had no lay sisters to spare, and the ailing sister Rosa, on her way home to Mexico, had suffered from drinking the foul water, on top of being deathly ill with malaria. Madre Pilar was bound to the sick nun's side, day and night.

Sirena had all her own chores to attend to as well as those of the two religious. One unexpected blessing was that her monthly periods had ceased. Both Madre Pilar and Consuelo assured her this was neither serious nor uncommon, but often happened to women in Manila until they became accustomed to the climate. Actually Sirena was grateful, for it spared her having to empty her chamber of such humiliating contents over the side, sometimes in view of a passing sailor.

After the water rationing in mid-July, Sirena began keeping a journal. One day, sitting on deck with Consuelo, who was optimistically knitting a baby's cap, she wrote: "August tenth. The winds are weak. We are in latitude 33 and 01 minute off the northern tip of Japan. Yesterday we sailed twelve leagues."

Two days later, wearing one of Su Mei's comfortably loose gowns in the stifling heat on deck, she wrote: "We lie becalmed. Water rations cut again by half. We are in a deadly race between water and wind."

A sudden breeze stirred the bone-dry gourds in the rigging and they began rattling like dice in a player's cup. Quickly she noted: "A brisk breeze is rising and may. . ." She stopped abruptly for Consuelo's hand suddenly covered hers. "Look, Sirena," she said breathlessly, pointing out to sea, "three ships just came over the horizon!"

Sirena stared at the strange sails. Having grown up on the frontier, where company was rare, her first response was pleasure at welcoming visitors. That notion was soon dispelled when a steward ran by, calling out to everyone to gather before the quarter deck. Only part of the many passengers were about, but Consuelo and Sirena were among those who reported at once to where the Captain stood, his sturdy legs astride the quarter deck, his craggy face flushed.

"My fellow voyagers!" he announced, cupping his hands to his mouth to be heard. "Three Dutch pirate sails are advancing rapidly on our starboard side. The wind is rising, so I'll try out-running them. If they overtake us, we'll stand to and fight. Thirty of our eighty cannon can still be fired."

His words brought home to Sirena the disquieting memory of him sealing fifty of his eighty cannon to make room for more merchandise. That accommodation could cost us our lives!

"We've ample stores of powder and grenades and we're well armed with pikes," he continued. "Every man aboard has at least one musket or sword. If we can't drive them off – well, they'll close in with grappling hooks to board us."

Terrified as she, herself, was, Sirena put a comforting arm around Consuelo, who was visibly trembling. She felt her already parched mouth and throat becoming even drier with fear, as all the blood-chilling tales of savage pirates rose up and paraded vividly before her.

"Only sailors, soldiers and gunners remain on deck. I order all passengers below. Barricade yourselves in your cabins and sell your lives dearly. As for the ladies and good nuns -- ," his bravado momentarily failed him. "I need not remind you, these are Dutch Calvinists. To them, we are hated Spanish Catholics first, fellow

Europeans last. I devoutly implore every man among you -- *see to it that no woman on this ship falls into their hands alive!*"

The captain led all present in a brief prayer, then with a brisk, 'Amen!' turned on his heel and rejoined his pilots at the wheel. Passengers scattered in every direction. Stark terror seized Sirena as she and Consuelo stood helplessly watching the nimble Malays swarm up the rigging in a race to unfurl the topsails and catch the gusting wind, even as they saw the same wind sweeping the Dutch ships closer.

A tall Dominican priest appeared, stark as the hour, itself, in his hooded white habit and full black cloak. His step was buoyant, his manner composed. Kissing the purple satin side of his stole, he placed it about his neck, drew up a straight chair near the Virgin's shrine and seated himself.

"I am ready," he announced in a loud, firm voice, "to hear gentlemen's confessions here now."

Sirena was aghast. The priest was as calm as though he were preaching a mission in Mexico's Cathedral! A line of male penitents queued up before his impromptu confessional, and she was struck by the cold truth of it: these men are not just confessing, they're getting ready to die! She blessed herself and silently begged God's forgiveness for all the sins of her entire life. She touched the place where the locket lay hidden, imploring El Santo Niño, Santiago and Tristán to lend her all their strength in the coming hour.

As Don Kevin rushed up and took Consuelo below decks, Lorenzo appeared at Sirena's side. "Take this with you to your cabin," he commanded without emotion, handing her his pistol. "Once you're inside your cabin, shove your heaviest trunks and boxes against the door. Fire at the first man who tries to force an entry. I'll keep in touch as I can."

They had not spoken a dozen words to each other since the night he expressed his love for her at the very outset of the voyage. But in the light of their present grave predicament his words now seemed trivial, and she felt great compunction at having treated him so cold-heartedly. "Lorenzo, I want to assure you, I bear no ill will for anything you said that night. We were both lonely and homesick and. . ." Looking down at the pistol in her hand, she gave him a nervous smile, " and, I thank you for this, with all my heart!"

"Sirena, I dare not leave Sister Rosa's side," Madre Pilar said, emerging from the hatchway as Sirena and Lorenzo started to go below. "Can you manage alone?" As always, her manner was brisk, her first concern the welfare of others. "I feel sure Sister will give up her soul before this night is through."

She clasped Sirena in a fierce, emotional embrace. "Don't worry about me, Madre," Sirena told her, trying to cover her fright with a show of nerve. "Lorenzo gave me his pistol. I'm a norteña, I know how to use it!"

"Good!" Madre Pilar said, and her black eyes radiated gratitude as she turned to Lorenzo. "Thank you, Maestro, for looking after the Condesa. God will reward you!"

ಌ25ೞ

In the few minutes since the Dutch ships were first sighted, the wind had risen rapidly, and as Sirena entered her cabin and locked the door behind her, she could feel the galleon ploughing ahead under what she knew was a full load of sail. Following Lorenzo's instructions was not easily done. Only with enormous effort, and pouring sweat, was she finally able to secure the door with trunks and boxes. She had never been so weak! Being on a quarter ration of water and eating only small portions of biscuit and broth each day had taken its toll of her strength.

Determined to remain calm, she checked Lorenzo's pistol. Making sure it was loaded and primed, she laid it within easy reach on the table by her bunk. As she took out a silver rosary her father had given her, the small world of her ship's cabin suddenly seemed to explode all around her.

It was a few seconds before she realized the Dutch were shelling the starboard side of the galleon, the side her cabin was on. When the *Santa Barbara's* cannon thundered back the great ship shuddered. She covered her head with a pillow as the galleon was raked by a second deafening cannonade. At this volley the *Santa Barbara* pitched so violently Sirena was thrown bodily from her bunk to the floor.

Blindly, on hands and knees, she struggled back to the relative safety of her bed, the cabin filled with dense black smoke. Unable to see a vara's length before her she cowered in the bunk's farthest corner, like an animal in its den.

"Holy Mother of God, pray for us now and at the hour of our death!" she prayed aloud, her teeth chattering with fright as the immediacy of those once routine words came home to her.

Another ear-shattering salvo swept the sides, and this time she was hurled halfway across the cabin against the door, striking her head on the metal corner of a trunk. She was dazed by the blow, but able to hear above the cannon's din the sound of running feet on the deck above, mingled with the shouts and cries of many men. Her whole body began trembling uncontrollably. Dear God, it was happening! The Dutch were boarding the galleon!

Sitting on the edge of her bunk, unable to see through the smoke, she heard the thud of repeated heavy blows on the hard wood of her cabin door. Her gaze riveted on the door, she was sure her trunks were sliding irrevocably toward her. Groping blindly for Lorenzo's pistol, her fingers finally closed around the handle. She braced her elbows firmly on the table and took careful aim at the door, as a sudden burst of light told her it had fallen.

A man's figure loomed, silhouetted briefly against the lighted companionway behind him. When he cried out and lunged for her, she fired. It was not until he was actually upon her and wresting the pistol from her hands that she panicked, knowing her shot had gone wild.

Mad with fear and utterly disoriented, she fought her captor with every ounce of strength she possessed as he dragged her from her cabin and along the smoke-filled companionway. At last, choking and blinded by the smoke, she gave up fighting. She had a vague sense of lying on a hard surface, then she tasted brandy on her lips. Parched for liquid of any kind, she gulped it down and begged for more. In one final effort she reached out for Tristán, and miraculously he appeared. Safe in his arms she let the numbing peace of sleep -- or was it death? -- close over her.

"I've just come from talking to the Piloto Mayor at the wheel," Don Kevin told Lorenzo, as the two men collided in the smoke-shrouded companionway. "No use your going up on deck. It's too rough to even stand. He ordered me below."

"The ship's been rolling so," Lorenzo said, "I figured we must have run into heavy seas."

"It's worse than that. The wind helped us outrun the Dutch all right, but thanks to one of the worst things that can hit a galleon at sea -- a typhoon!"

"But captain Eagle said we'd cleared Cavite so early we wouldn't run into any storms at all!"

"Typhoons happen when and where they will," Don Kevin said gravely.

"How long do they last?"

"Anywhere from twelve hours to a week, but the Captain says sometimes they come in clusters. It's a case of how many the *Santa Barbara* can withstand before she founders."

Lorenzo stared at him, feeling a great emptiness in the pit of his stomach. "It's *that* serious?"

"I've just made a general confession, so I'm prepared to die. My sole concern now is for my wife. Her father was lost at sea before she was born, when his galleon went down in a typhoon just like this. She's petrified. She's also worried sick about Sirena. Have you seen her? I tried her cabin but it was open and she was gone."

"I broke in and took her out when the Dutch began shelling that side of the ship. She was blinded by smoke and fear and judging from the way she fought me, I'm sure she thought I was a pirate and about to murder her. I finally got her safely to the Madre's." He paused a moment. "About your wife, I have a sedative that will calm her, something a religious friend in Manila concocts -- expressly for women."

"I'm willing to try anything," Don Kevin said. "We may only have a few hours left together in this world, but I'd rather she perished peacefully asleep in my arms, than see her suffer such agonies of fear."

Re-entering his cabin after giving Don Kevin one of Su Mei's vials, Lorenzo found Sirena in a deep sleep. He smiled at the pious lie he had just told Crowley. Hell no, he hadn't taken her to the nuns! What sane man would? He was glad for her sake the drink had calmed her, but at the same time he wanted her awake. God knew he was as scared of death as any man, and the prospect of dying alone and unmourned by any living soul struck him as devastating.

He lifted a *bota* of French cognac from his open trunk, uncorked it and began sipping, straight from the bottle. Ironically, he had been hoarding this rare vintage for some signal event, like the first sight of land. Well, *hombre*, don't count on it! This may be the last drop of cheer you ever taste! He took another deep draught and allowed it to burn his tongue fiercely before swallowing. With death all around him, his mind went back over the unsolved riddles of his life, a life littered with rejections and injustices. A slumbering rage at his dead criolla mother surfaced, as it always did when he drank. He pitied his poor grandfather, 'Old Martín,' who had failed at running La Torre and ended up selling out to Don Patrick. But by Christ, the old man was pure criollo and had the brains to marry one! So how could a criolla daughter of theirs so blindly betray her fortunate birth and class as to "marry down" to a bastard casta like Emilio?

As for Emilio -- damn him and all his mongrel breed! Damn him for trumpeting the news from Acapulco to the Apache frontier that he'd sired a son who could 'pass'! Don Patrick had done Lorenzo no favor, either: it took more than a fancy piece of paper to turn a casta 'white.' He could still see Emilio on the atrium of the Graciana chapel, weighing the newborn Sirena in his plate-sized hands, *"Small though she is, weigh what she will, the new patrona is born!"* Well, she's not my patrona and never was! I'm my own man!

But just who the Hell *was* that man? The best sculptor and portrait artist in the kingdom? Of course! But also a man barred from the mansions of the silver elite. Criollo and gachupín aristocrats pursued him to paint portraits of their women, but they'd rather see their daughters dead than let the low-born artist lay a finger on them!

Sipping steadily, he studied Sirena, lying in a deep sleep on his bunk. The sedative was working like a charm, but he was not about to forget its chief virtue, as demonstrated for him by Su Mei the night before he sailed. Holy Jesus, what a night that was! If her virtuoso performance was any gauge, this potion could trigger orgasm in a beata three days dead! Without her Sangley 'Spanish Fly,' not even a Paphian whore could have imagined *that* many ways to ball a man!

But, God Almighty, had he ever been so long between lays? Even in Manila, which crawled with whores, he found most Chinese women were like Chinese food -- an hour after he left their arms he was ravenous again! The storm was growing worse, the galleon reeling under the assault of mountainous waves that hit her sides like gargantuan battering rams. The cold fear of death gripped him again, and he lifted the comforting cognac to his lips, gazing greedily at his guest through the brandy's haze.

Lorenzo, all your life you've hungered for a silver bride, and this night, which may be your last, you've got her. Never again will the gods of silver offer one of their virgins on the altar of chance to a casta's son! Even if we live through this typhoon, she'll never be yours, just for the taking, this way again. The flame of desire dispelled the chill of fear. Daylight was going fast, and the artist in him deserved to see, as well as feel, the lushness of his own private Sabine Woman. Expertly he found and loosed the ribbon ties of her full Manila gown, then left her lying there, so his eyes could feast upon her nudity while he drained the bottle and stripped off his own clothes. Yes, he told himself appreciatively, as I expected she's the classic Greco-Roman female nude.

He did not remain the objective artist long. Darkness, which fell like a shroud, made the storm doubly frightening, as the galleon fought like a wounded titan drowning at sea. Holy Christ, if he'd ever needed a woman's arms to comfort him, he needed them now!

And never had any woman given him the matchless thrill he felt when, at long last, the First Condesa of Graciana lay naked in his arms. Of course, she transports you! She's the cream of the silver elite, not some *lépero* slut willing to pose and be laid so she can feed the child beside her bed, in that ever-present hammock which was *always* high with piss!

This Condesa's flesh was alabaster, ivory, noble Cararra marble, purer than white jade! Like the Conde's chapel itself, she had been put together with 'silver dust and Spanish wine!' Best of all, when his mouth found hers in the inky darkness she was already begging for his kiss. Eagerly his sculptor's hands went over every inch of her, then retraced their path with slow, provocative kisses, bringing her to a frenzy of passionate abandon.

"At last!" she cried softly, "You've come to claim me at last!"

Wasn't that exactly like a woman, he thought, rebuffing his advances like vile insults, when all along she'd been every bit as hot for his body as he was for hers? "You mean you've wanted me to take you this way?" he asked, mind and body flattered, his male ego hanging on her whispered reply.

"Would I let any *other* man be my -- conquistador?"

The appropriateness of her imagery and the marvel of her lust for him was electrifying. The brandy, the bestial excitement of the storm and Sirena's alternating passivity and passion drove him to madness. Nearing a climax of ecstatic bliss, he suddenly knew *why* this moment was so rapturous. You're not just plucking a random virgin rose here he exulted. You're humping *one of their own*! You're actually fucking the whole God-damned ruling class, lily-livered gachupínes, criollo bastards and frigging silver lords! "Yes!" he cried aloud, gloating over his revenge, "*THIS* pays all you sons-of-bitches back for the years of shit you've heaped on me!"

His passion spent, he fell upon her dizzily, far drunker than he thought. For a long while Sirena lay unmoving in his arms, then she began uttering delicious endearments. Lorenzo drank them in. Sweet Jesus, first she'd begged for and gotten his cock, now she was ravishing his very soul with expressions of courtly love, a pure tongue no woman had ever used with him before! Almost as exciting as sex, was hearing her describe him -- with every "thee" and "thou" of lofty prose -- as the gallant, noble, knightly lover she adored.

As he was coming down from these heady heights, Sirena seemed to sink deeper into sleep, murmuring what he thought were more poetic words, until at last he heard them right. Actually she was calling out to someone named 'Tristán.' He put off her entwining arms and drew away. Welling up within him, like black water in a deep mine shaft, was a malicious sense of envy, hatred and betrayal. Aphrodisiac or not, she'd been giving herself to some man of her own station all the time! She had made a mockery of his manhood, denied him entry even when he was already there, leveled his pride as no other woman had ever done -- or was capable of doing.

ɞ ʚ

When daylight penetrated the oilskin skylight once more, Lorenzo realized the storm was abating, the ship no longer pitching as before. When he was dressed he leaned over to cover Sirena, but was intrigued by her locket, opened it and saw the miniature inside. So it was that Tristán, her soldier kinsman, who had been so high-handed with him the day Don Patrick died! She was not merely calling his name, but all her courtly phrases had been addressed to him! In that case, Lorenzo, you won no spurs and lost no prize: I'm sure her Royalist stud's already serviced his luscious cousin well!

A tempting notion struck him. Instead of covering her, he took up his sketchbook and sanguine crayon, scrawling the words, *La Condesa Desnuda*, across the bottom of the page. With quick, clean strokes he laid out a rough sketch of the naked Condesa asleep, which he could paint later in oil on the best linen canvas. Since she robbed him of his conquest, he would hold her hostage. Who knows, she might care to ransom it someday!

ɞ ʚ

With daylight glimmering down on her from above, Sirena opened her eyes. Gradually realizing she was lying uncovered on her bunk, she drew the sheet up to conceal her nakedness. Seeing Lorenzo nearby, drawing in his sketchbook, she stared at him, amazed. "Lorenzo, what are you doing in my cabin?"

He looked up coldly. "This happens to be my cabin, Condesa," he corrected her, setting book and crayon aside.

"Then -- how did I get here?"

"I broke into yours when Dutch shells were due to blow it all to Hell." He grinned. "And if you'd been a better shot I'd be dead by my own pistol. As it was, you fought like a scalded cat 'til I gave you a sedative to make you sleep."

Disjointed bits and pieces of yesterday and last night began coming back to her, but everything was fragmented and unreal. No wonder! It had been a night of such unforgettably vivid, erotic dreams of herself with Tristán. "I was having nightmares," she ventured hesitantly, searching his face to see if, God forbid, she might have talked in her sleep.

"Neither of us thought we'd live through last night's typhoon," he stated candidly, in response to her questioning gaze. "I must admit that, lying on my bunk like that, you tempted me beyond my usual powers of resistance."

"I was asleep," she protested, her panic rising, "you just said you gave me a sedative."

"Ah, but happily for me, you were not entirely asleep," he said archly, sounding for all the world like the cad in one of those tattered tent-show melodramas which traveling actors used to bring to Monclova. "And, as you may or may not recall, this time you did nothing to parry my formerly unwelcome advances." With his satisfied smile, he seemed to be relishing a pleasant private joke. "In fact, for an inexperienced virgin you comported yourself quite creditably."

She flinched. "What gives you the right to address such insulting remarks to a lady?"

"Well, Condesa, you're not *quite* the lady you were this time yesterday," he replied sardonically. "You know the old adage, 'Lie down with dogs, get up with fleas'?"

She could only stare at him, appalled at his brass.

"However, I confess had our plight not been so desperate such a mismating of opposites would have been unthinkable. A mutual fear of death is a great leveler of class."

Rising to his feet, and ignoring the hate and horror in her eyes, he approached the bunk and lifted her hand to his lips in a gesture she found contemptible. "Condesa, you have my word of honor as a gentleman, I'll go to my grave denying anything happened here between us -- but being forever grateful it did." He turned and moved toward the door.

"How dare you even utter such words as 'gentleman' and 'honor' after what you've done to me!" She grabbed a bronze candlestick by the bunk and threw it at him, striking a glancing blow to his forehead and leaving an angry gash. *"I'd rather be raped by ten Dutch pirates than by one casta, posing as a knight!"*

"What about your other knight?" he sneered, "the one you kept calling for while making incandescent love to me?" Devastated by what he knew and how he must have learned it, Sirena was speechless.

"I'm sure Tristán's commander would be interested to know that one of his married officers of high rank is both committing adultery *and* carrying on an incestuous behind-the-barn affair with his own cousin!"

"God damn you, and your vulgar tongue!" she screamed, tears of hurt and rage streaming down her face. "If Tristán were here he'd drive his lance through your black heart!"

"The Bourbon Army has a strict moral code for its officers. If General Calleja knew what I know, he'd cashier your fuck-happy cousin out of the Tenth Brigade so fast he wouldn't have time to pull your skirts down first!"

Sirena hurled a second candlestick, but he was gone.

Closing her eyes, she pressed her brow against the bulkhead, all innocence dead within her. Sickened by her degradation at Lorenzo's hands, the bitterest gall of all, was knowing that somehow he had violated her in Tristán's name!

☙26❧

Captain Eagle managed to ride out the typhoon, but his ship had been severely crippled, her sails shredded and one mast lost. Life aboard the *Santa Barbara* now became a slow descent into Hell, with every demon known to a galleon's return voyage rising like a host of evil genies to assail her passengers and crew.

Millions of fleas hatched out in the spoiled ship's biscuits, infesting everything on board -- food, mattress, clothing, hair. Sirena was a mass of bleeding itching sores that made sleep impossible. The heat was brutal and relentless. Live maggots rose to the top of every bowl of broth or beans, until meals became a martyrdom, but it was eat or starve. More loathsome to Sirena than maggoty food and foul water, was having to sit at the Captain's table with Lorenzo, while he charmed Madre Pilar with good manners and gentlemanly solicitude for Sirena's welfare, knowing Madre Pilar could not even *conceive* of the truth.

While fever stalked the passengers, and scurvy cut down the crew, the worst storms galleon pilots had ever seen bedeviled their voyage. After the first typhoon, the *Santa Barbara* was struck by three more. Then, in late October, she was savaged by a full-scale hurricane. The deluge was Biblical, shrieking winds ripping away the galleon's topsails and tossing her mainmast like a matchstick into the boiling sea. At the hurricane's height, while the Captain fought to rig a jury mast, three sailors were swept from the deck by mountainous waves. One despairing merchant cut his throat, another went stark mad and threw himself into the sea.

But the havoc of the hurricane brought the first stroke of good fortune on the voyage. In a matter of days the *Santa Barbara* was blown across a vast expanse of ocean that would have taken weeks of sailing. On a calm November morning passengers awoke to the sight of pine-dark hills on Upper California's shore, their wounded galleon having limped into peaceful Monterey Bay and dropped anchor there in the night.

※ ※

On January fourth, six months and ten days after clearing Cavite, the galleon set out once more. The two-month layover in Monterey had revived everyone's spirits. Health was restored and new masts made from the straight, slim Monterey pines. Fresh food and water were taken on, and a packet boat, on its regular supply run up from San Blas, gave the galleon spare sail cloth and sound water butts.

Consuelo and Kevin Crowley had greater reason than most to rejoice, for Consuelo now knew for certain she was pregnant. Ironically, she told Sirena, she had conceived the night of the first terrifying typhoon, the same night sister Rosa died. Sirena recalled it only as the bitter night when Lorenzo drugged and ravaged her.

"That was such a *wild* night of love!" the blushing Consuelo confided. Then, jokingly she added, "I even told my Kevin, there must have been something more than we knew in that sedative which Maestro Lorenzo gave him to quiet me!"

But fate had saved its cruelest tragedy for last. The ebullient Kevin Crowley fell desperately ill, and a ship's surgeon diagnosed a ruptured appendix. Inoperable and incurable, Don Kevin faced its inevitable corollary, an excruciatingly painful death from peritonitis. Thirty-six hours later the body of the former Captain General of the Islands was respectfully consigned to the sea with a long drum roll and a twenty-one-gun salute.

Consuelo was not only grief-stricken, she became obsessed with the fear that she would die in childbirth, just as her own mother had done after her husband was lost at sea. Consuelo was raised in a Manila orphanage, and now with no living relatives to turn to, she was terrified her baby would suffer the same tragic fate.

To reassure her, Sirena went before Captain Eagle and the ship's notary, with Madre Pilar and Lorenzo as Consuelo's choice of witnesses, signing a sworn statement that in the event of Consuelo's death the First Condesa of Graciana would legally adopt, raise and give her child a loving home. This promise greatly comforted the distracted young widow.

When preparing to disembark from the *Santa Barbara* in Acapulco, Sirena looked at herself in the mirror and beheld a stranger. The sufferings of the voyage and the debilitating fever what she, Madre Pilar and several other passengers contracted in the tropical Port of San Blas, had reduced her to a wraith. Struggling to bathe and dress she noticed for the first time that her breasts seemed abnormally large and her abdomen distended. A week or so earlier Consuelo had shown her the physical changes which pregnancy had caused in herself. With a sickening premonition, Sirena now saw her own body exhibiting the very same signs.

Trembling, she sank down on her bunk, recalling that the Marquésa de Ávila had told her a lady could only become pregnant *after* marriage. Sirena believed that pious fiction, even when she saw lower class women having children out of wedlock all the time. Now she grasped the fact that the key word of that advice had been *'lady'*.

Oh, my God, she thought despairingly, I can't be pregnant! I'll die of humiliation! I'll never be able to face Tristán again! I'll kill myself before I give birth to any child of Lorenzo Santa Cruz!

In the end, like Madre Pilar and dozens of other fever-stricken passengers, Sirena was physically unable to walk off the galleon, and had to be carried ashore. There, Francisco's efficient agent found her, lying helpless on a shaded litter on the dock. She gave him her twice-checked list of purchases, and he promised to unload her cargo, clear it through customs, and take it safely back to Mexico for her.

Lying there under the canvas shade, she observed Lorenzo unloading Tolsa's bronze communion rail, and felt an implacable hatred for him. Dear God, she wondered, what has become of grace? Had she used up her life's supply surviving the voyage? It would take what little she had left to endure the killing trip back across the tierra caliente, transported on this litter, slung between two mules. Her sole triumph had been cheating death itself here in Acapulco!

"The Lord never gives us a cross heavier than we can bear," Madre Pilar called out to her courageously from her litter nearby. Sirena was shamed by her own self-pity. What about Madre Pilar? Think of how that brave woman is going to suffer on the road back, in her coarse woolen habit!

Later, approaching Sirena's litter, Lorenzo doffed his Panama grandly, and bowed. "Condesa, is there anything at all I can do for you before I go?"

"Thank you, no," she managed between clenched teeth, "I won't be needing any more help from you." He gave her a proud but puzzled look and turned away.

She had never known hatred before. Not even when Don Telmo locked her in her room and starved her, had she ever thought of evening the score. Although she now knew she was incapable of killing herself and her unborn child, she felt a murderous thirst for revenge. The sweet prospect of being reunited with the man she loved was all that had kept her alive these last Hellish months, and now, thanks to this low *canalla's* treachery, she could never face Tristán, or hope to be loved by him again. Staring at Lorenzo's back as he walked to his waiting cab she thought savagely, So help me God, if I had his pistol now, *my shot would not go wild!*

PART SIX

SILVER ROSES

1805-1810

*"It may help you
 to think of Grace as a silver rose.
 It can become tarnished by neglect.
 Sometimes blackened by mortal sin.
 But it is kept forever bright by
 Faith, Hope and acts of true Charity."*

Bishop Legázpi

27

"Excelencia!" Madre Pilar exclaimed, coming forward to greet Bishop Legázpi as he entered the visitor's parlor at Los Remedios. "It was good of you to respond to my letter so promptly."

"Madre, I would have come at once, but the difficulties threatened by the Crown's new "Act of Consolidation" made it impossible for me to get away."

"I can sympathize," Madre Pilar replied. "I returned from Manila three months ago to find my Order facing financial ruin if they impose this draconian tax."

He handed his hat and cane to the Indian lay sister who had admitted him, and seated himself in a friar's chair. Madre Pilar poured two tall glasses of lemonade and brought his lunch to him on a plate garnished with small white *besos*.

"The government's even demanding an account of my diocesan fund!" he confided, after the sister left the room. "It was only after writing directly to the Viceroy, himself, that I obtained an audience with him, which business brings me to the capital -- along with your own."

"Diego, you knew His Majesty when he was Crown Prince," she asked with visible distress, "what on earth would persuade him to impose such a ruinous tax on this kingdom?"

"He and Prime Minister Godoy have always regarded New Spain as their own private war chest, to plunder at will."

"But to call in the entire *forty-four million pesos owed the Church in mortgages and loans!*" Madre Pilar clasped her hands in an uncharacteristic gesture of exasperation.

"I know Madre, it could mean economic suicide!"

"Why, right here in the capital," she said, regaining her composure, "three-fourths of all urban property is mortgaged to monasteries, or to convents like mine. Where else will people turn for ready cash?"

"I believe the Viceroy knows he's risking open rebellion if he puts this tax through. But if he *does*, I estimate six thousand of the kingdom's largest landholders will be forced to liquidate their assets by selling off all their estates."

"That would be the biggest liquidation since The Crown seized all Jesuit estates and sold them at public auction!"

"But with *one* striking difference, Madre. Forty years ago there were plenty of buyers solvent enough to snap up three and four such bargain estates in a single bid. But after *this* tax, who would have any cash left with which to buy?" He sipped his drink thoughtfully. "The Prime Minister is seeking two things: total power for himself, and a financial windfall by confiscating all Church wealth in New Spain."

"But Diego that would be catastrophic! Church money *constitutes two thirds of all the operating capital in New Spain!*"

"This crisis helps me see now what I was too young to grasp at the time," Legázpi said gravely. "The expulsion of the Jesuits was a small foreshadowing of what has now become the Bourbon Crown's naked anticlericalism."

"As Sirena, herself, wrote the Viceroy last week, 'If the Church and the largest landowners are pauperized by paying today's royal debts, who will be left to pay the King's creditors tomorrow?'"

At mention of Sirena he leaned forward in his chair. "Despite my concern with this tax, I've been *very* worried about Sirena. Reading between the lines of your letter, she's suffered something much more grave than fever."

"I had to use great caution in what I wrote."

The large polished wooden beads of her habit rosary clicked against the leg of her chair. Madre Pilar reminded him of one of Zubaran's chiaroscuro paintings of a nun, lit by amber light from a window above. She was a novice mistress's paradigm, the ideal female religious, always with full custody of all her senses. But now he noticed severe emotional stress beneath that habitual composure.

"Sirena's been through a frightful experience," she said, "and is still suffering its emotional and spiritual effects." Steeling herself, she recounted to him key events of both outward and return voyages, closing with Lorenzo's apparently premeditated drugging and violation of Sirena.

"But Lorenzo, of all people!" Legázpi cried. "He's a lionized artist, a gentleman, not some brutish *cargador*! What on earth could have possessed him?"

For a moment she was too distressed to continue. "Unhappily, that's not the worst of it. Not until we made port at Acapulco did she realize she was carrying his child. The journey across the hotlands on a litter was such an ordeal, she didn't confide it all to me until we were safely here."

"Oh, Madre," he said sorrowfully, "as her confessor, only *I* know what a heartbreaking tragedy this is for her!" Afraid to risk exposing Sirena's secret by keeping her at the Asylum, Madre Pilar had taken both Sirena and Consuelo at night to her own private hermitage, a league distant from her Order's retreat house outside the city. There, safely hidden from everyone, both women passed the last weeks of their confinement.

"Fortunately, all Sirena's friends were out of town, including Don Francisco. Sirena wrote them she was ill with fever, a half-truth, but one that served her well."

"You've been very prudent, Teresita," he said gently, daring to use the diminutive of her baptismal name by which he had known her when they were sweethearts back in Spain. He left his chair and began pacing restlessly. "And did she have a safe delivery?"

She told him both mothers gave birth within hours of each other. Consuelo was delivered without incident, but Sirena's labor was long and the delivery so complicated she fainted, and was unconscious when the child was born.

"Because of the need for absolute secrecy I delivered both infants myself, with only the help of Beatriz."

"Beatriz?"

"She's the Indian lay sister who just now let you in."

"A shy rabbit, I must say! Never uttered a word in response to anything I asked."

Madre Pilar smiled indulgently. "That's because she's both deaf and mute. Her parents brought her to me about two years ago. We manage with signs and signals, and she's become an expert midwife."

"And Sirena's child?" he asked, seating himself again.

"First, Consuelo gave birth to a healthy boy," Madre Pilar continued, "then tragically enough, she died of child-bed fever." She studied her hands, folded in her lap. "As for Sirena's son -- *he* was *stillborn*."

The Bishop blessed himself and offered up a silent prayer for both Consuelo and the dead infant. "Sad as it is," he said, speaking deliberately, "her child being born dead was indeed providential for Sirena."

"Yes, it would have been a lifelong crucifixion to know that her son, even though sired by a casta rapist, was the true Graciana heir. Illegitimate or not, being her firstborn, he had clear and legitimate claim to both title and legacy."

"How is Sirena now?"

"Well, I believe Consuelo's little boy, Rafael, will prove to be for Sirena just what his name implies, 'The Medicine of God'. She's legally adopting him, but he'll stay here with me until he's old enough to travel."

"Is there the remotest chance Lorenzo knows or could someday find out -- that Sirena bore him a child?"

Madre Pilar's gentle expression turned savage. "Absolutely none! Because of the oppressive heat she always wore loose-fitting native gowns which kept her condition a secret even from me!"

"Above all Madre, Don Tristán de Luna, must *never* hear of this. He adores her, and I'm sure would not hesitate to kill Lorenzo if he knew what she's suffered at his hands."

"As God is my witness, only three people in this world, besides Sirena, know – yourself, sister Beatriz and me. Beatriz can neither read nor write, but most importantly, Our Lord Himself holds the key to her tongue!"

She informed him that Sirena had returned to her family palace on San Francisco Street six weeks ago. Her sister, Mercedes, was to be married in Guanajuato next month and she planned to attend. Also, due to the Act of Consolidation, she needed to reassess the financial status of La Torre hacienda and La Sirena mine.

"I'm not concerned about her finances," Madre Pilar observed. "It's her spiritual health that worries me. Even during labor, when she knew she might die, she flatly refused to confess to *any* priest but you."

She looked at him with open affection in her usually guarded gaze. "She has a very high opinion of you as a confessor – although I can't imagine why!" She tossed her head and gave him a teasing glimpse of the black-eyed half-gypsy girl he had known in his youth. It caught him completely by surprise and past became present – the sheepfold, the olive harvest festivals, the *jotas* they had danced together -- had those cherished days of youth been all of *forty years ago?*

"Madre," he questioned her gently, "in all these years I've never asked. How did you come to choose this life?"

"When you broke off with me to go to the seminary," she said forthrightly, "I made up my mind to either make you mad at me, or proud of me. I was deeply hurt, because I was young and -- as you may remember, head over heels in love."

"You're doing fine work here." He put his fingertips beneath her chin and lifted until her downcast eyes were level with his own. "Dear Teresita, you've made me *very* proud."

She gave him a youthfully radiant smile. "I'm glad. Even though my motives were spiteful, my vocation now means everything to me. But, as always, when Our Lord decides to build a fire, he uses whatever poor kindling lies at hand."

Rising he picked up his hat and cane. "Madre, I'll call on Sirena at once, and after my audience with the Viceroy, I'll come by and let you know if my arguments carried any weight." At the door he turned. "And I thank you again, my dear Madre, for all your kindness to Sirena."

"It was nothing," she murmured. "As you said, everything seemed to work out -- providentially."

⋄28⋆

Sirena gazed forlornly out the window of the Bishop's Episcopal coach as it rolled through the heart of the Bajío, the Bishop himself on the crimson velvet seat facing her. Everywhere were the sights and sounds reminiscent of her childhood. Scattered green islands of ash, elm and pepper trees still stood like honor guards around hoary cascos and haciendas. Spires and domes of countless ranch chapels rose above the treetops, symbols of bounty and peace, their pealing bells calling down God's benediction upon the land. Even the estates' names were melodious as chimes, and she recalled her father and herself reciting them aloud as they rode, and making them rhyme:

Santa Rosa, Santa Rita, Santa Fe!
Mariposa, Carmelita, Cristo Rey!

After that the Conde referred to them almost devoutly as the "Bajío's Litany of Saints."

The eighteen months between November of 1803, when she and Baron Von Humboldt rode through here last and this day, in early May of 1805, had been an eternity of loss, loneliness, suffering, and change. But the Bajío remained preserved in amber. If there were any change it was in its even greater fruitfulness. Crops were richer than she had ever seen them. Sleek coach mules fattened and blooded horses grazed in lush pastures, leggy spring colts frolicked with their dams.

The coach passed a slow, ox-drawn carreta filled with a bouquet of gaily dressed, carefully parasoled criollas, bound for a day in the country, convoyed by as many gallant young men on horseback, lent color and laughter to the pastoral beauty of the scene. Sirena's heart contracted at the bittersweet memory of her outings with Tristán. Dear God, had she ever been that innocent and carefree? Tears of grief and anger sprang to her eyes, as they did so often now. "Not only mystics and saints pass through the *'Dark Night of the Soul'*, my dear," Bishop Legázpi said comfortingly, daring to broach a subject she had been trying to avoid.

"I'm sorry to be such tearful company," she apologized.

She was deeply grateful to him for offering to travel with her to Guanajuato, and for giving her the comfort and privacy of his coach when she grew weary of the saddle. It proved a double blessing, for her health had suffered another setback with a severe reaction to the small pox vaccination Doctor Juan had given her before leaving Mexico.

Even in the confessional, where before he had easily touched her soul, the Bishop was unable to penetrate the protective wall she had built around herself. Within this fortress she dwelt in cold-hearted isolation, desolate over her loss of Tristán and embittered by hatred for Lorenzo. "What you're suffering is a form of spiritual aridity, Sirena. It's a time of healing from this tragic hurt." "I'm afraid it's more than that, Padrino. It's as though the silver rose of grace you spoke of no longer exists. I've not only lost Tristán and the love between us; I've lost my faith in God."

"It's a temptation against faith, but it's every bit as hard to bear." He glanced out the window at the passing landscape. "Nineteen years ago I made my first trip across this Bajío to preside at your christening. I so deeply regretted leaving family, friends and patria, I was sure I'd not only lost my vocation but my faith as well."

She looked at him in genuine surprise, incapable of imagining this Malta of spiritual strength ever having doubts or temptations of any kind.

"It was here at La Torre, when it was still a mesón, that we took shelter from the great hailstorm of '86. Here I first met Don Francisco. Here I gave absolution to an unknown muleteer, killed by lightning. From that night on I lost myself in others' lives -- and found my own." He reached across and patted her hand. "Our Lord withholds His consolations for reasons of his own, but trust me, you're not lost. He knows where you are."

Later he left the coach to join the others of the party traveling on horseback. Now she watched the four of them riding along the livestock trail paralleling the highway. Her brother Crispín and his shadow, Lucas Alamán, were twelve and thirteen now. Both students at the School of Mines, they were on their way to Guanajuato for their first summer of fieldwork in various mines there.

Father Hilario, riding with them, was a brother of Señora Alamán. He was also the priest secretly helping Crispín prepare for early entry into the seminary. Father Hilario was on his way to Guanajuato to become chaplain of the town regiment, which was under Don Antonio's Riaño's command.

With a scalding rush of envy and shame, Sirena realized that, at the tender age of twelve, her brother had enough faith to risk his mother's wrath and give up *everything* for God, while at nineteen she no longer had faith enough to utter a prayer!

When they stopped at La Torre for the midday meal, she felt her spirits lift a little. Old Martín told her how well they had done with the turnip crop, shipping five hundred cargas of seed to Don Francisco's mill to be pressed into oil for the lamps of Mexico. Then, as they were finishing their dessert, she was surprised to have her brother, Ramón, and Alicia's brother, David, suddenly burst in upon them.

"So what are you two doing this far from your beloved Queen's Regiment in San Miguel el Grande?" Sirena asked, when the initial greetings had been exchanged.

"We're on our way to join the Viceroy at the annual cantonment of regimental troops in Jalapa," Ramón replied enthusiastically.

"Is it true our Viceroy's gaining great popularity with the troops at these cantonments?" Bishop Legázpi inquired, for private reasons of his own.

"Of course it's true!" David Ávila responded. "He soldiers along with the rest of us, taking all the risks of field maneuvers. He even shares his table with men of lower rank, showing none of the haughtiness you'd expect from a man so close to the crown."

With the threatened Act of Consolidation hanging over everyone's head, Sirena realized her view of this Viceroy was jaundiced. But neither soldier seemed to have any inkling of how else this man spent his time when not playing war games.

"We're traveling with Captain Allende," Ramón replied impatiently. "So we only stopped for a quick visit when we saw Your Excellency's coach outside."

As everyone filed out of the dining room, Ramón drew Sirena aside, leading her into the empty overseer's office and closing the door behind him.

"Sirena, I just came from visiting Mamá," he began in a confidential tone. "She's beside herself with grief."

"Did she take the news of Felipe's death that hard?"

"She's in mourning for him, if that's what you mean.

 I'm talking about what's happened to Mercedes." He pulled her down beside him on a long bench. "You're going to be sickened by what I have to say," he began, in the patronizing tone of an older, wiser brother, "but I'll tell you how it came about, the same way Mamá" told me."

He explained that Don Telmo and Neto were gone for three weeks on business, and as soon as they left, Mercedes came down with fever. As she got worse, Doña Isabel recalled that she had refused the new vaccine, afraid the inoculation would make her too ill for the wedding.

"But then when the spots began to appear. . ."

"Oh, Ramón, she didn't come down with small pox?"

"Oh, yes she did! And the *worst* kind there is. It's called 'hailstones,' because it forms a solid mass of huge, white, suppurating sores. It covered her face and upper body. The sight was so revolting I had to leave the room."

Although Mercedes survived, Ramón compared her to a leper. Portions of her nostrils, lips and eyelids had been eaten away, transforming her into a grotesque parody of the pearl-skinned beauty she had been before.

"What will the poor girl do?" Sirena asked, dismayed.

"She's already done it."

Mercedes made Isabel swear not to call a doctor, or even let the servants know she had the pox. Too proud to face Neto or her friends, she had Isabel offer a fat fee that gained her quick entry to a convent of Carmelites in Celaya. The faces of these nuns were forever veiled, even to their own families, visiting only in 'speak rooms' from behind heavy black curtains and protected by a grille with iron spikes.

Instead of the customary farewell party with the nun herself presiding, Mercedes swore Matías to secrecy and had him retouch her wedding portrait, which showed her former beauty, but crowned now with flowers and wearing the habit of her Order. This *crowned nun's* portrait was displayed on an easel in the sala, replacing the real Bride of Christ, whom Ramón had just rushed to Celaya in a heavily curtained coach.

"The 'crowned nun's party' was eerie," Ramón continued, "all Mercedes' friends swallowing Mamá's pious fiction that she had 'answered an eleventh hour *call to religious life*!'

"And there was poor, dumb Neto, in a daze, wondering what in Hell had happened. For months Mercedes was climbing her stall for him, hotter than a Barb filly in heat, then overnight, he was jilted for Christ!"

As they walked together to his horse he told her coldly, "I know you've never suffered in your own life, Sirena, but try to understand what real pain is, and help Mamá through this tragedy."

As the two gasconading regimentals raced off, it struck her anew how callous Ramón was. No apology for the knife fight in the Coliseo! Not a word about Manila, or how she had survived what was infamous throughout the kingdom as the worst return voyage in the history of the galleon!

Sirena was chilled by a dread premonition. First there was Felipe in his Sangley den, and now poor Mercedes, locked in her cell. What sinister fate lay coiled, like a rattlesnake in the road, waiting to strike Ramón?

ஐ29ஐ

Tristán stood beside the pole man on the keelboat, his eyes scanning the Mississippi bank for a familiar landing. Then, her square sail shining in the sun, the boat swung out of the river's mainstream and made for the wooded western shore. With a warning blast of her ship's horn, she put in at the small private dock belonging to Captain James Lowell's Louisiana plantation, named after the Spanish saint, Santiago.

As Tristán stepped ashore with his portmanteau, he saw a well-dressed white couple standing in the shade of a moss-bearded oak. From their furtive glances and gestures he could tell they were discussing him. Having drawn the same curious stares downriver in New Orleans, he knew it was not merely because he was a Spanish officer in uniform. What set him apart, even in this backwater, was the mantle of notoriety that had settled upon him as soon as he set foot on the soil of what was now called 'Louisiana Territory.'

A moment later Captain Lowell appeared and enfolded him in an affectionate abrazo. "Welcome to Santiago, Tristán! I've been watching the river every day since your letter came from Natchitoches!"

Although the Revolutionary War hero's hair was a bit whiter than at their last meeting in the Riaño mansion, Tristán saw he retained his youthful soldierly bearing.

"I could get rich selling tickets to my neighbors if they knew you were my guest!" Lowell told him with a chuckle as they climbed the slow incline from the dock. They passed through a shaded aisle of over-arching giant elms that led to Santiago plantation's French-style main house, surrounded by white columned double galleries.

Lowell led his guest inside, and into his high-ceilinged library, which like Santiago's heavily shaded grounds, also gave the illusion of being pleasantly cool. Its bookshelves were filled with an impressive collection, and it was easy to see why Captain James and Don Gabriel were lifelong friends as well as brothers by marriage, bound as they were by their shared passion for books.

"I apologize for our stifling August heat," Lowell said, going to the high, bombe chest that held his hospitality tray of liquors. Lifting the tapered stopper from a red-glass decanter, he poured two drinks while they talked.

Tristán settled contentedly into a wing-backed chair overlooking the flower-filled back garden. "My dear captain, after two winters in New Mexico, I no longer complain about heat."

Handing Tristán his glass he lifted his own, "To your great achievement of capturing Zebulon Pike, and to your own New Spain!" The fine English crystal rang softly as their glasses touched.

"I'm afraid what you call my 'great achievement'," Tristán said modestly, "was actually due to the bad judgment of your own Territorial Governor Wilkinson. Entrusting his illegal expedition to his inexperienced young protégé -- was the classic case of sending a boy to do a man's job."

Seating himself nearby, Lowell asked, "Where did you finally intercept Pike's party?"

"A stone's throw from the Rio Bravo, close to Santa Fe and deep inside Spanish territory."

"Did they put up a fight?"

"Actually they greeted us as saviors. They had only light summer uniforms against bitter winter cold. If we hadn't come upon them brazenly building their military stockade they would have frozen to death and taken Baron Von Humboldt's plagiarized maps to the cold grave with them!"

Tristán relished his brandy while he reflected on the humorous irony surrounding his capture of what American newspapers were touting as Pike's 'lost' Legion.

"What was Pike's excuse for building a U.S. fort on Spanish territory?" Lowell asked.

"He said he *thought* he was on the Red River, not the 'Rio Grande', as he calls our Rio Bravo. But Wilkinson knew where he sent him, having mapped Pike's route in secret, without even Jefferson's knowledge or sanction. Pike was to reach Santa Fe and establish it as the entrepot of a lucrative trade between the isolated Spanish settlers and the money-hungry merchants of Missouri."

"I'm sure Wilkinson is a double-spy, but for years General Washington protected him in these shady deals."

"The Pike ploy was to bring about the steady eastward flow of New Spain's silver peso -- the soundest currency in the world today."

"Of course, marching Pike to Chihuahua made *you* a celebrated villain, and poor Pike a martyred hero."

"The case fell under my father's jurisdiction as acting Commandant General of the frontier provinces. Pike *had* to stand trial in that court. My father confiscated Pike's secret papers and warned him the next time they were caught they'd all be shot without trial." A wry smile played across Tristán's lips. "What made me a 'celebrity' was the thankless task of escorting the crestfallen young Pike all the way back to Natchitoches to set him free."

Lowell refilled their glasses and Tristán announced with a broad grin, "To cap it all, a note was sent me in my New Orleans hotel, inviting me to call on my old nemesis, the Governor of Louisiana Territory, General James Wilkinson!"

"You mean the old rogue had the gall to face you after all that?"

"He wanted to size up the enemy and somehow use me to cover his ass."

"He's a shrewd one."

"Yes, but like most ignorant Yankee frontiersmen, he's lordly proud of what he *doesn't* know."

"He claims he's the expert on New Spain's *Dons*, as he insists on calling you."

"Yes, I know. As I was leaving, he became the open-minded Baptist, inquiring of his Catholic neighbor. 'Please, Don Tristán,' he asked earnestly, 'can you tell me which of your Catholic Saints is *Sant Afee?*'" Captain Lowell roared with laughter.

Bent double with his own mirth, Tristán choked out, "Captain, I was appalled! I replied, 'General, you've been angling to steal the City of the Holy Faith for twenty years and you still don't know what its name *means* or how to *pronounce* it?'"

Later that day, in the stables where Captain Lowell was showing off his prize jumpers to Tristán, the talk turned to more personal matters.

"Perhaps we can meet again soon in Guanajuato," Lowell speculated. "This November, Don Antonio will be celebrating the completion and dedication of his Alhóndiga." He ran a hand over the blazed face of a favorite sorrel. "Sirena sent me this news in a note inviting me to attend a surprise reception and ball for the Riaños at her palace afterwards."

Tristán had to restrain his heart, which at mere mention of her name seemed to overflow with all the old forbidden dreams and desires. "Oh?" he said, trying to sound only mildly interested. "And, is Sirena well?"

"She seems so now, although both Gabriel and Antonio wrote a while back that she was very ill and despondent when she first returned from Manila. . ."

"My God!" Tristán broke in, "Sirena sailed to Manila?"

"Yes," Lowell continued, "There was something about her brother not being able to make the voyage."

Tristán fell silent, afraid to pursue this avenue of conversation lest he betray his own deep emotional involvement with Sirena to this perceptive older man.

"So, where do you go when you leave here?" Lowell asked.

"I'm carrying a secret dispatch on the Pike affair to the Viceroy in Mexico City. From there I report to General Calleja in San Luis Potosí, headquarters for the Royal Army. Thank God, I'll be stationed there now permanently; instead of always guarding the outer marches."

"Well then," Captain Lowell suggested, "on your way north from Mexico to San Luis, why not steal a few days of pleasure for yourself? Why not ride over to Guanajuato and help us celebrate?"

A week later Tristán took ship at New Orleans for Vera Cruz. In Mexico he gave the Viceroy a detailed report on the Pike incident and described the precarious state of the frontier. In an impassioned speech he told how American Indian agents were everywhere haranguing the tribes to break their treaties and alliances with Spain. Bribes of muskets and raw whiskey fired the Indians to increase their attacks on New Spain's borders, which for more than thirty years had been critically under-manned.

He made it clear that in the wake of Lewis and Clark's march to the Pacific and Pike's invasion of Santa Fe, an army of footloose trappers, traders and adventurers pouring out of Kentucky and Tennessee, were poised beside that main artery into the newly-opened American West, the 'Great Missouri'. Their greed for pelts and land, together with their still-bewitching dream of finding the mythical silver mines of Santa Fe, would soon place the Yankee crowbar firmly beneath the Spanish rock.

When he left the viceregal palace hours later, Tristán could only pray he had convinced this notoriously self-serving Viceroy that, whatever the cost to the Spanish crown, northern New Spain was irretrievably lost to United States' expansionists unless border defenses were tripled.

In October Tristán left Mexico for San Luis Potosí. He tried to keep his mind on his destination and the pleasant prospect of toasting Calleja's recent marriage to the criolla beauty, Francisca Gandera, heiress of an old Potosí family.

But the more he thought of the General's marital happiness, the more miserable his own life seemed, in turn, sharpening the pain of separation from Sirena which tortured him day and night. Lowell's seductive words, "Why not steal a few days of pleasure for yourself?" rang in his ears. The thought of seeing her made his head reel, the idea of holding her in his arms while they waltzed inflamed his senses.

He argued pro and con, but when he reached the turnoff where the trail branched, the man in love seized the reins. Even his long-legged palomino seemed in a hurry to get to where Sirena was, as quickly as possible! Or was it that his own spurs kept urging his mount from walk to trot to gallop?

⋐30⋑

"Hard at work as usual, I see!"

Sirena glanced up from under the wide brim of her leghorn to see Don Francisco walking toward her across the stone-paved floor of the processing patio.

"Where else would a spinster 'silver lord' be on a Friday afternoon except here among her arrastres?" she laughed, hastening to meet him. Tucking both hands in the crook of his arm she planted a fond kiss on his cheek. "So what brings you to visit my fine new Atocha refinery?"

"Merely checking to see if my protégé is doing her old maestro proud." He placed his hand over both of hers, as they strolled together to her office. "Actually my dear, it's a social call. I'm accepting an invitation to the reception and ball that you're giving the Riaños."

"Good! I'm so glad you stayed on, instead of returning to Mexico early with the summer students. It's going to be a grand reunion."

"Who's coming?"

"From up North there'll be Uncle Gabriel, the dear old Fourth Marqués de Àvila with Adrian, and a real treat for the Riaños -- Captain James Lowell is coming from Louisiana!"

"It's nice of you to bring them all together this way!" He looked down at her proudly. "I swear, you're the very image of that little girl I used to take to work with me every morning after we lost our dear Patrick, all dressed up in your pretty green dimity gown and flat black slippers!"

She blushed and glanced down at her empire dress and fashionable, but practical shoes. "You forget that little girl turned twenty-one a few months ago!"

"All the more reason you shouldn't be here. You should be out waltzing in the arms of a dashing young regimental!" She gave him the shadow of a smile. "Actually, I only dropped by for a while. Ricardo's taking over at five."

Despite his teasing, she knew he was not surprised to find her here. This newly built *hacienda de beneficio*, with its three large patios and seventy arrastres, was where she had her office and spent most of her time. Here she processed La Sirena's low-grade ore, as well as that of other mine owners who, not having their own processing patios, farmed the work out to her for a fee. The increased earnings enabled her to raise her workers' wages, now the highest in town, while still allowing each man to take home his *partido* every Friday night, just as Don Patrick had always done.

Arm in arm, they threaded their way among several spans of mules, each team treading its own circular torta of crushed ore. A workman asked her to check the primeness of the batch he was working. She stopped at his torta while he turned the mass over deftly with a short spade, lifting unmixed ore from bottom to top. Then she scooped up a sample with the large horn spoon suspended from a cord at her waist. Francisco watched with keen interest as she took a pinch from the spoon, rolled it between thumb and forefinger, and judged from its subtleties of texture if it was time to add powdered *magistral* or salt. The sharp metallic odor rising from the mixture lent a nostalgic quality to her work that never failed to remind her of the first time her father took her to visit his two bonanza mines.

"This batch needs one more day," she advised the workman, "I'll tell Ricardo to check it again tomorrow."

Reaching the far end of the patio, they climbed three stone steps and entered the cool interior of her office, its one wide window overlooking all three patios below.

Seating herself at what had been the Conde's carved red cedar desk she gave Francisco a mischievous grin. "Since my *azoguero* is off for the Holy Days, do you think you might be experienced enough to take on the job?"

He drew up a straight chair and straddled it, resting his chin on his folded arms as he studied her. "Probably not, but I'd certainly be working for the most popular mine owner in town."

"That depends on one's viewpoint," she said laughingly, removing the cord and horn spoon. "Don't expect Don Telmo to share your high opinion of me."

"You're fighting the same battle your father and I waged against him before you were born."

"He never dreamed I'd have the temerity to demand a seat as a voting member of the silver tribunal, and when I was elected Deputy

General for the next four years, I thought he and Neto would have a joint attack of apoplexy!"

"Naturally! By paying your men fair wages and the partido, you encourage all free workers to boycott him."

"But now he's hiring whip men and press gangs, forcibly dragging men in to work for him."

"It's rumored he's in dire financial straits. When the Act of Consolidation was enforced, it's said Don Telmo had to repay several enormous, long-standing Church loans."

"I'm grateful I was spared that fate by La Torre's seed crop and the huge profits I cleared on my Manila cargo."

"You bought wisely and well," he said approvingly, "but I can tell you now, I was worried over the severely despondent state you were in when you first got home. I'd been told some women never recover from a voyage on the galleon and, knowing the horrors of yours, I feared you were one of them."

"I was merely worn out -- with the fevers," she hedged.

"No need for me to know the cause. I just thank God you're well now. As the first woman Deputy General ever; elected by the silver lords themselves to this position of power, you're a dynamic force for justice in our city, a leader around whom men of rank and honor are proud to rally." Francisco left his chair and turned to look out the window, his customary way of concealing strong emotions. "And you've brought the Graciana palace back to life. The night Patrick's body lay there in state, I was sure I'd never see that ballroom lit again." When he returned to face her, tears still stood in his eyes.

"One reason I do so much entertaining, Francisco, is to reconcile hostile Spaniards and criollos. Every family here is made up of both, but Don Telmo has split them into two warring camps. My ballroom is like neutral ground where they can set aside their differences and even see how petty they really are. After all, not every Spanish immigrant is another Don Telmo -- as Captain Allende would have us believe! Nor *every* criollo the anti-gachupín rounder and gambler Captain Allende has himself become."

"I only wish Tristán could be hosting these receptions with you," he said with unexpected candor, searching her eyes. She sensed he was waiting for her reaction, and when there was none he asked, "Have you noticed his name's on every tongue, since he captured Lieutenant Pike?"

"I've heard," she said coldly. "That's his life. I've had to make my own -- without him."

Building this new life had not been easy. Returning to Guanajuato in the spring of 1805, she had faced the cruel truth she was no longer the innocent, hopeful girl who so blithely embarked on the galleon. But it took a visit from her mother's cousin, Inéz, to see the woman she was in danger of becoming. Inéz was a bitter, self-pitying spinster, who had let her unrequited love for Francisco sour her life.

With the Bishop's guidance, Sirena slowly forged a new identity, becoming a *viuda* of sorts, a never-married widow who nonetheless mourned a lost love and had buried a child. Taking her destiny in her own hands, she refused to look back. Locking Tristán out of this half-life, meant doing violence to herself, but she decided it was less painful to make a single agonizing renunciation of her love for him, than to suffer the endless torment of renouncing a little more of it each day.

But Francisco had helped her turn a corner earlier this year, by giving her a brass plaque commemorating the silver anniversary of the sinking of the Santa Cruz shaft in La Sirena. Beneath the dates 1782-1807, was engraved a portion of an ancient Aztec prophecy Don Patrick had repeated with a characteristic enthusiasm the very morning he brought in his second bonanza.

The Gods of Gold departed
When their sun dried up at noon,
But the Gods of Silver -- Never!
They vowed to stay forever
Till the Drowning of the Moon!

"I stumbled on this poem among some old papers," Francisco wrote on a card accompanying the gift, "May it keep the Conde's buoyant spirit alive, and help revitalize your own."

The daily sight of that poem on the plaque, which she had embedded in the stone collar of the Santa Cruz shaft, was a tonic that restored Sirena's zest for life and renewed her faith in the constancy of the 'Gods of Silver.' Throwing herself single-mindedly into developing the full potential of her mines, she began the herculean task of sinking the new Saint Patrick shaft, named for her father, in La Sirena mine. Recalling Francisco's signal gift, Sirena now regretted responding so sharply to his question about Tristán.

"My dear Francisco, the plaque and its poem helped more than anything to heal the wounds dealt me on the galleon."

"I'm glad. And hasn't your writing helped as well?"

"Yes, thanks again to you for letting me use the Hermitage. I'm able to steal away from the distractions of the palace and write there almost every weekend, undisturbed."

Sirena had shared the secret of her writing with no one, especially her mother. She was sure Isabel did not know this Hermitage even existed, but she was not about to tell her, since it was her only truly private retreat. The writing itself grew out of her loneliness for Tristán, hours when she yearned to pour her heart out to him in passionate love letters, an indulgence the Bishop forbade, lest her imprudent declarations of love fall into unfriendly hands.

"Captain Lowell told me there was need for a 'History of New Spain' for Yankee readers, so I'm hard at work on it," she told Francisco, adding with a flash of honest pride, "I'm writing it in English, too, but without the usual anti Spanish-Catholic bias of most British authors." She was silent a moment and then said, "That's one of several bittersweet reasons I'm not off waltzing in the arms of a dashing regimental this holiday."

Francisco rose to leave, "I'm glad my old retreat is of use to someone," he said with a pensive smile, "it's been years since I've been able to -- enjoy it."

The following morning, as Sirena rode off alone to a weekend of writing, a sense of *deep* spiritual distress came over her. She had just attended a memorial Mass for her father, celebrated as always on this Day of All Souls. She had prayed and received Holy Communion, devoid of all fervor. This continued resistance to every prompting of grace disturbed her. She had been a child of such abiding faith. Prayer had come as easily as breath. Where had it all gone? Killing her love for Tristán seemed to have sealed her inside a cold stone sepulcher, making her incapable of giving or receiving love from either God or man.

But stepping into the sanctuary of the Hermitage always quieted her troubled soul. Francisco had completely refurnished it for her, with a comfortable couch, chairs and writing desk, a small kitchen and a cozy bedroom. She had found a fine buffalo robe, packed away in a cedar-lined chest and, after shaking out the deep glossy fur, decided to use it as a coverlet for her bed.

After a late lunch she set herself to writing at the desk, and when darkness fell was still so deeply engrossed, she paused only long enough to light a second candle.

The profound silence of twilight in these dark hills was suddenly broken by an eerie wail. She felt the hair at the nape of her neck stand on end. What was it? A lost child? A panther's cry? Then it stopped as quickly as it began.

Laying the pen aside and taking up a candle, she moved to the door and opened it, the faint rustle of her silk damask skirt the only sound. In the doorway she listened. Nothing! Then the plaintive cry spiraled up again.

She scanned the hill's moon-washed incline leading down from the tree-hidden stable, and froze. There was no mistaking the figure emerging from those trees, his shadow stalking him down the blue-white slope: no mistaking the Cheyenne wooing song or the vibrant sweetness of a cedar flute. Tristán! It must not be him, but it was!

She panicked at the thought of letting that searing love live again. It would tear her apart. Every instinct of survival told her to blowout the candle and bar the door before he saw her. He'd only stumbled on this place, there was no way he could know she was here!

She snuffed the candle, but too late. He had seen her, and was begging her to come to him. For the space of a heartbeat she stood in the doorway, paralyzed. Then like an arrow shot from its bow she sped straight toward him, calling his name, aching to reach the forbidden haven of his arms.

Every barrier she had erected against him during the past four years, fell like straw before his touch. The fierceness of his welcoming embrace seemed to weld their very souls into one. His first kiss opened her entire being to him as the morning sun opens a rose.

"Forgive me for taking you unaware," he said in a rush of words, half-apology, half a fervent plea to understand how desperately he was driven. "I simply had to see you, hold you, kiss you once again – or die of longing for you!"

He carried her into the Hermitage, and sank down on the couch with her still in his arms.

"Oh, Tristán, I've lived whole lifetimes since the night you left for Santa Fe"

"God forgive me," he murmured, covering her lips and eyelids with expiatory kisses. "It cut me to the heart to leave you that way, but I dared not stay."

She pressed her cheek against his quilted cotton vest, secretly elated he had come to her wearing his frontier lancer's armor, spurs and sword.

"I wrote, but you never answered. In all my dreams I saw you lying like this in Adrian's arms. For the love of God, tell me those dreams weren't true, say you love me still!"

"Oh, Tristán, I love you and want only you! You'll always be my adored conquistador!"

"Thank God, thank God," he murmured gratefully, rocking her in his embrace. "This time I'll take you, make you my own!" He blew out the single candle's flame. "Surely you know I'd kill any other man I found doing half of what I'm doing to you now! If I'm such a jealous, envious protector, Sirena, it's because I know in my soul, God intended you for me!"

Throwing aside all caution and restraint, his hands were already inside her gown, savoring the never-forgotten sweetness of her body, seeking to reclaim the breasts she had given him that other night, eons ago. She abandoned herself to him with a wantonness that melted what small resolve he had left. Suddenly he was desperately afraid. That other night he had barely bridled the blind desire to ravish her that her innocent eroticism aroused in him. But now all self-mastery failed him, tonight he had rendered himself helpless by coming here and finding her every bit as wildly, blindly, recklessly in love with him as he with her.

What am I to do? He asked himself, appalled at the risks to which he was about to expose her. How could he hope to contain the fire of their passion, consummate their love, and at the same time keep himself from dishonoring her? Then, like words spoken by some Christian knight of Spain's Reconquista, the answer came to him. "Do you recall the recourse of Spanish lovers past," Tristán asked, "when priests could not be found on the Moorish frontier?"

"Yes," she replied, puzzled by his query. "Even here in New Spain, they married each other 'In the Sight of God,' as it was called, and the Church even recognized such vows."

As with those lovers, Sirena, our love, too, is pure in the sight of God," he said, rising to unsheath the short cavalry sword at his side. Then, sinking to his knees, he drew her down beside him. Holding up before them the wire-wrapped iron sword hilt, which formed a perfect Cross, he declared, "Here, 'in the sight of God' I, Tristán do solemnly take thee, Sirena, as my true bride. I swear upon this sacred Cross, and upon my honor, to always love thee, protect thee and cleave to thee alone, in this life and in the life to come. Amen."

"Upon this holy Cross," she breathed with a spiritual fervor she had thought lost to her forever, "I, Sirena, do solemnly swear to take thee, Tristán, as my true spouse, 'in the sight of God,' to love and honor above all others, to be true to thee alone, in this life and in the life to come. Amen."

Gravely, each kissed the sword-hilt Cross and then blessed themselves. Lifting Sirena to her feet in the quiet moonlit room, he asked in a hesitant whisper, "Will my lady do me the honor of removing my armor with her own hands?"

Accepting the weapon he gave her, she kissed the blade, set it aside and removed his quilted vest. Having herself been reared with the same chivalric code by her father, she understood what it cost a frontiersman to forfeit his role as trusted protector, for in so doing he imperiled the very knightly virtues that gave his manhood worth. Sirena knew it was a trust not lightly given nor one to be treated lightly by the woman in whose care it was placed.

"Your sword and armor are safe with me forever, my lord,' she told him softly. "Rendering yourself weaponless for my sake only makes me love you more." Then she shivered as the shadow of Lorenzo suddenly rose between them, "But, I'm afraid of – what if I'm not able to – please you?"

He smiled and gently placed her on her bed in the deep soft fur of the 'Comanche Peace' buffalo robe, as though restoring a fallen sparrow to its nest. "A wise adelantado never storms a beautiful wilderness. The more he loves and explores his realm, the more it pleases him." She was stunned that he was not demanding some hidden proof of purity as the Marquésa de Ávila had told her years ago every bridegroom had the right to do. For this tremendous grace she would be everlastingly grateful, and from somewhere deep inside her soul she felt an enormous wave of thanksgiving to God.

"Mi alma," she said her eyes misting over with emotion, "You've rolled away the stone from my soul. I know it seems a moral contradiction, but when I denied my love for you I shut out every other grace as well. Now at last I feel whole again."

"Do you intend to tell you confessor – about us?"

"No," she replied slowly, "Bishop Legázpi is my spiritual director, but in some things I know myself far better now than he. At least I know what I can live with and who I cannot live *without*." She felt her soul dissolve as his lips touched hers in a fervent grateful kiss. "Besides he cares so deeply for us both, it would be unfair to lay that heavy burden on him."

"You're quite a realist, my love," he sighed. "I confessed to that good man before I left for Santa Fe, so I know he would be even harder on me now, holding me entirely responsible – and he'd be right."

"I'm learning there are hard choices in life that don't always square perfectly with doctrine, but we needn't lose our Faith over them. As Papá used to say, 'God doesn't expect miracles from mortals. He asks only that they prize honor, love God and their fellow man, and have a heart that's pure.'"

"Would you have me break my word as a gentleman?"

"It had to be Francisco. He's the only one who could possibly have known."

"When I arrived in town today he was a fellow dinner guest at the Valencianas' with whom I always stay. At table he said you were at Linda Vista. But later, as I rode out the gate, he told me you were here, in his well-hidden retreat."

She smiled as she recalled Francisco's remark that she should spend the holiday waltzing in the arms of a dashing young regimental. Well, lacking only the music, he'd certainly seen to that! "For a confirmed bachelor, don't you think Francisco shows surprising insights into the nature of love?"

"Perhaps he's used this hidden nest for a trysting place himself in his time," Tristán speculated. "I noticed when I put my horse up earlier tonight, the stable has two stalls. You have to admit, this place is a perfect lovers hideaway."

"Tristán, how can you even *think* such a thing? You know how good and genuinely devout he is. It's like accusing Saint Francis of being – well – *Casanova!*"

Tristán arched a brow. "He could easily have a carnal side that no one else suspects. I must say, for a girl who was raised by them, you don't know very much about men!"

Smiling wisely, she kissed his shoulder. "Thanks to you, my lord, I know all I need to know."

☙31❧

The Graciana ballroom, brilliant under its five chandeliers, was crowded with splendidly dressed couples young and old, dancing to an orchestra hired to play only German waltzes the entire afternoon.

Waltzing with Adrian Ávila, Sirena gave a sigh of satisfaction as her gaze swept the room.

"I've never seen you look more radiant," Adrian said, "It's as though there were an argent lamp hidden somewhere inside of you."

She blushed and thought, dear God, my love must be showing! "Well, I'm pleased with the way things are going."

What an understatement! She had never been happier in her life. It was ten days since Tristán arrived and he was staying two more. Today's dedication of the Alhóndiga had gone off well, despite an outrageous breach of etiquette committed by her brother Ramón. And as planned, this ball had brought criollo and immigrant factions together, making her ponder anew why they were rivals at all. Uncle Gabriel said the split was formerly unknown, but was caused by the recent economic backwardness of Spain, which drove many more Spaniards to immigrate and vie with criollo males for land, mines and high posts in church and state. A major irritant to criollo men was their women's propensity for Spanish husbands, leading gachupíns to engage in a near Sabine rape of criolla brides. Well, the gachupín contingent was well represented here tonight, she thought. Stiff-necked Neto and his brother had both deigned to come, and even Don Telmo and Isabel!

Sirena was pleased that both General Calleja of the Tenth Brigade and General Flon of the next important Second Brigade, headquartered in Puebla, had surprised her by coming with their wives. Doña Victoria Riaño was overjoyed to have her last surviving sister, Flon's wife, Marianne, visiting her, as well as her brother-in-law, Captain Lowell. Sirena smiled to see General Calleja looking almost boyish as he whirled his lovely young bride, Francisca, with all the sprightliness of a twenty-year old cadet.

"I was surprised to see Don Tristán at the Alhóndiga with you today," Adrian remarked. "That Pike affair seems to have won him extra points. It's rumored he's being promoted."

Sirena was caught off guard. She and Tristán had taken great care not to be seen together, but today he arranged to meet her "accidentally" at church after Mass, and 'offered' to escort her to the Alhónidga. With this ruse they had spent all day together, Tristán even attending the ball earlier, but he risked only one waltz before prudently disappearing. Now with great caution she composed her reply to Adrian. "I wouldn't be surprised! General Calleja is as proud of Tristán as if he were his own son."

"And you?" Adrian asked.

She felt his eyes boring through her. "Naturally, I'm proud of him, too." A slow tingle of fear crept up the back of her neck. Did Adrian suspect something between them?

"Ever since I saw you two together during Humboldt's visit, I guessed you were more than fond of him."

Frightened, she snapped open her fan. "Well, like you, Adrian, I regard him almost as a brother."

"Forgive me, Sirena. I envy *every* man I see you with." He drew her closer to him. "As you can tell, I'm still in love with you."

There was an awkward pause and then she asked, "How are things going at La Soledad?"

"Life goes on pretty much as usual," he said without enthusiasm, "except I took the advice you gave me before leaving for Manila and got engaged." He colored slightly.

"Oh, Adrian, congratulations!" A flood of genuine affection welled up within her, for she sincerely wanted his happiness. "Do I know her?"

"You might. It's Juliana Amayo."

Adrian engaged to the Third Condesa de Amayo! Sirena was stunned. Juliana was heiress to one of the kingdom's greatest silver fortunes, quite a coup for a man as shy as he. The Amayos were norteños, but like many other nobles, Juliana's grandfather opted to move to Mexico, and his heirs preferred to stay there. That troubled Sirena. City life was not for Adrian. He was a born hacendado who was welded to the land.

"Of course the wedding's not for two years. We'll marry when she turns fifteen."

Hardly the anxious bridegroom, she thought. Was the aging Fourth Marqués having money troubles? Had the match been struck because the Ávila's needed Juliana's dowry?

"How did you come through the Act of Consolidation?"

"Papá was carrying quite a few church mortgages, so we were pretty hard hit. He shrugged, "But then, who wasn't?" After a pause he added, "He came down for this ball and to visit friends," Adrian said evasively, "but mostly to see Bishop Legázpi. He was hoping to get a substantial loan from his Diocesan fund, and was crushed to learn he was gone. Whatever possessed the Bishop to visit Spain?"

"He's been trying to get the King's ear," she replied. "Since letters got no results he went in person to persuade His Majesty to rescind the Act of Consolidation, the hated Indian tribute and several laws restricting commerce here."

"Papá prefers borrowing from an old friend, one who still believes he's good for it."

"Oh, Adrian!" she said in open dismay, "Of course he's good for it! A House as old and respected as Àvila? Why who *wouldn't* give such a loan!"

When the orchestra stopped for intermission she slipped away from Adrian and sought out his father. She saw him, standing dejectedly alone by the King's dais and throne. She made up her mind to offer him a long-term loan of thirty-thousand pesos. His pride would not be compromised, coming as it did from an old friend like herself. He declined her offer. When the music started up she declined to dance, making her way instead to the side of Don Fabian, the proud old Fourth Marqués of Ávila.

☙ ❧

"Well, I think everything went well today, don't you?" Sirena asked Alberta as she changed into a bottle green velvet riding habit after a refreshing bath.

"Everything except Ramón's disgracing his entire family by performing that low dance with Analinda in the Alhóndiga!" Alberta exploded. "And before the holy water even had time to dry from Father Hilario's blessing the place!"

"I know Alberta. The dedication was a solemn civic and religious ceremony. I can't imagine what possessed Ramón to humiliate Don Antonio in front of all his guests."

The blessing of the new granary had barely ended when Ramón, in full regimental uniform, and Analinda, barefoot and in low-cut peasant blouse and red flannel skirt, ran into the center of the patio, accompanied by four strolling musicians. There they proceeded to perform a dance depicting a barnyard rooster pursuing, and in the end, "covering" a hen. But even more out of place for the occasion, were the words of the song, lustily sung by their accompanists:

> *Hell has ceased to be!*
> *What have we to dread?*
> *So come, my love,*
> *Make free with me,*
> *For the Demons are all dead!*

When the dance ended, the couple fled the building.

General Calleja and Tristán had sought out Ramón's commanding officer, Captain Ignacio Allende. Later, Tristán told Sirena what had passed between them.

"What's the meaning of this suggestive dance by an officer of your regiment?" Tristán had demanded.

"Well, I think its meaning would be clear even to a eunuch!" was Allende's scornful reply. "We call it *pan de jarabe* since some find its real name unacceptably lewd."

"I know the jarabe well," Calleja put in, "it was born in a barracks and that's where it should stay! I don't question its doubtful merits, but I do question the intent behind staging it here. It was a premeditated insult to Don Antonio Riaños and the purpose of his Alhóndiga."

"Who put Ramón up to it?" Tristán asked.

Allende answered with a question. "Why don't you ask the 'prankster of Dolores', Father Miguel Hidalgo? It was idea, and the singers are potters who work for the priest!"

"If Ramón had a decent superior officer," Sirena said, as Alberta turned to leave the room, "he would have been cashiered from the Queen's Regiment without further ado, but Captain Allende encourages such impudence."

Since it was still daylight, Sirena was going to steal away to the Hermitage. She had told Alberta the plausible story that she was staying with Isabel tonight and riding over with her to Linda Vista tomorrow.

Setting her red-plumed tricorn on her head, Sirena studied herself in the mirror, remembering Adrian's remarks about Tristán, and Francisco's words about her being the highly respected Deputy General of the silver consulado. What if the mining elite and all her other guests today, should learn about Tristán and herself? What would happen to her sterling reputation and his? She sighed uneasily. Well, when she gave herself to him she knew it wasn't entirely without risks, and she knew many more problems would be posed by their secret affair.

Hurrying into the corner suite to pick up her riding gloves from the desk where she had left them, she found a gaily-wrapped package addressed to her. Inside was a crystal bud vase containing three exquisitely wrought silver roses on a silver stem, and a verse in Tristán's hand:

> *So rare are silver roses,*
> *My heart counts only three.*
> *The rose of Grace,*
> *The city where thy dear self repose.*
> *And thee.*

For a moment she was completely overcome, tears of love and happiness springing to her eyes. God in Heaven, what a dear man he was! What did it matter that their liaisons were fraught with danger? Being married to him, 'in the sight of God' was worth every risk!

Arriving at the Hermitage, breathless from a fast ride on her favorite white Arab racer, Emir, she opened the door to find a fire crackling on the hearth and Tristán in a silk lounge coat, seated in the bergere beside the desk, reading her *'North American's History of New Spain'*.

She stood there transfixed at the wonder of his being here, her heart swelling at the sight of his dark blue eyes gazing up at her, beckoning her to come to him.

"Don't move, my love," she said, "I just want to look at you, to remember you forever as you are -- here and now."

He smiled and rose from the chair impatiently. "If you won't come to me, I'll simply have to come to you!" he whispered, catching her in his embrace and tossing her tricorn aside. "I wanted to tell you my news earlier, but I didn't trust myself to survive a second waltz with you in front of everyone. God," he said, burying his face in her hair, "I was ready to rape you right there!"

"And I *wanted* you to!" she breathed, his long kiss leaving her faint, but still vaguely distressed by the seriousness of his tone. "What news?" she asked fearfully.

"General Calleja promoted me to the rank of full Colonel!" His eyes sought her approval, like a small boy seeking praise for a proud accomplishment.

"Oh, Tristán, how wonderful, and how well deserved!"

"It gets better. He's extended my furlough all the way through January!"

She kissed him frantically. "That's sixty glorious days together! I'll find ways to spend every minute possible here with you! We'll make love ceaselessly, day and night!"

"February first, I report back to San Luis Potosí. After that, my secret lady bride, God only knows how long we'll have to be apart."

Impetuously he began unbuttoning her blouse and kissing her shoulders and breasts as he bared them. "God, Sirena, how I've burned for you these past few nights we couldn't be together!"

Within minutes they were naked in each other's arms, heedless of everything and everyone, desiring only to unite flesh and spirit again in that sweetest of all unions.

"Oh, Condesita mia, I've so much love to give you and so little time! Promise you'll come to me here every night of my furlough? This time we'll store up memories of each other to see us through the lonely nights ahead."

"Tristán, Tristán," she begged, "*please* make love to me, in all of your many rapturous ways, over and over again, tonight! Don't give me time to even think of being torn from your side again."

The following morning as they rode the Dolores road to Linda Vista, Sirena's heart was so flooded with love, her mind so overflowing with images of last night's delicious intimacies and pleasures, that when she glanced across at him she was too choked with happiness to speak.

He reached over to caress her cheek. "I love waking in the night to find you in my arms. But I also love riding by your side like this. Just knowing I can touch you -- after all the time we've been apart -- means the world to me."

There was only one small cloud shadowing her happiness. He had told her when he was in Mexico City this time, he had stayed two days with Catarina. There was something she had to tell him about his wife that was difficult to put into words, but for his sake, it must be said.

"Tristán, does it bother you that I unwittingly met and befriended Catarina when I was living in Mexico?"

"Of course not. It's your nature to be kind. She told me all about you buying her candy and being such a thoughtful neighbor and friend."

He fell silent for a time, then he said, "Knowing now how much you love me, makes your kindness to her all the more remarkable in my eyes."

"The frontier never prepared her for city life, and the city has ruined her for the frontier. Ironically, because I was also a norteña, she insisted on opening her heart to me."

"Then I guess she told you she longs to have a child?"

Sirena nodded.

Deeply embarrassed, Tristán looked away. "Before God, I have tried to keep my word to Don José." His voice dropped to a whisper, "But perhaps this time, I've given her what she wants so desperately."

"Catarina is a child who wants a doll," Sirena said simply. "If it doesn't happen, *please* don't blame yourself."

"I shouldn't even be discussing this with you, but incredibly enough you're the only one who knows her! Even those who know I'm married, like Calleja, have never seen my wife."

Sirena was deeply troubled. "Tristán, there's something you must know, but it's so private -- how can I say it?"

Tristán seemed alarmed. "What is it?"

"Has she ever told you *why* she finds the marriage act so difficult to -- well, *endure?*"

"No," he said quickly, dropping his gaze, his face flushed with embarrassment, as though Sirena had somehow been witness to his fumbled attempts with Catarina, those failed sexual encounters that unmanned him, their only virtue being they remained his own painful secret. His humiliation would be complete if Sirena now knew, too.

"Did she ever tell you Apaches captured her as a child?"

"*Good God, no!*"

"She was only ten. They tied her to a stake and made her watch while they took a sixteen-year old girl, captured with her, and 'passed her on the plain.' She said there were seven warriors, so it took a long time, but she had to watch until death mercifully put an end to that captive girl's agony."

Sirena paused, mortified but determined to see it through. "Catarina was ransomed soon after, but the screams and pleas of that dying girl remained with her." Sirena reached over and laid a gloved hand on Tristán's thigh. Taking a deep breath she forged on. "She never dreamed I knew you, so she told me how she didn't really mind that her husband's visits were few, even though she wants a child. You see, Tristán, it's not that she doesn't like you. To her, just being touched that way by *any* man, means a *horrifying* form *of torture and slow death!*"

It was a minute before he could speak. "It's been one of the worst things about my marriage. I had no way of understanding *'why?'* All this time I thought I'd done something to make her hate me." He gave her a grateful smile. "I know telling me this wasn't easy for you. But I'm glad you did. It lifts a load of guilt -- and shame from my conscience."

He reined his horse in closer so their stirrups touched and her whole body thrilled at the intimacy it implied. She felt a wild desire to slip from the saddle and beg him to take her under the trees and make love to her right here by the side of the road.

He reflected on the earnestness with which she had told him she knew about and was using Alicia Àvila's 'secret recipe' to avoid getting pregnant, to relieve him of the concern for her that worried him most. And now this, "My dearest Lady-bride," he said, unconcealed admiration in his gaze. "In you I have not only found a noble wife, but a woman of many parts."

She tugged at Emir's snowy mane, her cheeks scarlet, completely disarmed by the full implications of his compliment. "Oh, I think I'm pretty single-minded," she managed at last. "After all, if I'd had my way, we'd still be in bed!"

32

"**Your copy of the Gacéta,** Don Francisco," the young clerk said, placing the newspaper on the desk before his employer in the office Francisco now maintained on the second floor of his mansion on Guanajuato's San Francisco Plaza. "It just arrived by courier."

"Thank you."

"Shall I work late this evening? There are still some mule freight bills to file."

"No need to bother, *joven*," he replied, smiling at the clerk through his gold-rimmed reading spectacles. "You've locked up both shops for the night. I'll file the bills."

When the clerk left, Francisco stopped his work to spread the newest Gacéta open on the desk before him, dreading today's headline:

NEW VICEROY TAKES OFFICE IN AUGUST

The paper was dated, *April 29, 1810*, which meant this Extra was only five days off the press. Well, at least today's news was a little less grim than most these past two years, as crisis after crisis rocked the old order in Spain. He sheaved through a small stack of landmark editions, which, out of a sense of duty to the history of these soul-wracking times of change, he kept at hand on his desk.

He glanced at the first, dated *June 9, 1808*, bannered with words that had never lost their initial shock.

HIS MAJESTY ABDICATES SPANISH THRONE

His eye ran down the long column of stunning sub-heads condensing the details:

King Charles IV Cedes Throne To His Crown Prince

French Troops Occupy Madrid!

New King Ferdinand Leaves Spain For Bayonne
-- To Meet On French Soil
With His August Ally, Emperor Napoleon!

The abdication had proved as farcical as a bad zarzuela. Both sorry kings -- father and son -- together with their respective families and Prime Minister Godoy -- had walked like blind sheep into captivity in Bayonne. As prisoners and political puppets, both Spanish 'kings' obligingly deposed each other, then bestowed the throne on Napoleon himself! Legitimate succession in Spain had been altered forever.

Then, on July 16, in the same year, the Gacéta printed the old order's death knell:

ALL SPAIN OCCUPIED BY FRENCH TROOPS

BLOODY UPRISING ON THE SECOND OF MAY

When this tragic news reached New Spain in July of 1808, the Viceroy, 'Godoy's creature', became alarmed. Fearing he himself might be deposed by restive elements in the kingdom, he sought to curry popular favor by revoking the heinous Act of Consolidation. But the damage had already been done. Hundreds of New Spain's most industrious landowners, great and small, had been ruined.

Although the Gacéta never printed it, Francisco knew that out of the vast fortune collected through the 'Act' by the Viceroy for Godoy, *two and a half million pesos*, came from the Archdiocesan fund of Mexico alone: another one million had been wrung from Legázpi's prosperous see of Michoacán. It was an open secret the Viceroy had pocketed *five percent* of all the loot under the Act, exactly as Godoy had promised!

From what the Bishop told Francisco, the 'Act' monies had then been duly squandered by the Bourbon court. A short time before the French occupied Madrid, Godoy's agent in Paris had personally handed over to Napoleon five million pesos, most of it squeezed from the Church, hacendados, silver lords and merchants of New Spain. No wonder one heard cries of 'Down with bad government!' on every side. After decades of remarkably upright viceroys, this one had stolen the horse, the carriage and the barn itself.

Utter confusion as to who ruled Spain sparked a bitter grab for power between criollo and Spaniard in New Spain. The venal Viceroy and his family were arrested in the palace in September of 1808, by a powerful criollo clique, fearful a group of 'foreign' gachupínes were plotting to take over the kingdom. 'Godoy's creature' was shipped back to a Spain in utter chaos, without its own king, crown prince, prime minister or even its infamous 'harlot queen.'

To crown all the other evils of this evil time, in September of 1809, Napoleon seized the aged Pope Pius VII, imprisoning him in a castle near Genoa, and decreed two new Calendar Holidays: 'Saint Napoleon' and the Feast of his own Coronation as Emperor!

Francisco restacked the papers and silently recited what had become his daily supplication; that the Protestant English -- *of all unlikely saviors!* -- would drive Napoleon from Spain and help restore order to the captive Old World and the seething political cauldron that was now New Spain.

Francisco placed today's Gacéta on top of earlier issues, recalling that the fighting in Spain was not only a harbinger of Armageddon, but for a merchant-aviadór like himself, it made trying to do business an economic nightmare. Communication with Europe was sporadic and unpredictable. In the wake of the Act of Consolidation, he had been forced to become a one-man banking firm, offering emergency loans to silver lords and hacendados who, a few years back, could have bought and sold him ten times over. This unforeseen aspect of his affairs had brought him back to Guanajuato in March, three months earlier than his usual return with the summer students. It might result in his giving up teaching to take up permanent residence here in his Guanajuato home.

"I beg your pardon, sir," the clerk said, reappearing in the open doorway. "There's a lady downstairs to see you."

Francisco removed his reading glasses. "Do I know her?"

Stepping forward the clerk handed him a small card. Francisco took one look and sprang to his feet.

"Of course! Show her up. I'll receive her in the sala."

Taking up a candelabrum, he hurried into the dimly lit sala, and after setting it down on a table, he went about hastily lighting wall sconces. At the sound of a light step on the parquet floor behind him he turned.

In a black chiffon gown with long snug sleeves and a sheer black mourning veil covering her face, Isabel stood framed against the blond wood of the closed double doors.

"Francisco?" she asked hesitantly, as though uncertain of her welcome.

"Please come in, my dear, sit over here by the fire." He was pleased, but shaken to see her. It was the first time she had set foot in his house in the ten years he had kept home and office here. "I'll stir up the embers."

"I've come to thank you in person," she murmured, her taffeta petticoats whispering as she seated herself on the salmon velvet sofa and lifted her mourning veil.

Francisco felt a stab of pleasurable pain at the sight of her copper-gold hair, caught in a chignon at the nape of her neck, still as bright as he remembered it, the same flawless complexion, the hooded grey eyes as intriguing as ever. Flustered as a schoolboy in her presence he took a chair facing her.

"It was kind of you to send that note of condolence," she continued, "and to have the friars offer so many Masses for the repose of my husband's soul."

"It was nothing," he said, "I know how trying this has been for you, especially given the manner of his death."

"Did you know it was I who found the body?" she asked, as though it was imperative he hear it from her.

"Oh, my dear Isabel, no!"

He knew Don Telmo had been found murdered near his own front steps early this past Sunday morning. Clad all in black, with cape, hat and cane, the same as in life, one man had described the body to Francisco as a 'giant, grotesque black spider, lying twisted and broken on the cobblestones.'

"I was on my way to early Mass," Isabel said, "The miner's pick had been driven clear through his heart and was buried fast in the cobblestones beneath him. Young doctor Daniel said it took several frightful hours for him to die."

She sighed, struggling visibly to compose herself. "I'm sure it was a Graciana crewman. Even the note stuck on the upright point of the pick, *'Death to the Gachupin!'* was scrawled on a sheet of good foolscap. And you know how scarce paper is in this kingdom -- thieves and vendors steal *every scrap* one doesn't keep under lock and key! Besides, as dear as miners tools are, the murderer even left his pick!"

Francisco's sensitive heart ached for her. To change the subject he asked, "And when will his lawyers read the will?"

"Not for several weeks. But that's not important."

Francisco had been concerned about Isabel's welfare ever since Sirena passed on to him what Felipe had told her in Manila about the terms of Don Telmo's will. Now, in his effort to console her, he found himself mouthing the tritest of cliches. "I was deeply saddened by his death."

"I was not!" she shot back coldly. Then, noting his shock at her candor, she continued. "Don't misunderstand. It was a slow and gruesome way to die, but I'm glad my years with him are over."

Grieved by the memory of his own fatal hesitations in the past, he reached over and took her hands in his. "Ah, Chabela mia! If only you'd given me a little more time – perhaps a year – or until Crispín was born."

All the explanations he had rehearsed silently over the years now came spilling out. "It was hard enough to live with myself after Patrick's death, but to have married you, enjoyed you in his own bed!" The pain of that time was still a white-hot spear through his heart. "Had I risked one more betrayal of that good man -- I swear on the Blood of Christ, Isabel, I would have killed myself!"

Isabel listened, transfixed.

"I wanted desperately to make a life with you and Crispín, but I needed time. You kept us at cross purposes, not seeing my pain for your own, then remarried in such haste."

She sighed. "I felt you had abandoned me, and I was spiteful. I knew marrying Don Telmo was the cruelest thing I could do to you."

It was a rare admission of fault on her part, the first time he had ever heard Isabel accept any responsibility for anything that had ever happened in her entire life.

"To think my own procrastination threw you into the arms of that vile. . ." he stopped short. "Forgive me, I didn't mean to speak ill of the dead."

"It's no use lying about how you feel. He was a bestial man. On our wedding night he bragged he'd gotten the Graciana mine out of me, and finally evened his score with Patrick. Those were the two noble reasons he'd married me! He told me he'd kept a mistress for years, so he had no sexual need for a wife. He thought his rejection would kill my pride."

Francisco covered his face with his hands. "Oh, Isabel!"

"It was only just and fitting that he returned from a night in that trollop's arms to be nailed to the street by cold steel on his own doorstep." Her hands made a tight fist in her lap. "But I owe that whore my thanks." She fixed him with her grey eyes. "Except for that one night with Patrick, which saved his honor and ours, she allowed me to remain true to you ever since the Hermitage."

He moved to her side on the sofa. "My poor Chabela, I promise to make it all up to you, if you'll have me."

She closed her eyes and then whispered, "I've waited an eternity to hear you say those words to me!" Tears coursing down her cheeks she fell into his embrace. "Please take care of me, Francisco! Without you I've been lost. In these terrifyingly uncertain times, I get so confused, and scared, not knowing who is Pope, King or Viceroy! Sometimes I don't even know who I am."

"You are who you've always been," he said, holding her, "my own dear Isabel. I won't let any more harm befall you."

His mind began racing. "I'll write Bishop Legázpi. He can dispense you from the full year of mourning so we can marry sooner. It's not a rare request, among older couples."

"I'm forty-seven," she said, slipping in a sharp sliver of irony, "safely past child-bearing age." She lay her head on his breast. "Oh, Francisco, when?"

"The wedding? Six months. We can have the banns waived and go off for a quiet ceremony, perhaps Dolores, where I'm sure Father Hidalgo --"

"No!" she cut him off, "Any priest but him! I never did like the man, but now he's the scandal of Dolores -- staging risqué plays, giving parties and dances, even gambling for stakes, *all in his own parish house!* His mistress lives there openly with him and plays female leads in his plays! Amantina says he's up to his elbows in political plots and schemes to destroy all the gachupínes. God forbid, I'd rather live in sin the rest of our lives than be married by an ordained rakehell like Miguel Hidalgo!"

"I had no idea," Francisco replied, wryly recalling his first meeting years ago with Hidalgo and Legázpi at La Torre mesón. And to think I had him pegged as a pious prude! Well, that shows how little we know about what makes each other tick! The Bishop then, Chabela? He could marry us in his house chapel and we could honeymoon in Valladolid."

"Oh yes, I'd like that!"

She pulled away gently and got up from the sofa. "So this is where you've lived alone for so long!" She strolled about the room, touching drapes, running her fingers over the carved details of tables and chairs. "I'm pleased to see you're not as Spartan and *monkish* as you used to be."

He rose, and leaned against the mantle, regarding her with a wise, wintry smile. "I've learned a lot about myself over the years, Chabela, and I'ves found that choosing one's own penances simply feeds spiritual pride."

She watched him warily.

"The crosses God sends, when humbly borne, are better." He paused, "But, as for us, I don't plan to wait six months." She caught her breath and stared at him in wonderment.

"After the Hermitage I took a vow of celibacy for life. Now I see I did it, not for love of purity, but because I was afraid of falling from grace. I regard that vow as dead. I've been faithful to you, but we've both been celibate too long." He let his meaning sink in. "At least this time the sin won't be adultery." He took her in his arms and put his lips to her ear. "Besides, Chabela, remember how we liked our love to be illicit, against authority? I think it was our way of hitting back at the king for martyring our fathers."

Her eyes lit up, as though he had made a mystery crystal clear. "Yes! Defiance of the rules always was our way!"

"You'll find I'm not as scrupulous as I used to be. Even then, I was more concerned with my betrayal of Patrick and sparing his honor than with committing the sin, itself."

Isabel was losing the thread. "But where can we meet? It's such a small town." She sat down again, "Discovery could ruin you."

"I've lived here for years with 'day servants' only. They come at ten in the morning and leave at five. And all this time, I've known, if you did not, that a short lane with a few steps is all that separates your back door from mine."

"I'll find a way to come and go alone."

"I'll write the Bishop tonight. When can you come to me?"

She lowered the black veil over her face and rose to leave. "Tomorrow evening? Five-thirty?"

"I'll count the hours." Taking firm grip of his own vaulting emotions, he gave a slight, formal bow. "Let me see you out safely downstairs."

"Oh, Francisco, there is one thing more," she said as they descended the stairs to the patio. "When you write the Bishop tell him I've given my consent for Crispín to enter San Nicolás Seminary this fall."

Francisco hugged her. "Oh, this will make the boy so happy! Only your refusal stood in his way."

"I know. But it was such a hard decision to make. With Felipe dead, and Mercedes entombed in her convent cell — ," she pressed a gloved hand to her breast. "Sirena has her own life, and Ramón's throwing his away on that negress, Analinda. Crispín's the only real child I have left. And he's been doubly dear to me because he's all I ever had of you."

"Now that's no longer true," he said softly.

"All I'm asking of Crispín in return, is that he wait until his birthday this coming August." She glanced up at him. "Can you believe it's been *seventeen* years?" Her fingers traced the long white scar running from his temple to his jawline.

"He'll make a fine religious," Francisco said, taking her hand and kissing it, "you'll see. Formed in Legázpi's own mold of common sense religion, he'll be a priest and a son -- we both can be proud of."

"And now I have you," she said as though reassuring herself, "it's not as though he were leaving me all alone in the world, with no one to care for me, is it?"

"Of course not! Tomorrow evening then?" he asked as they reached the door, unconsciously sliding his hand up to cup her breast, reaffirming the old intimacies between them. At his possessive touch she lost her reserve and lifted her lips to him imploringly. He raised her veil and gave her a slow, probing kiss, full of promises for tomorrow night.

"Chabela, if you didn't return home this very minute," he asked tremulously, "would the servants -- miss you?"

"No, they think I'm visiting someone else," she replied, eyes closed, nearly faint with desire. "I could stay another hour -- or two or -- three!"

He responded so swiftly to her surrender he was halfway upstairs with her before he thought what he was doing, her sheer mourning veil drifting over the black, wrought-iron balustrade, her loosened hair cascading down his left arm like bright silk floss.

The provocative sibilance of black taffeta reminded him temptingly of falling leaves. Soon she would begin shedding these mourning garments, as a white birch sheds its leaves. Not since their *idilio* in the Hermitage had he tasted the pleasures of carnal love, and his ravenous appetite for sex so long denied, increased with every step.

"We'll love as passionately as Abelard and Heloise!"

Isabel had never heard of them, being more concerned with something dearer to her heart. "And -- the games?" she asked, memory calling up the unforgettable playlets Francisco had improvised in the Hermitage -- being captured by pirates, being a virgin martyr cast in the arena with a Spanish bull. In these erotic tableaux she longed to lose herself again.

"Of course, we'll play the games!" he whispered, "and now at last we'll have time enough to drink our fill of passion's wine!"

ෲ33ෲ

"I don't think they suspect a thing, do you?" Sirena asked Francisco in a low voice as they rode behind the Riaño's open coach with some two-dozen other mounted members of this festive company.

"Not a thing! Don Antoñio thinks it's Amantina's annual harvest time fiesta." Francisco smiled at her appreciatively from under his black bicorn, "I must say, you and Gilberto are first rate conspirators."

"We had to be. As Gilberto said, his father would never knowingly approve of spending a *centavo* of municipal funds on something as personal as his own wedding anniversary. This way the silver consulado gives the party and foots the bill."

Sirena looked ahead at the open carriage in which Doña Victoria was riding with her sister, Marianne de Flon. Don Antoñio and General Flon, both mounted on spirited Spanish Barbs, rode on either side, chatting with each other and their vivacious wives.

"Just imagine!" Francisco mused aloud, "thirty years ago, in a double wedding ceremony in New Orleans, these two St. Maxent sisters married these two young Spanish officers who were there fighting beside French allies, to help the English colonists free themselves from British rule. And now, as we speak, the English are fighting on Spanish soil to help drive the French out of Spain! What an amazing change of alliances in a single lifetime!

Sirena nodded, but she was tired of thinking about the war and all the other political turmoil here and abroad. That was one reason she had worked so hard to arrange an event that could spread a little happiness instead of more gloom.

Manuel Flon, Governor of the distant city and province of Puebla, had not visited his Guanajuato counterpart and lifelong friend, Riaño, since the blessing of the Alhóndiga. A meeting between the kingdom's two leading Generals, Félix Calleja and Manuel Flon, had just been held in mid-August in San Luis Potosí. Being military commander of the city and province of Guanajuato, as well as its governor, Don Antoñio had attended as well. The double anniversary party for the two couples was held today because they had just come from that junta and the Flons were returning tomorrow to the General's command post in Puebla.

Twenty-eight-year old Gilberto Riaño, an only child, was here on summer-long furlough from his Mexico City regiment, his first visit in ten years. Sirena had seized upon this family reunion as an opportunity to persuade the quarreling criollo and gachupín factions to join in honoring Riaño for his two decades of selfless service as governor.

"Gilberto and I had a lot of time to plan this on our long ride north to San Luis Potosí."

"And were you able to see Tristán while you were there?"

"Yes, I saw him," Sirena replied slowly both happy and dismayed at the memories of those unforgettable two weeks.

Reflecting on that golden time, she still wondered if it had been unfair of her not to warn Tristán she was coming. Only two days before the Riaños' departure, Doña Victoria had asked Sirena to come along, 'to keep Gilberto company', as she put it with a disingenuousness that was not lost on Sirena. Being the two most eligible aristocrats in Guanajuato, Sirena's circle of relatives and friends, including the Riaños' had been fostering a serious romance between them all summer long.

Sirena found Gilberto an attractive man, with his mother's fair complexion and his father's gravity of manner. Given his good looks, charm and distinguished lineage, he ranked high among the most desirable marriage partners in New Spain. But he was as reluctant as she to move beyond the warm friendship they already shared. He had his eye on a political career, and with his connections could expect appointment to a high post in the viceroyalty, once Spain was liberated and life returned to normal. The arrival in Mexico this week of the new Viceroy, Don Francisco Venegas, a highly respected veteran of the Peninsular War, had everyone hoping the return of stable government to New Spain was finally at hand.

"With all of us old people," Doña Victoria had told Sirena, with a typical Gallic flutter of eyelashes and fan, "Gilberto will want someone near his own age to talk to."

Sirena was tempted. It had been three years since she and Tristán had said their vows 'in the sight of God.' They had stolen away to the

Hermitage as often as possible during his sixty-day furlough. But the time apart seemed forever, an especially troubled time of war abroad and rising political tensions here at home. Risky? Yes, but the prospect of being near him overcame every danger signal prudence raised.

Her first sight of Tristán in San Luis literally took her breath away. He was mounted on a magnificent palomino with white mane and tail, riding at the head of a brilliant squadron of cavalry on a parade ground just outside of town. The visitors arrived in mid-morning, surprising the Tenth Brigade in the midst of a cavalry drill. The St. Maxent sisters watched from their open carriage, while Sirena, Gilberto Riaño and Flon sat their horses at the field's edge.

When he first caught sight of her, Tristán's shock and dismay were so apparent to her that for one heartsick moment Sirena regretted she had come. Preparing a charge, he pulled up and wheeled his horse completely around. When he resumed his position at the head of his troop, she saw his jaw was set and his face had turned to stone.

For the first time she was seeing the other Tristán, a seasoned leader of men, secure in his own environment, a security her sudden appearance had clearly shaken. A full colonel now, he wore a black leather helmet with bright green woolen crest. His short-tailed tunic and trousers were crimson with black facings and gold lace, his padded 'shoulder rolls' almost medieval with their splendid gold lace slashes. A gold epaulet graced his left shoulder, a gold aguilette his right, while a green silk sash encircled his waist. She had never seen him look more heartbreakingly handsome.

At his back rose a forest of upright lances, each made of tough resilient ash, measuring eight English feet long and capped by a foot-long point of sharpened steel. The lancers were drawn up in close formation, their front ranks briefly broken as two or three unruly horses skittered out of line and had to be firmly reined back into place.

Tristán had written to her with great pride about these *Tamarindos*, a company of raw recruits he hand-picked and trained to form this crack *new* squadron of lancers. They took their name from the tamarind, a chamois-colored tropical fruit, the same shade as their own leather jackets. Today, mounted on matching blacks, with red pennants flying, they made a stylish troop. A youthful bugler rode a horse's length behind Tristán, his bright horn at his lips.

"Prepare to charge!" Tristán called, his lance upright, its heel couched in a leather pocket behind his right stirrup. "Lower lances!" As one man, he and every rider behind him grasped the nine-foot long lance midway down its shaft and, holding it poised close to his body, aimed it straight ahead. Sirena felt her heart stop beating.

"*Santiago y adelante!*" Tristàn cried, and chills ran up Sirena's spine. She had never before heard that famed battle cry of New Spain's conquistadores, *"Saint James and forward!"*

It was as thrilling as watching Cortes himself charge against Moctezuma's Aztec hosts!

The bugler blew a corresponding battle call and the tightly reined phalanx of horses and riders exploded into action, bolting as one, reaching full gallop in almost the first stride. The ground shook as they thundered past, every man's body tilted slightly forward in the saddle as he prepared to deploy his slim but lethal weapon in a disconcerting feint or deadly thrust at the imaginary foe.

Sirena's palms grew moist and her heart pounded at the gallant, but frightening sight of Tristán riding into battle. Never before had she grasped the terrifying vulnerability of the flesh and blood man she loved. What if this were a charge in a real war, shot and shell exploding on every side, as a real enemy slashed its way toward him and his Tamarindos?

Later, lunching at a long rustic table in the picturesque, beautifully landscaped garden of the Callejas' nearby hacienda, the General proved a gracious host, presiding over this intimate group of old friends which included Tristán.

"Had we known three beautiful ladies would have their lovely eyes upon us today, we would have staged one of our impressive mock battles," Calleja lamented, "but we'll have time for that in the two weeks you'll be here."

"I've never watched military maneuvers before," Sirena ventured, risking a brief glance at Tristán before giving Calleja her full attention, "but the lancers' charge left me breathless with admiration."

"I agree," Doña Victoria said, "they'd put the fear of God into any enemy who thinks it can invade us at will."

"We'll need the Tamarindos and a great deal more, if Napoleon decides to put his Austerlitz veterans ashore at Vera Cruz," the portly General Flon said pessimistically.

"Or Wilkinson's Kentuckians decide to storm across our northeastern border," Tristán added drily.

"The vast size of this kingdom is an *enemy* in itself," Calleja observed. "Distance alone would make it next to impossible for my Tenth Brigade, for example, to join General Flon's Second in Puebla quickly enough to repel a French landing, or for both of us to join forces in time to confront a land invasion in the north. God help us, Manuel, if we're ever attacked from *both* quarters at once!"

Sirena felt a rush of gratitude that Guanajuato was set squarely in the kingdom's heartland. Now that frail, five year old Rafael would soon be strong enough to leave Madre Pilar's care and come live with her at last, she knew why mothers worried about war. She silently thanked God that her beloved city did not lie open to attack on either of the two likeliest invasion routes, but was ringed by the same fierce mountains that protected the kingdom's richest silver mines.

"Don Tristán, why are you so sure the Yankees want to move against us from Louisiana?" Riaño asked.

"Sir, three years ago in New Orleans, General Wilkinson told me to my face he intended to invade us with between fifteen and twenty thousand Kentuckians," Tristán replied. "But the man's much given to bombast. I'm sure six thousand would be the most he could raise. The young republic has no standing army, and its civilians are as reluctant as ours to volunteer for soldiering, even though, to a man, these North Americans covet our land."

"You've had considerable contact with Yankees, Colonel Luna," Flon inquired, "How would you assess them, both as a neighboring country and a potential military threat?"

Tristán explained that hot-eyed rustics were pouring into the borderland region, political zealots all, who felt it was their patriotic duty to "free" New Spain from the yoke of 'European tyrants,' before, of course, annexing her temptingly close and empty northern provinces for themselves!

These *other* Americans are an intrepid, industrious people," Tristán said, weighing every word. "They seek first place among nations. Their fierce determination to rule from sea to sea springs from their unique racial-religious conviction that the Anglo-Saxon is a 'chosen race'. It follows that the Creator has bestowed on them their own 'Promised Land'. Given this premise, they revere their form of democratic government as though it were the revealed Word of God. To share this continent -- which God made *only* for them with a 'foreign' people and regal form of government," he spread his hands and smiled, "well, it's as unthinkable to them as renouncing our Catholic Faith would be to us!"

"With so much concern over invasions from without, it's easy to forget we have plenty of 'Moors on the beach' right here at home,"

Riaño commented, "the recent Valladolid conspiracy providing ample proof of that."

"True," Flon agreed, "but luckily that plot was betrayed by one of its own before it turned into a full-blown revolt."

"Not soon enough, Manuel," Riaño countered, "it has already sown the embers of rebellion throughout the Bajío."

"Well, whatever happens," Flon elaborated, "we have to keep in mind there are only *ten brigades* in all New Spain, barely thirty-thousand trained men in the entire Royal Army! Working out the best way to deploy these scant forces will be tactical challenge enough for us during the next two weeks. God knows, we can't look to Spain for more men and material!"

Calleja stood up, placing a protective arm about his Francesca, and raised his glass in a toast. "While we're here breaking our heads studying the art of making war, let us not forget New Spain's been *at peace* for nearly three hundred years. May Divine Providence extend that blessing to our own time, for ourselves and our children. *To peace in our time!"*

Lifting her brandy, Sirena saw the same dark anxiety she felt for Tristán, reflected in the eyes of the three other soldiers' wives. With the combined fervor of her love for him, and her passionate devotion to her own patria, she repeated with the others, 'To peace in our time!'

"There's still an hour of daylight left before sundown," their host announced, "long enough for us to show you around the grounds of our beloved hacienda, Los Bledos."

Calleja struck Sirena as a New World Cincinnatus, still young enough to soldier, but eager to retire so he could devote himself to his adored wife, their two small children and to improving his fine manor and its fertile lands.

"Your kinsman, Tristán, has become my dearest friend," Calleja confided to Sirena, when they found themselves briefly apart from the others, "he's also my most trusted officer. We keep a room for him here, which he regards as his own home, whenever he's free to visit us."

That conversation and the tour of the estate were cut short by a sudden summer downpour that sent everyone scurrying for shelter. When it was time to retire, Doña Francesca led Sirena to a bedroom suite, opening onto its own private secluded terrace. "This is the old wing of the house where I grew up. It's comfortable and very quiet, so you can sleep as late as you like without being disturbed."

Sirena was weary from the long journey and the strain of being so near Tristán without being able to have a private word with him. But sleep proved impossible. By ten o'clock the afternoon shower had escalated into what Bishop Legázpi liked to call 'one of Satan's tantrums,' with gusting winds, torrents of rain, and thunder resounding like cannon against the walls of the narrow valley in which Los Bledos stood.

As Sirena burrowed deeper under her covers, the French doors leading onto the terrace were blown open by the wind. Rushing from her bed to close them before drapes and carpet were ruined, she was startled when the doors suddenly closed by themselves. In the darkness she detected the pungent scent of wet wool and then Tristán's arms enfolded her, his cold, rain-soaked tunic pressed against her sheer silk gown.

"Oh, Tristán dearest, we dare not! Not here under the General's own roof," she whispered, "It's too dangerous!"

"No more dangerous than your coming to San Luis without warning me!" he retorted angrily, then quickly his sharp tone softened. "Surely you could guess when I first set eyes on you today I intended to ride through Hell itself if I had to, just to be with you tonight?"

"Yes, but forgive me! I didn't mean to compromise you in front of your Tamarindos, or before the generals."

"My own Condesita," he sighed, taking off his wet uniform and draping it over a chair. "I'm not angry with you, but with myself." He sank down on the bed and drew her down beside him. She sensed his eagerness to have her, but there was an underlying weariness and melancholy in his manner she had never found in him before.

"I've made such a mess of my life, trying to keep my vow to Don José," he cried brokenly, holding her warm body in his trembling embrace. "How I long to introduce you openly as my wife! How proud I'd be to tell them you're mine and that I have the love of such a noble lady! Oh, Sirena, I want so desperately for us to have the normal, fulfilling life the General and Francesca have here -- each other, a home, children, friends."

"I was never more proud of you than today, leading that charge," she whispered, "but also, I've never been more afraid of losing you!"

"These are desperate times we live in," he said, "and I'm afraid we have to face the fact that, sooner or later, war will come."

"Oh, Tristán, just for tonight, let there be no world outside this room," she pleaded, "No more talk of war and invasions, no 'Moors on the beach!' Let it be just the two of us again, losing ourselves in each other."

Greedily she ran her hands over his cold, muscular shoulders and back, kissing his nipples and pressing her radiantly warm breasts against his rain-chilled groin. Instantly aroused, he fell upon her, and suddenly his familiar cloud-shadow lips and hands were lovingly passing over the undulating wilderness of her body, melting her very soul.

"This adelantado intends to retake every inch of the realm that time and distance have tried to steal from him," he whispered teasingly, giving her a slow, deliberate kiss foreshadowing the exquisite pleasures of that thoroughgoing reconquista.

The tempest of their passion raged throughout the night, matching the pagan intensity of the Devil's spiteful storm that continued to assail the world all around them.

CB ЮD

"It's not easy for me to soldier with you here," Tristán confessed a few nights later, "always longing to lay my head in your lap, always hungering for the sweet taste of you." At midnight every night, when the house was asleep, he came to her room. Locked in each others' arms the whole night through, they made love repeatedly, or merely lay together talking about the little everyday things which they had never had time to discuss before. Each morning when the false dawn silvered the east, he returned to his own room.

"I've a gift for you before I go," Sirena told him on the last night before she departed for Guanajuato. "You can't see it in the dark, but these are your lady's colors." She handed him a diaphanous, silver-blue silk scarf. "When you lead your Tamarindos, always wear this inside your tunic, over your heart. Please God, it will protect you."

When dawn broke on this last day, he pleaded for 'one last stirrup cup of love,' which she could not deny him, or herself. It was the saddest of all their sad partings, filled with a deep sense of loss and foreboding.

"I have some private news to share with you before we reach Linda Vista," Francisco said, breaking the spell of Sirena's bittersweet reveries, and bringing her back sharply from her bedroom at Los Bledos to this brilliant, laughing company riding the sun-dappled road to Dolores.

"Oh? Gossip or confession?" she asked brightly, making a supreme effort to rise above the dull ache and sick premonition weighing on her heart.

"A bit of both I guess," Francisco admitted, acting surprisingly ill at ease, "you see, your mother and I are going to be married."

Sirena almost dropped her reins. *"Married?"* she gasped, so shocked she braced both hands on the swell of her saddle and stared at him. You and Mamá? I can't believe it!"

She tried to imagine them together, Isabel the creature of emotion, mood and whim, to whom any abstract idea was pure Greek, and Francisco, with his poetic nature and profound philosophical side. What under Heaven would they ever find to talk about? But of course there *were* other attractions, she thought, amending her first judgment. Isabel was still a great beauty, and Francisco a man to appreciate that. His quiet wit, dignity and exquisite taste might be just what Isabel needed after Don Telmo's crudities and his depressing 'executioner's black'.

"I hoped you would -- approve," he said, sounding hurt and disappointed.

"Of course I approve!" she cried, reaching over to lay a reassuring hand on his arm, "I'm simply bowled over, that's all. But now that I think about it," she cocked her head, "I remember seeing you waltzing together at my Alhóndiga dedication ball. She had a look in her eyes. That must have been the dawning of her love for you!"

Francisco permitted himself a secretly amused smile. "Well, I don't know about that, but I care about Isabel and she -- returns my affection. Just today the Bishop brought us a written dispensation from her period of mourning. The nuptials are set for two weeks from today."

"Oh, Francisco, this makes me so happy for you both," she sighed, "and I know Papá would be overjoyed! I'm sure there's no one in this whole wide world he would rather trust her to than you!"

Towns affected by the Hidalgo Revolution

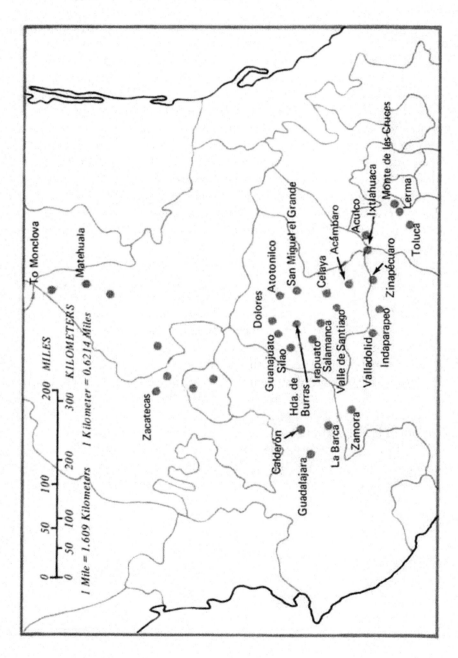

PART SEVEN

THE BLACK FLAME

1810

"Wealth has disappeared as if by magic in the black flame of insurrection."

Pedro Montes de Oca,
in a letter to the Conde de Regla, III.

34

"**I appreciate your staying** over the week end to help me tidy up from the fiesta," Amantina said, as she carried in two extra blankets to Sirena's bedroom at Linda Vista and set them down on her bed.

"I don't get over to see you often enough these days," Sirena said fondly, "this gives me an excuse to spend some time with you."

"I surely hope this cold spell doesn't bring frost," Amantina worried aloud, "the last two harvests were lean enough. From the look of the fields, we could have a bumper crop this year, but a bad frost at this time could wreak havoc with everything."

Sirena had spent all day Saturday helping Amantina put away her costly decorations for another year, and distributing the food left over from the feast among Amantina's large retinue of loyal *servientes* and their families. For most of them she had been the only patrona in their lives, and Linda Vista the only home they had ever known.

"You take very good care of your people, Aunt Amantina," Sirena observed as the two of them spread the blankets. "Yes, and I'm proud to say you look after your miners as well as your darling father ever did."

"Well, in spite of the wars abroad I've kept going. When the French invasion of Spain cut off our usual source of mercury in Alamden, I began importing it from Peru, so I've kept La Sirena at peak production, while other mine owners have been laying off half their crews."

"With that many more men out of work, the mood of the Bajío gets uglier every day."

Amantina spread the coverlet then stood up, both hands pressed to the small of her back, easing a twinge in her spine. "Well, God willing, we'll survive these times like all the rest. We got through the famine of '86 in one piece, although your mother's never been the same since."

"Weren't you amazed about her marrying Don Francisco?"

"Not really. He asked her first when she was fifteen."

"Do you mean to say he knew Mamá *that* long ago?"

"What I'm saying is, life holds more surprises for the young than the old," Amantina sermonized. "'The Devil's not wise because he's the Devil. He's wise because he's *old!*'"

Sirena smiled. There was no out-maneuvering Amantina! "So what Mass will you be attending in Dolores tomorrow?"

"With Father Hidalgo there, I'd rather drive to Mexico for Mass! Ugh! What that prideful priest has done to our parish!"

"Mamá was telling me he's giving great scandal -- staging French plays, gambling, keeping a mistress!"

"Scandal's not the worst of it! He neglects his duties *and* older parishioners like me, to cluck like a mother hen over every rag-tag Indian in the province. He and that *parandero*, Captain Allende, are now boon companions. They've joined some shady 'Literary Society' in Querétaro and Hidalgo spends all his time attending its secret meetings, leaving his assistant to say all the *cura's* Masses, as well as his own!"

"I think I'll go at seven. Will you be coming too?"

"No, because I have to spend the night in my new silk house over in town."

"Whatever for?"

"The weather's cold and we have to keep the graine and young larvae warm. Besides, there's always the danger of fire when we light that many extra lamps for warmth."

Sirena knew about silk house fires. Once, when she was a little girl visiting here, an oil lamp had tipped over in one of them turning wooden trays, leaves, larvae and graine into a daylong holocaust that was visible from leagues around.

"The fire hazard's one thing Auntie, but what about you? Isn't it time you eased up on yourself a little?"

Amantina's lean head came up sharply. "So you think I'm getting too old to run the place?"

"I didn't mean that. I just think you're working too hard for a woman of your years."

"I've never stopped to worry my head about age and infirmity," she declared, striding purposefully to the bedroom door, trailing the excessively long train of her blue broadcloth gown that even before the French Revolution had been dubbed an outdated 'dragger'.

"Why not let the new boy watch the silk house tonight?"

"I'm a lot more experienced at seventy-six than a night boy of sixteen. That's what staying alive is all about."

She stood a moment, framed in the doorway, her high, jeweled comb glinting in the light, both oval black velvet beauty marks in place on either temple. "I'll tell Melchor to bring the carriage around for you tomorrow early."

Sirena kissed her on the cheek. "Promise me you'll come home if you feel you're getting too tired?"

"Don't worry. The older I get the less rest I need. Besides, I've got the whole of eternity to sleep."

Shortly after sunrise on Sunday morning, Sirena saw the twin stone towers of Dolores church rising against the tender morning sky. The plaza in front of the church was so crowded Melchor had to force his team through it. A large number of vaqueros, mounted on both nags and Barbs, sat their horses in ragged ranks. Scores of other -- peons, ranchers and entire farm families, stood or milled about.

"Why are there so many people here for the early Mass?"

"Sunday's market day, Condesa," Melchor replied. "They sometimes come early and make a day of it."

The church was so packed there was no room left to kneel. Everyone was standing and, surprisingly there were far more men than women. *That* was a novelty! Well, it wasn't worth pushing her way down to the altar. Better stay right here, a few steps from the door where the air was fresh.

While an Indian server lit altar candles, Father Hidalgo appeared. A murmur swept the congregation as he hurried through the sanctuary and up the stairs to the wall pulpit on Sirena's right. Well, she mused, this Sunday he seems to be feeling priestly enough to preach the sermon himself. But something was wrong. The sermon comes after the Gospel, not before Mass begins! It was then she saw he was not even vested for Mass, but was wearing the clerical black suit he had worn Friday at the Riaños' anniversary party.

Lifting his arms high, palms outstretched, he quieted the murmurous crowd, his face suffused with an almost supernatural radiance. His voice, both strident and persuasive, resonated through the suddenly hushed church. "My friends, neither the Viceroy nor taxes exist for us any longer! For three centuries we've borne the Indian tribute as a sign of our enslavement to Spain. Now, at last, the hour of liberty has struck! Will you let the gachupínes hand you over to the godless Napoleon, to be his slaves? Or will you join me in my fight to take from the gachupínes the lands they stole from our forefathers? Will you follow me and, like true Mexicans, defend your religion and you homes?"

The answer, from hundreds of Indian throats, rebounded like a thunderclap: "WE WILL DEFEND THEM!"

Good God, she thought, what kind of rabble-rousing sermon *is* this? His incendiary words were tantamount to throwing a torch into a tinder dry forest, a potential firestorm!

Hidalgo raised his arms again in a mute appeal for silence. "In a few hours you'll see your Cura riding at the head of an army of men who take pride in being free." His tone was as ominous as the tolling of a mine's disaster bell. "I ask you to join my Reconquista, to fight at the side of our legitimate ruler, King Ferdinand the Seventh. Remember, *our cause is holy and God will protect it*! I cannot speak any longer, for all is being done in great haste and I must go!"

His green eyes flashing fire, an almost visible *potencia* of light haloing his white-fringed pate, he sang out a mesmerizing chant that electrified the Indian congregation:

> *Long live the Virgin of Guadalupe!*
> *Long live our rightful King Ferdinand!*
> *Down with bad government!"*

Then, he added with chilling finality: "NOW, LET US GO AND SEIZE THE GACHUPÍNES!"

The crowd echoed his chant, climaxing in a thunderous roar of "DEATH TO THE GACHUPÍNES!" which shook the venerable stone church to its lofty groining. "Follow your leader!" he cried like some avenging angel, "follow the priest who has always looked after you!"

He tripped down the pulpit stairs and took his place at the head of the howling, pushing mob that began closing ranks behind him, leading them straight to the doors of the church as they chanted:

> *"LONG LIVE THE VIRGIN OF GUADALUPE!*
> *DEATH TO THE GACHUPÍNES!"*

Holy God, Sirena thought, the old man's gone stark mad! But in the same instant she saw the logic of his manifesto, cunningly aimed at firing the emotions of illiterate, restless Indians. Now she knew it was no accident there was such a crowd at this hour. Everyone had been told to be here!

In an instinctive gesture of self-preservation she covered all but her eyes with her rebozo. In this Indian mob, incited to bloodlust, her fair skin could cost her life. As Hidalgo and his host surged toward her she bolted out the door and ran down the steps to Melchor's waiting carriage.

"Melchor," she hissed as he helped her into the open carriage, "Get us back to Linda Vista as fast as your team can go!"

"But Condesa -- ?"

"Trust me! Our very lives depend on it -- NOW!"

Melchor whipped his frightened team forward, scattering a crowd of idlers before them. Sirena thanked God and all His saints that Hidalgo's message had not yet been relayed from those inside the church to the waiting host outside. Under high, volcano-shaped sombreros, the stoic vaqueros still sat their horses with typical Indian patience.

"Condesa! Condesa!" a woman's voice called frantically from behind Sirena, "for the love of God, wait for me!"

Sirena turned to see a panic-stricken Analinda racing to overtake the moving carriage. Sirena reached out and pulled her in as Melchor's team finally cleared the crowded plaza and broke into a fast canter. Behind them the bells in both towers began pealing thunderously, a barrage of rockets soaring upward in a celebratory rush of racket and light. Looking over her shoulder Sirena saw hundreds of excited Indians come boiling out of the church, many carrying lighted torches, others brandishing the naked blades of *machetes*.

The horsemen who had been waiting, motionless as statues, erupted like a newly-lit, *castillo* of 'Christians and Moors,' darting wildly in every direction. Sirena caught sight of Father Miguel, mounted on a big blood bay, radiating power and pride. The bells, the rockets, the shouts of rebels filled the air, but drowning out every other sound, and as blood-chilling to Sirena as the ancient Aztec's throbbing sacrificial drum, was the relentless chant rising from a thousand throats:

"DEATH TO THE GACHUPÍNES!"

Melchor's horses, terrified by the sudden pandemonium, rose in their traces screaming with fright, and stampeded for the safety of Linda Vista's barn.

Sirena threw herself onto the floor of the carriage, huddled protectively over the nearly catatonic Analinda, as trees, buildings and aqueducts flashed past them with dizzying speed.

The chaos and din were not left behind until they entered Linda Vista's mulberry groves. There the runaway team streaked along the dusty road until sheer exhaustion reduced them, winded and heaving, to a loose-footed shuffling trot.

"Oh, Sirena. Sirena." Analinda sobbed hysterically, "Ramòn is one of the rebels!"

"Sweet Jesus, no!" Sirena exclaimed. "Analinda, tell me what is all this about? Why is a village priest leading an armed mob of Indians? How can such a monstrous thing be?"

"They've been planning it for months," Analinda gasped, between convulsive sobs, "Ramòn told me everything from the start, but swore he'd kill me if I told! Oh, Sirena, I'm so scared! At first I thought it was just a game, but they're not playing anymore. They really mean to kill the Spaniards, steal their silver and hand everything over to the Indians!"

"But Analinda, how? Is Hidalgo alone in this rebellion? Whose mad idea was it anyway?"

"The Cura and Captain Allende thought it up. At first they planned to proclaim the revolt at the big fair in San Juan de los Lagos, because so many horsemen buy and trade horses there. Hidalgo promised Allende an army of a thousand mounted men in *five* minutes, if he raised his banner there."

Sirena's mind was reeling. "Isn't the fair in December?"

"Yes, but the plot was discovered. They couldn't wait."

Weeping quietly now, Analinda explained that the bandmaster of Guanajuato's regiment, a key conspirator, had lost his nerve and told Don Antonio everything yesterday. Riaño dispatched an officer to San Miguel, with orders to jail the ringleaders on charges of treason. That officer carelessly divulged his mission to a member of the Queen's Regiment, who was a secret rebel. By taking a short cut and riding all night, the rebel streaked to Dolores ahead of Riaño's man to warn the ringleaders they should flee.

"At two o'clock this morning, Ramòn and I were at a dance in a private house in Dolores, with Father Miguel and Allende," Analinda hurried on, "when suddenly the rebel from the Queen's Regiment appeared at the door, white as a ghost, saying he had to see them privately at once. We all rushed back to the Cura's house, where they argued what to do next."

From Analinda's story Sirena gathered the rebel officer was petrified. His advice was to flee or go into hiding, warning if they staged the revolt now, they would be caught and hanged for treason.

The carriage reeled to a halt in Linda Vista's patio, the lathered team lowering their heads, as the trembling Melchor handed Sirena down.

"Melchor, saddle Emir at once and bring him around to me," Sirena ordered him, "I'm riding back to Guanajuato as soon as I've changed."

"But Condesa, it won't be safe on that road -- !" "Emir can outrun any horse in the province," she said quickly, "do as I say."

Gathering her skirts, she raced upstairs to her bedroom, Analinda at her side. "So what did Hidalgo do then?" Sirena asked, changing into her riding habit.

"He refused to listen to such 'cowardly advice'. He sat down on the bed, took off his dancing pumps and pulled on his boots, all very. . ." Analinda was at a sudden loss for words, then she added, "Well, you know how *dramatic* the Cura is when he's acting in one of his plays?"

"No, I *don't* know!" Sirena said hotly, pulling on her own boots. "I've never seen the man perform, until today!"

"So he got up and buckled on his sword," Analinda continued, acting everything out. "He stood there like this, looking at the others, then said in a commanding voice, 'Gentlemen, all may seem lost, but in action it can still be saved! *We now have no choice but to go out and seize the gachupines!*'"

"Sheer madness!" Sirena said in disgust, buttoning her jacket hastily. "How could Allende and Ramòn follow such stupid advice? The priest is a madman. He has no plans, no army, no weapons. . ."

"Oh, but he *has*!"Analinda cut in, "For the last six months his Indian pottery workers have been secretly making weapons for him -- leather slingshots, wooden swords and machetes -- hundreds and hundreds of them!"

Analinda handed Sirena the plumed tricorn matching her burgundy velvet habit, still talking compulsively. "Besides that, the Royal Regiments of Dolores, Querétaro and San Miguel have all promised to defect en masse to Allende!"

"Allende!" Sirena spat out the name. "That loathsome turncoat! What kind of black-hearted son would set out to murder his own father's people, handing innocent men and women over to a blood-thirsty mob?"

Estella, Amantina's faithful seamstress and Analinda's mother, stood in the doorway, her light bronze skin turned ash-grey with fear, her black eyes enormous. "But he's a *priest*," she asked in bewilderment, "how can a man of God lead an -- insurrection?"

"It's because the King is with him," Analinda said. "Last night at the dance Hidalgo told us King Ferdinand has come all the way from Spain to help him drive the gachupínes out of this kingdom!"

"Why would Ferdinand want to kill Spaniards?" Sirena asked, exasperated by Hidalgo's ludicrous claims and Analinda's credulity. "For God's sake, Analinda, *the King of Spain is a gachupín himself!*"

Running downstairs to the patio she found Emir saddled and waiting. Quirt in hand Sirena began firing off orders. "Melchor, take your fastest horse to Doña Amantina's new silk house and bring her back at once. Estella, you and Analinda gather up the house servants and lock up everything. As soon as Doña Amantina returns, all of you come at once to my palace in Guanajuato."

She mounted Emir and settling into the sidesaddle cast a fond last look at Linda Vista's patio, filled with so many sunlit memories of jotas and other happy times. Now the woebegone servants stood there huddled together, terror stricken as a band of orphaned children.

"May the Virgin watch over you, Condesa," Estella called out to her. Analinda rushed forward and, grasping Sirena's stirrup, burst into a fresh torrent of tears. "Oh, Condesa, please forgive me for not telling you before," she sobbed, "but I love Ramón so, and I was afraid he'd leave me!"

Sirena laid her hand on the girl's dark hair, and bending down so the others could not hear, murmured softly, "I understand, Analinda dear! Love is blind to everything but its own needs. What's done is done. Now take care of your mother, Doña Amantina and yourself. Amar a Diós!"

As Analinda stepped back Sirena touched her spur to Emir's side. Fresh and spirited, he lunged eagerly through the open gate. Knowing she had to pace him for the ride ahead, she deliberately held him to a steady single-foot, a ground-eating gait that was as easy as it was fast.

The trail wound upward, giving her a broad overview of Dolores. Looking back apprehensively, she saw the town swarming like an anthill that has just been kicked over. Everywhere Indians, criollos, mestizos, Spaniards were running through the streets, horsemen, soldiers and vaqueros pursuing and being pursued, the dust from that multitude of hooves laying a fine mist over the town's domes, towers and trees. The disquieting sounds of violence were borne to her on the light morning breeze -- gunshots, breaking glass, the shriek of frightened horses, a woman's piercing scream. Her blood froze. They had already begun seizing Spaniards!

Spying a plume of smoke, rising from a spot near the center of town, Sirena saw it explode into a pillar of flame, rising hundreds of *varas* straight up into the limpid sky. She watched in speechless horror: there was no mistaking what it was, she knew the site too well. Amantina's new silk house had been put to the torch!

"Amantina! Oh, my dear Amantina!" she moaned helplessly, a sob catching in her throat as she realized there was no way on God's earth anyone could escape that inferno alive.

Tears of rage and shame burned her cheeks. Ramón's unspeakable treachery, Allende's cold-blooded arrogance, the vanity that had tempted an obscure village cura to lead an Indian rabble against his own kind in a petty grab for glory!

Weeping uncontrollably, she forced herself to turn her back on Aunt Amantina's funeral pyre and face the road to Guanajuato. "Emir," she cried, talking to the animal in an effort to contain her rising hysteria, "take me to Don Antonio as fast as you can go!" Leaning forward in the saddle she twisted a long wisp of white mane around the fingers of her right hand to give her better purchase, and braced herself for the desperate ride ahead. "For the sake of every Spanish soul in Dolores," she pleaded tearfully, "RUN, EMIR, RUN!"

35

The door of this house is a heart always open!

Sirena read fresh meaning into that familiar salutation as she banged the bronze Moor's head knocker on the Riaño's front door. Stroking Emir's head, she saw his black muzzle was white with foam, his snowy coat slate-grey with sweat.

The moment a servant opened to her, she handed him the reins, shouting as she rushed past, "Blanket my horse and cool him down. I've nearly foundered him!"

Running across the patio, she called out to Don Antonio. He came striding toward her from the sala, deep concern on his always grave countenance, followed by the equally alarmed Doña Victoria and Gilberto.

Before anyone asked a question Sirena was already spilling out her shocking story. "I've just come from Dolores at a dead run," she sobbed, "Father Miguel Hidalgo is leading a mob of armed Indians and renegade Royalist officers in a revolt against the Viceregal government! They're seizing all the Spaniards and sacking the town!"

"God help us!" he murmured, putting his arms around her and holding her close. "I ordered Hidalgo's arrest yesterday. I thought he and Allende were safely in jail!"

"*Mon Dieu!*" Doña Victoria gasped disbelievingly, "The Cura broke bread at our table, he called himself our friend!"

As Don Antonio led her into the sala, Sirena's terror began to subside. Here in her second father's comforting embrace she felt secure again. All the assurance and power of his dominating presence flowed into her -- the veteran soldier, the prudent governor, the solid rock on which the city, the province and her own well-ordered world rested. She was filled with a euphoric sense of relief and faith renewed. He would muster his forces and crush this uprising in a matter of days -- perhaps even hours!

"Who else besides Allende is in this with Hidalgo?"

"Most of the officers from the Queen's Regiment of San Miguel and. . ." her voice broke, " -- my own brother, Ramón. He's been with them from the start."

Gilberto pressed a glass of brandy upon her, and she sipped it gratefully, trying to find the strength to express her deepest hurt. "Aunt Amantina – " she struggled to control her tears. "The mob torched her silk house. It was an inferno, and poor Amantina was *inside*!" Tears slid down her cheeks and she swallowed great gulps of brandy hoping to steady herself.

Riaño's jaw hardened. "That dear, good woman," he said stoically. "Such wanton violence!"

Regaining a degree of calm, Sirena took a long shuddering breath and pulled herself erect, aglow with the first confidence she had felt all day. "Of course, they're only a mob. How soon can your regiment march against them?"

"We need to move with great caution in this matter, Riaño said with uncharacteristic indecision. "The regimental bandmaster who betrayed their plot to me said Hidalgo would have ten thousand Indians at his back, twelve hours after raising his banner." Riaño paced the sala, his face a study in conflict and uncertainty. "At full strength my Regiment has only three hundred men."

"I know," she persisted, "but they're disciplined soldiers. Hidalgo doesn't have an army, Don Antonio. I saw it with my own eyes. *It's a horde!"*

"But ten thousand! New Spain's entire Royal Army numbers less than thirty. I have to think in terms of what's prudent -- what's possible." He patted her arm. "I'll send a courier to General Calleja. His Tenth Brigade is our best hope. Until he can come to our assistance we can only temporize and look to our own defenses."

Sirena stared at him, thunderstruck, reminded of the time as a little girl when she had begged her father to bring her dead pony back to life. "I'm only mortal," Don Patrick had said. "I cannot work miracles." His reply had stunned her then, as Riaño's did now. Somehow she thought the governor was capable of working miracles, but until this moment she had not grasped the full magnitude of the numbers involved.

The Campaign Route of Hidalgo and Allende (1810 – 1811)

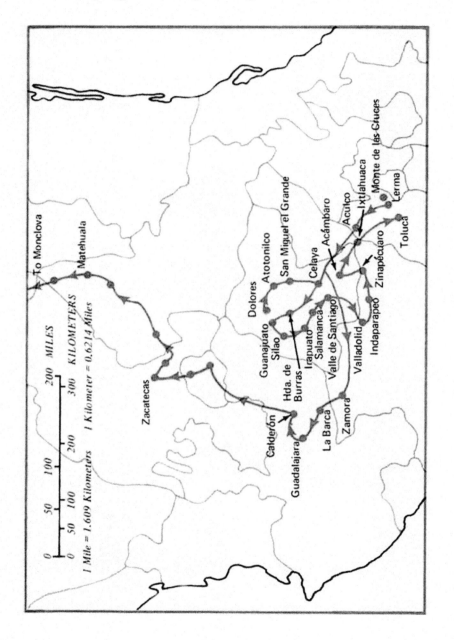

Did even Father Miguel realize the awesome force he had unleashed? Did he understand how explosive was this mix of ignorance, primitive bloodlust and plain human greed, that his promise of gachupín loot stirred in the breasts of thousands of Indians? Didn't he know he was as vulnerable to destruction at the hands of that wildly incited mob as any other member of the white race?

"Come," Don Antonio said gently, putting his arm around Sirena and leading her toward the stairs. "Let's go up to the house chapel. Father Hilario is about to say Mass, and God knows every Spaniard in Dolores needs our prayers."

⚃ ⚂

Gloriously naked in Don Francisco's arms, Isabel was rising to a new peak of ecstasy. They lay together before the fireplace in his sumptuous bedroom, on a paisley cover laid over a deep pile Chinese carpet, with a dozen velvet cushions strewn about. The twelve-panel Coromandel screen Sirena had brought him from Manila, closed off the other half of the room. The drapes were drawn, the only light cast upon the lovers by a fire blazing in the hearth. A carefully angled mirror above the mantel reflected their every movement, the firelight licking both their real and mirrored bodies. The whole mood of the room was sensual, a Cordoba Caliph's seraglio out of 13th Century Spain.

Although he was now past fifty, Francisco's body was still trim and firm. Isabel was more voluptuous, but also more satisfying to him. After years of mutually repressed sex, their hunger for each other was voracious. Scarcely a night passed without their meeting here, but they looked forward to Sundays, when they could be together all day long.

Now, from far away -- so distant it seemed to come from another world -- Isabel heard the urgent clangor of the bronze bell above the main door to Francisco's home. Enraptured, she pretended not to hear. Francisco did the same. The ringing persisted -- insistent, demanding.

"Damn it!" he muttered under his breath, "who can that be on a quiet Sunday morning?"

"They'll go away," Isabel panted, "don't leave me now!"

"It's probably a beggar," he said, rising and slipping on a robe. "I'll give him a few pesos and be right back."

Unable to tear himself away so quickly, he dropped on one knee beside her and took a fistful of her red-gold hair. "Do you realize you're riper and more luscious now than when I first lay with you at twenty-one?" he whispered.

"Please don't go!"

"I promise I'll have a new game for you when I return," he assured her, "one we can play all day!"

The bell grew more strident and he turned to answer it. "Hurry!" she called after him, "I'm ablaze!"

Settling back on a velvet pillow Isabel was irritated, but content. She was even more madly in love with Francisco now than before. Years ago, he had been in constant moral conflict with himself -- chaste as an anchorite one minute, hornier than a satyr the next. Now the satyr reigned supreme.

His love had built a secure wall around her. Apart from him she lived in a state of imbalance and fear. The wars in Europe and the political infighting at home frightened her, but here in this hidden harbor of his love, she was safe, world events becoming harmless ghost ships sailing past, unseeing and unseen. He had contested Don Telmo's will, and was working to restore the Graciana mine to her, but this practical side of the man she did not comprehend. She was obsessed with the Francisco who worshipped her body and wrote erotic poetry. She reached over and picked up the bound folio of odes to her that lay nearby, re-reading her favorite poem:

> *ISABEL*
> *Who is Isabel?*
> *A lighted Pascal candle,*
> *Burning in my name,*
> *And with my wick within,*
> *Her waxen flesh*
> *Is consumed*
> *By the flame.*

36

"It is now ten days since Hidalgo launched his rebellion," Don Antonio said with more than his usual seriousness. He stood with his back to the fireplace in his own crowded sala, addressing the assembled city council, officers of the mining consulado and leading merchants, mine owners and officers of the town regiment.

"I've called this emergency meeting to advise you that our situation is grave and growing more so every day."

Sirena, veiled and in mourning for Aunt Amantina, sat in the first row of straight chairs, between Don Francisco and Crispín. Observing Don Antonio through her sheer black veil, the weight that had fallen on his shoulders was clearly visible. Between lack of sleep and the crushing load of being responsible for the city's defense, he looked ten years older than he had ten days ago. Compounding his preoccupation with Hidalgo's stunningly successful insurrection, was his concern over Doña Victoria, who now lay in her upstairs bedroom desperately ill with a recurrence of malarial fever.

"Hidalgo's army moved quickly from Dolores to take San Miguel," he continued. "Rebels seized all the Spaniards in both towns, looting their homes and stores. The Cura has created a rebel war chest from their confiscated wealth, to finance the spread of his rebellion."

He went on to explain, that three days ago Hidalgo had appeared before Celaya's city gate with ten thousand men and seventy-eight Spanish prisoners in tow. When he threatened to cut the throats of every hostage if the city did not surrender, Celaya fell to him without a shot, half its regiment defecting to the rebel cause. Sirena closed her eyes to shut out the shame of it.

"I've sent word to General Calleja to come to our aid. Under my authority as governor, I have ordered all municipal funds, the monies from the Royal Tobacco Tax and the Treasury of the Mining Consulado be moved into the Alhóndiga for safekeeping." He explained that he intended to fortify the Alhóndiga, as it was the only building in town that could be adequately defended, or where the Regiment could make a stand. With its own well, and women inside to make tortillas, he felt sure it could withstand a siege of up to two months.

Listening to his words, Sirena wondered how she could fortify La Sirena mine. How would any of the people in this room seal their mines and shops and homes against such a huge invading army? The latest word from Riaño's spy was that Hidalgo was unstoppable everywhere, with a force of over twelve thousand men!

"My Regiment has now grown from three to five hundred men," Riaño said proudly, "and any of you who wish to join today will be welcomed into the ranks of Alhóndiga defenders."

Sirena stiffened in her chair as Don Francisco rose from her side and stepped forward. A second later Crispín and his lifelong companion, Lucas Alamán, joined Francisco at Don Antonio's side. They were followed immediately by the Conde de Rul, the Fifth Marqués de San Clemente, young Doctor Daniel Pinal, six School of Mines summer students, and a dozen other prominent mine owners and merchants, most well past middle age. Her pride strove against dismay as she witnessed this silent procession of volunteers. It was enough to break her heart. These boys were the flower of Guanajuato's youth, these men the very cream of her silver elite!

"Well, I for one don't intend to sit here in this indefensible bowl of hills and be butchered by Indians!"

All eyes turned to a wrathful Neto de la Huerta who had risen from his chair near the patio door of the sala.

"Do you have any better suggestions for your own defense?" Don Antonio asked with scathing courtesy.

"You're damned right I do! My brother and I are taking as much of our silver as a dozen mules can carry, and heading for Mexico!" He started for the patio, then turned in the doorway for a parting shot. "This is one gachupín who knows how to save his own hide. Guanajuato can go to Hell for all I care!"

"Go then, Neto!" Sirena shouted, springing to her feet, trembling with rage. "Why should men of courage and honor protect a craven coward like you? You've exploited your workers ruthlessly, and given the plebeians good reason to despise all Spaniards. You don't deserve to be counted a citizen of a city as noble as this!"

"I advise any others who share Don Ernesto's views," Riaño cautioned after Neto left, "the roads everywhere are filled with peril. A man would be wiser to face the enemy in the Alhóndiga than try to reach Mexico alive in times like these."

ଓଃ ଓ

"But Crispín will listen to you, Francisco!" Isabel cried, striding back and forth in the De La Huerta patio, wringing her hands and weeping. "He's only a child. I won't allow him to stay and fight as if he were a grown man! Francisco, *command* him to go the Bishop in Valladolid. He'll be safe there!"

"Mamá, you're asking the impossible," Sirena pleaded, trying to be sympathetic, but inwardly frantic because she was neglecting a thousand priorities at both her mine and palace to help Francisco cope with the hysterical Isabel. Ten days ago, returning to her own home, after bringing the news of Hidalgo's revolt to Don Antonio, she discovered little Rafael Crowley waiting for her, on that day, of all terrible days! Travel-weary and uprooted from his familiar surroundings at Madre Pilar's, he was requiring huge doses of her time, attention and reassuring love.

"Chabela," Francisco said wearily, his patience frayed from hours of such futile pleading. "Crispín may only be seventeen, but the times have made him a man. He refuses to flee the city in its hour of peril. I admire him for that. Surely you know, not even a mother has the right to deprive her son of honor?"

"*Honor!*" Isabel shrilled. "Good God, don't you men ever think of anything else?" She pressed her handkerchief to her swollen eyes. "How can you ask me to let the only son of whom I can be proud, throw his life away on something so empty and useless as *honor?*"

"Mamá, how can you say such a thing," Sirena cut in angrily, "when Papá prized honor above everything?"

"All right, so honor is worth dying for!" Isabel conceded. "Then let someone else's son die for it, *not mine!*" She turned to face them, vicious as a tigress at bay. "All I've heard from both of you for the last five years is that Crispín wants to become a priest. Well, I've given my consent and now *you* refuse to let him go!"

Wheeling on Francisco she threw herself in his arms. "Oh, mi corazon, *you*, of all people know why I treasure Crispín so! If you love me you'll see he leaves this very night in a closed coach for Valladolid!"

☙ ❧

Sirena awoke with a start from a night of little sleep, wondering what unaccustomed sound had roused her. It was Thursday, September the twenty-seventh and the rebel army was marching toward Guanajuato from Querétaro. She sat up in bed, listening intently. It was well past daybreak, but still no clitter of mules tripping beneath her window, bound for the upper mines. The life blood of the kingdom, those ceaseless mule trains had been moving for three hundred years. How could they have stopped in a single day?

She strained to hear the familiar banter between crewmen on their way up to the mines. Nothing. No vendors shouting, no servant girls' laughter. She shivered, knowing now it hadn't been a sound that had awakened her, but this eerie absence of all sound! The silence was abruptly broken by a small contingent of regimental cavalry clattering past, reminding her that Riaño was posting troops along every road leading into town.

Dressing hastily, she went downstairs and confronted her foreman in the patio. "Ricardo, why aren't the men going to work?" she asked irritably. She saw Ricardo was pretending not to hear, his face an expressionless Indian mask, a slate wiped clean.

"We *must* keep the mines going at all costs," she told him urgently, "we can't stop the malacates, even for a day, or the shafts will be flooded!"

"Condesa, the men are afraid to report for work," he said at last, "they're frightened of the rebels."

"Well, we can't let the world come to an end because a bunch of vainglorious maniacs have started a rebellion!" she snapped angrily. "Arrastres don't turn themselves, ore still has to be worked! Has everybody except me forgotten *this town runs on silver?*"

Alberta appeared, bringing Sirena a saucer with a cup of steaming chocolate, her hand trembling visibly. "There's word Hidalgo is nearing town," she said, spreading her dark hands on her fresh white apron, "when the men heard that. . ."

"But Alberta, a city of sixty-six thousand souls doesn't just stop like a clock someone forgot to wind!"

Ricardo looked apologetic and pained. "The poor plebeians are scared, they don't know what to do."

Well, she thought, they aren't the only ones scared, but *somebody* had to get the men back to work. Feeling panic rise within her, she set the cup aside and said decisively, as though it had been her intention all along, "I'm going to see Don Antonio about this!"

"The men are not disloyal," Ricardo said, "they simply want to -- wait and see."

He spoke as if Guanajuato's life and death struggle were a village cockfight! Able-bodied men should be taking up arms to defend their city, not standing around placing bets!

"The Aztec common people stood around watching Cortes and Montezuma this way, too," she cried, surprised at the heat of her ire, "that's how they lost Mexico! If we Europeans were fatalists like *you*, the Moors would still be ruling Spain and an Aztec sitting in the Viceroy's chair!"

Riding down into town she regretted her angry outburst at her understandably frightened servants. Church bells pealed urgently from every bell tower, and she stopped in at the Church of Our Lady of Guanajuato to pray, adding her own vigil candle asking for deliverance from the rebel army, to the hundreds of others blazing there. Reaching the heart of town she found confusion everywhere. Cavalrymen dashed recklessly down slick cobbled lanes on imperative missions, mothers collected their children. Merchants, silver lords and householders were busy barricading shops and homes to the best of their ability. Could it be true that *everyone* had forgotten the mines?

At the entrance to Las Pozitas street, she passed Gilberto Riaño, working with soldiers to erect barricades and dig moats on streets leading to the Alhóndiga. In his shirtsleeves, sweating and with pick in hand, he was too preoccupied to even look up as she passed.

An almost imperceptible darkening along the rim of the surrounding hills, reminding her of cattle grazing where no pastures existed, caught her eye. Slowly she saw that the spreading stain was actually people -- *hundreds of them!* -- Settling themselves on the slopes overlooking town. At first she thought it was the rebel vanguard, then in a sickening flash of recognition she saw they were local plebeians, many of them her own crewmen. What were they doing up there? Her skin crawled as the answer came to her: they smelled blood and were only waiting for the first signs of rebel triumph to close in for the kill!

Everywhere criollos and Spaniards worked at the desperate business of carrying all their valuables to the safety of the Alhóndiga. That imposing rectangular, neo-classic structure, built as a granary for wheat and corn, was now the central magnet toward which all of Guanajuato was inexorably drawn. Sirena had never thought of its high, stuccoed walls and flat roof as being fortress-like, but now as she rode closer she could see that it was. The exterior was utterly plain except for three long rows of small, square windows, evenly spaced about three varas apart. Each window marked the head of a stone-vaulted grain bin. Inside were fifty such bins opening off both the lower cloister and the loggia above.

A classical covered portal with large wooden doors and stone steps leading up to it, served as the main, northside entrance on Pozitas Street. Two blocks to her right, on higher ground and facing south, stood the Riaño mansion where Don Antonio's rooftop office gave him an unobstructed view of the Alhóndiga. Who would have dreamed, she mused, that his controversial 'palace for corn' would be put to such a use?

Dismounting, Sirena saw Don Antonio. Dressed in the dark blue uniform of Regimental commander, he was standing alone on the covered portico, an unwavering flame radiating confidence and hope in the midst of chaos. He called to Sirena to join him inside and then led her across the busy patio to his office. Their progress was impeded by men lugging sacks of food, Indian women cooking on *comals*, soldiers stacking arms and ammunition. Two red-faced, perspiring members of the consulado, whom she had never seen lift anything heavier than a snuff-box, passed in front of her, carrying between them a plank loaded with silver bars. Passing along the lower corridor and glancing through the open doors into the storage rooms, Sirena saw men bent double over the deep bins, burying ledgers, specie, bars of silver and the family jewels in mounds of corn and grain. The lean, black-cassocked Regimental Chaplain, Father Hilario, on his way to hear confessions, nodded to Sirena as he passed.

Riaño ushered her into a small storage room on the ground floor, which he had converted into his command post, fitted out with a table, a lamp, three straight chairs and a military cot. Once inside, he drafted her to write an urgent letter for him, pacing the small room nervously as he dictated it to her, his face a relief map of worry and strain.

*"To General Félix Maria Calleja,
      Tenth Brigade Headquarters,
         San Luis Potosí.*

"My Most Esteemed Friend and Commander,

I write you in an hour of dire necessity. The seeds of rebellion are spreading fast in this city, confidence in the legitimate government eroding. The plebeians scoff at authority and brazenly await the arrival of the Cura's horde.

"In the performance of my duties, I have neither rested nor undressed for the past nine days. In the last three, I have not slept a single hour at a time. To pacify the city's lower classes I ended the Indian tribute on my own authority, amounting to three million pesos in the fortified Alhóndiga.

The physical situation of the city, as you know, makes it impossible to defend, so I have told the people they must defend themselves, rich and poor alike. Criollos and Spaniards work at the task with zeal, but plebeians complain I've abandoned them, not comprehending that I have no choice.

Strong barricades fortify three points where the city might be attacked. The eastern gate is sealed and iron quicksilver containers converted into grenades. Rebel threats assure me my head will roll in the streets, but I do what I must. Spies inform me Hidalgo's forces march against us, twenty thousand strong. I count scarcely five hundred men. We are sure to be attacked by noon tomorrow, but I am prepared to resist as best I can, because. . ."

He searched for the proper words.

". . . because I am an honorable man."

He paused again and Sirena waited with quill posed, choking back tears. She had never admired and loved him more than now, as the pure nobility of his character shone through his simple, unpretentious words.

"I beg you, my friend, in the Name of God, to hasten to my aid: we can hope for no other succor short of a miracle!"

Sirena waited for the next chilling sentence, but instead he said quietly, "I'll sign it now."

As she watched him append his name and rubrica, Sirena tried to guess how soon an express rider could reach San Luis. Thirty hours? Twenty four?

Sensing what was in her mind, Riaño told her reassuringly: "This is my second request for help from Don Félix. In replying to my first he promised to be here himself by Wednesday of the coming week." He put his arm around her. "Take courage, my dear, the General and Tristán will not fail us!"

She turned to go, but he detained her briefly. "I must ask a great favor of you, Sirena, before we part. Please look after my dear Victoria. Husband and son are both here. . ." he glanced out the small window toward his office atop the nearby Riaño palace. "If anything should happen to either, or both of us, promise to get her safely to Puebla, where Marianne and General Flon can care for her until she makes *other* plans."

She promised, but was frightened by his prescient vision of the worst. She felt her heart breaking for him as she followed him out to Pozitas Street where he handed his letter to the waiting courier. Laying his hand on the lad's shoulder he admonished him, "Ride as though this city's very life depended on you my son, for in all truth -- It does!"

Sirena closed her eyes and tried to pray, but all that kept repeating themselves over and over again inside her head were four fervent words: the Tenth must come!

37

"All right, my dear," Francisco said in a loud whisper, "tell them to pass along the next one."

Sirena held a miner's torch for him to see by as they both worked feverishly at lowering heavy bars of silver into the covered well behind the Hermitage. It was shortly before dawn, the moon hidden by an overcast sky, and helping them in their nocturnal labors were Crispín, Lucas Alamán and the three summer students who had been working for Sirena since July.

As she signaled Crispín to pass another bar along the human chain, she found herself wondering how much silver they had managed to sink in this deep and completely hidden well. They had worked at it every night, foregoing sleep, but rest was the farthest thing from their minds. As things stood, time was their most priceless commodity, and there was precious little of it left. On Sunday, September sixteenth, Hidalgo had launched his rebellion. Now, a mere twelve days later, he was advancing on Guanajuato with some twenty-five thousand men, and was expected at the city gates by noon.

As Francisco waited, Sirena saw him wipe his beaded forehead wearily with the sleeve of his shirt. In the flickering light of the burning pitch the resoluteness of his will made his fine features seem carved out of granite. "Isabel and Rafael will be safer here than anywhere," he told Sirena, as though it were his first mention of it. They had been over the plan a dozen times this past week, but as the danger intensified, he needed to reassure them both. "If the rebels come in by this road they won't look twice at an adobe as poor and humble as the Hermitage."

"And I'm sure the rabble that has already sacked three towns has learned not to waste time on anything but the richest shops and palaces."

"The Alhóndiga's defenders have already sealed themselves inside," he remarked randomly, such tense, fragmented conversations between them having become commonplace, "They said I can be lowered down into the building by sharpshooters posted on the roof if I can get there by seven."

"Thank Heaven, you convinced Crispín to stay with Lucas and Doña Ignacia, to help defend the Alamán mansion," she whispered, "I dreaded the idea of his being in the Alhóndiga. But Francisco dear, I feel the same way about you."

He squeezed her hand. "I believe some things in our lives are predestined. This is what God asks of me today."

"But you're not a soldier. I've always seen you as a man of peace."

He shrugged. "When times change, men must change."

Reaching up he took the next bar Crispín handed him. While the two men balanced it on the stone collar of the well, Sirena wrapped it securely in a square of coarse *ayate*. Then, with Lucas and Crispín each holding a line, they lowered the heavy bar down into the stygian well. A moment later they heard the faint, familiar splash as it broke the surface of the water far below.

"That's the last one of the load," Crispín said, and Sirena looked up anxiously at the lightening sky.

"Perfect timing," Francisco exulted, taking out his pocket watch. "Fifteen minutes to four. You've all barely time to get back to your posts by sun up, and I'll make it to the Alhóndiga by seven."

❧ ❦

"Rafael, you and Doña Isabel are going to spend a wonderful day in the country," Sirena told the boy brightly, brushing his soft brown hair with her hand as she waited nervously for Ricardo to bring around the coach. She was anxious for them to be on their way so she could hurry downtown to the Riaño palace before the rebel host appeared. "Alberta has packed every good thing you can imagine for this picnic," she promised Rafael, and then, remembering herself as a child visiting the Royal Visitor's tent on the journey north, she added, "and you can even drink watered wine with the grown-ups. Won't that be grand?"

"Can we ride there in the coach?" he asked, his brown eyes shining at the prospect of such a treat. She looked at him fondly. He was such a beautiful child, with Consuelo's fair coloring and gentle disposition. He was strong and healthy now, but had been so frail as an infant and toddler, Madre Pilar had not dared send him up to live with her until this year. And what a year for him to come!

"Of course," she agreed, "A coach is part of every picnic's fun."

"And you'll be coming with me, Madrina?"

She hesitated. "Yes -- but not until later. I must go into the city first." Mother of God, she thought bitterly, ever since this poor child arrived I've done nothing but lie to him! How will he ever trust anything I say?

As soon as Ricardo drove the blue and silver coach into the patio, Rafael pulled open a door with the Graciana coat of arms emblazoned on it, and clambered up onto the seat.

When she knew the child was safely out of earshot, Alberta spoke to Sirena under her breath. "Condesa, I have some more bad news. Analinda has run away."

Although Estella, her daughter and Melchor had all taken refuge with her after Amantina's death, Sirena had not had time to miss Analinda. "Has she gone back to Ramón?"

"Of course! When she heard the rebel army was victorious everywhere and would soon be here, she went out to meet him on the road. She said she has to prove her love for him."

Sirena took a deep breath. "I'm not surprised," she said with a cryptic smile. In a way she was relieved. It was one less mouth to feed, one less soul to answer for. Then, as she watched Alberta and Estella climb in beside Rafael, Sirena realized someone was missing.

"Alberta, where's Mamá?"

Alberta looked up, surprised. "She was right behind me when I came down stairs."

Sirena raced up the stairs, and began searching every room. With the windows shuttered and the furniture shrouded, the house looked desolate as a church in Lent. She ran down the corridor, past the gallery of ancestors and paintings of her father's favorite saints, sending hasty wisps of prayer their way as she ran. Frantic that Isabel, in her present distraught state of mind might have tried to take her life, Sirena entered the last room left, the ballroom. There she found her mother, half-kneeling before the king's chair on the canopied dais, her head resting on the cushioned seat. Although everything in the room had been covered, Isabel had thrown off the cloth from the throne and exposed the hanging portrait of Spain's deposed monarch, Ferdinand.

In the dim light the scene seemed unreal -- Isabel in mourning dress and veil, with the shrouded harp, piano, harpsichord and other

313

musical instruments rising like ghosts all around her. "Mamá," she called softly, careful not to startle her, "Come, Mamá, it's time to go."

Isabel lifted her head from the chair and fixed Sirena with the unfocused gaze of a woman in a trance. "I can't go," she said dreamily. "Haven't you heard? His Majesty is coming to visit us, and I must be here to welcome him."

"Mamá, the king is safely locked away in a prison in France," she responded tartly. "Whoever told you such a silly tale?"

"All the servants know about him," Isabel said defensively. "That mysterious man wearing a silver mask who's been seen everywhere riding in the same coach with Hidalgo, is really King Ferdinand himself, *in disguise!*"

Sirena had heard the story too, for Hidalgo had been scattering it like seed corn among the credulous humildes of the Bajío, to prop up his fraudulent claim that he was *not* fighting to set up an independent nation, but merely to defend Ferdinand's rightful claim to the throne.

"Believe me, Mamá," Sirena told her patiently, "that story is a figment of Hidalgo's wild imagination. Come now, you have to go."

"Go where?"

Carefully, as though Isabel were made of fine porcelain, Sirena led her mother from the ballroom and downstairs to the coach, more deeply concerned than ever about her precarious mental state. Amantina's death and the failure of her efforts to make Crispín leave town, seemed to have unseated Isabel's reason. Then last evening, after taking their marriage vows before Father Hilario in the sala of Francisco's home, the harried groom broke the news to her they could not take a honeymoon because he had to help defend the city.

"No, no, you can't leave my side!" she had screamed hysterically, "I'm your bride at last! Carry me upstairs to the bedroom and make love to me! Oh, Francisco, *you know your love alone can make the world go away!*"

Francisco had been mortified and Sirena shocked to hear her mother commanding him with the shameless familiarity of a brazen, long-time mistress. Understanding his dilemma, Sirena had taken Isabel home with her, adding one more responsibility to all her others.

Now as Alberta and Estella settled Isabel in the coach with them, Sirena approached Ricardo on the driver's seat. "No matter what happens at the Hermitage, Ricardo," she cautioned him in a low voice, "whatever you do, *don't let Doña Isabel out of your sight!*"

On the stroke of seven, Francisco drew rein before the sealed Alhóndiga. The streets were deserted, the city quiet as death except for the movements of soldiers manning the barricades and trenches. Silent stores and palaces, many with doors barred and windows boarded up, all seemed to be holding their breath. He glanced up at the hills and saw the hundreds of plebeian spectators were still there, waiting with the savage patience of vultures for today's quick to become tomorrow's dead.

After being lowered from the roof, Francisco reported at once to Don Antonio in his command post. He had scarcely closed the door behind him and greeted his commander before Gilberto appeared with a dispatch in his hand. "This just came for you from Hidalgo, Sir," he told his father, the involuntary twitching of a muscle in his right jaw alone betraying the strain the younger man was under. "The rebel emissary says their forces have occupied the hacienda of Burros on the edge of town and know our position well."

"Come in, son, and close the door," Riaño said wearily, "let's hear what our erstwhile friend has to say." Taking the letter from Gilberto, he unfolded it and read aloud:

"The vast army I command elected me Captain General and Protector of the Nation in the fields of Celaya -- in the presence of fifty thousand men. I am legitimately authorized to undertake the projects that I judge equally beneficial to criollos and Spaniards.

I do not regard the latter as my enemies, merely an obstacle standing in the way of my success. Your honor will be pleased to tell the Spaniards gathered with you in the Alhóndiga that they can remain enemies or choose to become my prisoners, meeting with the same humane treatment as the Spanish hostages I bring with me. If they do not obey my demand to surrender, I shall use every means to destroy them, leaving no hope of mercy or quarter.

May God protect Your Honor.
Signed, the twenty-eighth of September, 1810.
Miguel Hidalgo y Costilla,
Captain General of America."

An enigmatic smile touched Riaño's lips as the former Cura's magisterial new title rolled off his tongue.

A second private message was enclosed and this Riaño also read aloud:

"The esteem I have always expressed for you is sincere and surely due to the high qualities which adorn you. The difference in our ways of thinking should not diminish it. We shall fight as enemies, if it be so decided, but because of her ill health, I offer Doña Victoria asylum and protection in any place she may select as her residence. This offer does not spring from fear, but from a sensibility I cannot discard from me."

Gilberto seated himself at the table, prepared to pen whatever answer his father dictated. Francisco was pleased when Riaño ignored Hidalgo's lordly new title, and now addressed him simply as --

The Señor Cura of Dolores, Don Miguel Hidalgo:

I recognize no other authority, nor is it evident that any other Captain General of New Spain has been established except our present Viceroy. My duty is to fight as a soldier, which noble sentiment animates those around me.

Guanajuato, the Twenty-eighth day of September, 1810.
Juan Antonio Riaño

No allowable reference to himself as Governor and Regimental Commander, Francisco thought, no adorning himself with high-flown titles. Riaño was indeed a man of true humility. Having finished his brief letter as Intendent, Riaño now addressed the personal --

To your private note, I make this reply:

The exercise of arms is not incompatible with sensibilities this demands of my heart the gratitude due your offer to shelter my family. But their lot does not disturb me on the present occasion.

Gilberto glanced at his father, eyes alight with pride.
"But before sending off this reply, I must consult the men who have pledged their lives to me."

Francisco and Gilberto accompanied Riaño into the patio where he called his entire force together. "My friends, Hidalgo has offered us the choice between becoming his humanely-treated prisoners, or fighting to the death, knowing he will grant neither mercy nor quarter. He has many more men than we. However, we have honor and a just cause. For this I am willing to give my own life. But I will not impose my decision upon you. Tell me how you feel."

Francisco gazed around at the men who stood crowding the corridors above and below and packing the center of the patio itself. As he did so he caught sight of his own son in that sea of faces! Having labored to make sure Crispín was safe from danger in the home of the Alamáns, he was heartsick at this grim turn of events, but helpless now to do more than weep in his soul. Jesus, Mary and Joseph, if anything should happen to this dear, chaste, utterly sinless boy, who had already given himself, body and soul, to God -- as Francisco had so often tried and failed to do! How would he ever live with the pain? And, Isabel? He was terrified to even harbor the thought, but he secretly believed that one more shock and his fragile, spun glass Isabel could quite easily lose her mind.

The silence that met Don Antonio's words was so suspenseful Francisco could hear the men breathing. Finally one man, Don Alfonso Mendizebal, swept the crowd with his flashing eyes and spoke for them all. "Your Honor, we will not consider the ignominy of surrender. For all of us here, let it be victory or death!"

The stout walls of the Alhóndiga shook as all five hundred men shouted,

"VICTORY OR DEATH! LONG LIVE THE KING!"

"Long live the King!" Riaño answered, giving their supreme act of courage his solemn "Amen."

It was only after Gilberto had taken private leave of his father behind closed doors and left to take up his appointed post defending the barricades outside, that Francisco rejoined Riaño in his cramped command post.

He found the commander standing with his back to the door, gazing out the small, square window at the nearly helpless city beyond. Wrapped in his own grave thoughts, Riaño remained there for some time after Francisco entered, and when, at last, he turned to face him, his dark eyes were flooded with tears. He came toward Francisco slowly and rested a hand on his shoulder. "Ah, my old and cherished friend," he said with a sorrow so profound it pierced Francisco's heart, *"whatever is to become of my poor, dear child of Guanajuato?"*

38

"**Oh, Doctor Juan, thank Heaven** you're here!" Sirena said in a low voice, answering his knock on the door of Doña Victoria's bedroom. "She's completely delirious. I've tried everything, but I no more than bring down her fever a point, than her teeth start chattering and she's begging for blankets."

"I understand. She contracted malaria years ago in Louisiana, and I've seen her through several of these savage recurrences over the years. I know exactly what to do."

Relieved that the lady she had sworn to care for was in such good hands, Sirena climbed the stairs from the second floor to Don Antonio's rooftop office, thinking how providential it was for her that Doctor Juan and his wife had arrived in town unexpectedly. The elder Pinals had set out from Mexico to visit their son, ignorant of the uprising in Dolores. Sirena met them by accident this morning when she rode past the Alhóndiga just as they were taking leave of Doctor Daniel, who was there assuming his post as Regimental surgeon. She immediately asked them to take refuge with her in the Riaño home and give Doña Victoria the professional medical care she needed.

Entering Don Antonio's sunny office, where his renowned library occupied three entire walls, she felt his presence all around her. The large rectangular window and two French doors opening onto a flat terrace, afforded a perfect view of the granary, only two blocks away. Looking down on it from here, one would suppose the siege of the Alhóndiga was a play being performed on a panoramic outdoor stage, a grim drama to which she had somehow been given a front row balcony seat. The rest of the household was gathered in the downstairs sala, but she felt compelled to follow the fortunes of war from here, where -- in spirit at least -- she felt closer to the valiant men huddled in the fortress below.

A short time later Doctor Juan joined her, saying he had given the patient quinine and hoped she would now begin to improve. "I swear if she weren't suffering so, I'd count her delirium a blessing. Somehow I can't imagine her sitting here, with all her faculties, watching her dear husband and son down there, fighting for their lives."

"I know," Sirena laid her hand on his arm, "I'm so grateful you're here, Doctor! I don't think I could have faced this day without you."

He pressed her hand. "'God's economy, as Bishop Legázpi would say! How were we to know this visit home to see our first grandchild would end like this?"

"Gilberto, too. It almost makes a person believe in predestination, doesn't it?"

"What about that Italian merchant from Milán? He came with us on the same coach from Mexico to set up a business here. Now he's inside the granary with a musket in his hand, defending a strange city he just laid eyes on!"

Sirena heard a distant rumble. She glanced at the small gold watch at her waist. Eleven-thirty! The rebels were expected at noon. Her pulse began to race. The rumble grew closer, reminding her of floodwaters rushing down a dry creek bed after a cloudburst. Wordlessly, she and the Doctor moved out onto the terrace to obtain a better view of Calle Helen, the main street leading in from the south.

As the sound increased she was certain it was not made by Hidalgo's rag tag foot soldiers. The steady cadence indicated the approach of a well-disciplined troop of mounted men, of well-shod hooves on cobblestones." Doctor Juan," she said tremulously, one hand pressed to her heart, the other gripping his arm. "It's them! It *must* be them! Thank God the Tenth has come in time -- *it's Tristán and his Tamarindos!*"

"Merciful Lord!" he whispered, blessing himself and reciting a silent thanksgiving. But when the lead horses and their riders finally came into view, Sirena saw it was not Tristán's proud, chamois-jacketed lancers, but the green-uniformed Queen's Regiment cavalry from San Miguel, traitors all! She thought she would die of disappointment when she recognized the stocky figure of Captain Ignacio Allende riding at their head, his face flushed with excitement, his bright hair worn *furioso* under a black fur shako with a bright red plume. She perceived a new air of triumphant rage crowning his customary arrogance.

Prudently the doctor drew her back into what was the more symbolic than real protection of the office, and closed the French doors behind them. Sirena picked up the rifle she had propped in a corner earlier, and leaned it against a nearby table, closer at hand. She shuddered. Hidalgo's dreaded attack had finally begun.

Her gaze was riveted on Allende as he unsheathed his sword and led his troop in a fierce charge on Gilberto's outermost barricade. Rifle fire crackled, wounded horses screamed in pain and several of Allende's men fell from their saddles before the defenders' hot fire forced the rebels' withdrawal.

Dividing his troop, Allende sent half up to occupy the heights of Cuarto Hill, a sugar loaf rising above and behind the Alhòndiga, and falling sharply to the bed of the Cata River directly below. From there, Sirena saw he could cut off all avenues of escape should the granary's walls be breached. They could also pour deadly fire on Gilberto's defenses and the Doloroso refinery abutting the Alhòndiga's west wall.

Allende led the rest of his men into a street one block over from the Riaño palace and a block nearer the Alhòndiga. Dismounting, they began systematically shooting out locks and kicking in front doors. Within minutes they were in possession of a dozen homes. Rebel sharpshooters appeared in the upper windows, or taking up protected positions behind the tile fretwork that trimmed the flat roofs. Each sharpshooter had a clear shot at the Alhòndiga.

Suddenly the door to the inside hall burst open and Isabel's spinster cousin, Inéz, rushed in. "They're storming houses only a block away!" she cried, beside herself with fear. "Doña Victoria seems to be out of her mind trying to run outside and warn Don Antonio he'll be killed if he attacks the British fort at Pensacola! Oh, Doctor Juan, what are we to do?"

He went at once to calm Inéz and go with her downstairs. From the doorway he cast a quick questioning look at Sirena.

"I'll stay here," she told him. Inéz was such a complainer, even in good times she was forever dramatizing every miniscule crisis in her life. Now, faced with more real life drama than she could comprehend, she was rapidly falling apart.

Alone in the quiet room, Sirena heard a new sound, and looking up Calle Belen beheld not so much an army marching as a massed horde of men *surging*, a tidal wave of Indians as uniform in height and color as a field of August corn. In white cotton *camisas* and *calzones* and hats of straw, they were armed with slingshots, lances and wooden swords. Here and there the broad blade of a machete flashed menacingly in the midday sun.

From their throats rose a wild, animal-like howl that froze the blood in her veins as they started running toward the granary. Gilberto's lethal fire mowed down their front ranks like machetes cutting cane, but when one wave broke, another crested right behind it. Without any visible leaders, the Indian tide rolled on heedlessly, men hurling themselves with fanatical zeal into the final abyss: and with each suicidal charge came a sound unlike anything Sirena had ever heard -- the raw, rasping whirr of a multitude of stones singing an eerie death song as they sped though the air.

Breaking into a cold sweat, her trembling hands clasped in an attitude of perpetual prayer, Sirena saw Don Antonio emerge from the covered portico, leading a dozen men to reinforce Gilberto's decimated ranks. She said a grateful prayer as she saw him return safely to the portico and then glance back quickly to see how his replacements were faring. A second later, he was reeling against the wall, his hands flying up to cover his face, before both legs buckled under him and he fell motionless across the threshold of the Alhòndiga's open door. Two men rushed out to carry him inside.

In the same instant, Sirena caught the indelible image of an Allende marksman on a nearby roof, hoisting his rifle above his head in an irrepressible gesture of triumphant glee. In a single motion she picked up her own rifle, pushed open the French doors, put the weapon to her shoulder and got the sniper fixed squarely in her sights. Cooly she squeezed the trigger. But the very moment she fired, a hand forced the barrel down. "Don't Sirena! For God's sake *don't*!" Doctor Juan commanded her, and the bullet ploughed harmlessly into the floor of the terrace.

She had not heard him re-enter the office, and now, enraged, she turned on him, "How dare you stop me? That murderous bastard would have been dead now! I intend to kill every black-hearted renegade on that roof!"

"You shoot *one* man, my dear," he said quietly, "and you'll have Allende's entire Regiment breaking down our doors looking for his killer." He took the weapon from her. "They would not hesitate to massacre every soul in this house."

"But what about Don Antonio!" she cried furiously, hot tears blinding her. "He's too good to die at the hands of a rotten criollo turncoat! I *won't* -- I *can't* let it happen this way!"

"Get hold of yourself, Condesa," he ordered her sharply. "There are other lives than your own to consider. There may be weeks of this ahead. A siege demands cool heads." Then he added more gently, "We don't know for sure, my dear, he may only be wounded."

She would gladly give her own life to avenge Riaño's death, but she had no right to risk the lives of the others under this roof. Biting her knuckles in frustration, and not yet able to speak, she nodded her tearful agreement.

"I must get back to Doña Victoria. Will you be all right here alone, or do you want to join the others?"

"I'd rather be alone for a while."

Whether Riaño had been wounded or killed, his fall put new heart into the rebel forces. Thousands of Indians were rushing toward the granary, waving small white banners bearing a crude image of the Virgin of Guadalupe, a symbol that had appeared like magic in every brown hand.

With an earth shaking chant of,

"LONG LIVE THE VIRGIN OF GUADALUPE! DEATH TO THE GACHUPÍNES!"

they overwhelmed Gilberto's last barricade. Sirena was sure he was wounded, because she saw him being helped back to the safety of the Alhòndiga by one of a handful of men who survived that bloody assault.

With the outer defenses gone, the Indians now hurled themselves against the stout walls of the fortified granary. The Royalists kept up a murderous fire from the roof and windows, also tossing down grenades, which wrought havoc among the closely packed attackers. The moats and trenches were glutted with dead bodies, and those in the front ranks at the wall, now attempted to break and run in an effort to escape the awful carnage there. But rebels pressing from behind, condemned them to a martyr's choice of being cut to pieces by enemy fire or trampled to death by their friends.

The virtually leaderless, but resourceful, rebel forces now tried a new tactic, forming a human chain from the bed of the Cata River, below the Alhòndiga, up the river's steep banks to street level. Some dug boulders from the riverbed, while others broke them into smaller stones and the rest passed them up to those members of Allende's troop on the heights of Cuarto Hill.

Armed with an endless supply of stones, slingers on the hill poured such a lethal barrage down on marksmen trying to hold the granary roof, that the defenders were forced to retreat inside. For a while Sirena heard nothing but the shrill whistling of sharp, newly-cut rocks slicing through the air and striking human flesh and bone with a sickening impact.

After an ominous lull in the defenders' fire, Sirena watched breathlessly as a Royalist officer, bearing a white flag, was lowered from a window of the granary. For a bewildering few minutes he tried to ascertain who in the rebel ranks was empowered to negotiate a truce. But Allende had disappeared into a nearby house at the outset of the siege, and Hidalgo had never shown his face at all. The sole of that poor officer's boot did not even touch ground before dozens of brown hands were pulling him down into their midst, there to be *machetasoed*: stabbed, stoned and literally torn to pieces by the wildly vengeful mob.

A rebel force stormed the nearby Doloroso Hacienda. The handful of defenders left alive, fled down the steep banks to the Cata River, only to run into the arms of Indian stonecutters there. A pitiful few escaped to the top of a knoll north of Cuarto Hill, where Sirena watched them take shelter behind a waterwheel and well. Trapped and out of ammunition, some threw themselves down the well. The rest were butchered by a band of rebels with machetes.

Another group of rebels were busily stacking bundles of flammable cactus fiber against the granary's wooden doors and torching it. Sirena sank to her knees by the window, heartsick with pity and concern for the brave men trapped inside.

This fire proved a decisive signal to the hundreds of undecided plebeians who, smelling certain victory at last, now came pouring down into town to get in on the spoils.

A dozen strapping miners drove a battering ram repeatedly against the flaming doors that finally came down with a thunderous crash. In that moment it seemed the entire rebel army went stampeding across the blackened threshold, to seize the fabulous treasure they knew was hidden there.

Sirena could only wonder what would happen now to Francisco, Don Antonio, Gilberto, Doctor Daniel and all the noble mariscales, condes and marquéses, merchants and silver lords whose industry had made this city the richest silver center in the world. It didn't seem possible it could be over! The siege Riaño thought he could hold out against for two months, had ended in a matter of hours. Allende appeared at eleven forty-five this morning. It was now five minutes to five!

Frantic with worry and fear, Sirena started downstairs to the sala, but found everyone gathered instead in the second floor dining room, whose windows offered the same view as the office above. All were staring in stunned disbelief at the grisly scene below. Inéz knelt by a window, saying the rosary, Doctor Juan's Emma, sat with her son's wife in her arms, both women softly weeping. Doctor Juan's face was a mirror of tragedy. Sirena wondered if she looked as stricken as the others. Does witnessing such horrors imprint itself on one's visage as well as one's soul?

Through the smoke surrounding the granary, which was now alive with Indians, Sirena sighted a column of Royalist prisoners being led out of the gutted building, all of them stark naked and roped together like animals. Indians cavorted along beside them, dressed in the uniforms stripped from the defenders moments before. Some were beating the helpless captives with swords or hacking away at their flesh with knives. Sirena spotted Allende, who appeared to be in charge of the prisoners, but all his efforts to stop the Indians from harassing them were useless.

Well, how could this mindless criollo blackguard turn loose his pack of staghounds to savage everything in sight, and then expect them to come obediently to heel at his very first command?

As Sirena was about to turn away, the most barbarous scene of this barbaric day was enacted before her eyes. Officers of the Queen's Regiment carried out the nude corpse of Don Antonio Riaño, his head still wrapped in a bloodstained dressing. With a rope slung across his chest and under his arms, they hoisted him to the cross arm of a pole in front of the same portico where he was shot. Indians gathered under this ghastly exhibit, making obscene gestures, joking about his private parts and laughing uproariously.

Inéz collapsed in tears. The Riaños' housekeeper fled the room. Doctor Juan laid his head in his arms and wept like a child. Sirena felt a vial of pure hate break open somewhere inside of her and spill its venomous contents throughout her whole being. She was sure there wasn't enough milk of human kindness or Christian charity in the universe to forgive this unspeakable desecration of Antonio Riaño's mortal remains at the hands of traitorous criollo officers! Her fury was so intense she did not realize she was sobbing uncontrollably until

Doctor Juan, still weeping himself, took her in his arms and tried to comfort her.

The coming of darkness brought new horrors. Rebels and plebeians were now roaring drunk and rampaging through the stricken city's streets. The Riaño household, like every other, huddled together listening to the looting all around them, fearful the next sound they heard would be their own front door being smashed in.

Liquor and food stores were cleaned out, homes and palaces sacked, shops plundered of everything of value.

Sirena's beautiful, beloved city, that Tristán had likened to a silver rose, was being systematically raped, amidst scenes of brutality and horror rivaling Alaric's sack of Rome.

Beneath her window, illiterate peons bought and sold bars of solid silver for a few centavos each or traded priceless family jewels for a bottle of rum. Drunken mine workers, who Sirena had always known excelled even Neapolitans in their love of finery and extravagant spending for fancy dress, now wrapped themselves in costly silks and danced around street fires like demons in a parody of Hell.

Barrels of spilled pulque, imported brandy and wine ran in the streets, mingling with the blood already crimsoning the cobblestones. Campesinos, blind drunk, fought and killed each other disputing the possession of a gaily-plumed bonnet or a Spanish merchant's captive daughter.

As they all knew it must, a band of looters finally began taking crowbars to the Riaño palace's brass-studded front doors. Sirena picked up her rifle, determined to make the rebels pay with ten lives for everyone they took.

"Wait!" Doctor Juan cautioned her in a whisper, laying his own pistol near at hand. "I have a plan. Let me try it first." Stepping out onto the balcony of the second floor he called down to the mob. "*Hermanos!* It is best for you to leave this house in peace. I'm a medical doctor from Mexico, here to treat an Indian servant woman inside. It is my duty to warn you, my patient is sick *with the malcehuatel!*"

As he hoped it would, mere mention of that well-known, deadly plague, the repeated epidemics of which had carried off millions of Indians over the past three centuries, struck a nerve. The whole group recoiled as if the walls themselves seeped death. One Indian, more sober than the rest, scratched a skull and crossbones on the wall with charcoal to warn others away. The rest had already vanished.

Satisfied that the obliging Indian's warning would continue to protect the palace from looters, Doctor Juan and Sirena put their heads together and worked out a scheme. While the rest of the household slept fitfully, the two of them took brown boot créme, staining their faces and hands. Sirena donned a dark cotton dress and mottled rebozo, while the doctor disguised himself as a poor campesino -- in camisa, calzones, worn serape and battered straw sombrero.

"But it's so dangerous," Inéz whispered, when she discovered their secret plan to go to the Alhóndiga. "If you get killed what will happen to the rest of us?"

"Inéz," he said sternly. "I will not let our friends suffer needlessly, as long as there is any way under Heaven Sirena and I can help them in this dark hour!"

Sirena waited at the door as he took from his black bag the medicines he thought might be most needed. When he was ready, she draped the dark rebozo over her head, and together they stepped out into the noisy, crowded street. Instinctively they blessed themselves and then, speaking for them both, Sirena murmured under her breath, *"In the Name of God!"*

39

As Sirena and Doctor Juan neared the granary, two Queen's Regiment men rode past, arguing heatedly in French, a ruse to keep the rabble from knowing what was said. "I don't give a damn w*here* you put them! I only know Hidalgo told me to get every Indian body out of sight, *any way I can!*"

"But both cemeteries are full!"

"Then throw them in the Rio Cata! Hidalgo won't have his Indians even guessing what their appalling death toll was here today! When they sober up, we'll be marching on Valladolid. We've got to keep their morale high for that."

Sirena was shocked by the criollo rebels' cynical treatment of the Indians, whose numbers they needed, but whose lives they were squandering with contemptuous extravagance.

The pillagers seemed to have moved to the part of town nearer her own Graciana Palace. The now familiar sounds of drunken looting were borne to her on the cool night wind. Her mind was a jumble of unanswered questions -- was everyone at the Hermitage safe? Who of the defenders were prisoners, wounded or dead? How was Crispín? The Alamáns? And *where* was Tristán? Something unthinkable must have happened to the Tenth, for Calleja to break his promise to come to Riaño's aid. From what the two officers had just said, the insurrection was far more widespread than she had dreamed.

Creeping into the Alhóndiga, they found it deserted, the rebels not even bothering to post a guard. A dying bonfire cast ghostly shadows on the smoke-blackened walls. Although she knew most of the granary's dead had already been carted off and dumped in a common grave, they found a few bodies lying where they had fallen, all of them naked, and horribly mutilated. One officer was sprawled near the foot of the stairway, a pitiful Saint Sebastian of multiple wounds, his splintered lance and tattered Regimental banner at his side. Lighting the candle she had brought, Sirena held it high, as they knelt to say an Ave over him. "He died bravely, God rest his soul," the Doctor said, covering the man's face and mutilated private parts with remnants of the Royal colors.

In Riaño's command post only the cot remained, one end of it soaked in blood. "With a bullet in his brain he died at once," he told Sirena simply, "and I pray God, without pain."

Sirena stood stock still in the middle of the room. "Doctor, listen! Do you hear someone groaning?" Having seen men hiding silver and jewels in the bins, she guessed a man, hoping to save his life, might hide himself there, too. They went through several storage rooms before they located the sound and, opening its bin, found a man lying face down inside, fully dressed but not in uniform. His back and shoulders bore cruel wounds where he had been lanced repeatedly. Still warm, and drenched in blood, he was mercifully dead.

Holding up the candle, while Doctor Juan lifted him out and laid him gently on the floor, Sirena uttered a low, broken cry as she found herself gazing into the sightless eyes and innocent face of her own dear brother, Crispín. Still the moans continued. Looking inside, Doctor Juan saw the upper body of a man, alive and half buried in corn. "I'll get you out," he told him evenly, "but first tell me where you're wounded, and how badly." "Doctor Juan Pinal?" the man whispered hoarsely, "In God's Providence, can it really be you?"

"Francisco Durán!"

"My left arm, Juan -- it's nearly severed."

"Condesa, bring me Riaño's cot!"

When she returned, Francisco was lying in the doctor's arms. She helped lift him onto the cot, placing the wounded man's feet where Riaño's head had lain. His face was waxen in the dim light and Sirena saw he was bleeding heavily. "Sirena?" he asked, his right hand groping to find and clasp hers.

"I'm here, my dearest Francisco, I'm here!"

"I swear I left Crispín at the Alamáns. . ." He winced as the doctor applied a tourniquet. "But he said he couldn't let me face *all this* alone. . ." He made a feeble gesture toward the bloodied central patio. "When the rebels overran us, my arm was slashed by a machete, Crispín carried me here and hid me in the corn. Knowing they would massacre us all, he placed his body as a shield over mine. The devils ransacked every bin, butchering everyone they found." Francisco covered his eyes with his hand. "Even dying, Crispín tried to comfort me, 'Please don't be sad about my going this way' he said, 'I'm proud to give my life for yours. As God is my witness, Sir, I couldn't love my own father more!'"

Sirena held him in her arms while Doctor Juan administered the opium. "This will kill the pain for a while."

"Would there were opium for the pain in my soul!"

"Don't blame yourself, Francisco," Sirena pleaded, her emotions numbed by this day of unrelenting grief and tragedy. "My poor Isabel," he sighed, gripping Sirena's hand, "Crispín's death will be the final blow. It will kill her!"

Before she could let herself think that far ahead, she heard spurs ringing, and a pool of light from a carried lantern flooded the small room. The boots that wore the spurs came to a halt on the stone floor beside Crispín's head. Sirena pulled the rebozo closer about her face and reverently closed her dead brother's eyes.

"So, what have we here?" the man asked, setting his lantern down.

Sirena looked up to see Captain Allende.

Casting off his disguise the doctor announced, "I am a surgeon, Captain, and this man is seriously wounded. If I can get him to a private home and operate, I can save his life."

"Since he fought in here, he's my prisoner."

"But he'll die if he isn't treated soon."

"Throw him in the public jail with the other gachupínes."

"But he's not a Spaniard!" Sirena cried.

"And you, Madam, are no Indian!" Allende retorted, yanking off the rebozo. "Well, I'll be damned! If it isn't the high-minded Condesa, my fighting virgin of Valladolid!" He scrutinized her with mild amusement. "Go back to your houses, both of you, or I can't guarantee your lives."

"This is my brother. Please permit me to bury him."

"He fought beside gachupínes. He'll share their grave."

"Very well, then," she said, getting to her feet and struggling to keep a civil tongue, "but I BEG you for Intendent Riaño's body, so he may have a Christian burial."

"Riaño may be dead, but he's still my prisoner!"

"On your honor as an officer, how can you desecrate the mortal remains of another soldier so shamefully?"

She saw a flicker of genuine chagrin through his cold facade, then he shrugged. "Our Indians think all Spaniards have tails. We're trying to disabuse them of that idea."

"But why *Riaño*?" she raged. "Was he too noble an opponent for the turncoat son of a Spanish father to face?"

Allende went white. "*You bitch!!* Get out before I have you both shot as spies!" While his men took Francisco away, Allende turned on his heel and went back to the patio.

After placing a kiss on Crispín's brow, Sirena followed Doctor Juan along the corridor to the patio. About to leave the building, she overheard Allende, from somewhere inside, storming at a fellow officer. "You'll never convince me the Indians took *everything* in here! I demand an accounting!"

"I did my best, Captain! I spread the rumor that a store of Royalist ammunition was about to blow up. That cleared the Indians out fast and it's kept them from coming back."

"But why weren't you watching when they first broke in? For God's sake man, Riaño had *three million pesos* in this charnel house! Where in Hell did all that treasure go?"

Although drowning in her own sorrow, Sirena took momentary satisfaction in this truly just retribution. The cynical rebel leaders *deserved* to be stolen blind by the very Indians they had incited to do their dirty work for them!

❦40❧

"The Captain General of the Americas will see you now," a rebel officer told Sirena, as he led her into the small crowded patio that was the town Regiment's former barracks. Here, Miguel Hidalgo now addressed only by his grandiose new title, had set up his command post. It was here, too, Sirena now knew, that he had sequestered himself throughout the five-hour siege, sipping chocolate with cohorts and receiving progress reports. He emerged only after hearing the Alhóndiga had fallen, and most of its Royalist defenders slaughtered without mercy or quarter, exactly as he had promised Riaño.

She had been waiting in line for an interview with the victorious rebel leader since daybreak, after a night of unmitigated Hell. The mobs had swept back through the heart of town again, even more violent and besotted than before, and this time whatever they could not consume on the spot was smashed or put to the torch. If Guanajuato had not been built of stone the entire city would have burned to the ground.

It was a night of hairbreadth escapes, helpless women leaping to the hoped for safety of a neighbor's roof, many with a child in their arms. In the dead of night, Sirena and Doctor Juan responded to cries for help from an adjoining rooftop, only to find the nearly exhausted man they finally pulled to safety was Father Hilario with Señora Alamán and young Lucas in tow! Escaping miraculously when the Alhóndiga fell, he had raced to his sister's aid to find her home being attacked. They barely escaped with their lives; crossing the entire town by jumping from roof to roof!

Later, over a fortifying brandy, the emotionally spent Regimental Chaplain described to Sirena and Doctor Juan the horrors he had witnessed in the granary. Riaño's death had shattered morale. Devastated with grief, Gilberto threw himself over the body, vowing to take his own life. Moments later he tried to kill himself with his pistol but, was persuaded to avenge his father's death instead, he proceeded to singlehandedly wipe out Allende's rooftop snipers, grimly satisfied with the knowledge that one of them had killed his father.

Last night's violence continued on into daylight and it was dangerous for anyone to venture out alone. Armed vagos and vandals were everywhere, prowling the littered streets, setting upon anyone well dressed, especially if they happened to be white. But Sirena had run that risk, as had all the other petitioners queued up with her on this narrow street. Mothers, wives, sweethearts, daughters, devoted servants -- they all wanted one of three things: to visit a prisoner and, if wounded, bring him home, armed guards to protect their homes, or a patent of safe conduct permitting them to leave town and flee to Mexico.

Sirena followed the rebel officer through the patio into a large, high-ceilinged room, where she had to wait in a shorter line for her turn. Coming and going were men and women of every social rank and class, but her eyes went first to the man who, *in twelve short days*, had risen from being an obscure village cura to supreme military commander, with the power of life and death over everyone in this room.

She found the gaunt, white-haired Hidalgo seated on a cot with a small portable desk set up before him. He was not in uniform, but wore his familiar black prunella cloth suit. Propped in a corner behind him, was a gold-fringed satin pilgrimage banner of Guadalupe, undoubtedly the one he had made his battle flag. Suddenly it came to her, Hidalgo was a political metaphor of the ubiquitous "pilgrimage captain," who bade men leave their plows in the field and follow in blind faith to some distant holy shrine. But the twin miracles Hidalgo promised the Indians at the end of his bloody pilgrimage were boundless wealth without labor and freedom from all authority, wonders they had never enjoyed, even in the palmyest days of their so-called Aztec glory.

In a corner to his left she saw a stack of silver bars, no doubt from the granary, for all were encrusted with dried human blood. She felt her gorge rise, and swallowed hard to keep from retching. Directly behind the Cura, her eyes came to rest on the most disquieting sight of all. Standing like honor guards at a hero's tomb, or guardian angels on an altar, were David Àvila and her own brother Ramón, each wearing the uniform of a lieutenant general! Judas priest! It had taken Calleja thirty years of tireless soldiering to reach that rank! Swollen with victory and vainglory, they watched with expressions of amusement and contempt as one after another titled supplicant paid unwilling obeisance to Hidalgo's omnipotence. The rattlesnake she had once feared lay waiting in Ramón's path, had turned out to be Ramón himself!

"Ah, my *dear* First Condesa!" Hidalgo exclaimed, when she reached first place in line. "Is there some favor I can grant you, in the name of your father, my good friend the Conde?"

"Before I ask anything for myself, Señor Cura," she replied, trying to keep her tone free of rancor, "I must speak for Intendent Riaño's grieving and destitute widow."

At mention of Riaño, his steady gaze wavered and he began busying eyes and hands with papers on his desk. "Oh? And what is it she asks?"

"First, to know the whereabouts and health of her son."

He glanced up. "Gilberto was badly wounded. I allowed him to be taken to a private home, but he died this morning."

Sirena caught her breath, as one more candle flame of life and hope was extinguished, but there was no time to grieve. "I also request a patent of safe passage for myself and a party of relatives and friends I wish to lead to the safety of Mexico City." She handed him a list of their names. She was half afraid to ask for more, but determined to try. "I also request custody of your prisoner and long-time friend, Don Francisco Durán. He lies gravely wounded in your jail and," she could not resist adding, "as you well know, he is not a Spaniard."

Hidalgo's impassive expression masked whatever remorse or compassion he might be feeling. "Sick or well, he is my prisoner. He took up arms against Ferdinand the Seventh, our rightful king."

"Sir, he was fighting *for* the Spanish crown!"

He shrugged. "As for the Intendenta, I know she's ill and I've already offered her an entire bar of silver to alleviate her swift and unexpected -- impoverishment."

It took every ounce of self-control Sirena possessed to keep from uttering the stinging retort that sprang to her lips. "That noble lady asks me to inform you, she has no need for your silver, finding herself rich in the charity of dear friends. But she does ask, as do I, for her dear husband's body, that we may give him a decent Christian burial."

His green eyes contemplated Sirena with almost Solomonic sagacity. "I will provide your party with a paper of safe conduct," he said gravely, "but Durán remains my prisoner and useful hostage. As for the late Governor's body, I regard it as a legitimate trophy of war. It will be cut down only at my order and disposed of however I see fit."

He gestured to Ramón, who sprang solicitously to his side. "Give me one of those forms you drew up last night for my signature." The document was in his hands almost as the words were spoken. While filling in the blank spaces with the names in her party, he addressed a hasty aside to David Àvila. "Send in the members of the city council next. They've had ample time to choose a new governor and *regidores* from the men I selected."

"But, Generalissimo," David muttered under his breath, "everyone of the five men you suggested refuses to accept the office vacated by Riaño."

Suddenly Sirena saw the lightning of anger flash across Hidalgo's countenance, a streak of intolerance from the seemingly clear sky of patient benevolence. "What reason do they give for refusing?" he demanded, scratching his signature savagely across the bottom of the document.

"They cannot reconcile the idea of Independence with their oath of allegiance to Ferdinand the Seventh."

"There no longer is a Ferdinand the Seventh," he announced, and Sirena was astounded to see how easily his mask of fealty to the crown was stripped away. "With the fall of the Alhóndiga we no longer need pretend we're preserving the crown for *any* Spanish king: We're fighting for *independence from that crown!* Go tell the town council that!"

Sirena reached out for the patent, fearful that in his rage, he might decide to snatch it back. As Hidalgo handed it to her, a rebel soldier burst into the room and rushed up to his leader. "Generalissimo," he cried excitedly, "Allende needs you at once! Some Indians are refusing to obey him!"

Hidalgo hurried from the room and, because it was the only way out, Sirena followed him. Once outside she found him and the unhorsed Allende, sword in hand, already arguing. Afraid they would see her as an unwelcome witness to their quarrel, she stepped behind one of the columns flanking the door.

"The bastards pulled my horse from under me, damn their black Aztec souls to Hell!" Allende raged, pointing his blade at a group of Indians ripping a wrought-iron balcony from a nearby mansion on the edge of San Francisco Plaza. "I warned you that first day in Dolores we couldn't stop them once they tasted Spanish blood and brandy. They're tearing the city down, stone by stone. At this rate there'll be nothing left to build an independent nation ON!" Sirena felt compassion for any soldier trying to impose order on anarchy, but the supreme irony of Allende's dilemma was not lost on her.

"We *must* indulge the Indians," Hidalgo pleaded. "You know how much we need their help. Liquor and looting gratify them until we can move on."

Allende handed his reins to a groom and limped back inside the former barracks with Hidalgo, "I agreed to lead an army, not a god-dammed horde of insubordinate savages!"

Free to go at last, Sirena stepped out onto the street, casting an anxious glance at Hidalgo's favored Indians, who were now stealing the mansion's front doors and rejas. In the same line of vision she caught sight of a familiar figure, a woman who was standing like a statue in San Francisco Plaza. *It was Isabel!*

She nearly fainted. What was her mother doing here? Why was she alone? How did she escape the Hermitage? Where were Rafael and the servants? Even as she imagined the best and worst of every possibility, she gingerly crept past the busy looters and hastened down the short street to take her mother in her arms.

"Oh, Mamá! Mamá, are you all right?"

Isabel made no response, and when Sirena held her at arm's length to search her face, she saw Isabel was staring fixedly at the ground. Following her gaze she realized they stood before the shell of what had once been Don Francisco's home. It had not only been plundered but, burned. Sirena felt a stabbing pain in her heart at the sight of Isabel, motionless as Lot's wife, rigid with shock, unable to grasp what had transpired. She could only guess the depth of her mother's grief as she, herself, viewed the poignant wreckage. Glittering shards of a fine mirror were strewn across the threshold, the handsome Coromandel screen from Manila lay blackened by flames. White down, spilled from slashed velvet cushions, drifted like snow over everything. Isabel picked up a half-charred folio lying on the ground, its inside sheets still unburned, and pressed it to her heart.

"Oh, Mamá, I'm so sorry -- !" The house that was to have been hers, the marriage not yet consummated, the man she loved perhaps dead or dying -- what words were there to comfort someone facing such loss? And still to come, the awful news of Crispín's death!

"Who is Isabel?" her mother asked blankly, and when Sirena could not bring herself to answer, Isabel started paging frantically through the sheets of the damaged folio, as though seeking something vital to her existence. "'Who is Isabel? A lighted pascal candle, burning in my name -- ?'"

Sirena was temporarily distracted by a drunken vago in the plaza who suddenly fixed his greedy eyes on Isabel. She felt her skin begin to crawl. "Come, Mamá, let's get out of here," she wheedled, pulling Isabel along, "Please! Hurry!"

"PAPEL! PAPEL!" the boozy vago called, producing a machete from under his serape and lunging after them.

"Oh, thank God, he only wants paper! Mamá give him that folio you're holding and he'll go away!"

"Never! "No one else must ever see this. It's mine!"

"But you know how they treasure paper! These are probably just Francisco's old freight bills anyway. Please, give them to the man!"

"You don't understand!"

Desperate, Sirena stopped in mid-stride, tore the folio from Isabel's grasp and confronted their pursuer, throwing it like a piece of raw meat to a wolf.

Catching the folio in mid-air the vago swept off his battered straw in a tipsy imitation of gallantry. "Gracias Señora! I'm the lucky man who found tobacco in the granary!" He tore a piece of paper from his hoard, rolled a cigarette, lit it with a brand from a nearby bonfire, then sat down contentedly to smoke.

The danger past, Sirena started to move on, but Isabel continued to stare at the vago, mesmerized by his cigarette's burning tip. Then, with a heart-rending shriek that would ring in Sirena's ears for the rest of her life, Isabel ran the few paces back to Francisco's house and fell to her knees on the burned Manila screen. Cradling a ripped pillow in her arms and rocking back and forth, she cried out repeatedly, pleading for an answer, "Isabel? Who is Isabel? Oh, God, I've lost her, I've lost her forever!"

41

Sirena now found her burden of personal responsibilities growing heavier with each passing hour. Doña Victoria was not merely weak from her bout with malaria, she was prostrate with grief. Sirena was taking her and her French housekeeper to Mexico and from there would see she got safely to her sister in Puebla. Also in the party were Doctor Daniel's wife and baby, Doctor Juan and Emma, and the six-year old orphan son of the Milanese merchant whom the elder Pinals had befriended on their recent journey by coach from Mexico. The boy's father died in the Alhóndiga and the poor child had no one else to turn to.

Father Hilario, young Lucas and his recently widowed and now homeless mother, Señora Alamán, were also coming, giving Sirena two more badly needed men to help Doctor Juan and herself with the pack mules.

With Amantina gone, Estella and Melchor needed to be looked after, and so were coming with her. They had learned Doctor Daniel was a prisoner, but did not know if he was wounded or whole. Since no one was allowed to visit the jail, his wife was frantic with worry, and her colicky baby cried around the clock. Cousin Inéz, orphaned years ago when her parents perished in an epidemic, was adrift without the Aunt who had raised her. Worse, she was plagued by a recurring nightmare in which every night, she witnessed Amantina's fiery death in the silk house inferno.

Then there was Isabel. No longer merely emotionally unstable, she had withdrawn into a shell of mute melancholia. She was unwilling or unable to tell them anything about the Hermitage. Sirena was nearly beside herself wondering if Rafael and her dearest servants were dead or alive. If it had not been for Lucas Alamán's unquenchable confidence and the rock-like support of Doctor Juan and Father Hilario, Sirena was sure she would have been as traumatized as Isabel.

Rumors, numerous as swallows, kept swooping down on the city. Royalist troops were coming from Spain, King Ferdinand was in Guanajuato with Hidalgo, and General Flon and his Second Brigade were marching north from Puebla. Sunday morning, Sirena confirmed with her own eyes one persistent rumor; that Allende was ordering the cavalry troops out of town by daybreak. She watched from Don Antonio's office as columns of uniformed horsemen clattered past the scarred Alhóndiga. Trudging along in ragged-step behind them was a horde of disorganized foot soldiers, white-clad farmers, peons, miners, plebeians, vagos and their women, some balancing wooden shutters on their heads, others lugging window grills, carpets and doors. All were heeding Hidalgo's call to descend on the great city of Valladolid, whose plunder, he promised, would be every bit as rich as Guanajuato's. As the same men who had sacked the granary left its silent shell behind, she wept again at the pitiful sight of Riaño's exposed corpse, still hanging there after thirty-six hours, now rigid and darkening. The helpless target of ravens and crows, as it turned slowly in the light morning breeze.

One rumor had it General Calleja and his Tenth Brigade, while riding to Riaño's aid, had been intercepted a week before by a large rebel force which had reportedly cut the Royalist ranks to pieces. This possibility filled her with such sickening dismay she refused to even think about it. Months later, she would learn that they were defending Queretaro.

But after the rebels moved out she felt more optimistic and her mind began to focus on the mines again. While a three-day stoppage was nothing any mine owner ever wished for, still its damage would be minimal. Doña Victoria would not be strong enough to depart for Mexico for another three days, which would give Ricardo and herself time enough to round up a few loyal men. A good skeleton crew would at least keep the malacates working and the shafts free of water. After she resettled her friends in the capital, she would return and restore La Sirena to full production. Sunday evening, with all this in mind, she and Lucas Alamán set out on horseback shortly after dark to visit her palacio and mine.

"Did you know Allende quartered his cavalry troops in the five largest mines, including La Sirena?" Alamán asked.

"I heard rumors," she replied, bracing herself for what they could expect to find. "Two thousand men and nearly three thousand horses will have made a pretty mess of our processing patios, I'm afraid."

"Just give me a good pitchfork, a team of mules and a buck scraper," he said brightly, "and I'll have those patios mucked out in a single day!"

She could have kissed him for being so irrepressibly cheerful in the midst of the universal gloom. Inseparable as they had been all their lives, she knew Crispín's death had been a crushing blow, but despite his own sorrow, he possessed such a generous, outgoing nature he radiated hopefulness to everyone around him. Although only sixteen, in the light of his manly courage, and being the male head of his house, everyone began addressing him as 'Don Lucas.'

Dreading what they might find at the Graciana palace, she was overjoyed to discover everything still intact. The well-secured gate had not been smashed nor the walls breached. Alberta and Ricardo had themselves just returned safely from the Hermitage and Rafael was already asleep in his own little bed. They had not been disturbed by a soul during the entire invasion, their only alarm, Isabel's mysterious escape.

Leaving the palacio they passed the family chapel, its lacy tower bright as a beacon in the silver light of an early-rising moon. She took comfort in finding it unharmed.

"If only they've left us our mules," she speculated aloud as they rode on up the mountain to the mine, "I'll be able to leave two or three teams to run the malacates and still have enough pack animals for our trip to Mexico."

She found that being able to talk with him about getting the mines back into operation lifted her spirits. Besides, after three years at the School of Mines and three summers of working for her at La Sirena, Lucas understood all the ins and outs of silver mining as well as she did, and she trusted his judgment implicitly.

The moon that had been waxing Thursday night while they lowered silver into the Hermitage's well, was now buoyant and full. It's clear blue-white light would make it easier to see conditions at the mine. Even though the invading army was gone, she still felt somewhat apprehensive.

"While you go inside and look around, I'll keep a lookout here for stragglers," Don Lucas said as they dismounted.

"Thanks, that's very thoughtful of you, Don Lucas," she said with a grateful smile. "I confess I'm still a little jumpy about being surprised by armed and drunken vagos."

Crossing the first processing patio she found horse droppings, empty liquor bottles, broken saddletrees and all manner of other debris. It stank worse than the Augean stables, and forking it out would be a task nearly as awesome. She picked her way into the shed that covered the new San Patricio shaft, which she had already deepened more than half way to its ultimate depth. But sitting on the broad stone collar, it began to dawn on her that something far more than stabling horses had gone on here.

The shed was littered with burned and twisted machinery. Costly horse whims and malacates had been deliberately dismantled and systematically destroyed. On every side lay broken *pointerolles* and slashed leather buckets, all of her prized underground forges had been smashed, everything that pertained to the operation of mining silver had been rendered useless.

Then, looking down the moonlit slope to the stone washing vats along the river below, she beheld a scene of truly Satanic devastation. Every piece of heavy machinery that could conceivably be moved by the brawn of men alone had been wrenched from its place and cast down that steep embankment. Expensive, irreplaceable wheels, drums, metal ovens, cast iron bells -- all had been sent hurtling down in a vast destructive torrent, battering and shattering themselves against the long row of stone vats below. Some pieces overshot the vats entirely and plunged into the river itself, where they now lay dark and silent in the water, torn and twisted mockeries of the productive miners tools they once had been.

Sick at heart, unable to believe that the inexhaustible silver mines of Guanajuato had been attacked by the very men who made their living from them, she sank down on the wide collar of the San Patricio. Caressing the finely cut stone as though it were a living creature, she took a secret vengeful satisfaction in the fact that the rebels were unable to destroy her shafts. Those at least defied them! Then, gazing down into the black cavern she felt her heart stop beating. What had been a black, reassuringly unfathomable abyss had assumed an alarmingly different aspect. Only a few feet down from the collar floated the bright reflection of tonight's full moon, glimmering like a lantern floating on the moving surface.

Black water in the San Patricio! One of the deepest mine shafts in the world -- FLOODED!

In total panic she raced across to the collar of the Santa Cruz shaft, her hands searching desperately for the silver plaque inscribed with her father's poem, which she had placed there in memory of its silver jubilee. The plaque was gone, ripped from the stones of the collar, only a dark oval hole where it had been. But she did not need to read the inscription to understand its portent, for the key words were emblazoned in letters of fire before her eyes:

> *But the Gods of Silver –*
> *NEVER!*
> *They vowed to stay forever*
> *'Til the Drowning of the Moon!*

And here it was again, here in the Santa Cruz! The evil moon, staring up at her like a drowned white ghost from the same black tide! This then was the final horror that could never happen, abandoned by the silver gods who vowed they'd never leave! She began to weep, quietly at first, then with great tearing sobs, as the horrors and sorrows of the past fortnight broke through all the dams of self-discipline she had erected to contain her emotions. Uncontrollably the tears flowed, tears for Don Antonio and Crispín and Gilberto, for Francisco and all the others wounded and dead in the Alhóndiga. She re-lived the nightmare of Hidalgo's call to rebellion in Dolores, and Amantina's frightful death in the silk house inferno. As grief piled upon grief she admitted to herself the last unspeakable calamity -- that her mother was irretrievably insane.

Bent double over the collar she stroked the stones, as though her hands could somehow heal the great shaft's mortal wounds. "The mines! How could they! Oh Papá, I tried so hard to do everything you asked! I cared for them so! How could anyone willfully destroy the mines?"

Suddenly strong arms were about her.

"Oh, my poor little Condesa," Doctor Juan murmured, giving her his handkerchief and rocking her in his comforting embrace. "Go ahead and cry, child. It's time you did!"

"They've -- they've wrecked everything!" she wailed, pulling back from him and gesturing wildly at the terrible destruction all around them, "Look! *Everything!*"

"Holy Mother of God!" he gasped, catching sight of the tangled wreckage strewn along the riverbank below. "All the machinery -- the whims, the bells, -- all of it -- smashed beyond repair!" She stared into the shaft, hypnotized.

For the first time he too, saw the moon, round as some buoyant silver peso, riding the surface below.

Blessing himself, he whispered hoarsely, "The great Santa Cruz -- flooded!" Looking across at Sirena, he tried to find words that could soften such a loss. "I know it must seem more than you can bear, -- Sirena -- but life on. It will go on.

Shaking her head in disbelief she lifted her tear-streaked face to his in the bright silver light. "I'm grateful for one thing," she choked out between convulsive sobs. "Thank God my father didn't live to see this night – 'the departure of the silver gods. The ruination of everything he worked for. *The drowning of the moon* -- '

⋄42⋄

On a bright Wednesday morning in mid-October, a month after Hidalgo's "grito" General Félix Calleja reviewed the army drawn up before him. Tristán, mounted on Conquistador, sat beside him. Many of the men before them had been green recruits a month ago, men whom the two of them had tirelessly hammered into this tough, disciplined force.

Calleja sat a big grey warhorse outside his training camp and spoke in an even, but emotionally charged voice. "Men, I know how anxiously you've waited for this day when our newly designated Army of Operations could cease its seemingly endless task of preparation and training and march out at long last to search for and destroy the enemy. I also understand that for those of you concerned for the lives and welfare of your loved ones, living in provinces overrun by rebels, this delay has been pure Hell. Now, thanks be to God, the ordeal of waiting and inaction is behind us."

He fixed Tristán briefly with his falcon's eye and Tristán felt his color rise. The two men had agonized together over these past weeks of sweat and strain. Their mutual horror at the news from Dolores and Guanajuato, and their shared helplessness and inability to crush the enemy committing these atrocities, had forged a common bond of trust, and compassion that would not be broken by anything short of death. Tristán was prepared to ride through the fires of Hell for this cautious, patient, resolute leader, and so was virtually every other soldier in the Tenth.

As he looked out upon the army assembled before him, Tristán recalled Riaño's first courier arriving at daybreak with news of a feared attack. Tristán had awakened earlier that morning in alarm, his every sense aware of Sirena's presence, even a trace of her Irish lavender sachet drifting on the air. He had reached out expecting to find her at his side. With a premonition she was in mortal danger, he had stepped from his barracks to see a lone rider, in the uniform of Riaño's Regiment, galloping toward him, an exhausted courier on a horse nearly spent.

Over the next ten days Riaño sent four couriers, his final communiqué bringing tears of compassion and rage to Calleja's eyes. Tristán, half out of his mind with concern for Sirena, had angrily told Calleja, he would ride south alone if need be, to help Riaño defend the city.

"I'll see you in irons first!" Calleja thundered, "I didn't send you to the best military academy in Spain to be machetasoed by some drunken vago following a lunatic priest! Don't be a fool, Tristán, there are nobler ways to die!" Cooling down, he continued, "My heart bleeds for Riaño and all his men, but don't forget, he's not my only charge. The entire kingdom is at stake, and it's my job to protect the life of every European man, woman and child in it! There is simply no way on the face of the earth to defend Guanajuato. I know that, you know it, and God help him, Riaño knows it too! To try and help him now, with a force as small as our own, would bury our men with his, and with them *every* hope of eventual victory." His craggy profile was as unyielding as his argument. Then, laying his hand on Tristán's shoulder his tone grew gentler, "My boy, the bitterest part of command in war is being made to drink the gall of temporary helplessness in the face of a morally inferior enemy. Right now, *one man or one thousand* would not have been enough to save the Alhóndiga, but it would still have been *too many* for me to lose in a battle I know cannot be won!"

Hidalgo himself soon made it clear how wise the General was to wait. The rebel leader feared the wily Spanish General more than any other man in New Spain.

One of his first acts after Dolores was to send two agents north to ambush and capture Calleja outside his Los Bledos home. Thanks to a last, minute change of route Calleja eluded their trap. But over the next three weeks rebel spies did everything in their power to foment a full-scale insurrection in San Luis Potosí. Had Calleja marched south to Riaño's rescue, the entire north would have fallen to the rebels. Worse, it would have laid the border open to easy invasion by Wilkinson's Kentuckians, and led to General Manuel Flon's dreaded nightmare of New Spain being attacked on two fronts by *two* foes!

The General was an effective politician as well as a shrewd strategist. He knew how to shame Spaniards slow to support his efforts to defend their own lives and property. He coaxed wealthy criollos to contribute much of their private fortunes to the commonweal. On his own cognizance, he raised the enormous sums needed to recruit, feed, outfit and train a decent army, with no help from the distant Viceregal government. Tristán had watched amazed as the old soldier -- who only yesterday was eyeing comfortable retirement -- did all this, while enduring long days in the saddle without complaint, although suffering the constant pain of a hernia caused by a recent fall from his horse.

Tristán thought it nothing short of providential that a man of Calleja's stature held high command at this hour in the kingdom's history. He himself was never more grateful than now, that his chief had sent him abroad to learn the European art of raising armies and assuming battlefield command. But as he listened to the General address the army, he admired most of all his ability to prepare fighting men psychologically for battle.

"We are now about to disperse this group of bandits who, like a destructive cloud, devastate our country because there's been no force to oppose them. I assure you I will march at your head. I will share the work, the danger, the sacrifices and fatigue. Our union requires only mutual confidence and brotherhood. Then, content and happy at having restored tranquility to our beloved country, we will return home to enjoy the honor reserved for the valiant and loyal!"

Tristán's eyes misted over as the troops sent up an enthusiastic cheer for the leader they had affectionately nicknamed, 'Boss Félix.'

"Let us go forward then, TOGETHER!" the General said, holding up his gloved hand and then bringing it down in a strong, decisive gesture. "NOW!"

With measured pace, the army moved past his appraising eye, marching southeastward in the direction of the Bajío, whose cities had been so cruelly scarred by what was everywhere being spoken of as "The Black Flame of Insurrection."

"Well, Colonel Luna," Calleja said, both pride and concern in his voice, "there they go, for better or for worse, our own pitifully small Tenth Brigade."

"Yes -- all three thousand cavalry, six hundred infantry and four cannon!"

"Not exactly a host to give Bonaparte sleepless nights," Calleja quipped, "but by Santiago, men brave enough to do the job. Mark my words, Tristán, the day we meet the deluded priest's turncoat regimentals and untrained rabble, these soldiers will make us proud!"

☙43☙

Walking back across the plaza to the Episcopal palace, after saying morning Mass, Bishop Legázpi brooded over his long and stormy relationship with Miguel Hidalgo. Was it rooted in the fact that he was himself a Spaniard and Hidalgo a criollo? His mind went back to his early days in New Spain, for the first time in twenty-four years, recalling the Viceroy's surprisingly flip remark about how jealous and wary its criollos were of every immigrant Spaniard.

"You'll find it easier to win the hearts of a thousand unlettered Indians, than to persuade one educated criollo to trust a Spaniard, even when he's a churchman like yourself."

But Legázpi had been so confident he would succeed where every other immigrant in history had failed! In those early days his optimism had been so boundless he knew if *he* could not find a way, God would work whatever miracles it took. How naive he had been at thirty-six! Or was he a greater fool now at sixty -- laboring to raise an army, cast cannon from church bells and defend his see city against a possible invasion?

Over breakfast with Monsignor Alonso Crespi, he expatiated on the topic. "Alonso, don't you think it's sheer folly, for us to see ourselves in the role of military commanders?"

"Oh, the role is not all that unusual," Crespi smiled, "think of us as shades of Cardinal Mendoza riding into battle with Queen Isabel, driving the last Caliph from Granada."

"Perhaps. But I still can't see how we came to such a pass! Wasn't there *something more* I could have done?"

"Believe me, Diego, you did everything humanly possible. You bore Hidalgo's many peccancies with saintly patience. As for the King, you sailed to Spain; you warned him to abolish the Indian Tribute and rescind the Act of Consolidation and he scoffed at your advice. The ultimate irony is that the very reforms you struggled to initiate are now being attributed to the great 'liberality' of Hidalgo himself."

Legázpi picked at his breakfast. From the day he first learned of the revolt he had lost his appetite. It seemed every frightened European and criollo, seeking refuge in Valladolid, had to pour out their gruesome tale to him. The barbaric desecration of the body of Riaño, his dearest and noblest friend, at the hands of one of his own priests, filled his soul with such sorrow and shame it pained him night and day, a pain he knew he would carry to the grave.

"As you know, Alonso, I hated having to take such drastic action against one of my own priests, but in the light of his unspeakable deeds, excommunicating him and his supporters was my only recourse."

A servant appeared and announced that Lieutenant Agustín Iturbide was in the sala requesting to see them immediately.

The two churchmen found Iturbide in his regimental uniform, gazing out the windows at the plaza, whose Indian laurel trees housed joyous choirs of larks.

"Have a chair, Agustín," Legázpi said warmly, but his visitor came forward with an air of great urgency. "Thank you Excelencia, but what I have to say can be quickly said."

In the briefest terms he told them the Intendent of Valladolid and his family, who had fled the city yesterday in a coach for Mexico, had run into and been captured by Hidalgo who was advancing on the city with an army of *sixty-thousand* men, and was only a day's march away.

"The rebels bypassed Querétaro, because General Flon was dug in there."

"Who brought this news?" Legázpi asked.

"Captain Allende himself! He appeared at dawn at my father's hacienda, where I spent last night. He even had the gall to offer me the rank of Lieutenant General in the Rebel Army if I'd defect with my entire regiment!" Iturbide gave a short bitter laugh. "I said I thought their revolt was ill-conceived and would produce only bloodshed and ruin, without accomplishing the noble ends they have in mind."

Allende told him Hidalgo had with him three coach loads of prominent Spanish and criollo prisoners. As was his custom, he promised to slit their throats at the city gate, unless Valladolid surrendered without a fight. Looking directly at the Bishop, Iturbide said, "One of those hostages is your friend, Don Francisco Durán. He lost an arm in the siege, but still Hidalgo's had him traveling as a hostage ever since."

The Bishop's jaw tightened. "If General Flon is in Querétaro, where is Calleja?"

"No one knows. He's no doubt trying to take the enemy by surprise, but the main reason I've come, is to ask you to flee to Mexico. Hidalgo is enraged by your excommunication. Second only to Calleja himself, he wants *most* to capture you. He vows he will publicly humiliate you in retaliation."

"But how can I abandon my see, the diocesan records and funds? And I'll die before I let our new Rare Books Library be used for cigarette papers by the rebel army!"

"My father leaves in an hour. He insists you come with him in a closed coach, so you won't be recognized. I will be your military escort. We'd only be massacred here, so I'm leading seventy steadfastly loyal regimentals to Mexico to offer our services to Viceroy Venegas."

"God reward you, Agustín, but I don't see how. . ."

"My father and I beg you, my Lord Bishop! He'll be here in an hour. You *must* go with us. There's not a second to lose." He shot a pleading look at Crespi. "Until then, Your Reverences, good day."

Legázpi sank down next to the Monsignor in a chair facing his desk. For the first time in his life he felt old.

"You must go, Diego," Crespi said, his usual common sense, artfully wrapped in tact. "In time the rebels will be defeated and someday you'll return. But what use would you be as Hidalgo's wretched hostage? Or lying with your throat cut outside some city gate?"

With a long, shuddering breath Legázpi turned his eyes to his Coat of Arms on the wall behind his desk. Every golden cross on that multi-quartered escutcheon marked some illustrious Legázpi forbear's cardinal victory over the Moors. "My courageous Spanish ancestors would disown me for such cowardice," he said, his hazel eyes still burning fiercely, despite weariness and age.

"Would they ask you to win a 'Cadmean victory?'"

"Pride of family was my greatest vanity," Legázpi said, surrendering the last earthly treasure he had left. "In the enigmatic priest, Miguel Hidalgo, God found the perfect instrument to humble me."

Knowing this meant his friend's capitulation, Crespi said, "I'll see to it your bags are packed." Then he turned and gave him a farewell abrazo. "Amar a Diós, dear Diego, and remember, true bravery doesn't always show. God sees the courage hidden in your soul -- and so do I."

Early the following day, Hidalgo and Allende entered Valladolid at the head of a pride of flamboyantly dressed and mounted generals, trailed by the rebel army. It was October 16th, a month to the day since Hidalgo raised his standard in Dolores, and the rebel leaders were welcomed by tumultuous crowds, salvos of artillery and jubilant church bells. A long active clique of crypto-rebels within the city government, along with turncoat officers of the local Regiment, had formed a welcoming committee to shower every honor on their triumphant heroes.

Monsignor Crespi, watching from a small choir loft window, saw the brilliant procession enter the main plaza and head for the spiritual heart of the province, the Cathedral. Allende, recently elevated to the lofty rank of Captain General, wore a resplendent uniform, but his chief outshone him. Gone was the black suit of cheap puckered prunella cloth from China. Mounted on a high-stepping, jet-black Prieto Azabache, Hidalgo was dazzling in a French blue uniform, its tunic marked by scarlet facings, gold braid and enormous, heavily fringed gold epaulets. A broad black velvet sash adorned his chest, bearing a huge gold medal of Our Lady of Guadalupe. All this finery underscored his awesome new title of *Generalissimo of America and Protector of the Nation.*

Both men dismounted, Hidalgo waiting while Allende went forward to open the Cathedral doors. Crespi himself had locked them for safety, but by the time he descended from the choir to open them, Hidalgo's wounded pride was seething.

"Tell the Bishop I *demand* that he sing a solemn *Te Deum* in celebration of my taking the city," he commanded.

"What a pity!" Crespi exclaimed, with apparent dismay. "His Excellency is on vacation, and our organist and renowned Cathedral choir just fled the city! And of course, I can't have Benediction, for as you well know, church law forbids exposing the Blessed Sacrament during an enemy occupation."

By now the Generalissimo was in a towering rage. He declared all canonical seats in the Cathedral vacant, confiscated two hundred thousand pesos in Church funds and demanded that the Monsignor rip the offensive bull of excommunication from the doors of the church.

Although the rebel chiefs had promised the welcoming committee that Spaniards and their property would be respected, they were unable to control the army for more than a few hours. Bands of looters began what had by now become their regular routine, plundering homes and stores. Crespi saw Allende fire on one band of pillagers, killing several. But for this attempt to restore discipline, he received a humiliating dressing down by Hidalgo, in the presence of his own men and in front of the openly disobedient Indians.

Still worse disorders erupted later in the rebel ranks. Having gorged themselves on brandy, pastries and candy, a large number of Indians became so violently ill a few of them died. An angry Indian spread the lie that Allende had poisoned the brandy. Allende met their challenge with his usual bravura: in full view of his accusers he filled his cup brimful of fiery brandy from the suspect barrel and, riding through the plaza, drained it in a few throat-searing gulps. That night at ten o'clock, the bell of the Bishop's door rang. Crespi opened to Ignacio Allende.

Once seated in the sala, his caller made it clear he was not there on political business. "To avoid being caught between Flon and Calleja, we're moving out tomorrow," he said forthrightly. "But I have a moral question for which I need a theologian's answer. And I ask that you keep what I say in confidence, as though it were confessional matter."

Crespi agreed, not surprised to find that Allende, like most criollos from good families, felt himself a true son of the Church, and was genuinely distressed at how the rebel rank and file were treating Spanish and criollo prisoners.

"It's a matter of conscience then?" Crespi asked.

"Perhaps. I need to know if what's held to be a sin in peacetime, might be considered as -- well, quite frankly -- as a noble *act of patriotism* during war?"

This was slippery moral ground and Crespi tried to draw him out, but the more he let Allende talk, the more he sensed that the real focus of his problem was the Generalissimo.

"Professional soldiers, like myself and other officers I know, have a high regard for personal honor and we feel the excesses Hidalgo permits his Indians to commit is beneath our dignity and degrades us all. We won't endure it, and we plan to remove him from command."

"You're giving him an ultimatum?"

"Yes, Monsignor. The idea struck me quite by accident today and I need to know if you think the Church would condone it."

"What is it you have in mind?"

"Poisoning his wine!"

PART EIGHT

REAPING HAVOC

1810 - 1815

*"Blood cried out for blood,
Atrocity for atrocity!"*
Lucas Alamán

44

Sirena rode south at the head of a party of three coaches and a dozen pack mules. Once past the rebel stronghold of Celaya, they were caught up in a torrent of carriage traffic. With the capitulation to the rebels of so many provincial cities, hundreds of small caravans like her own were fleeing south toward what seemed the only safe place left in New Spain – the City of Mexico.

She had never seen the Camino Real filled with such a concourse of plain black coaches, most with curtains tightly drawn. The more ostentatious carriages had either been left behind or their proud family crests, allegorical scenes and ecclesiastical coats of arms, prudently painted over. With crypto-rebels everywhere, any show of class or wealth could cost the refugees what little of value they may have salvaged, if not their lives. Most of the wealthy had done as Sirena, buried silver bars and hard currency in wells, cisterns, floors or walls at home, paying expenses with personal *libranza*s, drawn against the silver consulado in Mexico.

She noticed there were *no* lower class refugees: this was the wholesale flight of fortune, an all-white exodus of the interior provinces' mercantile, mining and social elite, for whom anonymity and a universal pretension of poverty was the new order of the day. For some it was not mere pretext: the insurrection had reduced many families to penury overnight.

She found the teeming Camino Real a conduit of sometimes heartening eyewitness news. A Spanish judge, taken hostage in Dolores, and dragged from town to town until he escaped, had known Francisco for a time. "Being jolted about, so soon after his arm was amputated, he was suffering constant pain." Poor, dear Francisco, Sirena sighed, but thank God he was alive! When she told her mother this news, Isabel uttered not a word and gave no sign she even recognized his name.

A criollo from San Miguel told her when Calleja's army re-took his town, a certain Colonel Tristán de Luna freed him from jail. He told Sirena, "I watched as this same Colonel ordered Allende's home there razed to the ground, and *with his own hands sowed the foundations with salt, Roman style!*"

Riding beside Don Lucas, while Doctor Juan took his turn driving a coach, Sirena kept scanning the horizon. Even with her paper of safe conduct it was frightening to pass through this once gracious region and find it fairly crackling with hostility. Every other paisano one met was either a rebel spy, a sympathizer or too frightened of rebel retaliation to offer any hospitality to escaping aristocrats.

When they passed her own La Torre, which was still secure and untouched by the rebellion, Old Martín told her Hidalgo was recruiting many hacienda supervisors of absentee landlords. Having grown up as one such supervisor's son, the erstwhile Cura knew their age-old gripes by heart and promised to cure them all. Knowing well that peons worked best by being told what to do at the start of each day, he urged each mayordomo to take his own field hands along. In this fashion clouds of unquestioning peons were recruited and then led into battle by the very same overseers who had bossed them in the field! So much for the Rebels' *liberation* of the Indians, Sirena mused.

The shrewder, more self-serving supervisors were not taken in by such panaceas, preferring to pillage and burn their home haciendas, whether its owners were absent or on the premises, even murdering them when expedient and stealing or driving off thousands of valuable horses and mules.

The ubiquitous mule trains, which had moved freight and produce throughout the vast kingdom for centuries, had all but disappeared, as arrieros jettisoned their lifelong trade to join the rebels, or better still, set themselves up as independent chieftains of their own bandit gangs. Each casta *jefé* staked out his own petty realm, terrorizing farms and villages into paying him an exorbitant tribute. Raiding fields and horse herds, raping countrywomen at will and shooting down any man who protested, these savage marauders had become a law unto themselves.

Luke-warm village priests were abandoning their parishes in droves, not a few hoping to emulate the Cura of Dolores' meteoric rise from the meekest of the meek to supreme overlord of the new political order.

Yes, Sirena thought, reflecting on the chaos that had swamped her beloved Bajío, it would be good to get to Mexico and sleep beneath her own roof again, without having to keep a loaded pistol by her bed.

Reaching a familiar bend in the road she recognized a small farm she remembered had a good well. She had stopped here with Adrian and Von Humboldt six years ago. The old criollo farmer proved far more courteous and hospitable than most along this route. He offered water for themselves and their animals, gratis, and was surprised when she insisted on reimbursing him with pesos for his generosity.

While Lucas and Doctor Juan helped Melchor water the coach and pack mules, Sirena inquired about conditions farther on. The farmer said the road ahead had seen no rebel activity at all. She was relieved until he went on to explain that a few weeks earlier, however, a rebel band had appeared right here on his own farm. He pointed out two small wooden crosses, painted white, crowning a knoll nearby.

"Two Spaniards stopped here for water, just like you, but with a long train of mules loaded with what was clearly silver. Then from nowhere came a huge band of rebel Indians, some grabbing their mules, others stripping the men of all their clothes." He scratched his head as though he still could not grasp the speed with which it had all happened. "They formed a circle, with the gachupínes in the center, took out their slings and *stoned* them to death! Then, so help me they tore to pieces what was left of them. Right before my eyes!"

Sirena suddenly felt nauseous. She did not want to hear one more gruesome detail, but her thirsty animals were still drinking, and the farmer seemed as parched for someone to talk to as her mules were for water.

"After the rebels rode off, I gave the poor fellows a Christian burial, up there on the hill with the crosses. But later I found this gold watch in the grass. Now me, I wake up, plant my corn and go to bed by the sun, so what use have I for a fancy time piece like this? But *you*, Señorita -- ?

She shrank from touching the dead man's watch, but the insistent farmer placed it in her hand. Gingerly she examined it to make a polite show of interest. It was indeed expensive, and engraved on the back she read the elaborate inscription: "To Neto, from your devoted Uncle -- Don Telmo." She felt her stomach turn over, and a terrible dizzying nausea overcame her.

"Six pesos says it's yours," the farmer chirped.

Now deathly ill, she ran blindly to a low wall of fieldstones and throwing herself on her knees, began retching. Great, gut wrenching heaves that left her weak, sicker than before and bathed in a clammy cold sweat.

◦ ◦

Arriving in Mexico, Sirena found the Graciana Palace on San Francisco Street colder than a Pharaoh's tomb, as she knew it would be, for there was no friend in the city to staff the place and warm the rooms in advance of her arrival. Alicia and Noel had never returned from their honeymoon and, with the continent torn by war, they had settled permanently in London where Noel was busy composing. Although bone weary from their rigorous flight, and sick with worry over the two invalids in her care, Sirena had hurried on ahead, bestirring the surprised porter to light braziers and cookfires.

Doctor Juan and Emma, with Daniel's wife and baby, returned at once to their own home, just off the plaza mayor. Don Lucas, with his mother and uncle, Father Hilario, moved into the centuries old San Clemente family palace, a luxurious but empty Mexico City residence, built by a pioneer Guanajuato silver lord. Both Señora Alamán and her priest brother were his direct descendants and two of several heirs.

Sirena's new household consisted of herself and her two servants, Cousin Inéz, two helpless women and two badly frightened little boys -- Rafael and the six-year-old Italian orphan, Caesare. One ray of light in her dark skies was that cousin Inéz took to mothering the boys as though born for it. And, perhaps because the children seemed to fill a lifelong void in her life she was more contented now than Sirena had ever seen her.

While the city itself was untouched by the revolt, the violence elsewhere was causing social turmoil. Mexico's broad streets and spacious parks teemed with refugees from the once prosperous war zones. These were mostly Spaniards, but there were also many Italians, Irish, French, Portuguese and some Austrian Catholics, nearly all with criollo wives and children. A few Protestant Germans, English and Scotchmen -- all captured aboard enemy or pirate vessels -- had converted to the Catholic faith, and settled happily in various provinces. Now all were seeking temporary lodging, suitable to their station, while trying to book passage on a neutral ship sailing out of

Vera Cruz. Their wait promised to be a long one, for it was hard to find any country in Europe that was not at war with, or occupied by, Napoleon's bellicose legions.

The rebellion had already disrupted the harvesting of many crops, and with the defection of so many muleteers, the transportation and supply of everything from pulque to lighting oil was sporadic. As the population swelled, demand and scarcity increased apace and prices soared. Freight rates, always high, had skyrocketed. Sirena found such staples as rice, beans, flour, soap and candles, in critically short supply and could only be had -- *if at all!* -- by going to every market in town. With only Estella to help scour these picked-over mercados, shopping became a full time occupation, made doubly vexing because she was buying for two very sick women who required special foods.

In this dilemma Sirena found help from a singular and unexpected source -- Tristán's wife, Catarina, and her dull-witted sister. Growing up frontier-scrawny, scratching for every grain of food as frantically as presidio chickens, basic staples which city dwellers took for granted, these fronteristas prized as rarities. They stubbornly continued to live desert-poor, camping out over in the patio, cooking an open fire, and sleeping in the porter's room beside the empty stables. They ignored the rest of the handsomely furnished Mendoza palace, keeping it shrouded and sealed, exactly as the servants of Tristán's great aunt had left it when she died. That was when the household staff quit en-masse; telling Tristán they could no longer live with and try to serve, 'these two uncivilized sisters from the North.' No new servants had ever taken their place.

Over the years, with precious little else to tempt her, Catarina had routinely spent most of the generous stipend Tristán sent her every month on items she was hoarding against the equivalent of an earth-scorching Apache raid. But as soon as she learned the Condesa was back and in need of such 'luxuries' as soap and charcoal and candles, she opened her cache to this trusted Norteña neighbor and friend. Sirena was astounded to find Catarina's packed shelves better stocked than any wholesaler's warehouse.

Two weeks after their arrival, Doña Victoria was at last well enough to leave for her sister's home in Puebla, and Father Hilario kindly escorted her. This allowed Sirena to give her full attention to Rafael, who appeared truly at home and happy with his Madrina. Part of the cure was the companionship of the spunky little *Italiano*, Caesare

Montini. Sirena now saw the troubles of the past few weeks had bonded the two orphans until they had -- become like brothers.

Father Hilario had surprised Sirena one day, by telling her that after the boy's father was shot in the Alhóndiga he had died in Don Francisco's arms. "I've assured Caesare his adopted father will be coming for him one day soon," Hilario explained, "because I witnessed his solemn promise to give the boy a home." Could it be, Sirena wondered, that in God's providence, little Caesare would help fill the emptiness left in Francisco's soul by the loss of Crispín?

Meanwhile, Isabel was daily becoming more morose and withdrawn, the only words she uttered, and kept repeating, were, "No! No! No!" and "Who is Isabel?" Sirena finally resigned herself to the inevitable and paid the dreaded visit to Our Lady of Remedies sanctuary.

"Of course I'll be glad to accept, your mother as a patient," Madre Pilar said, seated at the same plain desk in the same Spartan office Sirena remembered from her first meeting with this remarkable woman. "But, I can no longer give the level of care I offered a few years ago and which a woman of her rank has every right to expect."

She went on to explain how Godoy's Act of Consolidation had all but destroyed her Order's financial base. She had been forced to sell the hacienda in the valley, which supplied her sanctuary with all its milk, butter, eggs, vegetables and fowl. Her formerly reliable income from the interest on loans was virtually non-existent. Worst of all, at a time when she was inundated with new patients, she had to cut her staff because she could no longer afford to feed them all.

"You remember the deaf mute lay sister, Beatriz, who cared for you and Consuelo? I even had to send her back to her poor farm parents over in Cuautla."

"It's almost unbelievable the devastation that a corrupt Spanish court, a venal viceroy and a mad priest have brought down on this great kingdom in a few short years!" Sirena said with a heavy sigh.

"Much will be charged against Father Hidalgo's priestly soul in this bloodbath he's begun," Madre Pilar said darkly. "He has created a multitude of orphans and an army of widows and wives who, having witnessed scenes out of Hell, are now suffering mental breakdowns exactly like your mother's." Rising from the desk, Madre Pilar said firmly, "I shall pray Doña Isabel recovers soon, Sirena, but first we must begin. Bring the dear lady to me here tomorrow."

☙ ❧

"Oh, Condesa!" Catarina exclaimed, rushing into the palacio sala unannounced the following day, shortly after Sirena had returned home from the grim business of placing Isabel safely in Madre Pilar's care. "I just heard a rumor that the Royal Army is marching to Mexico! That means my husband, Don Tristán will be back with me soon!"

Sirena sank down on the sofa, suddenly weak as a kitten.

45

Catarina finally settled herself in a chair, after her usual indecision about which formidably fancy piece of furniture to sit on. "Did I ever tell you my husband serves in that army?"

"Yes, Catarina," Sirena replied awkwardly. "I recall you're telling me." Listening to Catarina talk to her about Tristán was pure agony. She sometimes felt she would go mad if this poor creature didn't stop recalling, confiding and describing her most intimate moments in bed with him. But by now Sirena was so obligated to Catarina for her neighborly generosity, she couldn't bring herself to hurt her feelings, which were as easily crushed as a sparrow.

In an effort to focus her mind on something else while she tried not to hear, Sirena studied the child-woman perched on the chair before her. Her swarthy face, framed in two long braids, was never without her dark rebozo. She wore a plain calico blouse and a skirt short enough to reveal thick ankles and gnarled, sandled feet. She was as plain as a roofless adobe after a rain. Only her eyes were pretty -- large, brown and brimming with a trust and affection that made it unthinkable to wound her in any way.

"I think the reason he visits me so seldom is because I find it hard to be a wife -- in bed, I mean."

Sirena colored, telling herself she was not hearing any of this, and trying desperately to distance herself from the topic of this bizarre conversation.

"But maybe this time, if I had a pretty silk gown to wear at night like ladies do -- ?" She cocked her head, question marks in both eyes. "Condesa, I'll tell you a *deep* secret! I've talked with a *real* witch, the kind of Indian *bruja* who can make and work powerful *hechizos!*"

"But Catarina, surely you don't want to cast a witch's spell on your own husband!" Sirena said, exasperated.

"Yes I do!" she said stubbornly. "This time when he lies with me, her spell will make it *possible* for him -- and for me -- to do what we must to make a child!"

After Catarina left, Sirena went upstairs to her bedroom, threw herself down on the bed and burst into tears. Alone in the darkened room, she was torn by great, heaving sobs. She was still suffering guilt and remorse over the ordeal of putting her mother away, even in an asylum as civilized as Madre Pilar's, but this encounter with Catarina was the final straw. Catarina's crude but graphic descriptions somehow marked the end of her patience, the outside limit of her endurance.

My God, am I to face the ghastly prospect of spending the rest of my life burning with love for Tristán, while his idiot wife lives six houses away and regales me with weekly reports on their most intimate acts in bed -- ! It's degrading, frightful, appalling! The only way out was to stop loving him, but she had been down that bitter road twice and knew it was as agonizing as yielding up her soul. It wasn't fair that he was married, she told herself as her sobs subsided, but then, what in life was fair? When she had reached this point before, she had thrown herself into her work, but now with all of Guanajuato's mines wrecked and flooded, she had no work to occupy her head and hands!

She lay staring up at the ceiling. Maybe she should go back up North as soon as it was safe to travel. She could help Uncle Gabriel run La Frontera until the war ended and the mines could be restored. At the thought of Don Gabriel's rocklike presence, of Frontera's solid walls and the everlasting Santa Rosa range always there to lean on, she felt an overpowering rush of homesickness. Yes, she would go back to La Frontera! Frontera was safe. It was home!

She responded to a knock on the bedroom door and Estella appeared. "Condesa, there's a gentleman waiting in the sala to see you."

"Who is he?" she asked, getting up and straightening her gown.

"He says he wants to surprise you," Estella said, "but I can tell you, he's an aristocrat and a Royalist soldier." Sirena caught her breath fearfully, then squared her shoulders and dusted her tear-stained cheeks with rice powder. Surely, Tristán isn't the *only* Royalist officer around.

When she entered the room the officer's back was to her as he stood gazing out a front window into the street. Although she still did not recognize him, she knew at once it was not Tristán, a realization that filled her with a curious combination of disappointment and relief. At her step, the man turned to face her.

"*Adrian! It's you!* Oh my dear, it's so good to see you!"

Adrian came forward eagerly, taking her two hands in his and kissing her affectionately on both cheeks.

"Dearest Sirena! You're as bewitching as ever," he murmured, stepping back a pace to admire her. "Even *mourning* becomes you!"

"Is there a woman in Mexico who's not wearing black?" she asked rhetorically, as they seated themselves facing each other before a flickering blaze in the fireplace.

He was wearing his sandy hair cut short and brushed forward in the popular new furioso style, with full sideburns filling what were his strangely hollow cheeks. She noticed the sideburns were salted with grey. She was shocked at his pallor. All his life he had been bronzed by exposure to the elements. He retained the same open, winsome quality she had always found his greatest charm, but he wore an expression of weary resignation that troubled her.

"What are you doing in Mexico? And in the army?"

"I've come to invite you to my wedding, early next month," he said without enthusiasm. "Juliana's now fifteen."

Suddenly she was back in her ballroom in Guanajuato waltzing with him, knowing that within a few hours she would be lying in Tristán's arms in the Hermitage!

"I can't believe it's been three years," she said unsteadily, "so much has happened since."

"I've been here six months, working with Juliana's father. As you know, her family's run the Royal Mint for generations. He's teaching me the family trade."

Oh, Adrian, she thought, not you -- not *there*! That explained his lack of color. The mint was a hive of bespectacled drones, scores of accountants poring over ledgers in dungeon-like rooms. It was no place for an hacendado whose love had always been for the land. What a price to pay for Juliana's dowry!

Aloud she said, "Somehow I can't picture you in that place. I always think of you outdoors -- in the saddle."

"I can't picture me a soldier, either," he said with a cheerless self-deprecating smile, "but here I am, a member of the Viceroy's own *'Distinguished Patriotic Battalion of The Desired One, Ferdinand 'the Seventh.'"* He laid his hand on the hilt of his sword in a gesture of mock heroism. "My sacred trust is to defend this 'Noble City of Palaces', should the Rebel horde attack!"

She laughed. "The Viceroy should save his strength for more likely disasters! Dear God, not even the 'mad Cura' is mad enough to march on Mexico!"

"I agree, but in war, as in love, others seem to dictate my destiny."

"Are things at La Soledad any better?"

"I must say your loan to Papá saved the day. If only David had taken hold and helped, I could have turned things around, but of course. . ." he shrugged helplessly, "David had to break his father's heart by turning traitor. I could strangle him!"

She nodded sympathetically. "I know. He and Ramón were at Allende's side in Guanajuato, relishing the spectacle of the rest of us having to *beg* Hidalgo's permission for everything under the sun."

"Oh, Sirena, I was worried sick about you there," he said, leaning forward. "Thank God you got through it unharmed. What about your home?"

"It was spared," she said, "but the mine. . ."

"Surely Hidalgo wasn't fool enough to touch the mines?"

She felt the horror of that night go through her again like a lance. "Oh, Adrian, I haven't been able to even speak of it to anyone -- the hurt was so great." Recalling it now, she realized that in some ways the aftermath was almost as bad as the siege. "On Tuesday, after most of the rebel army left, a band of my regular crewmen showed up at my door, saying they wanted to go back to work." She shook her head. "I asked them how in God's Name they could even face me, after they helped destroy La Sirena. 'But Patrona,' the foreman said 'it was like a fiesta, with the Cura of Dolores buying all the drinks and fireworks! Now the party's over, we've celebrated *San Lunes* -- and we need to go back to work in the mines!'"

She began to laugh, a bitter, sad, hysterical laugh.

"Were they serious?"

She nodded, dashing away the sudden flood of tears riding on the crest of her laughter. "I ordered them out, saying the ore was as good as dead in the ground. Then the foreman looked at me and said, in all his Indian innocence, 'But Condesa, silver is our livelihood! Your father always said, 'silver is a river no man can stop! *Silver is forever!*'"

Suddenly she was sobbing and laughing at the same time, "Oh, Adrian, Adrian," she gasped, "they demolished La Sirena mine -- everything Papá and I had built, *everything!*"

Adrian's arms were around her, his hand stroking her hair, his cheek against hers. She clung to him, grateful for the comfort of his love, soothed by his caring caresses.

Suddenly she was fifteen again, in the shade of the aqueduct, and he was kissing her for the very first time.

"Oh, Adrian, I want to go back to Frontera and Soledad! I want to go home! Please, take me there!"

"I've always loved you, always longed to care for you!"

"I'm sick of all the blood and death and mindless destruction. You can't imagine what it was like! The rebel army makes our frontier Apaches look like -- like *gentlemen!*"

"Of course I'll take you North, Sirena," he said impulsively, "I never wanted to go through with the marriage, anyway. I don't love Juliana, and I *loathe* the mint!"

He held her so tightly it almost took her breath away, but she felt safe. It was wonderful to be able to rest at last, to sink into the deep solace and security of his embrace. Dreamily, with her eyes closed, she saw the Fourth Marqués welcoming her to Soledad as Adrian's bride, with Uncle Gabriel, beaming at his side. How much those two had always wanted this! Joining the two estates was meant to be. And it would save Adrian from the mint, put him back on the land where he belonged. Her heart burned at the prospect.

Never had Adrian been so bold, his hands lingering over her every curve, his kisses no longer brotherly, but passionately possessive. To her deepening surprise, his ardor kindled an answering flame within her. She felt an overwhelming desire to love and be loved, to give herself to a man without the inevitable backlash, the mortal fear of discovery, the vague cloud of sin and guilt, the bitter price she had paid for every blissful moment spent in Tristán's arms.

"I love you, Adrian," she whispered, returning his fervent kisses with increasing passion and conviction, "I think I always have, but didn't know it."

"Neither of us belongs here," he murmured happily, pressing his lips against the gentle rise of her breasts beneath her gown. "Let's marry at once! In wartime it can be done in haste. Then I'll take you home, and we'll start a whole new life together, being what we were always meant to be -- fronteristas!"

Why not? There was never going to be a future with Tristán. She had deliberately deceived herself all these years. If a witch's spell were to remove Catarina in a puff of smoke tomorrow, there was still the severe Law of Consanguinity. Even marriages between royal first cousins for 'reasons of State' had to be submitted to high churchmen in the Vatican and were only rarely permitted.

"Adrian, meet me at the Cathedral tomorrow for the early Mass." His parting kisses drained her of what little resistance she had left and she found herself clinging to him, strangely afraid to be left alone, as reluctant to let him go as he was to tear himself away from her.

"Tomorrow then, my own dearest Sirena," he whispered, "Our lives begin tomorrow!"

46

Inside the great, soaring vault of Mexico's magnificent Cathedral, long shafts of golden sunlight poured through the windows, the mighty voice of the organ filling its vast interior with stately sound. Sirena knelt at Adrian's side and gave herself to God in a spirit of rededication and renewal. Her soul drank in the age-old beauty of the Mass -- gold vestments, candles, flowers, incense and the prayers addressed to God in reverential Latin. The faith and steadfastness of the Church filled her with new hope for a fulfilling future, after the long dark night of the soul she had been passing through ever since the voyage home from Manila.

Emerging from the crowded Cathedral into the sunny *plaza mayor*, Adrian offered his arm. Smiling happily, she allowed herself the luxury of leaning dependently upon him. He placed his white-gloved hand over hers and said softly. "This is how it will be for us, dear Sirena, for the rest of our lives."

Suddenly they, and everyone else in the crowded plaza, were startled when two pages, in scarlet and gold livery, appeared unexpectedly on the second story balcony of the Viceregal Palace that overlooked the square. Blowing two sharp flourishes on their trumpets, the pages alerted the surprised populace below to the fact that His Excellency, the Viceroy, was about to deliver an official proclamation.

Seconds later Viceroy Venegas, himself, stepped out on the banner-draped balcony in the splendorous dress of a full general. An expectant hush fell over the puzzled throng.

"My friends, it is with grave concern and regret," he began in a solemn voice, "that I inform you the rebel chief, Miguel Hidalgo and his army, have been sighted a day's march from this city, advancing rapidly along the Toluca Road."

Fearfully Sirena gripped Adrian's arm, as a murmur of alarm rose and rippled through the crowd.

"This traitorous priest has sent me an ultimatum that he intends to attack and invade our noble Capital! I implore you, good and loyal citizens, to gather all your resources for the city's defense. Please obey my instructions, which will be printed on broadsheets to be posted on designated public walls later today. You have my word, I will not surrender this city, nor this kingdom, without myself first fighting to the death!"

Sirena's eyes searched the Viceroy's face. She had never seen him before and found he looked much younger than she expected. His hair was grey, but he was every inch the soldier, veteran and decorated hero of the Peninsular War.

"Upon learning that the ancient shrine of Our Lady of Remedies lies in the path of the invaders," he went on, "I have ordered her image brought in solemn procession to be enshrined here in the Cathedral. I ask you to join me in beseeching Mexico'a most powerful *conquistadora* to save us from this enemy, even as she delivered Cortés from the Aztec host on this very spot three centuries ago."

He paused for a long moment before continuing. "In closing, I assure you -- we must rely on Divine Providence, for we have scarcely twenty-five hundred soldiers to defend us, while we face a rebel army now *eighty-thousand strong!*"

While Adrian hurried to the palace to receive orders from his military superiors, promising to see her later in the day, Sirena took a cab for home. Her mind and emotions, which had been soothed by the honeyed sweetness of the Mass, were once more thrown into turmoil. Suddenly there were a multitude of household crises clamoring for attention, the servants to advise, Inéz and the children -- Where should she send them that was safe? How would she fortify the house? The remembered horrors of the rebel sack of Guanajuato filled her with dread.

She was rushing through the wrought iron gates of the *cancela* into her patio when she noticed a man seated on the bench where tradesmen and vendors always waited. But he did not look like a tradesman, his dress was too fine -- tapered sage-green trousers, glossy black boots, a crimson waistcoat and black cutaway coat with exaggerated shoulders. Tossed on the bench beside him was an expensive fawn-colored woolen cape with black velvet collar. She could not see his face, which was in shadow above his white stock and frilled shirt. Well, whoever he was, she didn't have time for him now. But as she started past him, he rose and greeted her.

"Condesa?"

"Yes?"

He doffed his low-crowned top hat and bowed. To her astonishment she found herself looking into the magnetic dark eyes and saturnine face of Lorenzo Santa Cruz. "What business brings you here?" she asked sharply, marshalling every defense, but careful to mask her alarm.

"One more chance encounter!" he exclaimed, tucking his ivory-topped cane beneath his arm.

She hardly recognized him with his dark hair worn furioso. Now in his mid-thirties, the moody and insecure fellow-voyager of six years past had turned into a suave and sophisticated man about town.

"You recently requested a builder to give an estimate for adding on some small rental apartments along the front of your palace, did you not?"

"I did. But from an architectural firm, not from you."

"I'm a silent partner in that firm."

"I see."

Passing through the patio she invited him in politely. In total silence they climbed the stairs and entered the sala. She retained a coldly formal air, but he was an artist -- and she felt common courtesy demanded she treat him more as a guest than a tradesman.

"I suppose you've heard the terrible news?" she asked, by way of thawing the uncomfortable chill between them as they sat down near the fire.

"Yes indeed, and having been in front of the Alhóndiga last month, I don't look forward to a reenactment of that gory business."

"You were there, too?"

"Yes, quite by accident. Matiás had written he was ill. And, as he was living alone, I went to Guanajuato to see him." He leaned back in his chair with a reflective air. "It was a strange experience for me. I chanced to be on Calle Belen and so was caught up by the mob and carried against my will to the walls of the granary. And yet I wasn't a member of either side. How could I be? After all, what am I? Criollo? My mother, yes. Gachupín? Hardly. Indian? Not that I care to admit. Anyway, I got away alive and back to our studio to find the place had been sacked."

"Was Maestro Matiás hurt?

"Not hurt, just ruined. Later that night he died of a stroke, as dead as if the rebels had killed him.

She blessed herself. "I loved that old man very much! May he rest in peace."

"Although I still had the family atelier here in Mexico, the fine art of portraiture has fallen on hard times. Rich patrons are too busy burying their wealth to pose."

"What about your work with Manuel Tolsá."

Lorenzo's expression turned venomous. "He's a self-serving gachupín like all the rest of his breed," he said viciously. "He stopped work on everything but the war, refusing to make anything but Royalist cannon in our foundry. Naturally, that let me out."

She felt uneasy. Only his appearance has changed, she warned herself. He was still driven by the same old demons, still railing against the same barriers of race and class.

"The way you refer to Tolsá makes you sound like a rebel," she observed icily.

"Not yet!" he laughed. "So far, Hidalgo's turned no frogs into princes. He's only convinced the Indians the clock's been set back to a day before the Conquest. Now they can die for Hidalgo's greater glory -- in the name of an Aztec Reconquista."

Despite his scathing tone she was impressed by his political astuteness. "Hidalgo's mostly transformed a lot of muleteers into bandits," she observed.

"Yes, but *so far he hasn't turned a single mestizo or casta white!*" he said sardonically. "When he starts handing out fresh pedigrees, I'll be first in line." He ran his eyes over her figure, appraisingly, his gaze openly caressing her. Her cheeks began to burn. "When that day comes, Condesa, I'll have the same right to enter by your front door and ask you to. . ." he paused tellingly, " -- to *waltz* with me, as your high and mighty criollo cousin does now."

Her eyes blazed at his implication, but she would not give him the satisfaction of seeing he had stung her.

"And, which of the volunteer battalions defending Mexico have *you* joined?" she asked cuttingly.

"None of them," he replied. "You forget, Condesa it's not *my* war. It's *yours*. I'm still an interested spectator." Completely out of patience, she stood up. "Well, at the moment my first concern is to insure the safety of this household. I have people in my care for whose lives I must answer."

"Like that handsome little boy, Rafael, who let me in? Whose child is he?"

"He's my godson."

He studied her face closely. "He looks a lot like you."

"Nonsense!" she scoffed. "I'm sure you remember Captain General Crowley of the Philippines. When his wife died after Rafael's birth I gave him a home, as I promised to do."

"So, I understand you want to build several 'cup-and-saucer' apartments facing the street," he said, "without damaging the fabric of this building, correct?"

"Possibly," she hedged, not wanting him to think she *needed* the money from rentals. It was a way to hedge her bets against the mine being closed down, and generate enough income to meet her monthly expenses, by renting to aristocrats in need of shelter and a good address. "That's what I inquired about. But in the light of today's news, I'd rather you sent me a crew to fortify my house."

"I'll draw up a plan for securing the house and send my men over in an hour."

"Thank you. We can discuss the apartments later, when the threat of invasion has passed."

"*If* it passes, you mean," he said smugly. "This time next week we may be lining the streets, cheering Hidalgo as he rolls by in the Viceroy's golden coach."

Rafael came in and asked for his Madrina's blessing so he could go to his reading lesson. When she had given it and he was gone, Lorenzo moved toward the open door. "Well, my dear Condesa, I shall take my leave now, but without your blessing, I'm afraid." Bowing slightly he added with a knowing grin, "I still insist the boy takes after you."

Her eyes followed him as he tripped lightly down the stairs. What did he mean by that parting shot? Was he trying to tell her he *suspected* or *knew* she had borne a child -- his child? But how could he possibly know that? Was she never to be free of the fear he would betray her?

Suddenly she was distracted by the universal sound of hundreds of bells, tolling from church towers all over town, spreading the alarm of the impending invasion. Looking down into the patio she saw Adrian come rushing in, a huge bouquet of coral gladiolus cradled in his arms. He took the stairs two at a time and, finding her waiting for him at the top, swept her into his arms, kissing her wildly. "Oh, I almost forgot these!" he laughed, having nearly mashed the flowers in his ardor. "They're for you -- my *fiancée!*"

"Adrian I've been so worried about you! Whole battalions of men have been marching past my door all morning. Where are they all going?"

"Toward the Toluca Road. The rebels are entrenched there in a mountain pass some nine leagues west of here."

"But only twenty-five hundred against Hidalgo's eighty-thousand!" she cried. "Dear God, it's sure to be a massacre!"

"Maybe not. The Viceroy just told us that General Félix Calleja has joined up with General Flon near Querétaro. Their combined armies are rushing to our aid by double marches."

Tristán would be here, in days or hours! How could she face him, how would she tell him? Heaven help me, I could never lie to him. "But Adrian, what about you? Where will you be sent?"

"My Battalion has been assigned to guard the Viceregal Palace and the mint, so I'll be close by, and near enough to protect you if things get -- too hot."

"Deo Gracias! I'm relieved you'll be near and reasonably safe," she whispered. "God be with you, Adrian! I love you."

He kissed her goodbye, clasping her to him fiercely. "You can't imagine how much I love you, Sirena. It will take me an entire lifetime to show you how deeply I care."

Even with the assurance that Calleja and Flon were rushing to their aid, panic swept through the ranks of refugees who had seen other cities sacked. Every able-bodied male between sixteen and seventy was conscripted to defend the Capital. Veteran troops guarded the outer perimeters and causeways leading into the lake-ringed city from Toluca. Less experienced units, such as Adrian's, defended the inner core.

In Sirena's part of town, where there were so many palaces, the women and children of the white aristocracy were everywhere -- fleeing to the safety of Mexico's largest and most prestigious convents. But by day's end these luxurious sanctuaries were filled and the nuns forced to close their doors. Families left to fend for themselves were paralyzed with fear. Inéz took Caesere and Rafael by coach to Madre Pilar, each boy proudly brandishing the small wooden sword he had fashioned with his own hands, weapons that transformed their bearers into brave, crusading knights.

Lorenzo sent a crew of men around to seal the windows and doors. Estella and Melchor remained with Sirena. Then, at sundown, Sirena suddenly remembered Catarina and Gertrudis. She couldn't leave the poor frightened creatures alone! She ran down the street and insisted the sisters leave the unfortified Mendoza palace and take refuge with in her palacio.

As her last errand of the day she went to the Cathedral to attend the enshrining of the small, robed statue of the Virgin of Remedies. She and everyone else wept openly as the Viceroy, with trembling hand, lay his baton of office at the Virgin's feet, solemnly proclaiming her '*Captain General of the Royal Army*', Protectress and Guardian of Spanish arms in this Kingdom of New Spain!"

For the next two days Sirena and the entire city kept a harrowing vigil, hearing rumors that a bloody battle was being fought between Royalists and rebels in a rugged mountain pass west of town. But no one yet knew who was victor or vanquished. The entire city was holding its breath.

Then, late in the afternoon of the second day, Sirena heard the slow beat of drums, and the uneven tread of marching men. Rushing out onto a small balcony overlooking San Francisco Street, she saw armed men passing, but they were hardly an army. She watched in stunned silence as the ragged column shambled past in the direction of the Plaza Mayor.

Were these the same soldiers she had watched marching out so purposefully three days ago? She noted their haggard faces, their leg-weary pace. She started counting as they straggled by – twenty-five, fifty, a hundred-and-fifty, two hundred. She looked westward in vain. The street was empty. Were these the sole survivors of the battle, then? *Only two hundred men out of more than two thousand?* Jesus, Maria, and Joseph! What had happened up there in the mountains above Toluca?

After the column passed, the street became deathly still. What had been fear now turned to dread. A book lay open in her lap, unread, as she sat in her sala listening for every sound, watching Catarina and Gertrudis on the floor playing 'jacks', unconcerned as two children. At the sound of someone ringing the small street bell below, she jumped as though a canon had been fired into the patio. Cautiously she stepped to the front balcony, and without exposing herself looked down. A Royalist officer stood below.

"Please identify yourself, Sir," she requested politely.

"Condesa! Lieutenant Agustín Iturbide, here from the *very* loyal Royalist Regiment of Valladolid, at your service. I beg a brief audience, if I may."

Her first thought was of Bishop Legázpi. She had heard a rumor he had been escorted safely here by Iturbide and his men. Her second was the memory of dancing with him in Valladolid, the night he announced his engagement. "Lieutenant Iturbide, of course. I'll have my servant admit you at once."

She ushered the sisters into another room, and received Iturbide alone in the sala. "Please be seated, Lieutenant," she said, noticing his obvious fatigue and the dusty and disheveled condition of his uniform.

He accepted with a quick nod. "It's been a long while since we met, Condesa, but I confess I never forgot you."

"I'm afraid I have a thousand questions," she said, while she poured two glasses of her best Hennessey brandy.

"Is Bishop Legázpi safe and well? Have you seen Generals Calleja or Flon on the road?"

He raised his hand in a half-playful gesture, as though warding off her flood of queries, but she saw his smile was fleeting, his expression sober.

"His Excellency is well and residing with the Viceroy at the moment," he said, taking the glass she handed him. "I do thank you for this, dear Lady. I needed it." He took a welcome sip before continuing. "I've seen nothing of the generals, for I have just this moment returned from a fierce battle with rebel forces at a pass called Las Cruces to the west of here."

"You were *there*? I saw some of our men returning from there this afternoon. They looked exhausted -- beaten."

As Iturbide described the Battle of Las Cruces, the Royalist forces had been routed, but not utterly defeated. Still they suffered heavy losses with more than two thousand killed and wounded. "Although there were eighty-thousand rebels, only about a thousand had firearms, and they were untrained in their use." He shook his head in disbelief. "The Indians are so ignorant of warfare, they ran up to our gun emplacements and covered the mouths of our cannon with their straw sombreros to keep the balls from coming out! Naturally, the slaughter among them was frightful."

"Did you halt Hidalgo's advance?"

"No," he said candidly. "But the Indians' ignorance of weaponry cost him dearly. On top of that there were wholesale desertions. Almost half his army fled."

"Do you think he'll invade us in spite of all that?" she asked, beginning to wonder why Iturbide had chosen to visit her, nearly a stranger, worn out as he was from fighting for two days.

"Yes. He's promised his Indians plunder."

He drank deeply of his brandy and, as if the right moment had finally come, said with sudden gravity. "Condesa, I've brought you a message from that field, as I promised to do." She could see him visibly steeling himself. "It's from the Fifth Marqués de Àvila."

For a moment her eyes held his then, with a sigh of relief, she sipped her brandy and smiled politely. "But Lieutenant, there's some mistake. Adrian's stationed right here in the capital. His Battalion is at this very moment defending the Viceroy and the mint!"

"That Battalion was called out to reinforce my own," he told her. "The Marqués fought bravely at my side, even stormed and took a gun emplacement manned by Allende himself. But in that action he was mortally wounded. He died soon after in my arms." He hesitated. "His last request was that I tell you he grieved only because death overtook him before you two could be married." Iturbide bit his lip. "I'm deeply sorry to be the bearer of such tragic news."

Sirena tried to speak. Her lips formed Adrian's name, but she was unable to utter a sound.

Iturbide reached into the breast pocket of his tunic and handed her a small object wrapped in a snowy linen handkerchief. Unfolding it with trembling hands, she lifted out a shield-shaped gold ring engraved with the ancient crest of the House of Àvila. Stoically she slipped the crest-ring on her finger and stared down at it, dry-eyed but riven.

"Thank you, Lieutenant Iturbide," she managed at last, reaching deep inside herself to find some secret hoard of strength and courage hidden there. "Tired as you are, and with so many worries of your own, it was more than gallant of you to do this for Adrian -- and for me."

Iturbide rose to go. "Would to God I had come on any other mission but this, Condesa," he said slowly. "Will you kindly inform his family? I don't expect to have time for anything in the foreseeable future except fighting rebels."

She stood up to see him out. "Of course," she said numbly, "I'll notify his poor father -- and sister."

"Thank you. I'll let myself out."

☙ ❧

For two more agonizingly suspenseful days the city waited, Hidalgo and his army encamped a few leagues distant, the ranks of their own Royalist defenders cut to pieces at Las Cruces, old men and boys alone left to protect the helpless Capital. Sirena watched through her sala window as one rebel envoy after another raced past on his way to the Viceregal Palace, a white flag streaming from the upright blade of his sword. The Viceroy turned each envoy back, refusing even to discuss terms of the city's surrender.

"What will the léperos do? Where will they place their loyalty?" That was the universal terror. Sirena remembered only too well the plebeians on the hills around Guanajauto. More encouraging was the news that the Aztec Indians of the Valley of Mexico had closed their homes and stubbornly refused to give Hidalgo or his army comfort or aid. The ever faithful Tlaxcalans, earliest allies of Cortés, remained steadfastly loyal to the Royalist cause as well.

Late on November 2nd, the Day of the Dead, which cast a double pall over the capital, the Viceroy's spies brought incredible news, shouting it like old-fashioned town criers as they galloped through the streets. *"Hidalgo is falling back! The Rebel Army is retreating! THE CAPITAL IS SAVED!"*

But why? With the city prostrate before him, why would the merciless conqueror of Guanajuato withdraw? Was Calleja's army on his heels? Whatever the reason, the miracle was real. Church bells thundered, people ran into the streets praying, weeping, cheering. Sirena joined the thousands thronging the Plaza Mayor to follow Viceroy Venegas into the Cathedral where a Mass of Thanksgiving was offered on the magnificent Altar of the Kings before the plucky little Virgin of Remedies.

Returning home, Sirena was met at the door by a weeping Estella. That hardly surprised her for virtually everyone in town was in tears, tears of sorrow for the many men lost at Las Cruces, mingling with tears of joy because Mexico City had so miraculously been saved.

"Condesa, I've something to tell you."

"Don't cry, Estella. Whatever your news is, somehow everything's going to be all right now!"

It's about my Analinda," Estella said. "She's been following the Rebel Army with Ramón, but now she's come back to give the baby she's expecting, a home."

Sirena stopped dead. "Ramón's child?" she asked, already knowing the answer.

Estella nodded.

She put a comforting arm around the weeping woman's shoulder. "You know this presents no problem to me, my dear. Tell Analinda she has a home here for herself and her baby for as long as she needs or cares to stay."

"Bless you, Condesa," Estella said fervently, and then added, with tears coursing down her cheeks. "There is one thing more. She asked me to tell you -- Ramón was killed in the fighting at Las Cruces.

ᛞ47ᛟ

"General Calleja, Sir?" Tristán ducked his head inside his commander's lamp lit field tent, knowing the saddle-weary Calleja had stretched out on his cot for a brief rest before tomorrow's battle.

"Yes, Colonel?"

"Our informant from the rebel camp is here."

In a single movement Calleja swung his booted feet to the ground and turned up the wick in the kerosene lamp on a portable desk by his cot. "Good! Come in, both of you." Nodding to the young lieutenant from Allende's Queen's Regiment, Tristán held back the tent flap to let him pass, then followed him inside. They seated themselves across the small desk from Calleja.

The General unrolled a rough sketch of the battlefield, and with typical attention to precise details, penned in the date and hour at the top – 10:30 p.m., January 16, 1811.

The informant was a criollo from San Miguel who had, very early on, defected with Allende's troop and turned rebel. He was still Allende's dedicated follower as recently as last month, when Hidalgo occupied Guadalajara and made it his Capital. They had set about rebuilding the rebel army after its catastrophic losses in dead, wounded and massive desertions following their near-disastrous victory at Las Cruces. Rebel morale was further shaken by Hidalgo's inexplicable withdrawal from defenseless Mexico, when he had that city, and the plunder of a lifetime, securely in his grasp.

But like many criollo officers, this spy became disgusted with the constant quarreling among rebel leaders and repelled by the savage character of the peasant recruits he was expected to turn into disciplined soldiers. Above all, he was appalled at such routine barbarisms as slitting hostages' throats, herding together dozens of bound captives to be cut down with volleys from behind, and severing the heads of Spanish prisoners with a saw. Tristán had even found himself wincing when the spy described such atrocities. Disillusioned and remorseful, the officer finally slipped away to meet the Royalist army secretly at night, as it was advancing on Guadalajara. After asking for and receiving amnesty from Calleja, he offered his services as a spy.

"Well, lieutenant by how many tens of thousands do they outnumber us this time?" Calleja inquired, indulging in a bit of macabre humor.

"You face an army of eighty-thousand," he replied, pointing to key points on the map. "They're dug in here, backed up against steep heights on the opposite bank of the Rio Calderón, and moated by the river in front. Their position is inaccessible except by open attack across this grassy plain that separates the two armies."

"How are they organized?"

"Six thousand cavalry and five thousand infantry-archers, but not nearly as skilled with bow and arrow as the Apaches. The remainder of the horde is armed with the usual lances, clubs and slings. Foot soldiers march in divisions of a thousand men each."

"Cumbersome," Calleja observed drily.

"Allende wanted smaller, more manageable units and part of the troops held in reserve. But the Cura insists on throwing the entire army against you and, as usual, his views prevail. But spirits are high again, everyone assured of victory. Yesterday, when he led his host from the city to the bridge, Hidalgo vowed, *'I'll breakfast in Guadalajara. Dine at the Bridge of Calderón and sup in Mexico City!'*"

But the spy said rebel troops had only six hundred muskets in all. They had cast more than a hundred cannons of medium caliber, but poor quality, with few able cannoneers to man them. To compensate, they had produced a great quantity of rockets, such as were commonly used for religious fiestas, but armed with steel points. These erratic, but damaging missiles, would be fired into Royalist ranks. As for funds, he said the rebel treasury held more than half a million pesos, most of it taken from convents and the confiscated wealth of Spaniards.

"But I confess, gentlemen, the last straw for men of honor among us is the old priest's ultimate folly; his boon *'compannera'*, who goes with him everywhere in his private, curtained coach. He passes her off as a boy soldier, but she's actually a young woman, dressed in a Captain's uniform! The men all call his pretty whore *La Fernandita*!"

After the lieutenant departed, Tristán stood in the chill darkness outside the tent with Calleja and General Manuel Flon, whose Second Brigade had now joined the Tenth. The three men gazed pensively across the vast open plain at rebel campfires twinkling on the hillside beyond the river.

"Eighty-thousand men over there, against six-thousand of us," Flon mused aloud.

"What do you think has happened to General Cruz and his reinforcements?" Tristán asked. "They should be here by now."

"I'm not waiting an hour longer for more men, much as we may need them," Calleja said. "Hidalgo *expects* us to wait. We'll surprise him tomorrow by attacking at dawn."

The Battle of the Bridge of Calderón

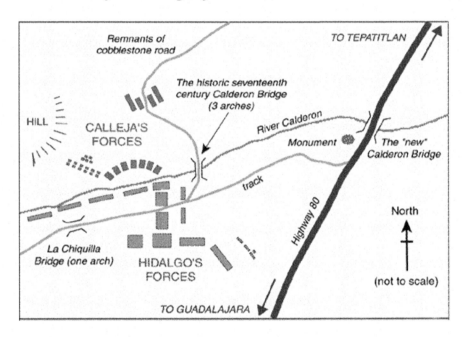

At first light on this bitterly cold winter day, Tristán was already astride Conquistador at the head of his lancers. Calleja's carefully formulated plan of attack branded on his mind. Knowing the rebel force was cumbersome and the terrain uneven, Calleja placed his hopes for victory in mobility, dividing his army into three groups. Flon would attack the enemy's left flank, while Tristàn's cavalry engaged their right.

Calleja positioned himself squarely in the center, his troops poised to support either wing as needed.

The cavalry charge across the plain, in the face of intense enemy fire was a resolute, naked assault on a nearly impregnable position. Tristán's eye noted an eagle circling a bufa above the old stone bridge, heard the chafing of the plain's tall, dry grass as the icy wind at his back rustled through it. His blood raced as Conquistador's flashing hooves thundered toward the enemy.

When rebel cavalry streamed out to meet his Tamarindos, Tristán caught sight of General Flon being driven back after engaging a powerful battery on the left. Calleja sent reinforcements. Then, seeing that Flon was being overwhelmed, Calleja coolly took all of his reserves and ten pieces of artillery and hurled himself against the rebels' strongest point. Tristán joined his commander in repulsing the murderous assault on Flon.

At this same moment, Royalist artillery fire scored a direct hit on a rebel wagon loaded with ammunition. The wagon and its contents went up in a stupendous explosion, ballooning into an enormous fireball that ignited the brush around it. Fueled by the thick sere grass and whipped by a rising wind, flames began licking across the plain, turning that portion of the battlefield into a roaring wall of fire under a pall of blinding black smoke. As his lancers regrouped for another charge, Tristán drew rein briefly on a low rise and watched what little discipline had existed among Hidalgo's vast army disintegrate. Terrified by the explosion and grass fire, the untrained Indians were fleeing in utter panic before it. The flight of individual thousands swelling the ranks until it became a universal rout. The impregnable rebel position now lay open to the enemy.

Seizing the fortunes of battle, Calleja and Tristán pressed their advantage, reaching the tops of the cliffs behind the rebel entrenchments with only sporadic resistance. The General swept the rebels before him toward the river, while Tristán's Tamarindos drove the last stragglers from the field.

When Tristán and Calleja took the final count, they estimated the enemy had lost twelve hundred dead to the Royalists' fifty! But the real rebel devastation at Calderón was the irreplaceable loss of three quarters of its army to panic and flight. Most would never soldier again. The Battle of the Bridge of Calderón where Hidalgo had promised to dine as the valorous victor -- lasted six hours.

It was late afternoon before Calleja discovered General Flon was missing. Weary as he was, Tristàn climbed back into the saddle and rode over the battlefield, far beyond where he himself had earlier given up pursuing rebel stragglers.

It was nearly twilight when he finally found him. Recognizing him by his uniform, Tristán dismounted and knelt beside the fallen general.

From the almost unrecognizable condition of his face and body, Tristán judged he had been overtaken and surrounded by a group of vengeful Indians, as he was driving more frightened rebels from the field. Pulled from his horse, he had been brutally stoned, stabbed and machetasoed to death. Carrying the body, wrapped in his own *capa de agua* and covered by his own cloak, on the saddle before him, Tristán recalled the warm gathering of old friends at Los Bledos only five months ago, repeating Calleja's toast of 'Peace in our time!' Now Riaño, Gilberto and Flon were all gone, and the last two of the beautiful St. Maxent sisters widowed. He reached inside his tunic and fingered the blue and silver silk that Sirena had given him. Had her colors protected him? Would he be in Flon's place now without them? The ecstasies of their stolen nights together at Los Bledos blazed within him again. How he longed to repeat them! Suddenly he was sick to his very soul with the slaughter and ruin of war. In the deepening darkness his tears fell without shame on the cloak that covered Mañuel Flon, the Spanish hero who, long ago had helped a daring young Antonio Riaño drive the British from their 'impregnable' fort at Pensacola.

48

"**Accepting amnesty doesn't mean** you're obliged to bear arms for the Royalists," Tristán told the blond criollo captain seated across the desk from him in Don Gabriel's upstairs office at La Frontera. "You need only swear not to fight for the rebels or give them comfort and aid."

He hoped he wasn't favoring this repentant insurgent because he was the youngest son of his old friend, Don Fabian, Fourth Marqués de Ávila. Some sixth sense told him there was more in this rebel's defection than met the eye.

"You needn't worry about me giving aid to the enemy," David Ávila said venomously. "I wouldn't give either rebel leader the sweat off my balls!" He gave a shrug. "I was prepared for an honorable war, something like the gentlemanly war games our regiments used to stage at the cantonments in Jalapa. How could we know Hidalgo was obsessed with Indians?"

Tristán had heard it all before from others seeking amnesty. What made Ávila's case more fascinating was the deep personal hatred he bore Allende and his passion for evening the score.

"After Guanajuato, I put all my hopes in Allende," David confided, as though purging his conscience in the confessional. "But I saw then, Hidalgo had all the clout. After Valladolid, Allende tried poisoning Hidalgo's wine, but they don't call him 'The Fox' for nothing! He suspected skullduggery right off, and appointed an official taster, who tested everything he touched."

"Is it solely your dislike of Allende that prompted you to desert the rebel cause?"

David took a moment to respond. "Not entirely. Ramón Munroy was my closest friend. He died senselessly at Las Cruces because Allende let the Cura run things. Then, I got a letter from Ramón's half-sister, Sirena, telling me my brother Adrian, died in that same battle, fighting for the Royalists. When I learned it was Allende who killed him, a lot of old slights and injustices at his hands suddenly began to come together."

Tristán caught his breath at mention of Sirena, and felt a twist of grief at the thought of the Fourth Marqués losing his beloved son and heir.

"Odd as it may seem, I loved my brother and respected him greatly. For the first time I felt remorseful, unclean, and guilty -- with a lot of innocent blood on my hands."

"I'm sorry to hear of Adrian's death," Tristán said. Then, after a brief inner struggle with himself, which he lost, he asked impulsively, "And where is Sirena now?"

"She wrote me from Mexico." A faint smile touched his lips. "She told me the surprising news that she and Adrian were going to be married in a few days. At least he must have died a happy man. He's been in love with her forever."

Tristán was seared by the hot fires of his deathless jealousy. About to marry Adrian? But what of their own vow? Had she stopped loving him? Well, why shouldn't she? What had he ever been able to offer her except a life of scandalous and illicit love, guilt and shame? With great effort he put her out of his mind for the moment to follow David's thread. "So, how did you know I had set up secret headquarters at La Frontera? Do the rebel leaders know I'm here?"

"No! They don't even know I've defected. Lots of men in the ranks took this lull in fighting to visit home. Allende was glad to have fewer mouths to feed for while. I came to visit my father and saw you one day in Monclova. I fought against you at Calderón, so of course I recognized you. It made sense to me you were here on a covert mission."

For a moment Tristán hesitated to trust David. On the other hand, the truth might prove irresistible bait. "Well, you were right. I'm here to rally the northern provinces. While they went over to the rebels in the first flush of victory, now they're sorry and want to prove their loyalty."

"I know. Even Texas threw its empty weight Hidalgo's way at first, but our defeat at Calderón changed things."

"So what happened to the leaders after Calderón?"

"They fled separately, any way they could. I rode with Allende, who cursed Hidalgo's soul with every breath."

According to David's passionately told tale, when the leaders finally came together at an hacienda near Zacatecas, their feud reached flash point. After a violent quarrel Hidalgo's three subordinates officially stripped him of his command. As David pointed out, this had been Allende's alternative to the 'poison plot' all along.

"From then on Hidalgo travelled as Allende's prisoner," David continued, "threatened with certain death if he tried to escape. But they needed his priestly image and charisma, so they still paraded him publicly as their leader in order to hold the Indians."

At this point, Tristán learned the real reason for David's final break with his former idol. As the new rebel chief, Allende began handing out illustrious titles right and left. Having fought beside him since before Dolores, David felt he deserved the rank of full General. But Allende repeatedly passed him over for others. To rub salt in pride's open wound, he saddled David with the dangerous job of sowing the seeds of rebellion in Monterey. Riding north, still not the General he longed to be, David's resentment festered until it became an all-consuming passion for revenge.

"Allende was dead set on rebuilding his army in Zacatecas. He had salvaged three-hundred-thousand pesos on the field at Calderón and swore he'd never again let Indians tarnish his honor."

"Is it true Zacatecas had cooled to the rebel cause and Allende now had to alter his plans?"

David agreed and said the first he knew of this change was when Allende brought back to his headquarters a dozen hand-picked bawds from the local zona and announced, "We're taking these whores along for solace during the long dearth of women that lies ahead."

"When I asked where we were going, Allende said, 'We're crossing the northern desert to the United States. I'm going to get President Madison's official support.'"

Tristán sucked in his breath. "God Almighty, Sir, do you mean to say he expects *Yankees* to help his cause?"

"He's already sent an envoy on ahead with a hundred bars of silver. With this he hopes to gain diplomatic recognition and buy arms."

Tristán welcomed this news as if a live rattlesnake had been thrown in his lap. "He expects to recruit and bring back thirty-thousand Yankee mercenaries to help him crush Calleja."

"Imagine General Wilkinson being given a princely bribe to help himself to New Spain! How the old double agent's eyes would light up to see his fondest dreams of empire come true!"

"But I want to level with you, Colonel Luna. I want nothing of Allende except to even the score. I've been guilty of treason, I've betrayed my class, disgraced my father, and dishonored the Ávila name." David's voice broke and it was a moment before he could continue. "That, Sir, is why I'm not content to simply receive amnesty and go home. I need to redeem myself, privately and publicly, for my father's sake. Surely, Colonel, you can understand? A man has to win back the honor he lost -- or deliberately threw away!"

Suddenly Tristán saw David as the long-missing piece he needed for a complex plan he had been trying to put together for the past two months. Working with Don Gabriel, the Fourth Marqués de Ávila, and his own father, Octavio, who was still Commandant General of the Northern Frontier Provinces, he hoped to create a strong frontier army comprised of hard-riding hacendados and their retainers. What he had lacked was a man who the rebel leaders believed to be unshakably loyal, but one who had in fact turned secretly against them. David Ávila was the key that fit the lock. "David," Tristán said, carefully baiting his hook, "would you rather settle your quarrel with Allende with a duel or avenge your honor by destroying the cause that means everything to him?"

"Do I have such a choice?"

"You do."

"That's easy. As I said, honor is a public as well as a private matter. I'd rather destroy everything he holds dear."

Drawing a map from the desk drawer, Tristán spread it open between them. "Point out to me the route you think he's most likely to take going north through Texas."

David studied the map briefly and then put his fore-forefinger squarely on target. "Right here at the Wells of Beján, half a day's ride north of Saltillo. Hidalgo told me himself it would bring them luck to go north by way of the *Wells of The Virgin of Guadalupe de Beján.*"

49

On the morning of March 21st, the principle chiefs of the Hidalgo Revolt, with the lightest of mounted escorts, rolled northward in the vanguard of their army toward the Wells of Beján. Astride Conquistador and well-hidden behind a purported 'honor guard' lined up to welcome them, Tristán waited patiently to catch sight of the lead carriage. He now knew more about the rebels' line of march, and who rode in which coach, than they did themselves. He had worked tirelessly for weeks preparing his fellow norteños for this decisive day and hour.

Monclova, the town that Allende believed to be securely in rebel hands, had been secretly retaken last night by Don Gabriel, the Fourth Marqués de Ávila and their private lancer retainers. The genial alcoholic officer Allende had appointed rebel commander of the town, had been easily captured while grandly drunk in a local cantina. Don Gabriel and his lancers spent the rest of the night combing the road to the south between Monclova and Saltillo, making sure no word would be leaked to the advancing rebel leaders that the town they were nearing had changed political stripes overnight.

David Àvila rode south at sun-up to confer with Allende in Saltillo. As the Generalissimo's most trusted emissary, David told his chief he had arranged a special 'honor guard', lining both sides of the road at the oasis of the wells, to hail their passing through. He also recommended that Allende space his large force of fifteen hundred men all along the route, so the wells of Beján would have time to refill between thirsty contingents. As a final bow to his chieftain's comfort, David suggested the Generalissimo and other high-ranking officers ride in the *first* carriages, so as not to be inconvenienced by waiting for water. Everything done, David told Allende he was riding on ahead and would meet him later at the wells.

Meanwhile, Tristán concealed himself, Don Gabriel, the Marqués de Ávila and their men, behind the so-called honor guard that waited in full view. The oasis itself was hidden from anyone approaching from the south by a series of low hills, and now, as Tristán watched from his cover, the first of fourteen carriages began rounding the nearest hill.

As expected, the two lead coaches contained Allende's private stock of gaudily-gowned jades, who were clearly flattered when several gallant norteños stepped forward to personally escort them to the wells. The occupants of the next coach, one of whom was the rebels' treasurer, Hidalgo's older brother, were quickly taken, bound and led away.

Tristán watched with bated breath as the next coach rolled up, for inside were the unsuspecting Generalissimo and a handsome young man -- Allende's only son. This coach David Àvila had claimed for his own. Stepping forward, pistol in hand, David yanked open the door. "Welcome to Beján, Generalissimo!" he said. *"Now, I order you to the surrender in the name of the King!"*

Seeing the trap and who had betrayed him, Allende opened fire with his pistol and lunged for the door. David's simultaneous fusillade killed the younger Allende instantly. Tristán and Don Gabriel closed in to overpower Allende, who fought his captors with all the ferocity of a bloodied bull, while David Àvila sank slowly to the ground.

By the time Tristán had securely manacled Allende and returned to the empty coach, David was already dead in his father's arms, his white tunic crimson where Allende's bullet had pierced his heart. Deeply moved, Tristán doffed his shako and bowed his head. The Fourth Marqués de Àvila looked up at him through tears. "My son died in Royalist uniform. Tristán," he said proudly, " he bought back his honor with his own Àvila blood."

When the key coach, the one assigned to Hidalgo, himself, rolled to a halt Tristán found it empty. Mounting Conquistador he road quickly back down the rebel column, wondering how the wily 'Fox' had managed to elude him. Then, half a league to the south he sighted the white-haired Hidalgo on horseback. He was still wearing his resplendent Generalissimo's uniform, but was bareheaded and lounging carelessly in the saddle, chatting with an aide, at the head of a small troop of equally relaxed cavalry. Tristán waited out of sight until Hidalgo and his troop had passed safely between the 'honor guard,' then he came forward and ordered Hidalgo's surrender. The forward thrust head came up with a start, Bright green eyes ablaze, he drew his pistol then, realizing the futility of resistance, he heaved, what to Tristán seemed like a great sigh of relief, and gave himself up without a struggle.

At that moment an alarmed Royalist officer rode up from the south on a lathered horse. "Colonel Luna! An insurgent artillery unit in the rear refuses to surrender and threatens to open fire!"

Tristán saw Hidalgo, square his shoulders, his eyes burning with the light of ultimate triumph.

"Sir," the doughty Fourth Marqués of Àvila said, striding up to the officer. "Go tell that cannoneer the minute I hear his guns, I start slitting rebel prisoners' throats!"

"GOOD GOD, NO!" Hidalgo cried, horrified at such a ghastly prospect. "Spare the hostages! I'll command that unit's surrender!"

Only by the end of the day did Tristán and the others begin to grasp the full magnitude of their victory. Besides the painted ladies from Zacatecas and all the rebel chiefs, they took a thousand prisoners, twenty-four cannon, vast stores of military supplies and over one million pesos in coin and silver bars. Only the rebel rear guard escaped, fleeing back to Saltillo in complete disarray.

Then, as darkness fell, and Tristán was going through the insurgents' baggage, he came upon an item that underscored the little ironies of war. Hidden in Allende's portmanteau was that little vial of poison intended for Hidalgo, carried all the way from victory's high tide in Valladolid, to the bitter end here at the lonely desert Wells of Beján!

⌘50⌘

As the highest-ranking Royalist officer, Tristán headed the convoy escorting the rebel leaders northwest to Chihuahua to stand trial in the court of his father, Don Octavio.

It was the only sane choice, since the risk of such prime political prisoners escaping on the long march to Mexico City made it foolhardy to take them there. Tristán had explained the wisdom of his decision to Viceroy Venegas, in the same letter describing the norteños' capture of the rebel army. The only sour note in his triumph was that the main insurgent leaders in the south had escaped this trap. Most dangerous of all was the renegade priest, and Hidalgo's former student at San Nicolás seminary, Jose Morelos, who was already terrorizing the hotlands south of Cuernavaca.

In Chihuahua, Don Octavio appointed Tristán as Hidalgo's official jailor, afraid to assign that critical post to anyone less trustworthy. It was an ordeal for Tristán. The trials ground on for months and he was made daily witness to Hidalgo's suffering and transformation under the strain of questioning and long imprisonment.

The pranks, histrionics and romantic posturings of his mischievous days as Cura of Dolores and later as captain General of America, had all been shed. He addressed the court with gravity and candor, admitting that he knew it was unjust to seize the criollos' inheritance, which they had received from their Spanish fathers. He confessed that 'none of us thought anything of sacrificing what others had legitimately earned or inherited.' The Hidalgo Revolt, as it was now called, that began as *opera buffe* was ending as a Greek tragedy. As such, the chastened Cura was confronting it.

Not so Allende. He remained as bullheadedly rebellious as ever. During one session, driven into a series of frustrating legal cul-de-sacs by the prosecutor's cross-examination, he summoned his tremendous physical strength and burst his heavy manacles, beating the judge about the head with his chains, before guards could subdue him. Even then the indomitable insurgent used the occasion to deliver a fiery speech that rocked the complacency of his captors.

You can kill us," he shouted, "for after all we're only men, with all the faults and sins of mortal man. But the seed we've planted you can never kill! The blood we shed here will only serve to water that seed. And, from it will rise a free and independent Mexico in which the children and great-grandchildren of you, our executioners, will be proud to call us heroes!"

Later, when one of the guards remarked to Tristán that Allende was a madman, Tristán corrected him. "No! He's a damned fine soldier. If he hadn't been hobbled by Hidalgo's military inexperience the rebels might have swept the field at Calderón. I wish we could have had him on our side!"

Allende was executed in June, shot with his back to the firing squad, as was the rule for traitors. But Hidalgo's sentence was delayed until July when the Bishop of Durango could attend, because the prisoner first had to be ceremoniously "degraded" from the priesthood. For this reason Hidalgo suffered the pain of seeing his beloved older brother, Mariano, and all his former comrades-in-arms meet their deaths, one by one, day after day.

The night before Hidalogo's execution, Tristán was playing mus with his prisoner. Losing, Miguel tossed in his cards and suddenly broke into tears. He spoke with such artless contrition it touched Tristán's heart.

"Now, facing death, I see the destruction of my beloved country which I have wrought," he confessed bitterly. "The property I've ruined, the countless widows and orphans my actions have made -- all the blood which has flowed with such abundance. Ah, for all this, may the good God forgive me!"

After a moment Tristàn remarked. "In all these months, Señor Cura, I've never once heard you say you regretted the Insurrection itself."

Hidalgo raised his head from his folded hands and a spark of the old rebelliousness flashed in his green eyes. "Regretted it? Never! Remorse for the suffering I've caused is one thing. Recanting my belief is another. I go to my death convinced our Cause was right!" He sighed heavily. "The ox that cuts the furrow may never taste the corn. So, I and the men with me, will not see the harvest. But those who follow in the furrow we have plowed. . ." He gazed out the window a long while. "I promise you, Tristán -- they will taste the corn!"

By the following morning Hidalgo's composure and wit had both returned. Pointing out to Tristán that his breakfast pitcher of milk was not as full as yesterday's he quipped, "Just because it's the last -- need it be less?"

In the courtyard, seconds before he faced the firing squad, he asked Tristán to fetch him a bag of sweets to distribute among his executioners, remarking, "As a sign that I forgive you."

With a sick feeling in the pit of his stomach, Tristán recalled being told that the first shop in Guanajuato to be looted by the mob was a candy store!

Allowed to face the firing squad -- out of respect for his, even now degraded, priesthood -- he seated himself in the chair in the courtyard of what had once been a Jesuit College. He told his executioners he would hold his hand over his heart, so they would be sure to see their target in that dim morning light.

The first volley blazed -- and Tristán was horrified to see that all except one shot had gone wild. A single bullet had lodged in his hand, which bled profusely. Hidalgo remained erect and praying, until the second volley toppled him from the chair to the dust of the patio.

Tristán was glad to be done with his grim assignment. He was also grateful he did not have to carry out Calleja's personal orders regarding final disposition of the rebel leader's remains. He knew only too well what those instructions were, for he had stood beside the general when he formulated them.

That had been the day the Tenth re-took Guanajuato. Both Tristán and Calleja still thought that two hundred Spanish and criollo prisoners were being held in the Alhóndiga. They had rushed there first to free them. But as Allende fled the city, he issued one last impulsive order to the rebel guard in charge of Spanish prisoners, "Why don't you just finish off your gachupínes, once and for all?"

By the time Tristán and Calleja reached the granary the massacre had already taken place. Never in his career as a soldier had Tristán come so close to being unnerved before his own men. The helpless victims had all had their throats cut, their bodies had been stripped, broken and mutilated. The patio floor was literally slick with flesh, blood and bone. The sight was so gruesome and pitiable he was barely able to gather the remains and direct the burials.

Beside him, viewing the carnage, Calleja stood, trembling with rage. "Someday I'll repay the rebel leaders for the barbarities they've had committed in this granary. As God is my witness, I'll entomb them here forever."

"Another soldier carried the severed heads of Hidalgo, Allende, Aldama and Jimenez, packed in salt, from Chihuahua southeast to Guanajuato. There the rotting skulls of the four rebel leaders would be placed in separate iron cages and hung at the four comers of the Alhóndiga, everlasting reminders of the atrocities perpetrated there.

In this fashion did Félix Maria Calleja avenge the death of his friend, Antonio Riaño, and all the others who had suffered and died within its once chaste and noble walls.

Spent with the brutal excesses of this vengeful war, Tristán felt he had no emotions left. But dutifully he rode south to rejoin Calleja in San Luis Potosí. He was needed there to rebuild the Royalist Army's morale after the havoc wrought in Guadalajara during a lull in the fighting by what Calleja described as 'the heat and the whores.' Tristán knew that ahead of him lay another relentless pursuit of rebels in the south, being led by the wily mulatto ex-priest, José Morelos, whose mobile and brilliantly led guerrillas were overrunning the hotlands and threatening Puebla and Mexico City itself.

⌘51∞

On a bright May morning in the spring of 1813, Sirena alighted from a cab before Don Francisco's new townhouse in Mexico City. Approaching the handsome building she was surprised to see a plaque on the door, spelling out in blue and white tiles: CASA CRISPÍN: This House is a Heart Always Open. The sight of it brought a sharp stab of painful memories and it took her a moment to overcome the threat of tears before venturing to strike the black iron knocker.

For the first time since that fateful Sunday in Dolores, Sirena was not dressed in mourning. Today she had set out on her weekly round of social calls wearing a brand new and festive old-rose faille silk walking dress Estella made for her. It had a low, square neck, long close sleeves, fashionably puffed at the shoulders, and three wide rows of shirred ruffles on the ankle-length skirt. The latest fashion engravings from Paris showed this new and more flamboyant-style gown being worn with plumed turbans or beribboned bonnets, but Sirena preferred the classic white mantilla over a high comb, set off by a ruffled pink parasol to parry the sun.

Francisco opened the door himself, hugging her to him with his right arm, the empty left sleeve of his dove grey waistcoat tucked neatly into his left pocket. "My dear, what a welcome surprise! You look as pretty as a page out of Holland's fashion plates!"

He led her into the flower-starred patio, heavy with the scent of potted orange and lemon trees in bloom, where they seated themselves at a small round table near the beautifully-tiled Mudejar wall fountain.

"You look very elegant yourself," she told him, closing her parasol. "From outside appearances neither you nor Casa Crispín give any clue that you take in orphans."

Francisco was white-haired now, his brown eyes doubly dark under silver brows, his figure slightly stooped to favor the missing arm. Although Doctor Daniel's prompt and skillful amputation saved his life, it had been done under unspeakable conditions, with no anesthetic, in a filthy rebel jail. It had aged him dramatically, but he was still as courtly as ever.

"Of course! That's the whole idea behind Casa Crispín," he said proudly. "My little ones paid a high price for being the children of nobles. There were asylums for sons of the poor and for Indians, but 'no room at the inn' for small aristocrats."

Sirena understood. It was now known that the Insurrection had cost the lives of eight thousand Spaniards. New Spain lost many of its finest European minds in Hidalgo's bloodbath, a loss from which it would take decades -- if ever, to recover. But the death of that many fathers had also cast a host of homeless upper-class children in the streets, especially in Mexico, which had been the final haven for so many refugees. Casa Crispín was one more proof of the true selflessness of Francisco's charity. Instead of brooding over his own personal tragedies, he had opened up his heart to these youngsters. He had even set up a 'Prix Riaño,' enabling his wards to study the classics, to carry on the tradition Don Antonio had established in Guanajuato.

"Today I took in a brother and sister whose father was shot as a hostage. Their mother still lives, but her mind was unhinged by the horrors of war, exactly like our Isabel."

"I just came from visiting Mamá at Madre Pilar's," she told him, glad he could speak of Isabel at last without breaking down. The first months after he and Doctor Daniel were re-captured from Hidalgo by Calleja, Francisco had been unable to resign himself to the hopelessness of her condition. He visited her two or three times a week, convinced she would one day recognize him. But that day never came, and now he had reached a point of acceptance, if not resignation, to the fact that it probably never would.

"Did she know you?" he asked, the old hopefulness alight in his eye.

"No, but she is talking a lot more. Today she still took me for a stranger, but delivered an eloquent speech. 'Our world was a fragile peristyle of silver filigree,' she told me, 'easily toppled by a storm'. It's as though she's become an oracle for the others like her, who cannot speak."

They both fell silent for a time, sorting through their private memories of Isabel, while half a dozen golden songbirds in bamboo cages warbled and chirred.

"So how is our dear little *Italiano*, Ceasere? Rafael and I miss him so!"

"He's still my trusted aide. When a new child arrives he takes charge, and puts them at ease. By the time Inéz and I take over, the hardest part's been done." He gave a slight smile. "I needn't tell you, he's the light of my life since I lost Crispín."

"And Inéz? She seems so happy working with you here."

"She's right as rain. In fact, she's a changed woman."

Sirena couldn't help but wonder if Inéz were still in love with him. As though answering her unspoken question he remarked insightfully, "I believe she always wanted children more than she ever wanted a husband. And of course her presence here spares me having to separate brothers and sisters, for now we can take in girls as well as boys."

He plucked a fragrant lemon blossom and gave it to her. "So what are you doing with yourself these days? Still studying with Don Cosmé?"

"Yes. Thank Heaven he reopened the School. I've never been idle in my life and I nearly lost my reason that first year here with nothing to do." She leaned toward him with an air of repressed excitement. "But I have a surprise for you: Don Lucas and I have come up with a workable plan!"

"A plan? To do what?"

"To help bring Guanajuato back to its former glory."

He recalled Riaño's stricken face and heard his last tearful words: *What is to become of my poor dear child of Guanajuato?* Didn't she understand? Guanajuato's past glory died with him!

"We've figured out a way to share the work and cost of digging adits to drain our mines' flooded shafts." She tapped her fan. "I can hardly wait, but we can't leave except with the convoy General Calleja keeps promising to send north.

The Bajío's alive with bandits like that barbaric 'El Lobo'."

"I'll soon be leaving town myself," he said softly.

"*You?* Leaving for where?"

"New Orleans."

She was speechless. "What on earth would you do there?"

"Well, Doña Victoria Riaño and Doña Marianne Flon, have gone back to Louisiana to take over the St. Maxent family properties. Recently they wrote to say there's been a tremendous influx into that city of refugee aristocrats missing from the wars of Independence that have torn all of Spanish America. There's a great need for another Casa

Crispín and the two widows have offered me their New Orleans townhouse if I'll come and set it up. I don't plan to stay but, you must agree, it widens Crispín's singular – priesthood."

Although she admired his charity, the thought of losing this dear man was like losing her father and Don Antonio all over again. "I feel like the last leaf on the tree," she said. "Don Cosmé announced in class that he and Doña Sophia are going back to Spain." She spun her closed parasol absently. "His leaving will be a tragedy. Mine owners were just beginning to see the results of all his labor."

"I agree, Sirena, but the truth is, he's convinced the silver industry in New Spain is beyond hope of recovery."

Her jaw hardened and she lifted her chin defiantly. "I refuse to accept that, *even from him!*" she said hotly. "You told me yourself he was proven wrong once before with his famous 'Born method'!" She pressed his arm fondly. "You'll see, Francisco! Trust me! Don Lucas and I will prove to him that 'silver is forever!'"

He smiled. She was *just* like Patrick when she got off on silver! No common sense at all! "Well, for your sake, I pray that's so. But until Royalists can break Morelos' ninety-day hold on Cauatla, *nothing* can get back to normal."

"Have you heard any news about Calleja's siege?" "Only that the *tierra caliente* is sapping his men's strength and morale. Is Tristán with him?"

"I don't know *where* Tristán is!" she said without feeling. I haven't heard from him since the war began."

Suddenly the strident sound of chords being repeated doggedly by an earnest piano student upstairs, reminded her of the main reason she had come. "Francisco I need your advice. I've just received a shocking letter from my former tutor, Noel Leclerque, in London. Something terrible has happened to him."

"What is it? His health? His career?"

"No. Much worse. Remember, I told you I wrote Alicia when Adrian died? She never answered. I thought it was because the wars on the continent had delayed the mails." She rose from the table and walked restlessly about the patio. "The truth is, she's left Noel for another man!"

"Divorced him?"

"No, just up and left him, penniless, to run off with a dashing French deserter from Napoleon's elite guard!"

Noel was stranded in London, while Alicia, blindly infatuated, was traipsing all over Europe, living openly with her paramour like those new "free love" couples who called themselves 'Romantics', while he gambled away her fortune.

"Poor Noel hasn't even fare home. I'd send it to him gladly, but you know we must find a way around his pride."

"When I leave, Inéz will need an experienced male tutor to work with her here. I'll send him passage money as an advance against his salary. That way he'll know I really need his help and talents and he'd not be accepting charity."

"I knew you'd think of something!" Then, turning to go she said, "Oh, Francisco, how could Alicia do such a thing? Apart from the moral disgrace, the inheritance the old Mariscal left her could have saved La Soledad for the Fourth Marqués a dozen times over!"

Resting his hand on her shoulder, he said proudly, "Not every noble father is lucky enough to have a noble daughter the way Don Patrick did."

Walking home, her mind went back to the endless war. Even with him dead, Hidalgo's revolt kept growing like a hydra-headed dragon. For every head the Royalists cut off, it sprouted three more. Rebels and bandits were picking off armed silver trains bound for Acapulco, as easily as if they were lone virgins on their way to the well. Closer to home, Mexico had been bled white with wartime taxes. Even so, the cabildo was reduced to civic penury, causing a catastrophic breakdown of public services; streets and canals stacked with garbage, dog packs everywhere, the city bankrupt. Today's Gacéta had said, 'conditions are the most calamitous in three centuries.' There was also an outbreak of typhus in the poorer outskirts, an epidemic Doctor Juan said was straining the protomedicato's resources to the breaking point. As though to illustrate the city's plight, Sirena saw a starving rat, dying in the gutter right here on elite San Francisco Street! When she stopped at the Mendoza palace, a starving dog lunged across her path and finished off the rat. Sirena shuddered.

In the small basket on her arm were two jars of convent-made guava jelly which Madre Pilar gave her this morning, one of which she was giving to generous Catarina. Now, as she stepped through the always open front door, and called out their names, both sisters rushed forward to greet her.

"The angels must have sent you at this very moment!" Catarina cried. "We were just on our way out the door to the farmacia to buy medicine, but we need..."

Knowing Catarina was easy prey to witch's spells, homeopathic medicines and voodoo cures, Sirena broke in cautiously, "But do you have a proper doctor's prescription? Which one of you is ill?" "Oh, we're not sick! We need you to stay here with the one who is! *My soldier-husband just came home -- wounded!"*

⌘52☍

Sirena felt the floor of the patio moving beneath her feet, and for a second she thought one of Mexico's frequent earthquakes had chosen this moment to strike. In an effort to steady herself, she sank down in a rickety chair beside the crude table on which Catarina displayed her candies.

"Don Tristán?" she asked, speaking his name as reverently as a prayer. "Is he -- seriously wounded?"

"We don't know," Catarina said. "They brought him by ambulance wagon from Cuautla, but the army's hospital ran out of beds, so I guess someone knew he had a palace here and sent him home." Catarina collected her slow-witted sister and her shopping basket. "Condesa, he's asleep in the master bedroom at the top of the stairs. All you have to do is sit by him 'til we get back." In a whirl of hastily tossed-on rebozos they both covered their heads -- which with them was *de rigueur* for going into the street -- and hurried out.

Sirena leaned on the table, still in shock, her heart thundering in her ears. Just up that stately flight of stairs -- which she had never climbed -- and through one door, lay Tristán! How near and yet how far it was from this bedroom to the one in Los Bledos. Those long passionate nights, that wine-sweet last stirrup cup of love! It all lay across a wasteland of war, blood, death and endless longing for him.

Frightened at what she might find, but magnetically drawn to that room, she started up the stairs slowly. Nearing the top she found herself almost running. When she reached for the wrought-iron latch, her hand was trembling so badly it took three tries before she opened the door.

She entered a handsome master bedroom, its walls covered with a rich burgundy silk damask. Oyster-white drapes at the tall windows were drawn against the light. Tristán lay on his back in the center of an enormous carved and gilded 17th Century Venetian bed, with a wine-colored damask coverlet under a matching canopy. As she crept closer she saw his chest was heavily bandaged. His right arm, resting on top of the coverlet, was in a sling made from a plain flour sack.

She tiptoed to his bedside and stood frozen there, looking down on him. How good it was to gaze upon that finely modeled manly face again! But he looked so weary and worn. A yellow pallor had replaced his natural sun-bronzed color and shadows black as charcoal dust underlined his eyes. She succumbed to an overwhelming desire to kiss his clean-shaven cheek and as her lips rested there she caught the familiar heart-melting scent of sage and wood smoke. Her lips also told her he was on fire with fever.

At her kiss he stirred and slowly opened his eyes. Seeing her above him, he closed them again.

"It's all right my darling," she whispered brokenly, kissing his closed eyelids tenderly, "you're safe, I'm watching over you."

"Condesita mia!" he murmured, "You're here! You're real! My God, I thought I must have died and gone to Heaven!" He struggled to lift himself on his elbow, winced with pain and fell back, exhausted. "Where have they taken me?"

"You were wounded and they brought you from the military hospital here, to your own Mendoza townhouse." Then she smiled wryly, trying to lighten with bitter humor the bizarre circumstances under which they found themselves reunited. "You, the lord of the manse, are lying here in your very own matrimonial, and I, the good samaritan neighbor from a few doors away, sit charitably by your side, having promised your wife I'd watch over you!" She was trying to make a jest of it, but at the same time tears were pouring down her cheeks. With his free hand he reached up and tried to brush them away with his thumb. "It's raining while the sun's shining," he said, his trailing fingers gently retracing the well-remembered path along her throat to where the swell of her breasts began. "Isn't that supposed to be a sign there's a rainbow somewhere?"

She moved closer and he drew her near enough to touch his lips to hers, kissing her slowly, repeatedly. "I heard you were going to marry Adrian," he breathed between kisses. "I guess that means you must have really given up on me?"

"I was sick at heart, sick of the war, and we were both so lonely for home! But, Tristán, I never stopped loving you, not for a moment!"

"Nor, I you." His eyes feasted on her. "You look like an angel in your pretty pink gown and white lace mantilla." Then his eyes clouded over. "Oh God, how I hate the war for keeping us apart! Even during this long hellish siege, Calleja has had his own Francisca with him. I envy him that. I'd fight Morelos for the rest of eternity, if I could have you at my side."

"Where were you wounded, Tristán? How badly?"

"I don't honestly know. I think this arm was broken when poor Conquistador went down with me in a charge. And I vaguely remember taking a nasty saber wound in my chest."

"You're also burning up with fever," she said. "I'll notify Doctor Juan and have him come and look at you."

"It's just the fever that comes from wanting you so," he joked weakly. "Another kiss or two might cure it.

In spite of all the cupping, rinses and salves that Doctor Juan prescribed, Tristán's wound festered, stubbornly refusing to heal. The fever he had picked up in the military hospital sapped what little strength he had. Sirena was at his bedside night and day. Much of that time he was delirious. One entire night she sponged his brow with cooling witch hazel, listening while he pleaded with an invisible Calleja to let him go alone to Guanajuato and fight beside Riaño. Another night, putting compresses on his wound, she was astonished to hear him engage in an hallucinatory conversation with her own father.

"You know it's the little Condesa I would choose to be my bride in ten years or so, when she's sixteen and I, not yet thirty. But since that can never be, he broke off and sitting upright in bed he cried out, "You were right, Don Patrick! I've never set eyes on the girl!"

To add to her anguish, she dared not let Catarina out of her sight or leave her long alone with Tristrán. In a city virtually devoid of medicines, Catarina managed to find a rich supply of shamanistic cures -- brewed corn-silk, powdered witcheries and wizened human organs in bottles, anyone of which was enough to kill him.

By the time Tristán's wound finally did heal and the fever left him, Morelos had slipped out of the Royalists' trap at Cuautla and was threatening Puebla. Félix Calleja, his own health broken by fever and the protracted siege, retired temporarily to a rented palacio in Mexico City to recuperate. As the best-known Royalist figure in the kingdom, it was natural that a government faction sprang up around him during his convalescence. When Viceroy Venegas resigned and retired to Spain, it came as no surprise to those politically in the know, that the man appointed in his place was "Boss" Félix Maria Calleja.

"Calleja's appointment as Viceroy leaves me as the most experienced, highest-ranking Royalist officer in the field," Tristán told Sirena, stopping by her palacio shortly after reporting to Viceroy Calleja for his new assignment.

She forced a smile. "I'm happy to hear the new Viceroy's first act was to raise you to the rank of Field Marshall. You deserve it."

She was proud of his promotion, even while she regretted it, knowing his greater responsibilities would only serve to keep them apart. But already an estrangement seemed to have taken place between them, a distance greater than the half block separating their palacios. After his first irrepressible expressions of love, he had kept his feelings for her strictly guarded. She realized how awkward his position was because of Catarina, but even now, when he was completely well, he had not given the slightest hint he wished to engage in a discreet but passionate lover's rendezvous.

A strained silence fell between them, his face a study in perplexity and distress. "My words may seem hollow," he said at last, "but every night since I've been well, I've dreamed of stealing over here to be with you again, as we were in the Hermitage and Los Bledos." He stared at the floor in a torment of shame. "I did not do so because I felt it would be more honorable to free you from any promises you ever made to me. My illness gave me time to think about what kind of man I am and what I've done to you. My love for you -- which is all I've ever had to offer -- has only served to grieve and dishonor you. I've risked your ruin and disgrace repeatedly, selfishly and without conscience. I've robbed a pure soul of its right to live in a state of grace. At this point, I wish to God Adrian Ávila were still alive to give you the marriage and happiness you deserve. As for me, I *have* a wife I do not love, but to whom I'm morally and legally bound. Somehow I must accept that fact -- and still live with myself. You, dear Lady, owe me nothing. This time I'll be riding out of your life for good."

As he rose from his chair to go, she took a small step toward him. He drew her close and laid her head against the heavy gold braid of his Marshal's tunic. Pressing his lips into her hair he quoted, *"'Love is like war: you begin when you please and leave off when you can.'"*

He was gone. Sirena would have found this parting unbearable, had she not been overwhelmed by the universal suffering that followed it like a thunderclap. The city entered into a municipal *agonia factum*. What had been alarming became catastrophic. Torrential rains filled the lakes, flooding whole sections of town, already awash in tons of uncollected garbage. Typhus crept in from the outskirts to become a citywide epidemic, raging out of control. Municipal monies for relief were exhausted.

Doctor Juan told Sirena twenty thousand people had died in the past six weeks! The Viceroy forbade the tolling of bells for the dead, because it spread panic among the living. Since all the cemeteries were full, many bodies were buried in shallow graves in the streets. Packs of starving wild dogs running loose at night, dug up the corpses, scattering their bones. Finally the Viceroy ordered out volunteer night crews with guns, knives and poison to hunt down the dogs. For two weeks Sirena's nights were filled with ghoulish shrieks and howls as scores of dogs were rounded up and slaughtered.

Repeatedly, she warned Catarina and Gertrudis to keep the Mendoza palace's front door locked. "Believe me! These dogs are vicious, they can kill!"

"I like dogs," was the younger sister's response.

"Sometimes I lose all patience with Gertrudis," Sirena told Catarina irritably. "She's such a simple -- *child!*"

Catarina fixed her with a dreamy smile. "Ah, Condesa, soon Gertrudis won't be the *only* child in this house."

Sirena spun around to face her, astonished at the news, but also sick with pity for Tristán, knowing the terrible cost to his own manly pride her simple statement implied. "Yes, the witch's spell worked! I'm three months along!"

Because of Catarina's pregnancy, Sirena increased her vigilance over the sisters. They can barely fend for themselves, she thought frantically, how will they ever care for a helpless infant? But, it was Tristán's child and she found herself trying to make sure Catarina ate well. She also began keeping careful track of the passage of time. It was two months to the day after Catarina announced her pregnancy that she found a frantic Catarina waiting in the Graciana patio, weeping and twisting her apron in her hands. "Condesa! Please come at once. It's Gertrudis! You'll know what to do."

Sirena raced to the Mendoza palace to find Gertrudis in the porter's room, sitting on the edge of the bed, holding her bleeding hand over a basin of water. "Did you cut yourself with a knife?" Sirena asked.

"No Señora," the girl replied guiltily, "it was a dog bit me through the window grille. But I didn't let him in, because he was sick."

"How was he sick?"

"He staggered about and his mouth was all -- foamy."

Years ago at La Frontera Sirena had seen a shepherd boy who had been bitten by a bat, die a slow and agonizing death from rabies. There was no cure and there was no doubt in her mind that the dog that bit Gertrudis was rabid. To Catarina she said, "This time there's nothing anyone can do."

Gertrudis suffered cruelly and it seemed to take forever for the end to come. Catarina was so desolated by her sister's death, Sirena worried the grief might cause her to lose the baby. After the funeral she brought her home to the Graciana palace, insisting she stay with her for the next three months, until the baby came. That night Estella fixed a fine dinner and Sirena staged an impromptu concert, singing old frontier ballads, while accompanying herself on the guitar. Catarina perked up, greatly consoled by the uplifting verses of *"The Mines of Glory"*, especially the closing one:

> *This world's ore is transitory,*
> *Seek an everlasting prize!*
> *For it's in the Mines of Glory*
> *That the deathless fortune lies!*

She asked to hear the final verse several times and afterwards even got a sudden craving for the fresh tunas from which she made her candies. Estella reminded her tunas were out of season, but promised to have fresh strawberries for her breakfast instead. To Sirena's relief, before retiring Catarina told her she felt truly resigned to her sister's death, because she now had a child of her own to look forward to.

When Sirena sat down to breakfast the next morning Analinda told her Catarina had apparently left sometime in the night. "Guessing she had gone 'back home' to the Luna-Mendosa palace, in the morning, Estella took a big basket of strawberries to her. It's not good for a pregnant woman to get a craving for something that can't be had," Analinda observed, now the wise mother of a two-year-old boy. "I hope the strawberries work."

"Well, God simply doesn't make tunas this time of year," Sirena said crossly, worn down with care. "Of all people, Catarina must know that."

"Patrona! Patrona!" Estella cried hysterically, rushing into the dining room, tears streaming down her face. "I just found Catarina!"

Sirena rose from the table, her own eyes enormous with fright, apprehension clutching at her heart. "What is it?"

"She's dead! She's hanging from the Mendoza's front window's wrought iron grille! The door was open, so I thought some vago had come in and murdered her. But -- Oh, Madre de Diós! Then, I saw what had really happened!" She covered her face with her hands.

"Patrona, there's blood everywhere! She miscarried in the sala sometime in the night, while she was there alone. I think when she finally realized that she had lost her baby and with no reason to go on with her own life and nothing to look forward to, she just -- despaired! And, in a moment of blind, mindless panic she took a sash of black crepe off the front door, and that's what she used…"

53

"I'll be happy to grant you permission to travel under the protection of this first convoy going North," Viceroy Calleja told Sirena across his gilded desk when she called on him in the Viceregal palace. "But Condesa, are you sure you want to return to Guanajuato?"

"Oh yes, Excelencia, I do," she replied emphatically.

"My good friend, young Lucas Alamán, and I are really anxious to get our family mines producing silver again."

She saw that the piercing falcon's eyes had dimmed. He studied her with an expression of great weariness and, it seemed to her, disillusionment.

"But are you prepared for what you'll find? Less than six thousand people live there now. The finest homes and palaces are in ruins or boarded up, most of the mines unworkable and abandoned."

"Yes, I realize that, Excelencia. But Don Lucas and I are convinced that Guanajuato needs mine owners who are bold enough to set an example of faith in the future. People need to see machinery being put back to work, flooded shafts drained in order to *believe* things are *possible*."

Describing her reasons to him this way also revealed to herself for the first time that what she was instinctively planning to do for Guanajuato's miners in her own lifetime -- was exactly what her family's foundress, the indomitable Doña Graciana, had done for the mines of Zacatecas in the 16th Century. When all the rest deserted, she had kept the silver flowing, defying the burning, rapine and bloodshed of the Chichimeca War that raged around her for fifty years.

Calleja accorded her youthful enthusiasm a grudging half-smile. "Well, it's no secret we've a desperate need for silver. Only yesterday I denied permission to a large group of Spaniards asking to return to Spain, because with them would have gone half the coin left in the kingdom." He gave a light sigh. "Perhaps God will smile on your efforts, my dear. Young people like you and Don Lucas carry the same torch of fire and faith that inspired your conquistadorial and pioneering forefathers."

After handing her his signed letter of permission, he came around the desk and took her hand. "I wish you luck, Condesa. Perhaps, in God's providence, we'll meet again."

She sensed finality in his tone. "I'm sure you and Doña Francisca are eager to return to your beloved Los Bledos when your term of office ends?"

He bowed his head thoughtfully, put his hands behind his back and walked slowly to a window overlooking the Plaza Mayor and the massive bulk of the Cathedral. "Like many other Spaniards, I've put down deep roots here," he said emotionally. "I've learned to love this land and I've found many true friends. But I've also known more than my share of treachery and betrayal. The politician begging favors with one hand, all too often carries a knife in the other."

He turned and faced her again. "Remember what I once said about fronteristas praying to God for what only the Viceroy could give, and begging the Viceroy for what not even the Almighty can bestow? Well, having sat in this chair for a while I can tell you, it's true of the *entire kingdom!*"

"I pray you continue to make your home here, where your valor earned you the title of *Conde de Calderón!*"

"Did Tristán tell you he has been awarded the equally distinguished title of *Conde Luna-Mendoza de Cuautla* for his heroism and wounds received during that long, bitter siege?"

"Sir, you both deserve your titles!" she said proudly. "I'm sure you won't be one of those going back to Spain!"

"With all the Hell I've witnessed in this war I've truly learned not to be too sure of anything," he said soberly. "From the ruin I see all about me, I'm no longer certain where my future home lies."

ଔ ଓ

As the Royalist convoy neared the safely reconquered Bajío town of Celaya, Sirena felt her pulse quicken. Not even the disquieting signs of the rebels' destructive occupation of Celaya could dampen her excitement at being so close to home. Don Lucas Alamán, now grown into a handsome, black-haired, grey-eyed silver lord of twenty years, felt it, too. He had turned down his mother's offer to send him on the Grand Tour -- now that Ferdinand the Seventh once more occupied the Spanish throne, and Napoleon was safely imprisoned on the isle of Elba -- because he had his heart set on working together with Sirena. Like herself, the Alamáns had cached enough silver bars before the sack of the city, to help finance the costly project of digging adits to drain his own very old and still fabulously rich San Clemente mine.

Their plan was for Don Lucas to escort Estella and Analinda and her little boy, on to Guanajuato. There he would stay with Alberta and Ricardo in the Graciana palacio until he could examine the mines' tunnels and shafts. Meanwhile, Sirena would set up headquarters for support operations at La Torre. Old Martín had just written her that all through the war La Torre's tough old walls and casco had repelled rebel bandits and Royalists alike. Its mule herd was intact and a big corn crop in. Soon, she and Old Martín would begin bringing trains of sound young mules, loaded with corn to feed them and other needed supplies, to the upper mines. By spring they should be able to commence the hard work of drainage.

"Are you sure you'll be safe riding to La Torre with only Melchor?" Don Lucas asked when the convoy disbanded at Celaya and its fewer civilians began going their separate ways.

"It's only two leagues west of here, Lucas," she assured him. "I'll be there in an hour."

While she appreciated his gentlemanly concern, they both knew the Bajío now was far safer than the south, where the Morelos' guerrillas were still putting whole regions to the torch. She had even heard Acapulco had fallen to him and the great Manila Galleon would never again make its centuries old voyage across the vast Ladies' Sea.

Sirena found that distance and time had mossed over many of the remembered horrors of the sack of Guanajuato while memories of earlier, happier days were wooing her back. Most of all she was beguiled by the siren song of silver, calling her as it had her father and his mother's people -- all the way back to Doña Graciana herself.

Sirena was actually starting a new life; one without Tristán. While Catarina's death had freed him to remarry, the obstacle of consanguinity remained. And now, another barrier had arisen between them. Ironically on this trip north she overheard one officer pass along to another some recent news about him that made many things clear. "I served under Field Marshal Luna since before Calderón," the first man said. "He's been a confirmed bachelor all these years, but during the long siege of Cuautla he became quite smitten with the young widow of an officer who was killed serving under him. Now they say she's here in Valladolid and barracks' gossip has it they'll marry soon."

Heartsick as this news made her, it at least explained his silence. She had not had any word from him since he left New Spain and she was too proud to write. She did not begrudge him happiness if he had found it with someone else, but she was hurt to learn there was something more than the noble reasons he had given her for riding out of her life.

Well, she thought resolutely, the herculean task of restoring the Graciana and La Sirena mines would keep her too busy to even think of anything else. And silver was not quite as volatile as human love. Despite the awful night of 'the drowning of the moon,' deep in her heart she still shared her father's boundless confidence that 'Silver is a river no man can stop! Silver is forever!'

To ease Don Lucas' concern, she promised to send him word by courier of her safe arrival at La Torre. She also agreed with him it would be prudent to stain her face and hands brown, to look as much like a poor campesina as possible. A proud horse, fine clothes or any show of wealth, drew highwaymen like honey drew flies. In native dress and wearing sandals, she set out with Melchor after dark, taking the path that ran beside the highway. A waxing moon cast sufficient light to travel by and there was no traffic at all on the Camino Real.

She guessed it was shortly past eleven when the tower of La Torre hacienda appeared, looming reassuringly above its grove of elm and fresno trees. Knowing Old Martín always posted a night guard, Sirena and Melchor approached stealthily, prepared to identify themselves to his sentinel. They found the corral gate open and a swarthy mestizo on foot talking with a vaquero who was mounted on a big chalk-eyed bay pinto. She could not hear what they were saying.

Finally she heard the horseman shout, "Si, mi Jefé!" and striking savagely-spiked spurs to the pinto's sides, he came bolting through the gate toward herself and Melchor. "Out of my way, you stupid Indian!" he shouted at Melchor, quirting him across the face. Sirena jumped back to escape the pounding hooves, which were almost upon her, but the big pinto's shoulder dealt her a glancing blow as he thundered past, throwing her against the stone wall.

Sirena had no idea how long she had been unconscious, but when she came to she found herself safely inside La Torre's monastic dining room. Still half-dazed, she looked around and saw the place was almost unrecognizable except for the Dominican pulpit in its old place on the wall.

Rifles, lances and ammunition were stacked everywhere. Each corner piled with sacks of feed for horses and mules. An open fire burned in the center of the room, around it several cannon that appeared to be in the process of being rebuilt. The whitewashed walls were blackened from the smoke of campfires, and obscene verses were scrawled over every inch of open wall space. Her consoling certainty that La Torre was a safe haven in the crucible of war turned to ashes. It seemed certain the Rebels were in charge.

Gradually she became aware she was half-lying on a hard straw-filled mattress with her wrists tied together to a post at the head of the crude bed on which she lay. A lantern on a table by the bed added its meager light to that of the fire. The only other person in the room was a tall man with dark, shoulder length hair, bending over one of the cannon, examining its bore. He was dressed in knee breeches of good, dark cloth and his shirt, although without a stock and open to the waist, was of fine linen. Maybe rebels hadn't taken over. This man might even be a gentleman of culture.

When he heard her stirring on the bed the long-haired man straightened up and swaggered over to her, his hands resting lightly on his narrow hips, appraising her as though she were a whim horse at auction. She caught her breath when the lantern shed its light upon his face.

"Lorenzo!" She cried. "Oh, thank God it's you!"

54

Sirena hadn't thought it possible she could ever be glad to see Lorenzo Santa Cruz, but compared to falling into the hands of a monster like 'El Lobo', she welcomed him as the very flower of chivalry. But she was surprised to find him here and needed to find out what he was doing at La Torre.

"I came to see Old Martín?" she asked. "Do you know where he is?"

"He's resting in the churchyard with a bullet in his shoulder."

"What happened? How was he wounded?"

"He was foolish enough to put up a fight when we came to take the place. He should have known better."

"Good God, Lorenzo!" she cried, aghast. "He was your own grandfather!"

He never flinched. "It's not who you are anymore," he replied serenely. "It's what side you're on."

She waited in terrified silence.

"And what in God's name are you going about in that get-up for?" he asked sarcastically, pulling back her rebozo to reveal her plain skirt and blouse.

"I thought I'd be safer on the road if I looked like a campesina," she said simply, ignoring his derisive tone. "I had no way of knowing La Torre had fallen to rebels."

"Not rebels! Free citizens! Mexicanos!"

"I see." As she watched him she found it incredible he could be the same man. He was like a chameleon. The English fashion plate architect who had called on her in Mexico was gone. His clothes now were expensive, but soiled. His hair was long, neglected and shot through with grey. His eyes held an expression she found hard to describe in any other words except jaded brutality.

"So you decided to join the Rebels after all?" she asked, determined to maintain her dignity even though trussed up like a pig in a vendor's stall.

"Well, I heard Morelos was finally handing out new pedigrees to outcasts like me. I figured if a mulatto like him could send the entire kingdom running for cover, he could damn well set my feet on the 'white man's path' as well."

Picking up a short knife from a plate of fresh pears on the table by the bed, he speared the moist flesh of the fruit and lifted it to his mouth on the blade. Scrutinizing her, he scowled in displeasure. "I won't have you dressing like a vago whore in my camp, understand? You'll wear expensive clothes here, worthy of your rank."

He strolled over to an open trunk, overflowing with dresses and jewels. "I'll find something here about your size. We've got piles of loot to choose from." Rummaging through the clothes, he held up one elaborate ball gown after another. At last one struck his fancy. "Here we are," he said, walking back to her. "This is some Condesa's wedding dress." He tossed a froth of white ruffled lace onto the bed beside her.

Then, without a word', he stepped forward, yanked off her rebozo and cast it onto the flames. A moment later, holding her blouse tautly away from her body with his left hand, he slashed the fabric with the knife in his right. Remnants of blouse and skirt followed the rebozo into the fire, leaving her naked with only a shred of petticoat. She was too stricken to speak, too proud to cry out. Lorenzo's no savior, she thought desperately. He's madder than Hidalgo ever was!

"Now, you can just lie there and wait 'til I finish work." He went back to the cannon, ran his hand along the inside bore, and fixed her with his most winning smile. "You always did like to watch me work. Remember?"

"You were carving saints and angels then," she said hotly, furious at being unable to cover her breasts because both hands were tied. "The last time we talked you told me you despised Manual Tolsá for making Royalist cannon. Now you're doing the same thing."

"Yes, and forging *three* rebel cannon to his one!"

"Where will making weapons get you? What kind of 'new order' will you build on the ruins of the one you're so determined to destroy?"

"A world of power! Your class was on top for centuries. Now a society of classless folk like me is about to replace you."

"So what of honor then, and charity? Who will care for the sick, the poor, the mad, the orphans? What will become of civilized society?"

He spat into the fire. "Fuck civilized society!"

"You barbarian!" she hissed. "You've got more greed than ten gachupínes and without a drop of their piety!"

He shrugged and she decided to change her tack. Sweet reason might not work, but maybe throwing herself on his mercy would. It was worth a try. "Lorenzo, I don't want to fight with you. If you have any chivalry left you'll let me go. Please give me some riding clothes and one good horse!" *Oh God*, she thought. *I can't be sitting here stark naked in my own hacienda, with a thousand head of my own prize mounts, begging this blackguard to loan me a horse!* "Please?"

"But that's not in my plan for you, Condesa."

She eyed him suspiciously. "What is your plan for me?" He busied himself oiling a musket. "I have a hobby. I collect extraordinary female camp followers. For a time I had an Indian hunchback with a cleft lip -- you know, the kind the moon takes a bite out of during an eclipse when they're still in the womb? Anyway, she was a damned good lay." Sirena began to tremble with fear and cold. There was a good blanket at the foot of the bed, but out of her reach.

"Next I had an albino bitch, all white, head to toe, and even her eyes." He laid the knife down and lit a cigarette. "Then, when I joined Morelos at the siege of Cuautla, picked up an Indian deaf mute. Calleja's massive bombardments brought her long-lost hearing back. She even learned to speak again. She told me some fascinating tales about life in a convent in Mexico." He studied Sirena's face. "But, like all the rest, the novelty wore off."

Sirena felt all circulation in her arms stop. Her head throbbed and her body ached. Numbly she wondered if the deaf mute was the same Beatriz she knew at Madre Pilar's, but would not flatter him by discussing his sorry conquests.

Lorenzo exhaled slowly. "But now *you* are something else. A real collector's gem. No bandit or rebel leader has ever had a real honest-to-God silver heiress as his own private whore." He pulled on his cigarette. "So it's important to me you dress the part. You're living proof the castas have won!"

He kept glancing over at her as he worked. "You'll find I'm not a selfish master. I'll share you with special friends. But I admit I'm hard on horses and women, and I have to change both often. I get bored having the same piece of ass twice a day. When that time comes for you, I'll see what your illustrious cousin is willing to pay to get some well-used Royalist baggage back."

Sirena thought she was going to faint, but refused to give him that satisfaction. *I'll stay upright if it kills me!*

"You still look exactly like my painting of you."

"I never sat for you in my life!" she snapped.

"You're right. You were actually lying on my bunk aboard the galleon."

All the air went out of her lungs in a single gasp.

"I call it La Condesa Desnuda, and I carry it with me in a tube in my bed roll." He lit another cigarette and looked at her, slit-eyed through the rising smoke. "Sometimes when I feel horny and there's no female handy, I put up that painting and get myself off quite pleasurably in front of it." He sighed. "But now *I have the real thing*."

Sirena closed her eyes, wishing to God she had never regained consciousness.

There was a heavy pounding on the door. Sirena was torn between the dread of having another man see her, and the hope that some gentleman might come to her aid. To her dismay Lorenzo merely glanced up and called out "Pasé!"

When the door opened all she could see was a great shadow on the floor, cast by a man whose large frame filled the doorway. She glanced up fearfully as he entered the room, enormous roweled spurs growling at his heels. Emilio!

Catching sight of Sirena, Emilio stopped short near the foot of the bed. She looked at him pleadingly. "Emilio! It's me, Sirena!"

His blue eyes ice cold and devoid of all compassion, he leaned down, picked up the blanket and threw it over her.

"For Christ's sake, Lorenzo, do you want the bitch to die of distemper before you even hump her? You treat women worse than a *sambo* treats a mule."

"I've got half a night's worth of work here before I can get around to her," he said irritably.

She shut her eyes, and when she opened them Emilio was bending over her, cutting the hemp that bound her wrists. As she pulled the blanket tightly around her Emilio stood nearby, surveying her as though trying to decide what to do with his prize. She held his gaze, terrified but alert, positioning her feet beneath her, ready to make a run for the door if he made a move in her direction. Finally Lorenzo stepped forward.

"Don't touch me!" she warned.

His huge hand closed around her upper arm, but she wrenched free, making a reckless dash past him for the open door. Emilio grabbed her around the waist and she had a glimpse of Lorenzo, head thrown back, laughing uproariously at the amusing spectacle of his father chasing a naked Condesa around the room. Infuriated, she drew her right arm back and struck Emilio with all her strength. A split second later she saw his open palm coming down upon her, knowing the heavy blow would fall, but helpless to escape.

"Hitting a woman hard enough to knock her cold, without breaking her jaw," Emilio bragged. "that's the trick!"

Lorenzo shrugged. "You should know. You've had enough practice." Then headded, "When you're through with her, have her put that lace dress on her." He pointed to the wedding gown. "What good is it having a bona fide Condesa if she goes around looking like a common rebel whore?"

"Thanks for your generosity," Emilio said slyly, lifting Sirena's blanketed form lightly from the bed.

"For nothing," Lorenzo winked. "It will broaden her experience. God knows, after experiencing an old casta bull like you, she'll appreciate me fucking her with style!"

Emilio shot him a venomous look. "That, Lorenzo, remains to be seen," he said, walking out and kicking the door shut behind him.

○○ ○○

The night sentry raised his rifle, primed it and challenged the lone rider approaching Royalist field headquarters. "Who are you?"

"A courier from nearby La Torre," the horseman replied, nodding at the white cloth tied to the point of his upright lance. His lathered mount was mute testimony to the speed with which he had come. "I bring a valued prisoner to your commanding officer."

Seconds later two mounted cavalrymen emerged from the trees, closing in on either side of the courier. "Surrender your weapons first." The man handed them over wordlessly.

The three rode in silence through a long, tree-shaded lane leading to the casco of a 17th Century hacienda. Although well past midnight, a light still burned in the commander's window. Now, at the sound of horses' hooves ringing on the flagstones, he opened the door of his office on the second floor and descended the curving stairway to the patio. "Well, Corporal, what have we here?"

"Sir, this courier from the rebel stronghold of La Torre claims he's bringing you a hostage."

The commander walked over to the courier who held a blanketed figure in his arms. The two men held each others' gaze for the space of an Ave. Then the commander told his soldiers, "Leave us." The sentries withdrew.

"Well, Emilio, which rebel prisoner of mine are you so eager to get back in exchange for this one?" he asked softly.

"It's no swap, Don Tristán. This one's yours, free as a yearling calf without a brand." Tristán looked closer at the blanketed form in Emilio's arms. "Has he been wounded? Who is he?"

"It's not a soldier," Emilio said, leaning down from his saddle and placing the hostage in Tristán's arms. "It's the First Condesa de Graciana. I took her from a bandit stud who planned to make her his private whore. I had to knock her out first to make taking her look real." He grinned proudly. "She'll have a sore jaw when she comes around, but I didn't break it. I never do."

Accepting the burden, Tristán was speechless.

"Careful. She's slick as a newborn colt. That blanket's all I had time to grab."

May I ask you why you brought her to me?"

"Well, as the old saying goes, 'Courtesy steals nothing from valor'. I gave Don Patrick my word of honor she would be my patrona, and no man alive harms my sworn patrona. Not even if that man were *my own son!*"

"Don Patrick would salute you for this very noble deed if he were here," Tristán replied.

"Like him, my word is my word of honor!" Emilio said firmly, frankly accepting Tristán's compliment. Then, with a deprecating smile he confided, "But then, as they say, 'Even a stone's been known to roll downhill!'"

Tristán summoned the sentries and ordered them to return the courier's weapons and escort him safely back through Royalist lines. "And if any man so much as lays a finger on him -- *I'll have that man shot!*"

Emilio reined his horse about. Touching two fingers to the brim of his sombrero that formed an enormous black halo encircling his head, he said, "Amar a Diós, Don Tristán!"

"Amar a Diós!" Tristán replied.

⋄55⋄

Tristán's spurs pinged softly as he entered Valladolid's sumptuous Cathedral. Of all New Spain's many fine churches, he found this the loveliest, its neo-classic interior bathed in the soft glow of daylight filtered through windows of pale ocher onyx. Enriched by religious paintings and statues, the work of the kingdom's greatest artists, each soaring reredos wooed the soul upward to lose itself in God's own crowning storm of glory.

Although it was only minutes past six on this quiet weekday morning, the first Mass of the day was being celebrated, and the lofty vaulting was fragrant with the smoky sweetness of incense and hot bees wax. Kneeling near the sanctuary, Tristán was pleased to see Monsignor Crespi was offering a Mass in honor of Saint Martín of Tours. Tristán had taken this noble Roman soldier-saint for his model as a youth, but never in all his years of campaigning had he been able to receive Holy Communion on his Feast Day. Taking it as a sign, he addressed a fervent prayer to his valorous Roman friend, for today he was in desperate need of supernatural guidance and grace.

After Mass and a devout post-communion thanksgiving, he passed through the sanctuary gate and into the spacious sacristy. Monsignor had already removed his vestments and was the picture of sacerdotal elegance in his black cassock with cerise piping and a wide bougainvillea-colored sash.

At the sound of spurs, Crespi cast an apprehensive look at the door, then seeing who it was, his face lit up in recognition. "Tristán!" he cried, coming forward to embrace him. "It must be a year since you were last here to re-take the city from the rebels!"

"Longer, Monsignor!" Tristán assured him, returning Crespi's abrazo. "I dearly love this Cathedral and it warms my heart to find you and it safely back in Royalist hands."

"Well, rebels aged me a bit," he jested, "but the church came through unscathed." Crespi swept Tristán and his gallant uniform with a discerning eye. "Your new rank of Field Marshal becomes you, my friend, but you look as though you've just made a marathon ride."

"Indeed I have. I just arrived from Celaya, in record time."

"Come, Tristán," Crespi offered, leading him out a side door, "Share hot chocolate and hot salsa with me and we can talk." Together the two men crossed through the park-like plaza, its Indian laurels, as always, lyrical with larks.

"I'm anxious to see His Excellency, too," Tristán said, "for I need his advice on an urgent personal matter." Crespi halted in mid-step. "Ah, but you've missed him!"

"He's gone?" Tristán was stricken.

"Gone to Madrid," Crespi said, resuming his measured pace. "He sailed from the port of San Blas a week ago."

Tristàn felt the same sinking sensation he felt when a horse went down under him in a charge. "I was afraid he might return to Spain like many of his countrymen, however, knowing how he loves this kingdom -- "

"Oh, he's coming back," Crespi assured him, "his heart lies here. He's even reserved his own crypt beneath the sanctuary floor." At their approach a watchful servant opened a side door into the palace dining room. Crespi seated himself and waved Tristán to a chair across the table from his own. "But you know what a crusader he is! He felt it would help the crown avoid future rebellions if King Ferdinand were given a first hand report on the war from someone who had witnessed it all from the start."

Tristán was bitterly disappointed. He had ridden like a man possessed to reach the Bishop and seek his advice before Sirena's expected arrival in Valladolid by coach. Now what was he to do?

"I trust it's not another rebel threat that brings you here in such haste?"

"In part, Your Grace," Tristán admitted, as an Indian servant brought them the ranch-style breakfast of fresh tortillas, eggs *rancheros*, and fiery red salsa, favored by this unassuming mestizo son of a Bajío hacienda supervisor.

Tristán's cold dismay at not finding the Bishop here began to thaw. "I've seen many good men blighted by this war," he confided. "Its cruelties have tainted even such a moral cedar as Calleja himself. Blood calls out for blood, atrocity for atrocity! We've been brutalized by the very barbarisms that shocked us so at first."

Sensing in Tristán's tone a rising storm of emotional and moral conflict that might crack even a Field Marshal's steel reserve, Crespi tactfully led him into the greater privacy of the sala, where they seated themselves in chairs facing the Bishop's desk and the Legázpi Coat of Arms.

During the hard fighting and difficult negotiations of the retaking of this City, Tristán had come to know and respect Crespi's judgment and compassion under fire. Now, in the privacy of the sala, he found himself opening up his soul to this understanding priest.

Impulsively he returned to the subject of Sirena who, he explained, was now under the care of Doctor Daniel Pinal, his army surgeon.

While recuperating in Celaya she had been dealt another blow in a letter from Lucas Alamán. He wrote that, having surveyed the full extent of the damage to the silver mining industry in Guanajuato, he had been forced to abandon their brave plans. He advised her to give up hope of ever salvaging her tunnels or shafts, adding that he was leaving for London to spend several years studying abroad. This news left her heartbroken and adrift, with no real purpose in life.

"To my everlasting sorrow," Tristán told Crespi, in great emotional distress, "I admit that much of Sirena's suffering has been brought about by me." He poured out the unhappy circumstances of his marriage, his illicit liaisons with Sirena, the risks of pregnancy he'd let her take, his inability to live without her. "And now that I'm presented with yet *another* Gordian knot -- that of our still being too close of kin to marry even though my former wife has passed on." Tristán bowed his head over his folded hands. "So help me God, I would ride through fire and brimstone to make this woman my wife, but I've been blocked at every turn! *Please,* Your Grace, what should I do? Dare I even hope? Is there ANY way -- ?"

"I'm fully aware of your dilemma, Tristán," Crespi informed him gently. "The Bishop told me before setting out for Spain." Crespi rose and went quickly to a corner safe. "Not enough to break the seal of confessional, of course," he assured him, while he worked the combination, "but enough to prepare me to give you -- this." He drew out a letter on parchment and handed it to Tristán. "It bears his official Episcopal seal and is valid even in his absence."

Puzzled, and daunted by its canonical language, Tristán read the document slowly. "Does this say what I *think* it does?" he asked brokenly, suddenly dizzier than if he had just downed a whole liter of scaldingly raw Santa Fe brandy.

"It's the Bishop's official dispensation, granted to the two of you as second cousins, because of the 'intelligence, high rank and moral character of the parties involved', and because the kinship is on the paternal side only." A slow smile flickered across Crespi's face. "This gives you the Church's canonical permission to marry the First Condesa -- provided, of course, you still desire to do so."

Tristán was struck dumb with the wonder of this totally undreamed of blessing, and he silently thanked Saint Martín for giving him such an incomparable Feast Day gift.

"Later, of course," Crespi was saying, "there will be time to go into the matter of marriage contract, dowry and the disposition of your respective houses, lands and mines."

All at once the full, heady impact of the dispensation hit him. Merciful God and all the saints, he thought, what did silver mines or property or barracks' gossip matter now? After all these years we're free!

"Monsignor, would you be willing to say a private nuptial Mass for the Condesa and me on very short notice -- providing she accepts my proposal?"

Crespi laid a hand on Tristán 's shoulder, "Nothing would please me more! I'll even waive the banns. I shall also offer my own Mass tomorrow for all your intentions," Crespi said sympathetically. "God does not sow thoughts of grace in a noble heart for nothing."

"And I do thank you, Father, for -- hearing me out."

"For this I was ordained," Crespi replied quietly.

"Sirena is staying at Las Flores and I'll let you know her reply. Meanwhile, I ask one more favor of Your Grace." He drew an envelope from his tunic and handed it to Crespi. "My poor wife, Caterina, recently died, as she had lived, under very tragic circumstances. It is my wish that one hundred Masses be said as soon as possible for the repose of her soul. My *libranza* for this ultimate solace is enclosed."

"I shall offer my Mass tomorrow for all your intentions, Tristán," he said sympathetically, "God does not sow thoughts of grace in a noble heart for nothing."

☙ ❧

Tristán returned to the Iturbide hacienda to find the patio abuzz with the lilting laughter of guests who had just alighted from the few coaches lining Las Flores' spacious drive.

After paying his respects to his host, Tristán went in search of Sirena. He did not find her in the patio or sala. He stepped inside the brightly lighted ballroom, where he found elegantly gowned couples engaged in the quaint curtsies and courtly bows of an old-fashioned minuet. The juxtaposition of years struck him like a blow. It was as though the war had never happened, as though all the clocks had suddenly stopped that summer night, on the eve of his own and General Calleja's 1803 Inspection of Provincial Regiments! Now, as if it were that same night re-lived, he saw the corner arch where Captain Allende had whirled out of this very room with seventeen-year-old Sirena in his arms.

Following where memory led, he entered the secluded Grecian garden, enclosed by black cypresses, against whose dark ranks the garden's white columns shone softly in the light of an early moon. Sirena sat on a stone bench, her profile to him, gazing down into the murmuring waters of the artificial stream. She looked utterly chaste in a blue velvet gown and elbow-length white gloves, her hair loosely drawn back and caught in a soft chignon at the nape of her neck. He felt his heart melt.

Hearing his step in the coarse gravel she looked up. "Dearest condesita mia," he said tenderly, "I thought I might find you here."

She gave him a wistful smile. "The ballroom held so many memories of the last time I was here, so many ghosts, I had to get away. They were all in there again -- my poor misguided brother, Ramón, and David Ávila -- and Adrian." She looked back down at the glistening water. "And out here I found still another the shade of that rash, irrepressible Captain Allende, who thought he was God's gift to women!"

Tristán seated himself on the bench beside her. "There are two other ghosts in this garden tonight," he said, trembling as he took her in his arms. "This is where I first saw you as a grown woman, where you told me you had always loved me, and where I first realized I could never love any other woman but you." A shining tear slid down her cheek and he brushed it away. "But those star-crossed lovers are now only two more ghosts from another lifetime past, because we. . ." He hugged her to him, "Oh, Sirena, we've been reborn, we've been given whole new lives to live. . ."

"What new lives? What sort of life are you day-dreaming about?" she asked him, completely bewildered. "Congratulations on your 'coming marriage to the young widow. Is this the news you bring me." Sirena had stopped him cold.

Then, he remembered the rumors."But that's sheer gossip!" he protested. "The God's truth is that I had called on the lady three times only to press a difficult suit for an officer in my command. He had been her late husband's closest friend. The suitor loved her, but did not want to appear too eager to supplant his former comrade. Father Hilario married them as he had that authority as the Chaplain of the Royalist Army.

"I apologize, Tristán," she had said unemotionally. "It was unfair of me to credit gossip and believe you would ever lie to me." But her warmth stopped there.

No, Condesita, listen, to me. I have a letter," he admonished her gently. "The Bishop has given us an ecclesiastical dispensation enabling us to marry each other! When you read it, you'll understand. I'm asking you to marry me for the second time in the sight of God, but this time it will be in our favorite Cathedral, with our own nuptial Mass and Father Crespi as the witness to our vows! Thanks to our good Bishop, at last we will be a happily married couple, free to love each other openly and can begin raising the family we've always longed to have together."

"The Bishop has granted us a dispensation!" he whispered, unable to contain the wild excitement he felt when uttering those magical words. "Will you marry me a second time, 'in the sight of God'? He held his breath.

Sirena looked deeply into his eyes. "Was there ever any doubt?"

ଓଃ56ଓ

On the day after Monsignor Crespi married them, Sirena and Tristán rode up a narrow mountain trail that spiraled upward through sun-shafted aisles of blue-green cedar and pine. Tristán was riding his golden war horse, Conquistador, Sirena her milk-white Arabian, Emir. Following at a discreet distance was Amantina's lifelong servant, Melchor, on one of La Torre's good coach mules leading four others bearing packs. The animals' hooves fell soundlessly on the deep carpet of pine needles cushioning the trail. Amber and lilac-hued wild orchids bloomed among the trees while wild canaries, clarines and mocking birds filled the forest with their song. Sirena had never seen any region more beautiful than this heavily timbered sierra northeast of Valladolid.

She was dressed in a full-skirted royal blue riding habit, her long black hair caught up in a Spanish *maja's* snood of blue-green wool. She had not forgotten Tristán liked her best in blue. Riding at her side, he looked almost as she first remembered him, wearing the plain campaign dress of a Border Army soldier; the high black stock, sleeveless vest of light-weight quilted cotton armor and the black, wide-brimmed, flat-crowned sombrero worn by norteño lancers. The only vestige of his new rank of Field Marshal was a broad sword, carried in a saddle scabbard under his left leg and his lance, resting upright in a leather boot behind his right stirrup.

"I'm glad you are not giving up your Border Army position, and that in your later retirement years you will be moving with me back to La Frontera."

He smiled down on her. "It's not something I decided in haste, but it's not the place for us to be right now. Besides, raising livestock and defending the frontier against Indian raids, it will always be as vital to New Spain's survival as chasing Morelos through the tropic's jungles, and *much* more rewarding!"

"I was so proud of you, Tristán, when I read the Viceroy's letter."

"Well, I knew he'd decided to retire to Spain, but I never dreamed he would recommend me as his successor!"

"Do you think you might ever look back and wish that you'd accepted such an honor?"

"Trust me, my dear, there's more pride to be taken in being *offered* the post of viceroy than *filling* it." He reached over and laid his hand on hers. "I'm utterly content being with you. Are you happy, my lady bride?"

"Oh, Tristán, happier than I've ever been in my whole life!" Then after a moment she added. "I still worry a little about the mines. I keep thinking I should save them. They're like poor noble orphans with no Don Francisco to watch over them."

"But Don Lucas was right about Guanajuato. It would break your heart to see it. I'm afraid the gracious world that silver lords like Don Patrick -- *and* his feisty First Condesa -- once took such pride in, is gone forever."

"But the other night at dinner Monsignor Crespi said foreign investors -- especially from England -- are pouring into the kingdom, seeking to buy up and joint-lease silver mines, derelict or not. If *foreigners* see a future in the mines, how can I justify not -- ?"

"They don't know it yet, but they're buying economic nightmares," he cautioned. "Frankly, I think our best revenge for 'perfidious Albion's' centuries of pirating New Spain's silver, is to let the British *have* the mines! I'd like to see them lose all their stolen silver by throwing it right back down the now-ruined shafts they came from!"

Her chin went up and her eyes flashed angrily. "I'll never let any foreigner set foot inside a Graciana mine!" she cried defiantly. "I'd dynamite them first!"

"Now, don't get your Irish up," he said affectionately, brushing her cheek with his gloved hand. "You've had to fight too many battles alone. As I said a long time ago, you need someone to look after you. That's why I'm here."

She gazed at him lovingly. "Thank God you are, Tristán, but it's hard for me to let go of that precious world."

Just before sundown they entered a hidden mountain meadow enclosed on three sides by a forested ridge. A shingle-roofed cabin built of peeled, squared logs was built up against the ridge, blending so naturally into the rustic setting, Sirena had to look twice to make sure it was real. An open veranda ran the cabin's length supported by hand-hewn and brightly painted pine columns.

"How peaceful it is here!" she cried, pulling up on, Emir's bit, transfixed by both the cabin and the breathtaking panorama that spread out endlessly below. "Oh, Tristán!" she exclaimed passionately, "Peace is such a precious thing!

His deep blue eyes were thoughtful as he drew rein beside her.

She sighed. "It's like looking out on all eternity."

"This cabin has been in the Tarascan Indian side of the Monsignor's family for generations. His aunt keeps it spotless and completely furnished for any guests he sends along. He sent me up here to rest for a couple of weeks after we retook Valladolid from the rebels. I never forgot the place."

Sirena felt his eyes upon her. "This is where I hoped to spend our first night together -- as man and wife," he said almost shyly. "That is, if it pleases you."

"Oh yes, Tristán," she breathed, "It pleases me!"

He signaled Melchor toward the barn and servants' cabin situated a short distance away, on the banks of a small rushing stream. Dismounting from Conquistador he lifted her down gently from her sidesaddle. After Melchor led their horses away, they walked slowly up the slope to the cabin.

He drew her eagerly into his arms. "The only thing I ever found wanting in this paradise was you."

"Could we stay for more than just one night?"

"I was hoping you'd want to. After all, condesita, this is our honeymoon! I'm in no hurry for anything else but loving you."

"That's such a bright little river."

"It has a low waterfall dropping into a secluded pool just downstream from here. That's where I used to swim and dream of you." His voice fell to a whisper. "We can swim there tomorrow, if you wish, or by moonlight tonight."

As he pressed his cheek against her own she closed her eyes. "Oh, Tristán, belonging to you at last, and being able to have the family we've always wanted. I promise not to even *think* about my poor ruined mines. Our happiness is all the 'silver dust and Spanish wine' I'll ever need!"

Slipping his hand about her waist he led her gently up the rustic steps and through the door, her head resting lightly against his quilted armor. "Remember, Condesita, God put that silver in the ground. He'll let you know when it's time to start taking it out again."

LA FRONTERA

November, 1822

Years had passed and she could still clearly remember their delectable honeymoon. Her heart sang in gratitude for their seven years together. She had never known a moment of unhappiness with this dear noble man, their love growing deeper and richer with each day.

Tristán proved to be as gentle a father as he was a lover. Born in their first year of marriage were twin sons, Damian and Marcos. The title of Second Conde fell to Damian, born three minutes before his brother. Three years ago they had welcomed blonde, blue-eyed Patricia, named after Don Patrick. Little 'Tricia inherited from Tristán her title of First Condesa de Luna-Mendoza de Cuautla. Tristán had also legally adopted Sirena's godson, Rafael, who lived with them here at La Frontera, when he was not attending school in New Orleans or Saint Louis, under Don Francisco's watchful eye. The near total collapse of the kingdom's educational institutions during the last twelve years of constant civil war, had made sending him to the United States for schooling imperative. Because Rafael planned to become a diplomat, she and Tristán felt gaining fluency in both languages was crucial. Thoughts of Rafael always reminded Sirena of his mother, Consuelo, and their harrowing return voyage on the galleon. Memories, which, brought her back to the imminent arrival of that miscreant, Lorenzo, who had written to her, threatening her with exposure and scandal, with yet another threat of blackmail.

Where for the past weeks she had longed for Tristán's imminent return, she was now praying he would not arrive until Lorenzo had safely come and gone. But until Lorenzo was actually on her doorstep she had to keep functioning, for this afternoon she was hosting a small bon voyage party for the Fourth Marqués de Ávila. Tomorrow he would leave his ancestral home of La Soledad -- now foreclosed and incorporated into Sirena's own vast northern estate -- to take up residence in the Ávila family palace in Mexico. She was glad she had wrung this last concession from the local notary, making sure that certain incomes from his former estate continued to support him, while all his other creditors wanted to send the aging nobleman begging in the streets. Well, Sirena thought, with both sons dead and his daughter, Alicia, living scandalously with her paramour allover Europe, that was the least a lifelong neighbor and friend could do for the proud old man.

ങ ഌ

"Sirena, is it true young Lucas Alamán is coming back from Europe?" the Fourth Marqués asked.

"He's already back," Sirena replied. "In fact, I received a long letter from him today from Mexico. The San Clemente heritage ran dry, due to the wreckage of the mine, and his mother called him home because they're bankrupt. But you know Don Lucas! He'll land on his feet. He's enthusiastic as ever and God knows, he's had a superb education."

"Yes, he's been active in government in Spain," Don Gabriel said, "and speaks fluent Italian, French and English. He's formed strong business and diplomatic contacts in Rome and Paris and been especially effective in London, persuading banks and private financiers to invest British apital in reactivating New Spain's damaged mines."

As dessert was being served Melchor appeared, with a whispered message that a visitor had arrived. "Please excuse me," she said, "And please don't delay the after-dinner musicale. I'll join you later."

"It's that cut-throat rebel chief who captured you at La Torre!" Melchor hissed, horrified, as he escorted her down stairs to the old refectory.

"Yes, Melchor, I know."

"I'll be right outside the door if you need me."

Sirena crossed the patio and turned into the stone-paved cloister that led to the old refectory where her retainers dined. This corridor was also La Frontera's armory, and now, passing between double rows of steel-tipped lances, upright in their racks, each beribboned with the Graciana colors of silver and blue, fresh courage flowed into her. Then, seeing her reflection in a large pier glass to the right of the refectory door, she realized she was wearing the Graciana colors, too. The festive gown she had chosen for the party was powder-blue velvet, trimmed with silvered chiffon. Well, she mused, lifting her chin defiantly, if lancers and Indians can ride into battle wearing full tribal regalia, why not I?

Entering the high, narrow room, she found a brilliantly uniformed Lorenzo standing at the opposite end of the long trestle table. Benches flanked the table's length, with carved friar's chairs at both head and foot. A large, freestanding wrought iron candelabra stood on the floor to her right, all two dozen tapers ablaze. Seating herself at the table's head, she gave Lorenzo the slightest nod of permission to take his place opposite her, glad to have considerable space between them.

"So, here we are," she said icily, her spine barely touching the back of the chair, her hands folded before her.

"My, my what a chilly welcome. And I have such warm memories of you!"

"We needn't discuss our memories of each other. Mine are all exceedingly unpleasant."

"But we're here to delve into the past, and you'll find I know a great more deal about yours than you supposed."

"So which secret of my past is so *provable* and worth telling, you want me to pay a king's ransom to buy it back?"

"Well, last time we met, Emilio snatched you before I finished about Beatriz, the deaf mute I knew in Cuautla." Sirena stiffened slightly at mention of Madre Pilar's Indian nun.

"Beatriz was my sole diversion during Calleja's loud bombardment -- so loud in fact, she got her hearing back the same way she'd lost it, with an overdose of explosives. I taught her to talk again by ticking off the names of my more memorable conquests, and having her repeat them back to me. Amazingly, when I got to you, and mentioned I'd laid you on the galleon, Beatriz got jealous as a cat."

Sirena sat in frozen silence.

"By putting her story together with mine and doing a little simple arithmetic, I found out I was the go-to-Hell proud father of a silver plated Second Conde!"

"All right! What if I did bear the child of your rape?" she parried boldly, poised for the lunge that would drive her blade deep into his heart. "I guess Beatriz forgot to tell you one small fact! *Your son was born dead!*"

He did not flinch. "Someone has misled you, Condesa," he said, eyes burning with a dark triumph. "Beatriz helped deliver both infants, and she swears on the Cross, the Crowley child was stillborn. *Yours* was the son that *lived*!"

Sirena clutched the arms of her chair.

"Think about it. Beatriz was sworn to secrecy for what was done. Madre Pilar could hardly let a noble title descend to the bastard son of a casta muleteer, now could she? Once she saw fate had dealt her the right cards, she decided to play God. You'd raise your own son as another woman's orphan, get high points for charity and neatly cloak your shame."

Then, clutching the arms of her chair, she faltered. "I've never known a more ignoble man."

"Nobility's not the issue here. Money is. I'll collect half a million pesos in exchange for something you regard as noble. One thing this war's taught me -- ideology is a powerful force in the affairs of men."

For the first time she noticed how coarse his once handsome features had become, how his fair complexion was darkened by exposure. Despite his effulgent uniform, she beheld Emilio's swarthy visage in the face of his son.

He winced as though she had quirted him across the face, but he regained his composure quickly. "A lot, if I can put them to political and financial gain. If I were in your shoes, I'd say Rafael's true identity is well worth what I'm asking, and a bargain at that."

My baby died, I know he did, she thought wildly. But how could she know? She had fainted -- was still unconscious when he was born. Doctor Juan's words came back to haunt her: "Madre Pilar had something of great importance to confide refused to put it in a note -- *too confidential*."

He left his chair and walked around the table to her side, his shadow falling upon her. "Your generous 'donation' to support his army will buy me the political equivalent of a seat at the right hand of God."

"So, you're making blackmail work both ways?"

"With Independence a casta's now as good as a Conde. Just look at our mulatto hero, Morelos! See what he became!"

"A renegade priest, shot for treason, dead before his time?" she fired back. "Some achievement!"

He lifted the quill from an inkwell on the table and laid a sheet of foolscap before her. "Sign this and life for you goes on as before. Your husband still thinks he wed the Immaculata."

Cornered and helpless, she took the sheet, wrote out her libranza against the silver consulado in Mexico for the ruinous sum, and signed it with her rubrica and seal. "How long do you think you can keep on changing sides?" she asked.

"Not sides. Horses," he grinned. "A man doesn't get very far riding *one* horse. However, there is another matter we much come to an agreement on," he smiled, pulling out another piece of foolscap.

"Augustine Iturbide, will now receive your 600,000 in taxes for the Army of the Three Guarantees," Lorenso said, "but unhappily that windfall would not be mine alone. But, I do deserve the 400,000 additional pesos *per annum* that you will pay me for NOT showing my Manila galleon painting of La Condesa Desnuda, which I would otherwise exhibit as a posed portrait, painted in oil from life and handsomely framed in a major European gallery. I'm sure it will become a prized collector's item. That tidy sum will be entirely mine. "Since, we finally agree that my son, was truly stillborn, and proof that he ever even existed, is not at hand, I am at least able to make my own art work earn serious money for me."

So, you're making blackmail work for you both ways," she asked.

"Yes, and happily for me I still possess the painting, securely stored in my raincoat on the back of my saddle." he replied. "And remember, art lives so very long -- like -- forever!"

She rose from the table and faced him, standing straight as a Spanish lance, and refusing to show any sign of vanquishment she signed the second document.

He took her libranza and kissed it ceremoniously. "Who knows? In this age of revolution, I can even become Emperor." Tucking the valuable paper safely inside his tunic he asked theoretically, "After all, Condesa, who's to stop me?"

She fixed him with a baleful eye. "Only God, I'm sure."

CS ΒΟ

Still too shaken to rejoin the group, Sirena climbed the narrow stair that led to the mirasol above the gate. Picking up her field glass there she scanned the surrounding plain. The norther that had remained stalled beyond the mountains for several days, was now moving down upon La Frontera. Sheets of grey rain billowed like sheer curtains in the open window of the darkening sky, distant thunder rumbled, feeble lightning flared.

In his scarlet uniform and astride a cinnamon-red sorrel, Lorenzo made a bright stripe across the drab grey-green landscape as he galloped out to meet his troop of supporters. Some of them lounged in their saddles others sat on the ground, holding their horses reins while the animals grazed, manes and tails blown about by the wind.

Gazing through the field glass, her eye was drawn to another movement, a cluster of bright colors cresting a nearby rise to her left. Her heart leaped. It was Tristán! He and Don Octavio were accompanied by a band of about two dozen Indians. Judging from his ornate war shirt, braid wrappings and feathered weaponry, one of them was a Comanche headman, probably Ecueracapa's son himself. From what passing Indian trader had told her about the proposed ambush, the younger Ecueracapa must have ridden with them as protection against Tristán being killed by tribal renegades.

Having reached his Imperial troop just as the Comanches topped the rise, Lorenzo appeared openly alarmed. His men mounted hurriedly, all apparently jumping to Lorenzo's same false conclusion that the Indians were hostiles. Of course he would, Sirena thought! He knows nothing about, the nomadic tribes up here, their history, customs or dress. But in spite of his ignorance he was ordering his men into battle formation.

It was sheer madness for him to attack a band of peaceful Comanches! They weren't a war party! Such an attack by an Imperial troop could set the whole northern frontier aflame, and unravel the fragile peace Tristán had worked so hard to keep intact! She wanted to scream, to tell Lorenzo to stop before it was too late. Instead, she watched helplessly through her glass as he drew his sword from its scabbard and raised it in his command to charge.

Watching Lorenzo advancing at full gallop, brandishing his silver blade against the roiling charcoal skies, she was suddenly a little girl again, seeing another blade against a dark sky. "No! Lorenzo, No!" she cried, seeing again the memory of the Royal Visitor's French chef drawing down from Heaven the lethal fire that would consume him!

She watched, unable to move, as the shimmering blue-white lightning bolt touched Lorenzo's upright sword. She saw him open his mouth in a long, soundless cry, saw his body, stiffen as he stood rigid in his stirrups for what seemed an eternity. Then the sword dropped from his hand as he was pitched from his running steed like a sack of seed corn. Sirena clenched her eyes closed to save herself from the sight. She slowly steeled herself to open them to gaze at the plain where a mound of horseflesh and leather smoldered next to Lorenzo's motionless body.

Minutes later in the patio she watched as Melchor opened the gate to admit two solemn riders bearing Lorenzo on a tarp slung between their two horses. In the quiet group slowly dismounting were Tristán and his father, two members of Lorenzo's troop and one *very* old Comanche. Sirena ran to Tristán the minute his foot touched the ground. He swept her into his arms, shielding her from the icy north wind by wrapping her in the dark folds of the ample wool serape he wore.

Together they watched in silence as a trooper and the old Indian, whom, Tristán told her was a Comanche healer, lifted Lorenzo from the tarp to the cot that Sirena had Melchor bring out from the porter's room. The Indian bent over the motionless form, and when the old man spoke she understood enough Comanche to know he was asking her to remove Lorenzo's tunic. Impulsively she sprang forward to peel away the red tunic before the trooper even knew what had been spoken.

At sundown, Lorenzo's troop set out for nearby Monclova to find a doctor, Lorenzo, still unconscious and wrapped in blankets, traveling in the Graciana-Mendoza coach that Tristán loaned them. The Fourth Marqués left at the same hour, to pass the last night in his venerable Ávila frontier casco.

☙ ❧

"So tell me, what was Lorenzo doing way up here?" Tristán asked, tossing aside his quilted cotton vest and pulling her down beside him on the sofa before the fireplace.

"Oh, some sort of forced loan to finance the new Emperor's Army of the Three Guarantees," she said quickly, and then to fend off more questions, she asked one of her own. "Do you think Lorenzo's going to survive?"

"Doctor Daniel and I had a case much like it during the siege of Cuautla," Tristán said reflectively. "The bolt travels down the arm and into the chest cavity, acting like a massive heart attack. Our young soldier died. The old Comanche says his people rarely suffered fatal lightening strikes before the Spaniards gave them steel, but with hatchets and swords, now they're common. From the strikes he's seen he says *if* Lorenzo lives he'll be paralyzed and never speak again."

An involuntary shudder went through her as she recalled their last prophetic words, Lorenzo's cocksure, "Who's there to stop me?" and her engimatic reply, "Only God, I'm sure."

She got up nervously and walked around behind the sofa to the chair where Lorenzo's tunic lay. She had made sure it stayed in her hands. She quickly drew out her signed libranza and, moving unobtrusively to the fireplace, she stirred the smoldering logs until they blazed up brightly. She dropped the agreement into the orange and violet flames, then taking Lorenzo's extortionary note from her pocket she tossed that in after it. She watched spellbound as they wilted, flared and slowly turned to blackened ash. In seconds that small flame consumed the terrifying fear of Lorenzo's blackmail.

"That's sweet of you, Condesita, to stir up the embers," Tristán said lazily, his eyes closed, his booted feet stretched toward the warmth of the blaze.

Returning to Tristán, she curled up on the sofa beside him, tucking her hands tightly around his waist, resting her head contentedly on his breast, drinking in the familiar scent of cedar and sage that clung to him.

He drew her closer, his lips playing across her hair, his hands stroking her body through the sensuous velvet of her gown. "Such a lovely wife," he murmured contentedly, "And such a lovely fire."

"Yes," she responded, gazing at the flames and breathing a long and tremulous sigh. "I think it's just about the loveliest fire I've ever seen!"

෴ FIN ෨

BIBLIOGRAPHY

Chevalier, Francois, *Land and Society in Colonial Mexico: The Great Haciendas*. Translated by Alvin Eustis. Edited with a forward by Lesley Bird Simpson. University of California Press, 1970. Paperback edition.

Harris III, Charles H. *A Mexican Family Empire: The Latiundia of the Sanchez Navarros 1756-1867*. University of Texas, 1975. Cloth edition. This is a study of a family in the North of Spain who owned and successfully operated multiple large haciendas. It serves as a historical model for the Graciana Family Empire treated in this book. They were also closely involved in capturing the Insurgents in 1810.

Ladd, Doris M. *The Mexican Nobility at Independence 1780-1826*. The University of Texas Press, 1976. Paperback edition.

Schurz, Lyle. *The Manila Galleon: The Romantic Story of the Spanish Galleon Trading Between Manila and Acapulco*. E.P. Dutton, 1938. Paperback edition.

Von Humboldt, Alexander. *A Political Essay of New Spain*. Edited with an introduction my Mary Maples Dunn. Translated by John Black, abridged. Alfred A. Knoph, A Borzoi Book on Latin America, 1971. The Paperback edition.

Author's Note: This handful of titles represents the core of a total of two hundred works dealing with various aspects of the history of New Spain in the late 18th Century Colonia Spanish and early Independence periods. The author spent a total of ten years on the ground in Mexico, studying all the regions touched upon in this book. Another twenty-five years were devoted to researching all of the historical personages and relevant scholarly works that became available during the same time. Five years were devoted to the actual writing of *The Drowning of the Moon*.

GLOSSARY

Place Names	439
General Spanish Terms	440
Art Terms	446
Ecclesiastical Terms	447
Mining Terms	449

PLACE NAMES

Acapulco:	(ah-cah-<u>pull</u>-co) -- home port of the Manila galleon or China ship for almost three centuries.
el Bajío:	(el Ba-<u>hee</u>-o) -- Rich alluvial farm region in central Mexico.
Cuernavaca:	(kwer-nah-<u>vah</u>-ka) -- Indian term signifying 'the place at the side of the woods.'
La Graciana:	(lah grah-see-ahn-a) - Family-owned silver mine and title of nobility.
Guadalajara:	(guad-ah-lah-<u>har</u>-ah) -- major city in Jalisco.
Guanajuato:	(guan-ah-<u>hua</u>-toe) -- ancient Indian name for 'The Place of the Mountain Frog.'
La Sirena del Norte:	(lah see-<u>ray</u>-nah dell nor-tay) – 'The Siren of the North', a silver mine named after a legendary mermaid, siren or enchantress who lured and bewitched seafarers.
Monterey:	(mon-tair-<u>rey</u>) Military capital of Upper California.
Querétaro:	(kay-<u>rhet</u>-ah-ro) Major city of the Bajío.
Rio de los Brazos de Diós:	(<u>ray</u>-os-day-los-<u>bra</u>-sohs-day-<u>dee</u>-ohs)The River of the Arms of God in southeast Texas, now known simply as the Brazos.
Valladolid:	(va-ya-do-<u>leed</u>) -- see city of the Bishop of Michoacán, named after a city in Spain. Later changed to Morelia to honor Morelos, who was born there.
Zacatecas:	(zah-cah-<u>tay</u>-cas) -- site of New Spain's first major silver strike in 1546.

GENERAL DEFINITIONS

Abrazo:	(ah-<u>brah</u>-sohz) -- a hug or embrace upon greeting or parting, especially in Spain and Latin America.
Adelantado:	(ah-de-len-<u>tad</u>-o) – one who discovered and pacified formerly unclaimed territory; must have had sworn witnesses to prove that he was indeed the first to enter the realm he claimed.
Alhóndiga:	(al-<u>hon</u>-dig-a) -- a public granary, or storehouse, of corn; in Guanajuato, often referred to as Riaño's Alhóndiga and a primary and important building famous in that city.
"Amar a Diós!"	(ah-mah ah-dee-<u>os</u>). . ."love God!"
Amigo mio:	(ah-<u>mee</u>-go mee-oh) – my friend.
Angelita mia:	(oh-hey-lita mee ah) – term of endearment: my little angel.
Arriero:	(ah-ree-<u>air</u>-o) -- a muleteer.
Ayate:	(aya-te) -- linen fibers made from the Maguey/Agave cactus. Used to make bags or sift flour.
Barb:	(barb) -- Spanish term for an Arabian horse.
Los barbaros:	(los <u>barb</u>-ah-ros) – barbarians. The term given nomadic Plains Indians (Apaches, Comanches, etc). Hunters as opposed to the sedentary planter Indians of New Spain.
Bruja:	(<u>bru</u>-hah) – a witch.
Bufa:	(bu-fa) – a very small bluff.
Camino Real:	(kah-<u>mee</u>-naws re-<u>ahl</u>) -- Literally, the Royal Road or the King's Highway. Usually refers to the historic 600-mile road connecting the former Alta California's 21 missions, four presidios and three pueblos, stretching from Mission San Diego de Alcalá to Mission San Francisco Solano. Once Mexico won its independence from Spain, no road in Mexico, including California, was a *camino real*.
Camisa:	(k-aa-m-<u>ih</u> sah) – a shirt or undershirt for men or women.

Campesino:	(cahm-pey-<u>see</u>-no) -- poor farmer or farm worker.
Cancela:	(can-<u>say</u>-la) -- a kind of gate in a wall or fence.
Carga:	(<u>car</u>-gah) -- a mule load of ore or produce.
Cargador:	(<u>car</u>-ga-dor) -- a strong mail laborer whose only job is carrying large burdens. In Aztec times there were whole chains of them lowly, perhaps brutish, laborer who carried large bundles.
Casta:	(<u>cah</u>-sta) -- person of mixed Indian, European and Negro blood.
Cempasuchitl:	(Chem-paz-sue-ch eel) -- Mexican marigold flowers. The word comes from the Nahuatl/Aztec language. Referred to in Mexico as *flor de muerto*, which means flower of the dead, because they figure prominently in Mexican day of the Dead celebrations.
Cigarro:	(ci-ga-rro) -- The Indians planted a native tobacco, the leaves of which were dried in the sun, crushed and smoked by everyone- Spanish men, women and even children from ten years old. These crude cigarettes were made with paper wrappers one inch wide and the length of a finger.
Cohetes:	(<u>guet</u>-ays) -- fire-crackers, skyrockets.
Comals:	(co-<u>mahl</u>-z) -- A flat griddle typically used in Mexico to cook tortillas, sear meat and generally prepare food. Some are concave and made of 'barro' or clay.
Compadre:	(com-<u>pah</u>-dre) -- godfather of one's child.
Compañera	(com-pan-<u>yair</u>-ah) -- a bedfellow, sexual partner, companion, wife.
Cortes:	(<u>core</u>-tes) -- ruling political body comprised of representatives of various Spanish provinces.
Criollo, (m): Or	(cree-<u>o</u>-yo) -- [Eng. Creole] – male person born in the Americas whose parents are of pure European blood.
Criolla, (f):	(cree-<u>o</u>-ya) – [Eng. Creole] – female person born in the Americas whose parents are of pure European blood.
Cuidado:	(cui-da-do) – take care and/or be careful.

Fanega:	(fah-<u>ney</u>-gah) -- Spanish measure of dry weight, (corn, wheat, etc.) -- about 1.5 bushels.
Frontierista:	(fron tier <u>ees</u> tah) -- a settler of the northern provinces of New Spain.
Gachupín:	(gah-chu-<u>peen</u>) -- derogatory Aztec term for a person born in Spain. Sometimes translated as 'The spur (or boot-heel) that stings.'
Guitarrónes:	(gui-ta-<u>rrón</u>-aas) – Spanish name for a big Mexican guitars often used in mariachi bands.
Hacienda:	(ah-see-<u>en</u>-dah) --a large, productive landed estate traditionally comprising 21,500 acres.
Hechizos:	(he-chi-zos) -- a witch's spell. Sorcery, witchcraft.
Hidalgo:	(ee-<u>dahl</u>-go) - a gentleman of honorable, but not always wealthy, family. Also a family name.
Huizache:	(wee-sä-<u>chee</u>) – species of acacia tree. Slang for an 'unqualified' lawyer.
Humilde:	(oo-<u>mill</u>-days) -- a genteel or polite term for country folk or the unlettered poor. A lowly, simple-minded peasant.
Idilio:	(ee-<u>deal</u>-ee-oo) -- secret love affair, an idyll.
Jeremiad:	(jer-e-mie-ad) – a long, mournful complaint or lamentation; a list of woes.
Jipijapa:	(hih-pea-<u>hah</u>-bah) -- a Panama hat made from the young leaves of a tropical American, palm-like plant, Carludovica palmate.
Jotas:	(<u>hoe</u>-tas) – a folk dance from northern Spain, danced in couples in fast triple time.
la Indiada:	(In-dee-<u>ah</u>-da) -- the general Indian population.
Latifundio:	(lah-tee-<u>fun</u>-deo) -- a very large landholding, commonly containing three haciendas or more.
League:	(leg guaw the Spanish league was equivalent to 2.6 miles.
Lepero:	(<u>lep</u>-ero) -- term applied to poor city beggars.
Matrimonial:	(mat-ri-mon-i-<u>ahl</u>) -- the marriage bed shared by a husband and wife.
Mayorazgo:	(my-yor-<u>ahz</u>-go) -- an entailed or legally indivisible family estate, favored by New Spain's silver and landed nobility.

Mestizo:	(mess-<u>tee</u>-so) -- person in Spanish Americas of mixed Indian and European blood.
Mesquite:	(mess <u>keet</u>) -- a small, thorny tree found in the tropics whose sugary pods (mesquite beans) are used for animal fodder. From the Nahuati mizquitl.
'Mi alma':	(me-<u>al</u>-mah) -- term of endearment, 'my soul.'
'Mi consentida':	(mee-con-sen-<u>tee</u>-da) -- term of endearment: a pampered or spoilt little girl. 'Daddy's little girl.' 'Apple of my eye.'
'Mi preciosa:'	(mee-<u>pre</u>-cio-sa) -- term of endearment: my precious one.
Mesón:	(may-<u>zone</u>) -- an inn, tavern or hostel.
Molinillo:	(mo-lee-<u>nee</u>-lio) -- a Mexican kitchen utensil, whisk or stirrer made of 'turned' wood and used to froth warm drinks.
Muchas gracias:	(moo-chus-<u>gra</u>-cie-us) -- thank you very much.
Mucho gusto:	(moo-cho-<u>guz</u>-toe) -- literally means 'I like much.' Can be used in many contexts. Most commonly used to mean, 'very nice to meet you' or 'it's a pleasure to meet you.'
Mulas:	(<u>mulas</u>) – mules. Slang: tough guys.
Mullata:	(mul-<u>yah</u>-ta) -- a female of mixed white and black ancestry.
Mus:	(moush) -- a Spanish card game widely played in Spain and Hispanic America for 4 players using 40 cards. The name may be derived from the Basque 'musu' which means 'kiss', describing the lips or face and suggests that the name of the game could have derived from the facial gestures used while playing.
Palacio:	(pa-<u>la</u>-cio) -- a private residence equivalent to a mansion. Also the country seat of a count, duke, etc. or an important official building.
Presidios:	(pre-<u>see</u>-th-yaws) – garrisoned forts or military posts.
Paso atras:	(pah-sow-<u>aa</u>-traz) -- a step backward.
Patria:	(pat-rea) – one's native country or homeland.
Peons:	(<u>pea</u>-yawns) -- a Spanish-American day laborers or unskilled farm workers. Persons of low rank.

Pemmican:	(pem-i-kan) – a paste of dried and pounded meat mixed with melted fat and dried fruits or berries, pressed into a loaf or into small cakes, originally prepared by North American Indians.
Prieto azabache:	(<u>Pree</u>-ah-toe ha-bah-chee) -- a strong, solid, jet black breed of horse.
Pozole:	(po-<u>zo</u>-le) -- from the Nahuatl: a traditional soup or stew of pork or chicken, hominy, mild chile peppers and coriander leaves. Traditionally served at Christmas and often favored as a hangover remedy.
Pulque	(pul-<u>kay</u>) – a Mexican alcoholic beverage made from the fermented sap of various agaves.
Quince año:	(kin-sea-ahn-yo) – a celebration of a girl's fifteenth birthday in the Latino culture. A coming of age acknowledgment.
Rejas:	(re-jahs) – a grill or screen usually made of wrought or cast metal and used in Spanish architecture to protect a window in a house or to enclose a chapel or tomb in a church.
Remuda:	(re-<u>mu</u>-da) – a source of relay horses that travels with .the herd of horses that travels with from which those to be used for the day are chosen.
Sambo:	(sam-bo) – a term for a person with African heritage and, in some countries, also mixed with Native American heritage, more black than white.
Serape:	(sa-ra-pe) -- a blanket-like shawl or wrap, often of brightly colored wool, as worn in Latin America.
Sereno	(s-ur-<u>ree</u>-n-oh) -- night watchman.
Sericulture:	(sari-cul-<u>ture</u>)The raising of silk worms and the manufacture of raw silk made from the wool of their cocoons.
Sombrero:	(som-<u>brer</u>-row) -- a broad-brimmed felt or straw hat, typically worn in Mexico and the Southwestern US.
Tapadera:	(<u>ta</u>-pa-dare-ra) -- the leather covering for the stirrup on an American saddle.

Tunas:	(tu-<u>nas</u>) -- the edible fruit of a prickly pear cactus.
Vago:	(<u>vah</u>-go) vagabond, drifter, migrant worker.
Vara:	(<u>vah</u>-ra) -- Spanish baton or wand of office, symbol of authority and official rod of measure in Spanish America, about 33 inches in length.
Verdad	(ver-<u>dah</u>-d) -- truth.
Zarzuela:	(zahz-<u>zway</u>-la) -- a Spanish musical comedy/opera also having spoken dialogue and usually of a satirically treated tropical theme.

ART TERMS

Agate hook: (ah-gah-u) -- A tool used by artisans to burnish gold leaf on statues and carved altarpieces.

Atelier: (ah-til-lee-<u>ay</u>) -- a tool used by artisans to burnish gold leaf on statues and carved altarpieces.

Azulejos: (ah-su-<u>ley</u>-hos) -- colorful, brightly-patterned and glazed tiles used to decorate fountains and church domes throughout New Spain.

Estofado: (es-to-<u>fah</u>-do) -- a tooled, gold-leafed and painted embellishment of carved religious images.

Pointerolles (poh-tey-<u>roll</u>-yea-zah) -- engraving tools comprised of a long beveled blade and a rounded handle. wedge, tapering wood or metal blocks.

Ratablo: (rey-<u>tab</u>-lo) -- an altar screen.

Reredos: (<u>reyr</u>-dos) -- a multi-tiered screen rising behind a church altar, usually peopled with wood-carved statues of Catholic saints.

Santo: (<u>sahn</u>-to) -- carved image of a Catholic saint.

ECCLESIASTICAL TERMS

Beatas	(bay-yah-tahz) – overly pious women always obsessively praying and attending church.
El Señor Osbispo:	*(bee-cia) -- Ruling official of a Catholic diocese.
Cathedral:	(cah-thee-dral) -- Not necessarily an imposing edifice but the official church or chair of the bishop of a diocese.
Law of consanguinity:	Church law forbidding marriage between blood relations in the direct line.
Diocese:	(die-yah-seas) -- An ecclesiastical territory and jurisdiction governed by a bishop.
Dispensation:	(deez-pa-saz-cian) -- Relaxation of ecclesiastical law in certain cases, a power usually reserved to a Bishop.
Dominican friars:	Religious followers of Saint Dominic, early Indian missionaries in New Spain.
Episcopal:	(aa-peez coh-pahl) -- Pertaining to the duties or powers of a bishop.
Excommunication:	(x-com-mu-nah-kay-see-on) -- A penalty or censure by which a Catholic is banned or excluded from the "communion of the faithful". (The official act of a Bishop, pope or other high-ranking church official.)
Feverinos:	(fev-ah-ree-nos) -- Newly ordained priests filled with apostolic zeal.
Franciscan friars:	Followers of St. Francis of Assisi, and pioneer missionaries to the Indians of New Spain.
Friar:	(frah-yah) -- a religious who preaches and serves the faithful, as opposed to a *guitarrones* is a member of a reclusive, monastic or contemplative order.
The Holy Office:	An ecclesiastical court appointed to guard the purity of Catholic doctrine, especially to investigate charges of heresy or immoral conduct of members of the clergy.

Jesuits:	(<u>jed-u</u>-eatz) -- members of the Company of Jesus, followers of Saint Ignatius Loyola, renowned in New Spain as educators of the aristocracy and for their Indian missions throughout Spanish America.
Monsignor:	(man-<u>scene</u> yah) -- title of distinction granted to certain members of the clergy as a mark of papal recognition of their services to the Church.
Ordinandus:	*(oar-di-<u>nan</u>-doz) – an overseer. One who keeps order.
Sacristy:	(<u>sac</u>-<u>ris</u>-ti) -- the anteroom adjacent to a church sanctuary where celebrants and their assistants vest for religious services.
Sanctuary:	(<u>sahn</u>-shoe-air-ree)The immediate area surrounding the altar where Mass is celebrated.
See:	(si) -- Another name for diocese.
Zona:	(zoe-<u>nah</u>) – a specially designated area. For example: A section of a city.

MINING TERMS

Azoguero: (ah-zoe-<u>gay</u>-lo) -- a workman who incorporates quicksilver (mercury) etc. with pounded silver ore to extract the silver.

Arrastra: (ah-<u>rahs</u>-tra) -- a circular, mule-powered ore crushing mill.

Aviador: (ah-vee-ah-<u>dor</u>) -- financial backer and investor in silver mines.

Barrateros: (bah-rah-<u>ter</u>-os) – mine workers, pick-men.

Barrenadores (bah-ren-ah-<u>dor</u>-es) – mine workers, blast men.

Cajero: (cah-<u>hay</u>-ro) -- an apprentice merchant or clerk in store or mine office.

Desazogaro: (dez-ahz-o-<u>gar</u>-o) -- expert at testing ore during the 'patio process' of amalgamation.

Hacienda de beneficio: (ah-see-<u>en</u>-dah dey ben-e-<u>fee</u>-ci-o) -- a large refining mill, an hacienda that processes ore.

Quinto Real: (<u>keen</u>-to ray-<u>ahl</u>) – the 'King's Fifth.' Crown tax or a fifth of the value of each real of silver mined in Spanish America paid the crown.

Malacate: (mal-ah-cah-te) – a horse-powered whim used to raise water from deep mine shafts.

Patio process: Processing the ore in open patios by means of several mule-turned arrastres or crushing mills.

Silver Road: The Kingdom's main Camino Real or Royal Highway, over which all of New Spain's silver moved to Mexico and to seaports for shipment.

Tenateros: (ten-ah-<u>ter</u>-os) – mine workers, specifically ore carriers.

Torta: (<u>tor</u>-tah) – 'cake', i.e., the raw ore being amalgamated with mercury, pyrites, salt, etc.

Veta Madre: (veta <u>mah</u> dray) -- the mother load.

ABOUT THE AUTHOR

Diana Serra Cary is the former child star: Baby Peggy" She began her career in 1920 at the age of twenty months and starred in more than 100 two-reel comedies and five feature films. As an adult she became a historian, writing articles for such major magazines as Wild West, American Heritage, American West, American History, Saturday Evening Post and Readers' Digest. She is also the author of four popular nonfiction books: *The Hollywood Posse: The Story of a Gallant and of Horsemen Who Made Movie History*, *Hollywood's Children, An inside account of the child star era*, *Jack Coogan, The Boy King* and *Whatever Happened to Baby Peggy?*

CPSIA information can be obtained
at www.ICGtesting.com
Printed in the USA
BVOW06s2034010118
504157BV00011B/343/P